The Classical Plot and the Invention of Western Narrative

From Homer to Hollywood, the Western storytelling tradition has canonised a distinctive set of narrative values characterised by tight economy and closure. This book traces the formation of that classical paradigm in the development of ancient storytelling from Homer to Heliodorus. To tell this story, the book sets out to rehabilitate the idea of 'plot', notoriously disconnected from any recognised system of terminology in recent literary theory. The first part of the book draws on current developments in narratology and cognitive science to propose a new way of formally describing the way stories are structured and understood. This model is then used to write a history of the emergence of the classical plot type in the four ancient genres that shaped it – Homeric epic, fifth-century tragedy, New Comedy, and the Greek novel – with new insights into the fundamental narrative poetics of each.

N. J. LOWE is Lecturer in Classics at Royal Holloway, University of London.

The Classical Plot
and the Invention of Western Narrative

N. J. Lowe

Royal Holloway, University of London

CAMBRIDGE
UNIVERSITY PRESS

PUBLISHED BY THE PRESS SYNDICATE OF THE UNIVERSITY OF CAMBRIDGE
The Pitt Building, Trumpington Street, Cambridge, United Kingdom

CAMBRIDGE UNIVERSITY PRESS
The Edinburgh Building, Cambridge CB2 2RU, UK   www.cup.cam.ac.uk
40 West 20th Street, New York, NY 10011-4211, USA   www.cup.org
10 Stamford Road, Oakleigh, Melbourne 3166, Australia
Ruiz de Alarcón 13, 28014, Madrid, Spain

First published 2000

Printed in the United Kingdom at the University Press, Cambridge

Typeface 10/12 Plantin   *System* QuarkXPress™   [SE]

A catalogue record for this book is available from the British Library

Library of Congress Cataloguing in Publication data

Lowe, N. J.
The classical plot and the invention of Western narrative / N. J. Lowe.
    p. cm.
Includes bibliographical references and indexes.
ISBN 0 521 77176 5 (hardback)
    1. Classical literature – History and criticism – Theory, etc. 2. Classical
literature – Stories, plots, etc. 3. Narration (Rhetoric) 4. Rhetoric, Ancient.
    1. Title.
PA3014.N37 L69 2000
880'.09–dc21   99-052857

ISBN 0 521 77176 5 hardback

Contents

Figures

Tables

Preface

'Plot' is an unloved word in narrative theory: no longer quite the four-letter vulgarity it was to critics a generation or two ago, but still not much used in polite conversation.[1] Largely bypassed by narratology, it remains for many theorists a suspect term, worryingly slippery to define, and tangled up with lines of theory that have not fared well in the history of postwar criticism. Part I of this book tries to soothe these suspicions, arguing for the rehabilitation of 'plot' as a central term of narrative theory, and putting forward a model that seeks to repair the difficulties felt in definitions and analyses from Aristotle on. With the help of ideas borrowed from narratology and cognitive science, I argue that the vernacular notion of plot is anything but a disposable and methodologically suspect abstraction – that, on the contrary, it marks an attempt to describe a fundamental component of the mental machinery we use in the construction and reading of fiction.

But this is not centrally a work of theory. Part II is historical and text-specific, and the theoretical model proposed in Chapters 1–4 is there chiefly to make such a history writable. Rather, however, than a 'history of plot' in general – something nobody, let alone a classicist, would be easily persuaded to take on – it seeks to track the emergence of one very particular kind of plotting, which has held a position of extraordinary dominance in the traditions of Western literature for close on three millennia. If it has been comparatively neglected by modern criticism, that is partly because it has tended to be associated since the Romantics with 'low' or 'popular' narrative forms – farce, detection, adventure. But with

[1] 'What do we mean by the melodramatic phrase "heresy of plot"? Nothing very sensational; it is the notion that in a poem or a play or a novel there is an order of events that may be thought of in complete isolation from other structures and that "somehow" exists independent of the language of the work. So described, the idea is revolting; no self-respecting literary critic is guilty of this. Crude hypostasizing of plot and separation of plot from expression is a nineteenth-century error, left behind with character sketches and the well-made play' (Brower 1952: 48). 'Plot has no strong place in the pantheon of acceptable literary terms' (Dipple 1971: 1). 'In the great efflorescence of study of narrative in recent years, plot has been slighted as something apparently too old-fashioned to deserve prolonged attention' (Miner 1990: 147, and cf. Merrill 1999).

postmodernism's dissolution of the boundaries between high and low art; with the sophisticated, ironic embrace of genre narrative traditions such as the mystery; and especially with the high cultural and critical status allowed to popular cinema, there is every sign that this system of narrative values is returning in esteem. It seems the right time to try writing the story of its roots.

What I here call *classical* plotting is, broadly, the idea of plot we associate with Aristotle (a quite different thing from Aristotle's own idea of plot, which is only glancingly addressed here).[2] Its principles were in fact well established in narrative practice by the time Aristotle tried to articulate them in the fourth century BC; and though, like Aristotle, we may not always find it easy as readers to make these principles explicit, we are all of us well trained in recognising their effects. 'Classical' plotting is felt to evoke, for example, an impression of elegance, economy, and efficiency in the deployment of narrative resources. There is a strong sense of unity and closure to the narrative structure, with particular importance attached to a firm and satisfying ending. At the same time, the audience or reader is teased with guessing-games over what is to happen: twists, surprises, mischievously thwarted expectations. And yet, classical plots play fair: they do not allow us to feel cheated by the turn of events taken or the means used to achieve them. This book sets out to explain how these impressions are achieved, and why this way of making stories, despite all fluctuations in fashion, has remained the most resilient narrative paradigm in Western storytelling to this day.

Clearly, I use the term 'classical' here in its historical as well as its cultural sense, because I want to argue that for the study of plot the two senses merge into one. Classical plotting is an invention of the classical world. By the third century AD, the classical plot paradigm had already been refined and adapted to the three narrative forms in which it was passed on to the Renaissance, and which remain the basis for subsequent developments: epic poetry, tragic and comic drama, and the novel or short story. Its applications since the Renaissance, which have brought into its domain narrative media unknown or unimaginable to antiquity, are nevertheless modifications and extensions to ancient patterns, rather than essential

---

[2] The difference is well illustrated by the way Aristotle's name is widely taken in vain in creative-writing handbooks, often for concepts that bear only the most parodically distant relationship to anything Aristotle wrote. Screenwriting tutors, for example, invoke Aristotelian authority for the now-canonical three-act model (for which see e.g. Field 1979: 56) of Hollywood film structure: 'You have a beginning, a middle, and an end. In other words, you get your character up in a tree, you throw rocks at him for a while, and then you get him down. And that's your basic three-act structure in the Aristotelian terms' (Francis X. Feighan, co-author of the interactive screenwriting program Collaborator, on *Moving pictures*, BBC2 6/2/94).

departures from them. To understand the basic grammar of classical plotting, it is necessary and sufficient to understand plotting in the classical
world – and, in practice, a surprisingly narrow canon of genres and works
within that world. That, at any rate, is the argument of this book.

To put this case, I have had to wade further into the mainstream of theoretical debate than classicists are normally expected to go, though it will
be all too evident that I have managed to keep my amateurism intact. It
remains impenitently a classicist's book, mired in what will seem to some
a crudely archaeocentric view of the Western narrative inheritance –
according to which all literature is crumbs from Homer's banquet, and all
criticism footnotes to the *Poetics*. Nevertheless, my approach sits with the
small but swelling number of literary studies that see implications, not
just for the redemption of narratology but for the future of their entire dis-
cipline, in the methods of cognitive science[3] – in the empirical study of
how the human mind organises information in the operations of perception, memory, and thinking, and the structures or 'schemas' of mental
representation we use as frameworks for knowledge, inference, and
understanding. At the same time, I have tried to make the text sufficiently
modular, and the theoretical model sufficiently accessible, for a reader
innocent of any interest in these issues still to be able to make sense of the
discussions in Part II.

Readers in a hurry are welcome to peek at the ending, but in outline the
story is this. Chapter 1 reviews some main lines of approach to the theory
and definition of 'plot', and the complex of questions such attempts have
tried to address. Chapters 2–3 then describe the model proposed here to
deal with those questions, beginning with a general consideration of the
different mental operations involved in the reading of fictional narrative,
and moving on to a detailed discussion of the descriptive mapping proposed between the representation of narrative universes and certain kinds
of structure in games. Chapter 4 then uses this model to try to explain the
distinctive qualities of *classical* plotting; and Chapter 5 looks briefly at
each of the principal genres of Greek narrative excluded from the historical survey that follows, and at the rival possibilities they propose to the
classical paradigm. Part II then deals in turn with the use and evolution of

---

[3] An ambitious manifesto in Turner 1991, who notes that the cognitivist project is that with
which Western literary theory begins; see also Spolsky 1993 (on the cognitive underpinnings of poststructuralism), and good narrative casebooks in Britton and Pellegrini 1990,
Ryan 1991 (with a valuable emphasis on work in artificial intelligence), Branigan 1992,
Gerrig 1993, Emmott 1997, and a useful introduction in Semino 1997 (esp. 117–224). The
term 'cognitivism' is mainly bandied in film studies; see e.g. Andrew 1989, Bordwell and
Carroll 1996 (index s.v.). In literary studies the cognitivist trend is most evident in stylistics, humorology, metaphor theory, and *Lesengeschichte*; a wide range of applications regularly appears in *Poetics*. I reserve my misgivings for the Conclusion (below, pp. 261–2).

that paradigm in the four successive narrative traditions of antiquity that I argue embody its historical development: the Homeric epics (Chapters 6–7), fifth-century tragedy (8), Greek and Roman New Comedy (9), and the Greek love-novels of the Empire (10). It is largely a Greek history: aside from translated New Comedy, Latin literature remains marginal to this narrative, for reasons sketched at the end of Chapter 5.

It will be all too apparent from this summary that the very attempt to tell this story has wound up espousing the values of its subject: a totalising, teleological narrative with a beginning, middle, and end. 'It is not yet clear', says a recent textbook of narratology, 'what a history of narrative as such would look like';[4] this book is one attempt to imagine an answer, but some nettle-grasping is required. To come clean, I do not think that narratology can survive its postmodern critiques[5] without embracing the full implications of its (often tacit) cognitivist underpinnings. But the new cognitivism itself is an unabashedly positivistic, neo-Aristotelian response to the poststructuralist stance,[6] which has tended (for example) to minimise the closural, systemic elements in storytelling; to stress the anthropological otherness and distance of the ancient cultures which produced and consumed it; to mistrust the dehistoricising tendency of formalist approaches; and to recoil with alarm from any notion of confronting literary works as products of compositional processes, something that cannot be entirely evaded in a survey of writing on plot. These are embarrassments that need to be left at the door. It is a weary truism that *fin de millénium* aesthetics is caught between the classical values of order and closure still privileged in popular narrative culture, especially in cinema, and the postmodern values of polysemy and pluralism that our information- and irony-saturated world celebrates. One of the themes of this book is the centrality of that tension to all human narrative – including, obviously, attempts to tell the story of narrative itself.

I have done my best to keep jargon to a minimum, but a good deal has slipped through; the worst is collected for reference in a glossary at the back. Bibliographic references have been brutally compacted: wherever possible, I have made do with a single reference to a recent discussion through which the full literature and debate on a subject can be accessed. Most Greek words are translated or transliterated; Greek names other than Menandrean titles have been Latinised as severely as I could bear ('Posidon', but '*Oresteia*'), and other words transcribed for visual intelligibility rather than phonetic puritanism (*tyche* rather than *tukhē*). Unattributed translations are my own.

[4] Onega and Garcia Landa 1996: 12.   [5] See below, p. 21 n. 17
[6] But not necessarily at odds with it: Spolsky 1993 argues attractively that the poststructuralist model is itself cognitively well-grounded.

   This book owes so much to so many colleagues in London and elsewhere that I blush to elide most of their names. But Chris Carey, Pat
Easterling, Barbara Goward, Vassiliki Kampourelli, Andreas Markan-
tonatos, and John Morgan read parts or all of the text at a variety of
stages; Michael Silk, David Wiles, and especially Malcolm Willcock
planted early seeds whose fruit they will not easily recognise; and Pauline
Hire and the Press's readers surpassed all duty in helping to knock a ten-
thousand-stade text into eusynoptic shape. My deepest debts are to students and colleagues in the Classics Departments of Westfield College
and Royal Holloway; and to Margaret Welbank, who has shaped this
project from the start, and will be glad to see the back of it.

Part I

The Classical Plot

I   Approaches

Everybody knows what plot is. 'Readers can tell that two texts are versions of the same story, that a novel and film have the same plot. They can summarize plots and discuss the adequacy of plot summaries. And therefore it seems not unreasonable to ask of literary theory that it provide some account of this notion of plot, whose appropriateness seems beyond question and which we use without difficulty.'[1]

Yet in recent practice such an account of what we understand by 'plot' has proved extraordinarily elusive.[2] Narratologists, especially, have been unhappy with the word (and such equivalents as *intrigue/intreccio*, *trame/trama, action, Handlung, Fabel*). Some standard textbooks avoid the term altogether (Genette 1980, Bal 1985/1997); others push it to the margins (Prince 1982) or treat it as a casual synonym (Bordwell 1985ab; cf. p. 6 below), while some openly question whether it carries any useful meaning at all (Rimmon-Kenan 1984: 135). To find any extended, unembarrassed discussion of the concept one has to look underground: to the fascinating but rarely acknowledged literary-theoretical ghetto of creative-writing handbooks, with their deviant reception of Aristotle and forbidden fascination with the poetics of authorial composition. It may not be too late to reclaim the word, but the task has been made stiffer by the emergence in the last quarter-century of a widely accepted system of narrative categories in which 'plot' plays no recognised role. And yet, the idea of plot, in Aristotle's *mythos*, lies right at the centre of the theoretical system from which narratology begins. It is also probably the narrative term most people untouched by formal literary theory would find it easiest to use in everyday analysis; and this very intuitiveness makes it

---

[1] Culler 1975: 205.
[2] Prince 1987: 71–2 and Wales 1987: 355–7 are useful starting-points, but the only extended treatments are the exemplary and complementary discussions by Egan 1978 (on prenarratological theories) and Ronen 1990a (on narratology and after). There are many surveys of broadly relevant theories of narrative structure and content; see especially Scholes 1974: 59–117, Culler 1975: 205–24, Chatman 1978: 43–95, Segre 1979: 1–64, Rimmon-Kenan 1983: 6–42, Ricoeur 1983–7 ii.17–91, Martin 1986: 81–129, Stewart 1987, Jonnes 1990: 1–54.

tempting to suspect that the idea of plot is a flag for something innate in our mental apparatus for understanding narrative. How, then, has it managed to fall through the terminological net?

Much of the answer must lie in its very ease of use. 'Plot' is a vernacular term, and as such not only resists formal definition, but is in a way designed to substitute for it. We use the word to talk about a variety of things we recognise in the way stories are put together, and the way they affect us. But like 'heaven', 'common sense', or 'a federal Europe', it is really a tag to identify a *hidden* quantity – a quick answer to a question too loosely formulated to have one. Its usefulness and persistence lie precisely in the fact that it is a label for the absence of a more formal representation. To define one, it is not enough simply to lay down a definition *ex cathedra*, or to negotiate a diplomatic middleground between competing uses, or to hunt for some superinclusive formula that can encompass the range of applications. We need to look beyond, to the questions about the way narrative works to which the idea of 'plot' is part of the answer.

The difficulty here is that there are a number of competing priorities, not always clearly articulated, for what we want a notion of plot to do. Take what seems like a simple case. In a common, perhaps the commonest, vernacular usage, 'plot' is used as a synonym for *story*: what happens in a narrative, the sum of the events the storyline recounts. When we speak of 'summarising the plot' of a novel or play, we mean a paraphrase of what we perceive to be its basic story content, the events abstracted from the text that recounts them. Here, for instance, is Aristotle's summary of the 'story' (*logos*) of the *Odyssey*: 'A man being away from his home for many years, under the hostile eye of Posidon, and alone; and the situation at home, moreover, being such that his property is being wasted by suitors, and they are plotting against his son – the hero returns after great hardship, and after revealing his identity to certain persons makes his attack, saving himself while destroying his enemies' (*Poetics* 17.1455b17–23).

But there is one difficulty here already. How do we agree on what constitute the essentials in a story outline? Why does Aristotle feel that the wrath of Posidon is part of the *Odyssey*'s *logos*, and the support of Athene is not? Why does the suitors' wasting of Odysseus' property get a mention, but not their pursuit of his wife? Why does Aristotle, in contrast to most modern readers, feel the essence of the poem is concentrated in its second half, and that IX–XII contain no details significant enough to deserve explicit mention?[3] What makes the essentials essential, and how do we recognise their significance?

---

[3] In fact Aristotle's distillation is extraordinarily acute. For answers to these questions see respectively pp. 139–40, 142, and 137.

And there is a more subtle problem as well. Even when we perform this everyday act of synopsis – of summarising the 'plot' of a book or a film – we convey far more than mere events. Inevitably, we find ourselves simultaneously trying to say something about those events' narrative *articulation*. We tend to distinguish, as Aristotle did in his abrupt shift of construction, between preparatory set-up and main action ('It's in 1943, when France is still occupied but the African colonies are technically outside Nazi control; and he runs this bar where all the refugees hang out while they're waiting for American visas to come through . . .') Like Aristotle, we use the present tense, as though we are living through the unfolding of the narrative over again ('. . . and Peter Lorre passes him a set of exit papers, but then gets shot, so he hides them in Sam's piano . . .') And we easily succumb to a further temptation that Aristotle resists only by straining both summary and syntax: we report events not in their own internal chronological sequence, but in the order they were reported to us ('. . . and it turns out they were lovers in Paris, when she thought her husband had been killed, but she never told him back then that she was even married . . .')

What we are already doing here, of course, is making an instinctive separation between the *events* of the story and their *telling*: what the Russian formalists distinguished by Shklovsky's famous terms *fabula* and *sjuzhet*. This distinction is a cornerstone of modern narrative theory, even though there has been huge disagreement over the precise definition of the two terms and the boundary between them, and scarcely less over how to present them in English. *Fabula* (in English, usually 'story') is the series of events the work recounts, but imagined stripped of all the artifices of storytelling: a series of actual events in their natural order, in what merely happens to be a fictional world. In contrast, *sjuzhet* is the account of those same events that we actually get, reordered and reshaped in the process of telling to reach and affect the audience or reader in a particular and deliberate way.[4] (The best of the English equivalents proposed is 'narrative', though it is a long way from ideal: see pp. 18–19. below, and the Glossary.) In some kinds of fiction – tales of detection, for instance – the reconstruction of the *fabula* from the *sjuzhet*, a hypothetical 'objective' story from the story told, is the *raison d'être* of the whole work. And when we run the two together in our attempt to describe the 'plot' of *Casablanca*, we are

[4] Ironically, this terminology works in every language but Russian, where the formalists' choice of everyday words to pressgang into technical service is the wrong way round to deal with some nuances we would nowadays want to include in the distinction. In ordinary Russian usage, *fabula* can mean a story in its actual manifestation as a text, but *sjuzhet* cannot; it can, however, as its etymology implies mean the 'subject' (whether story or theme) treated by a narrative, something *fabula* cannot cover.

expressing our instinctive sense that there is something more to what we mean by 'plot' than simple story – that what is told may be less important than the shape it is given in the telling.

But if our sense of plot is inadequately covered by *fabula*, still less can it be explained as a synonym for *sjuzhet* – which is unfortunate, as 'plot' has become the accepted English translation for the latter,[5] despite the strange nonsense it makes of the word's native usage. It is disconcerting to be told in a classic textbook of film theory: 'The term *plot* is used to describe everything visibly and audibly present in the film before us . . . The film's plot may contain material that is extraneous to the story world. For example, while the opening of *North by Northwest* is portraying rush hour in Manhattan, we also see the film's credits and hear orchestral music.'[6] (By analogy, the 'plot' of *Middlemarch* would presumably include the chapter numbers, and perhaps that of *Little Dorrit* the Phiz illustrations.)

Nevertheless, a distinction of this kind has long been felt important to pinning down a definition of plot. It is hinted at already in Aristotle, particularly in his use of the terms *logos* and *mythos* – the terms in the *Poetics* regularly rendered in English as 'story' (sometimes 'argument') and 'plot'. But it would be misleading to claim (as still suggested, for example, by Prince 1987 *s.vv.*) that Aristotle anticipates the formalist distinction. For one thing, both terms are polysemic in Aristotle's actual usage: *mythos* means sometimes 'plot', sometimes 'myth', sometimes both,[7] while *logos* (never formally defined) means 'speech' much more often than it means 'storyline'. What is more, the two terms are only once juxtaposed,[8] and never explicitly contrasted;[9] on the contrary, the distinction between story and narrative is blurred at least as often as it is observed. And most

---

[5] Lemon & Reis 1965: 68; cf. Wales 1987: 357.

[6] Bordwell & Thompson 1993: 67.

[7] See the careful analysis by Downey 1984 (who properly points out that the problem is as much in our use of terms as in Aristotle); cf. Halliwell 1986: 57n16.

[8] 5.1449b8: Crates is describes as the first comic playwright to have composed 'stories and plots', a statement that does nothing to clarify the distinction (if any) between the terms.

[9] The closest is 17.1455a34 with 1455b8, where Aristotle summarises the *logos* of Euripides' *Iphigenia in Tauris* and then labels as 'outside the *mythos*' the reasons for Orestes' Crimean voyage. But the passage can equally be invoked to support the view that *mythos* and *logos* are in fact synonymous (as argued by Belfiore 1992a: 108,128, cf. 1992b: 362). Ἔξω τοῦ μύθου is usually taken to mean either 'outside the primary action' (but this is also true of other events narrated in the prologue to *IT* and apparently accepted by Aristotle as part of the *mythos*) or 'inessential to the chain of causality in the play' (in this case, a debatable claim). The phrase occurs only here, though we find 'outside the play' (ἔξω τοῦ δράματος) at 14.1453b32 and 15.1454b2, and similar expressions at 15.1454b7, 18.1455b25, 24.1460a29. If consistency is to be found in Aristotle's usage, we must posit a *threefold* distinction between *logos* (the story or *fabula*), *mythos* (the set of events that constitute the essential causal chain), and *drama/tragoidia/mytheuma* (the subset of plot events included in the primary action of the play). See the thoughtful treatment by Roberts 1992.

importantly, Aristotle has *two* quite separate terms to describe the story the narrative recounts, depending on whether he is interested in its ability to be summarised (*logos*) or its internal unity (*praxis*); and it is the latter term, not the former, that is used contrastively for the definition of *mythos* itself.

In fact, like so much else in the mosaic of elliptical jottings and afterthoughts that is our *Poetics*, that definition of *mythos* is let fall almost in passing. It turns up in the middle of an ungainly sentence whose main purpose is to complete the famous list of the six qualitative elements of tragic drama. Spectacle, music, and diction have already been explained; there remain the three elements of *mythos*, *ethos*, and *dianoia*, all of which are now derived from the earlier definition of the object of tragic representation as a particular kind of action. Aristotle's deeply embedded periods, essential to the logical structure, are not reproduced in any English translation I know.

Since it (tragedy) is a representation (*mimesis*) of an action (*praxis*),
  and it (the action) is acted out (*prattetai*, cognate with *praxis*) by particular agents (*prattontes*, participle of the same verb),
    who will necessarily be particular kinds of person in respect of their moral character (*ethos*) and their ideas (*dianoia*) –
      for it is through these (character and ideas) that we assess people's actions,[10]
      and it is through their actions that all people succeed or fail –
  and (since) THE PLOT (*mythos*) IS THE REPRESENTATION (*mimesis* again) OF THE ACTION (*praxis* again) –
    for BY 'PLOT' HERE I MEAN THE ORGANISATION (*synthesis*) OF THE EVENTS (*pragmata*, passive cognate of *praxis*: 'things done' as opposed to 'doing'),
      by 'moral character' that which makes us say that the agents are particular kinds of person,
      and by 'ideas' passages of dialogue in which they argue something or express an opinion –
then there are necessarily six qualitative parts of every tragedy: these are plot, moral character, diction, ideas, spectacle, and music. (6.1449b36–1450a10)

Now, Aristotle clearly does here recognise the importance of a distinction between story and its narrative presentation. For Aristotle, and the current in early Greek critical thought to which he is responding, the distinction is expressed in the idea of *mimesis*, literally 'imitation'. The essence of art is to create *images of things*, and in the elegant opening chapter of the *Poetics* Aristotle has sketched out a general typology of the arts on the triple differentiae of what the things are, what the images are

---

[10] At this point a marginal gloss has infiltrated the text as a parenthesis: 'there are two causes of actions, ideas and moral character'.

made of, and – a third criterion for the special case of narrative – how the image is created. In the case of drama, for instance, the *things* are human actions; the *images* are made of words, music, and movement; and the images are *created* by real people pretending to be those imaginary people.

Yet the kind of higher-level 'organisation' of story events Aristotle denotes by the term *synthesis*[11] has little to do with the interface between story and narrative as narratologists nowadays conceive it – the selection of what events to report, in what order, from what viewpoint, and with what kinds and degrees of emphasis or colouring. Aristotle's 'organisation' turns out to be something quite different, and to come much closer to our vernacular understanding of 'plot'. It is the *internal articulation of story events:* the composition of a story whose individual events link closely together in a satisfyingly coherent and interesting way.

But what does make a story interesting? What *kind* of organisation makes a set of story events cohere? This question is one that has risen high on the agenda of recent theory about the basic semantics of fiction: the problem of *narrativity*, of what distinguishes a story from a non-story, or makes one story more interesting than another.[12] And Aristotle's own solution to this fundamental question is surprisingly complex, protean, and finally elusive. But its consideration will take us right through a range of variously sophisticated modern views that attribute the coherence and affectivity of plot to a whole hierarchy of different narrative levels.

The simplest view would locate interest entirely in the choice of story *incidents* in themselves. After all, certain kinds of story event clearly do carry an intrinsic affective payload, irrespective of their structural context and narrative treatment. A kiss, or a punch on the nose, is intrinsically a more charged event than a handshake. And Aristotle himself did recognise that some kinds of affectivity could indeed reside at this level of the narrative process. Tragedy's delivery of pity and terror, for example, could be increased by the simple inclusion in the story of an element he called

---

[11] Sometimes *systasis*: the terms are used interchangeably over the course of the treatise.

[12] 'Narrativity' (sometimes 'tellability') is necessarily a relative rather than an absolute term; good discussions in Prince 1982: 144–64 and Ryan 1992a, 1997. There have nevertheless been some engaging attempts to draw a line around what exactly constitutes a non-story. As a minimal instance, Leitch suggests an eventless narrative such as 'Once upon a time they lived happily ever after' (1986: 10). Ryan, however, suggests there can be failed stories even with a process of conflict and resolution: 'Mr Fox was hungry, so he asked the crow to give him some cheese. "OK," said the crow, "let's share it and neither of us will be hungry." Moral: sharing makes good friends' (1986a: 319). The classic showcase is Meehan's collection of 'mis-spun tales' from his pioneer program TALE-SPIN, which offers several enchanting clinkers: 'Henry Ant was thirsty. He walked over to the river where his good friend Bill Bird was sitting. Henry slipped and fell in the river. He was unable to call for help. He drowned' (1976: 94).

pathos – defined, in splendid deadpan, as 'a destructive or painful action (*praxis*), such as deaths in public view, agonies, injuries, and all that sort of thing' (12.1452b11–13).

But it is hard to imagine, and Aristotle was at pains not to propose, a view of plot that would attribute the interest of a story *entirely* to the kind of isolated events recounted – except perhaps in certain narrative forms of very limited affective range, such as pornography or slapstick. The nearest thing I know to such a theory is Polti's remarkable *Thirty-six dramatic situations*, much the most entertaining of the largely unrewarding modern attempts at a taxonomy of plot patterns,[13] which attempts to explain the intrinsic interest of all serious drama by the inclusion of items from an *à la carte* of affective predicaments. Yet even there many of Polti's 'situations' are concatenations of events rather than minimal or isolable motifs,[14] and it would be the height of perversity to claim that stories derive no significant part of their impact from the way groups of incidents *combine* in succession. If that were so, the most tragic tragedy would consist of nothing more than a pageant of executions or a plotless gladiatorial spectacle.[15]

Then does the affective component lie in the surface-level *sequence* of events? This has certainly been claimed in our time, and was tried out by Aristotle in one celebrated chapter (13), the bravura analysis of reversal patterns in tragedy. By careful consideration of how well each possible combination of categories delivers the prescribed emotional pay-off of pity and terror, Aristotle is able to identify one particular pattern that carries the strongest available affective charge – a good or morally undistinguished (but not evil) character whose fortunes take a turn for the

---

[13] The most respected have been Crane 1952, Friedman 1955, Frye 1957; cf. Wright 1982: 108–36. The *Poetics* itself well illustrates the hazards of such an approach in the two systems it offers for tragedy, their relationship to one another obscure: the famous distinction at 10.1452a12 between 'simple' and 'complex' plots; and the notoriously problematic typology of tragedies at 18.1455b32–56a2 into 'complex', 'tragedies of suffering', 'tragedies of character', and a fourth category shrouded in textual corruption whose tantalising exemplars are '*Phorcides*, *Prometheus*, and all plays set in Hell'.

[14] *e.g.* 'Vengeance taken for kindred upon kindred' (4), 'Murderous adultery' (15), or 'Discovery of the dishonour of a loved one' (27).

[15] In a Souriauesque final chapter of considerable sophistication, Polti himself freely conceded that his 'situations' were not in themselves *elementary* structures, but could themselves be described in terms of an underlying system of three 'actors' – which he ingeniously equated with the Thespian protagonist (or hero), the Aeschylean deuteragonist (or opponent), and the Sophoclean tritagonist (the crucial complicating agent or object). Moreover, the thirty-six situations could themselves be concatenated by an '*Art de combiner*' to generate more complex scenarios (which Polti whimsically offered to supply on order to 'dramatic authors and theatrical managers' by the gross or dozen at prices to be negotiated, 1895: 182–3) – and to support the arresting claim that 'we cannot, however great our simplicity, receive from the drama, or from life, more than one thousand three hundred and thirty-two surprises' (178; Ray's translation).

worse (not the better) as a result of a gigantic mistake (μεγάλη ἀμαρτία: not a moral flaw or offence).

But the difficulty all such surface-structural theories of plot have to face sooner or later is the challenge of explaining *why* their particular sequence should work better than any other. It is possible to evade the question by claiming a correlation outside the realm of narrative altogether, such as a sub-Frazerian ritual pattern (as in Raglan's *The hero*), or a sub-Jungian archetypal allegory of psychic growth (as in Joseph Campbell's *The hero with a thousand faces*). But solutions of this kind have not won much credibility among theorists (though Campbell's model has been consciously adopted by story *tellers* as the template for some well-known American heroic fictions, most notably John Barth's novel *Giles Goat-Boy* and George Lucas's films *Star wars* and *Willow*). Without clear empirical evidence for the existence of the pattern claimed, such models find it hard to escape the charges of being arbitrary, methodologically naïve, poor in actual explanatory power, and insufficiently generalisable to account for more than a modest class of traditional or traditionalist narrative types.

A more ambitious solution is to look for a *deep structure* underlying the production of individual story patterns. At two points in the *Poetics* Aristotle himself attempts a limited version of this for particular constellations of plot motifs, by breaking them down into a system of elementary constituents and running through the permutations in which these can be combined.[16] But the attempt to extend and generalise this procedure to the analysis of narrative as a whole is largely a phenomenon of the structuralist era, inspired in the fifties by the pioneer projects of Propp and Souriau,[17] but driven by the new and initially attractive hypothesis that stories, like other kinds of mental and cultural structure, are organised and understood through syntactic mechanisms similar to those of natural language. This quest for a workable *grammar* of fiction became the Grail of narrative theory throughout the 1960s and 1970s – initially among French literary theorists, but increasingly and internationally amongst workers in the new disciplines of semiotics, cognitive science, and artificial intelligence,[18] who were looking for ways of designing and imple-

---

[16] *Changes of fortune* are classed by moral status of subject, direction of change, and mechanism of change (13.1452b34–53a12); *pathe* or acts of violence by relationship of subject to object, subject's awareness, subject's intent, and degree of fulfilment (14.1453b14–54a10).

[17] *Morphology of the folktale* appeared in Russian in 1928, but its Western influence begins with the 1958 translation. On Souriau's *200,000 situations dramatiques* see Scholes 1974: 50–8, Elam 1980: 126–31, de Toro 1995: 129–30.

[18] In the mid-seventies, early AI researchers took on the ultimate challenge of *generating* story texts automatically by computer – an enterprise marked by some dramatic early successes, in particular the remarkable (though now very dated) computerisation of Propp by Sheldon Klein's team at the University of Wisconsin (Klein *et al.* 1974), and the

menting formal models of how narrative is apprehended by the mind. Some milestone works came out of this enterprise in the sixties, including Todorov's *Grammaire du Décameron*, Barthes's 'Introduction', Kristeva's *Texte du roman*, Greimas's *Sémantique structurale* and the classic papers that became the kernels of his two collections *Du sens*; while the seventies saw the proliferation (especially in North America) of the 'story grammar' model of narrative that sought to reduce the principles of narrative construction and comprehension to a formal syntax.[19] But by 1980 the story-grammar model was generally felt to have failed, and with it the prevailing linguistic model of narrative structure – partly because of doubts about its actual explanatory resilience, partly from disillusion with its tendentious assimilation of narrative forms to syntagmatic structures, partly in the face of stiff competition from rival event-based models,[20] but above all out of frustration with its worryingly arbitrary application of what were supposed to be rigorous formal categories.[21]

If there is a deep structure, then, to the syntax of well-formed narrative utterances, so far it has proved discouragingly elusive. Does this leave any hope for the story-structure view of plot? As it happens, a quite different principle of story organisation is suggested by a number of forceful passages in the *Poetics* itself. The clearest is 9.1451b33–5: 'Of simple plots and actions (*mythoi* and *praxeis*) the worst are the episodic ones. By an episodic plot, I mean one in which episodes follow one another in a way that is neither probable nor necessary.' This famous 'probable-or-necessary'

still classic TALE-SPIN program by James Meehan at Yale (Meehan 1977/1980, 1981). Klein's approach was structuralist and linguistic; Meehan's, in practice far the more successful and influential of the two, adopted the quite different technique of programming a story 'universe' of characters, environment, props, and rules, and allowing stories to be generated by the characters' strategic interactions within that universe as they pursue the goals (such as the satiation of hunger) assigned them. Such work had fallen from fashion in AI circles by the time its significance began to trickle through into narratology: see Ryan 1986a, 1986b, 1988, 1991, and for related work Klein *et al.* 1973, Fournel 1977, Correira 1980; Dehn 1981; Lebowitz 1984, 1985. A fascinating recent development, independent of this earlier work, has been a vogue for commercial software assistants for film plotting, of which the best-established are Collaborator (a simple questionnaire-based knowledge-elicitation program acknowledging Egri's published and unpublished writings; cf. Brown 1994), Plots Unlimited (a moderately sophisticated combinatorial situation-generator inspired by Cook 1928), Blockbuster (formerly Storyline), and the extraordinary Dramatica (cf. Phillips and Huntley 1996).

[19] The principal attempts are Rumelhart 1975, Thorndyke 1977, Mandler and Johnson 1977, and Stein and Glenn 1979; important review symposia in special issues of *Poetics* (9.1–3, 1980) and *Journal of Pragmatics* (6.5/6, 1982).

[20] Schank 1975, Schank and Abelson 1977; Wilensky 1978; Beaugrande and Colby 1979; Black and Bower 1980; Lehnert 1981, 1982; Habel 1986; Seifert, Dyer, and Black 1986; Ide and Véronis 1990.

[21] Black and Wilensky 1979 (cf. replies by Mandler and Johnson 1980, Rumelhart 1980); Ryan 1979; Brewer and Liechtenstein 1981; Johnson-Laird 1983: 361–70; Wilensky 1983; Ronen 1990a. For attempts to revive the model see Mandler 1987, Shen 1989ab.

formula turns up regularly in Aristotle's discussion of the linkage between story events,[22] and is clearly crucial to his idea of their 'organisation'. Several key passages place judgemental stress on the *causal* connection between story events: the famous prescription that a well-made plot have a beginning, middle, and end (*sc.* of a causal chain); the rule-of-thumb recommendation for story length; the incisive remarks on what does and what does not constitute narrative unity.[23] And in one perceptive aside the principle is extended further: tragedy's affective payload of incidents arousing pity and terror 'will occur most, or more, when they occur because of one another but contrary to expectation' – in other words, when the *audience* can see the catastrophe coming, but the *characters* cannot.[24]

Yet even Aristotle stops short of claiming that the surprise (ἔκπληξις) generated by such tight causal programming is the sole or even the primary source of *interest* in a plot. More often, in fact, Aristotle's plea for a naturalistic mimesis of causality seems to be concerned not with affectivity or *surprise*, but with the principle of narrative *transparency* – avoiding the kind of obtrusive contrivance that might call attention to the artificiality of fiction, and thus snap the audience out of its narrative trance. It may be a necessary condition of successful plotting, but it is hard to see how it could be sufficient; and it is at this point in the search that the *Poetics* runs out of general answers.[25]

Even so, Aristotle's emphasis on the *causal* connection between story events has long been felt to touch something essential in our modern understanding of plot. Not surprisingly, then, the idea of causality stands at the centre of what is perhaps the most celebrated maverick definition of 'plot' in our century. Like Shklovsky's closely contemporary formulation, it is one of a contrastive pair: best remembered, and most often quoted, in its famous illustration.

We have defined a story as a narrative of events arranged in their time-sequence. A plot is also a narrative of events, the emphasis falling on causality. 'The king died and then the queen died' is a story. 'The king died and then the queen died of grief' is a plot. The time-sequence is preserved, but the sense of causality over-

---

[22] An exception is 9.1451a36–8, where the emphasis is on the plausibility of the story events selected or invented.   [23] 7.1450b26–7; 7.1451a11–15; 8 *passim*.

[24] 9.1452a3–4. Else *ad loc.* thinks it is the audience, not the characters, who are surprised; Lucas's note on 1452b7 puts a strong, though not watertight, case against this view. Aristotle does not, of course, mean that plots have to be rigidly predictable and pedestrian: twice in the treatise he approvingly paraphrases a paradoxical couplet of Agathon's to the effect that unlikely things are quite likely to happen.

[25] To advance the argument for the special case of tragedy, Aristotle has to argue that the form – apparently uniquely – targets a specific affective range of narrow frequencies on the emotional spectrum. It is hard to see how any such claims might be made for, say, epic.

shadows it. Or again: 'The queen died, no one knew why, until it was discovered that it was through grief at the death of the king.' This is a plot with a mystery in it, a form capable of high development. It suspends the time-sequence, it moves as far away from the story as its limitations will allow. Consider the death of the queen. If it is in a story we say: 'And then?' If it is in a plot we ask: 'Why?' That is the fundamental difference between these two aspects of the novel.[26]

Narratologists like this celebrated paragraph, but find it hard to do much with it. Forster pretended to no academic rigour; his attractive distinction remains an isolated *aperçu*, floating free of any wider theoretical system. But there are some surprisingly clever things about his formulation, and they have pointed the search for an understanding of plot in one of its most important directions.

Forster's chapters on 'The story' and 'The plot' move away from Aristotle somewhat, by proposing two contrasting (though not exclusive) ways in which narratives can organise fictional events to produce an affective response from the reader. The first, story, builds its response on the affective interest of the bare events. Strong storytelling involves the minimum possible refraction of the fictional events through the prisms of narrative gimmickry. No gaps in the story, flashbacks and fill-ins, no mischief-making with sleights of viewpoint and narration: the text presents the tale with pure transparency, the flow of words evoking the life in time.

But a plot is different. In a plot, the text becomes a game of detection. The narrative snips, elides, or conceals key elements of the story, and the reader is challenged to piece it together again. There is just one clue: all events are linked by the logic of natural causality. By applying our own experience of cause and effect, we can rebuild a personal model of the story events from the text. Those events still carry their native charge; but the activity of repeatedly answering questions of 'Why?' has exposed a structure of dominating causes, and with it a sense of the life of value. For Forster, not surprisingly, this is incomparably the higher goal.

Forster's 'story/plot' division is clearly close in scope, as well as in time, to the formalists' *fabula/sjuzhet*. (The difference lies chiefly in Forster's debatable insistence that a story can exist without the higher levels of narrative organisation implied by his 'plot' – whereas formalists would argue that the story is always mediated through some kind of narrative recasting, however persuasive the *illusion* of transparency.) But the real strength of his formulation – and the reason, surely, for its impressive longevity – is the importance it places on the hermeneutics of *reading*. For Forster, plot is that property of narratives that forces us to read actively and intelligently between the lines: to use, to value, and ideally to extend our human understanding of people and causes through the process of making sense of events, whether real or imagined. The affective power of story may indeed, therefore, *reside* in its internal causal structure; but it is only *activated* by first being cast in the form of a hermeneutically challenging narrative, and then being worked on by an intelligent reader.

This is clearly a powerful and sophisticated solution, and its reader-centred model of how plot works has inspired – with varying degrees of directness and acknowledgement – some classics of modern narrative analysis.[27] But we have moved some way from a view of plot that treats it as a synonym for, or even a property of, story in the narrow sense; and we should consider whether the nature of what we think of as 'plot' does not lie entirely on the farther side of the categorical fence straddled by Forster's definition. If plots only become plots by being cast in a certain form and read in a certain way, is plot a property of stories at all? or simply a quality grafted on to them by the art of narration and the act of reading?

This is why the most recent views of plot have shifted attention away from the story content *per se* and on to the way it is *processed*: the way readers respond to stories as their texts unfold, and in particular the way our expectations of certain kinds of narrative fulfilment are manipulated from moment to moment as we read. A powerful example, and probably the best-known, is Brooks 1984, which uses a loosely Lacanian notion of 'desire' to analyse the pervasive and complex ways in which novels lead us on and, in the process, develop meanings of a uniquely *narrative* kind.

The main drawback of such a perspective, of course, is that it seems to make any *formal* definition of plot impractically difficult. In a sense, it is really an anti-definition, since in this view plot is necessarily *all* pattern read, or readable, in a narrative text: 'the logic and dynamic of narrative, and narrative itself a form of understanding and explanation'; 'a structuring operation deployed by narratives, or activated in the reading of narratives . . . the logic and syntax of those meanings that develop only through sequence and succession'; 'the global dynamic (goal-oriented and forward-moving) organization of narrative constituents which is responsible for the thematic interest (indeed, the very intelligibility) of a narrative and for its emotional effect'.[28] It is hard to see what, if anything, such a definition might exclude. In its extreme formulation, it obliterates the distinction between narrative and other textual forms: thus one occasionally encounters claims for the 'plot' of a non-narrative poem or essay.[29]

---

[27] Explicitly Forsterian: O'Grady 1965, Falk 1965, cf. Sternberg 1978: 10–14. Other important reader-centred studies: Ruthrof 1981; Brooks 1984; Branigan 1992.

[28] Brooks 1984: 10; ibid. 113; Prince 1987: 72. For a book-length defence of such a view, see Pinnells 1983, and cf. Sturgess 1992 (who is careful to define this quality *not* as 'plot' but as 'narrativity').   [29] See *e.g.* Leitch 1986: 139–43 on 'Plot in the English sonnet'.

But we should be careful of falling victim here to a form of 'textual fallacy' – a reductive assumption that the properties of texts can be sufficiently described in terms of their internal linguistic or other textual structures, rather than of the interaction of those structures with the worlds in which they are created, transmitted, and consumed. On the one hand, plot is undeniably an attribute of *texts*, something that lies on a page (or in some equivalent public space) for the eventual use of a human consumer. Plots reach us not as events, or as conceptualisations of events, but as words (or other equivalent signs); and if our model cannot at least find room for this then clearly it is a failed, or at best incomplete, description. Yet at the same time plots, like every other property of texts, have to be *decoded*, by being processed in the brain of a reader. And when we attribute 'plot' to a text, we are describing not a property resident *in* the text, but an aspect of our *experience* of that text. The strength of Brooks' model lies precisely in its recognition that plot is not an inert assemblage of printed words but a complex, dynamic phenomenon constructed during and in the activity of reading. But his particular chosen approach has its self-set limitations too: its acknowledged distrust of formal methods (and especially of the achievements of narratology),[30] and its not unrelated preference for a Freudian model of the reading mind over more recent and empirically sanctioned research on mental processes.

Now, on the face of things, it might indeed seem attractively economical to assume that we use just the same decoding mechanisms on plots as we use to process any other set of squiggles and dots on a page of paper into the affective world of mental phenomena. All types of linguistic event, after all, share a common vocabulary and syntax; unfold identically in real time, in an orderly linear sequence; and depend similarly for their decoding on a background of semantic and cultural assumptions in the reader's experience. So a theory of how we understand plot would ideally be able to explain how we make sense of many, perhaps all, other kinds of dynamic organisation in discourse: persuasive arguments, say, or formal structures, or networks of imagery and verbal association. We might even wonder whether there is anything unique to the organisation of *narrative* that requires the specialised label of 'plot' to describe it.

But the evidence of cognitive science seems increasingly to argue that there is. Empirical studies of narrative comprehension and recall, which have returned from the wilderness with the resurgence of cognitive studies in discourse analysis, suggest that we do represent events in a way qualitatively different from our processing of language. Unitary models of discourse comprehension have proved inadequate and unwieldy, and

---

[30] See the remarks by Pavel 1984 (esp. 361); Bal 1986 (esp. 558); Prince 1988: 361.

since the 1970s there has been growing acceptance of the inconvenient
principle that the mental structures we use to apprehend events and propositions seem to involve a different *kind* of mechanism to those that
process text.[31] In particular, the event-based empirical models sometimes
lumped together as 'schema theories', whose achievement and remaining
drawbacks are discussed in the next chapter, have largely killed off the
earlier story-grammar approach. It seems increasingly unlikely that we
can make sense of plot without invoking a mechanism of this kind –
despite the once unthinkable Cartesian separation this seems to demand
between the flesh of the text and what Aristotle resonantly dubbed its narrative soul.[32]

What seems needed, then, is a view of the process we call 'plot' that can
make graspable sense of what increasingly looks like a complex, multi-
tiered, and as yet imperfectly understood *cognitive* phenomenon; a view,
moreover, which will somehow find room for the notions of affectivity,
causality, and structure that seem so important to our sense of what plots
do, while simultaneously respecting the family resemblances in traditional usage, preserving the provenly useful categories of mainstream narratology, and answering the practical needs of analysing and comparing
how plot works in complex literary texts and other media. In the next two
chapters, I try to suggest a way in which these very diverse specifications
may perhaps after all be met.

---

[31] The literature is very large; a useful early review in Johnson-Laird 1983: 356–95, with
more recent surveys in Gerrig 1993, Semino 1997, and especially Emmott 1997. Major
contributors include Gordon H. Bower, William P. Brewer, Jean Matter Mandler, David
S. Miall, and their respective collaborators.   [32] *Poetics* 6.1450a38.

2 A cognitive model

First, some key terms. Basic to modern narrative theory is a distinction between two or more levels in any work of fiction. Unfortunately, they are variously labelled, and even more variously defined. For reasons explained shortly, I favour the scheme (but not the terminology) of Bal 1985. First, there are the *events* of the story itself; next, there is the way those events are *told* to the reader; and finally, there is the actual *text* that the reader reads. I use, with misgivings, the three terms STORY, NARRATIVE, AND TEXT; these words will be used only in the senses here defined.[1]

STORY is the favoured Anglo-Saxon term for the French *histoire*, the Russians' *fabula*, and Aristotle's *logos*.[2] In respective opposition to *discours*, *sjuzhet*, and *mythos*, it marks the most fundamental distinction in mainstream narrative theory: between the *content* of a tale and its *presentation*, the things that are supposed to have happened in the world of the story as against the way the reader actually learns of them.

'Story' is not an ideal label for this specialised concept. It is, of course, vernacularly used to mean a narrative *text* – as in 'an O. Henry story', 'a story I wrote at school'. Some important cognitive work, in particular, has used the term specifically in this sense, to the extent that Schank and Abelson's Yale AI group was teased for its doggedly textual (and minimal) definition of a 'story'.[3] Others, confusingly, have reserved the term for the *presentation* half of the antithesis: Bal preserves Shklovsky's *fabula* for the first element but uses 'story' to translate *sjuzhet*. Still, 'story' has the

---

[1] A comparative table of terms in O'Neill 1994: 21 (to which should be added the English translations of Shkhlovsky's *fabula* and *sjuzhet* as 'story' and 'plot', and Lanser 1981's 'story' and 'fiction' for Bal's first two terms). Note that Shklovsky is followed by Tomashevsky 1925, Bordwell (1985a, 1985b), and Bordwell and Thompson, 1993, and Lanser by Branigan 1992 (with 'story world' for 'story'); Todorov's terminology is also that of Barthes 1966; while classicists tend to follow Bal 1985 (so de Jong 1987a, 1991; Goward 1999), whose strengths are diluted in the more discursive 1997 edition. Most narratologists have been content with two or three strata, but O'Neill goes to four, Lanser six, and Branigan eight; the deeper levels sit somewhat uncomfortably in the hierarchy.
[2] Chatman 1978: 19; Rimmon-Kenan 1983: 3.   [3] Wilensky 1982: 346.

authority of two of the three major English-language syntheses, as well as the standard English translations of Barthes and Genette. I use 'short story' for the first sense of the term above.

NARRATIVE is a less easy term again. I follow Lewin's rendering of Genette's *récit*,[4] but there are bewilderingly many rival labels in English for the form in which a story is presented to the reader. To take only the three canonical introductory textbooks, Bal, confusingly, uses 'story'; Chatman (who follows Barthes rather than Genette) prefers 'discourse', 'expression', or even 'plot';[5] while Rimmon-Kenan, for reasons amplified below, actually subdivides it into 'text' (including, but not limited to, my own usage of that term) and 'narration'. For different reasons, none of these six is usable for this book. Three (plot, story, text) are spoken for; the others are for my purposes imprecise or opaque.

Worse, the term 'narrative' itself is used in a number of competing senses. It is not, I think, particularly troublesome that in ordinary parlance we often use 'narrative' more widely and loosely to mean 'storytelling', the process in which all our three levels of fiction combine. Since I will be arguing that the heart of this process is precisely the *packaging* of story content, nothing essential is lost by imposing the sharper sense proposed here. 'Narrative' is simply 'recounted story', a 'narrative text' a 'text' carrying a 'narrative'.

Potentially more serious, however, is the disagreement over the technical scope of the term. 'Narrative' is also the normal rendering for Plato's διήγησις,[6] denoting the presence of a narrative voice outside and beyond the direct speech of the characters (*mimesis*). Drama has normally no such voice, so that we often appropriate the term 'dramatic' as a convenient label for this directly mimetic mode of storytelling in general. European narratologists prefer to exclude dramatic and iconic storytelling from the term 'narrative', and to centre their studies in the text-linguistics of narration;[7] in the US, where literary and film studies are on closer speaking terms, the tendency is overwhelmingly to treat 'narrative' as a global category, and to stress the generalisability of narrative models across the whole range of storytelling media. It will be clear that I subscribe wholly to the second view; indeed, I can no longer see a sustainable defence for the first.[8] In this book, therefore, 'narrative' is used in its

---

[4] Genette 1980: 25n.   [5] Above, p. 6.

[6] *Republic* III.393d-4c. Confusingly, *diegesis* is also widely used in Genettian narratology and film theory in a sense close to *sjuzhet*; this book uses only the Platonic sense. Aristotle prefers the term ἀπαγγελία (*Poetics* 3.1448a21, etc.).

[7] The principal dissident is Ricoeur 1983–7, who in any case emphatically distances himself from narratology as such.

[8] The nearest thing to a statement of case is Genette 1988: 15–17. Attempts at an equivalent 'dramatology' (though none is comfortable with the term) include Pfister 1977,

larger sense. In particular, I shall be arguing for very close technical and historical continuity between the successive narrative systems of epic, drama, and the novel.

As usually defined, the narrative repackaging of story has two main effects. First, it reorganises story *time* (by flash-back and flash-forward, manipulation of pace, selection and omission of episodes and events). Second, it imposes a more or less restricted *point of view* (by choosing and changing who observes the story, what they see, how much they know, and what they choose to pass on to the narrator – who will then, of course, filter the account of events through a second level of editorial screening).[9] In essence, these are one principle, not two. The experience of narrative time is determined by what the textual viewpoint selects. If we jump forward three years in time, it is because the character or author through whose eyes we see the story feels they are not relevant to the narrative he or she is concerned to tell.

TEXT seems in some ways the most straightforward term of the three; but in others it is also the most contentious. For one thing, even if we resist the various poststructuralist attempts to dissolve or globalise the boundaries of the term, there is a lively dispute within narratology itself over what counts as a narrative text in the first place. Bal (1985: 5, 1997: 5) glosses 'text' as 'a finite, structured whole composed of language signs'. But narrative can be carried by many other media besides the word. Some, such as film, mime, and comics, need not have any words in them at all. Though narratologists disagree on how to treat these non-verbal

Ubersfeld 1977 and 1991, Elam 1980, de Toro 1987, Carlson 1990, and Aston and Savona 1991, with a useful survey in Carlson 1988 (cf. 1984). But the Aristotelian polarisation of storytelling between these two modes is itself made obsolete by the invention of film and comics – which already had a foot in the door of Chatman's system in 1978, since when he has argued strongly for the unity of verbal and non-verbal narrative (1980, 1990). A general cross-media model remains a desideratum; it may well come from film narratology (disowned by Bal 1997: 173), where Branigan 1992 is the most ambitious synthesis to date.

[9] This careful separation of what literary narratologists call *focalisation* and *narration* has been one of the seminal achievements of Genettian narratology. In treating both as aspects of the narrative level, I offend against every existing version of the tripartite model: even Bal treats narration as an aspect of text. This seems to me to introduce a dangerous confusion. De Jong confronts it, but does not, I think, resolve it in her own version of Bal's definition: 'The text, consisting of a finite, structured whole of language signs, is the result of the narrating activity (narration) of a narrator . . . A narrative text de facto derives from an author, but for purposes of narratological analysis it is thought of as the result of a narrator's narrating activity' (1987a: 31, 32). This is a fudge: the boundaries between worlds cannot simply be erased in this way. 'Narrators' are every bit as much an abstraction from the text as their extended kinship group of 'implied authors', 'implied readers', 'narratees', 'focalisers', etc. They exist in the world on the other side of the textual window: in the interior domain of narrative, not in the top-level world of text, author, and reader.

forms, this book necessarily takes the broader view. A general theory of plot needs to explain what *kinds* of things can have plots in the first place. It is not self-evident why we can regularly speak of plot in epic, drama, the novel, comics, and film, but not routinely in music, dance, sculpture, or painting. The obvious answer would be that the first list can carry *narrative*; but this only shifts the question. Why can some media, but not others, convey 'narrative' (in the sense above, or any other)?

There are, I think, two conditions to satisfy. First, the medium needs to be able to represent *events* – not states, images, abstractions, or free-floating emotions. An 'event' may be mental rather than actual, but it has to connect to *something* in the world of concrete experience. Music cannot carry narrative because it has no way to represent the experience of the outer world.[10] The melodic ascent of the 1–3–5 major triad can convey 'an outgoing, active, assertive emotion of joy';[11] but there is no musical utterance to translate 'escaping certain death' or 'scoring against Juventus'.

Second and, for the view of plot proposed below, crucial: the medium must be *linear*. Stories happen in time; and narrative, in ways discussed at length below, likes to mimic this flow of time in telling its story. This in turn requires a textual medium that is capable of being processed, or 'read', in a linear sequence – ideally, one that *compels* its consumer to travel through it in one particular order. The classical, absolutely unilinear text is the spoken utterance: a series of phonemes produced and processed one-by-one in real time. But the literary work may offer a close fascimile: a string of words assembled in a single unambiguous order, and designed to be read in that order from first to last.

Needless to say, we may not always, perhaps ever, read this way in practice.[12] Even normal reading activities such as skipping, skimming, and retroversion distort the linearity of the text. Some texts artfully allow for this, by ensuring that the reader's eye is subtly directed to essential nuggets of text by typographical or structural cues – in the layout of dialogue, for example, or in the length and structure of paragraphs. But it always remains possible for readers to 'cheat' the intended textual order by time-honoured subterfuges such as peeking at the ending or leafing to the juicy bits (though some texts adroitly plan for this reader tactic as well). There are also, increasingly, experimental alternatives to the classical unilinear model of literary fiction. Some postmodern fictions, such as Cortázar's *Rayuela* and Pavic's *Dictionary of the Khazars* and *Landscape painted with tea*, are explicitly designed to be read in more than one possible sequence; while the rise of interactive fiction and hypertext opens intriguing new possibilities for plotting that have been imaginatively

---

[10] Not all musicologists would accept this. For 'narrative' and related issues of representation in instrumental music see the essays in Scher 1992 (cf. McClary 1994).
[11] Cooke 1959: 115.   [12] So, famously, Barthes 1975: 10–11.

exploited in electronic literary texts,[13] as well as by the games market in children's books and multimedia.[14]

Nevertheless, all narrative texts, in whatever medium, present a series of signs to be processed in a definite sequence – whether of the author's choosing, of the reader's, or of some sly pact between the two. Some kinds of text have a *double* information track, of words and images: so with drama, film, comics. The first two of these sustain linearity by unfolding before the audience in real time, but the third has much less direct control over the order in which the reader chooses to process the signs on a page. Yet even here a set of subtle conventions has evolved to impose a *sequence* on the static page[15] – whence Eisner's coinage of the term 'sequential art' as the defining characteristic of this medium.

For this book, therefore, a *text* is *a set of representational signs with a directional linear structure*. The signs may be words, images, or even (as in Andrew Sachs' BBC radio play *The escape*) inarticulate sounds, but if they can (a) represent events and (b) be processed in a determined order, then they can carry a narrative. To avoid ugly terms like 'processing', as well as to stress the essential unity of the narrative media, I describe the consumption of all such texts by the verb 'read'. I hope references to audiences of plays and films as 'readers', and to wordless performances or picture series as 'texts', will not seem needlessly polemical or perverse.

But there is a second, more serious difficulty with the TEXT level to Bal's model of the narrative process. Is it even meaningful – let alone useful – to draw a distinction between narrative and text at all? Can we really separate the presentation of the story to the reader from the words or images in which it is couched? The 'crisis' of narratology, proclaimed in the late eighties by some of the the the field's celebrities[16] and subsequently the basis for some powerful postmodern critiques,[17] stems above all from a recognition of this problem. Many theorists, especially French or

---

[13] As of writing, Joyce 1990 remains the touchstone work (print discussions in Bolter 1991: 123–7, Douglas 1992 and 1994: 165–72, Aarseth 1994: 69–71 and 1997: 85–96, Landow 1997: 192–7, and cf. Joyce 1995); but this is a rapidly-evolving field.

[14] Ryan 1988: 174 first noted the similar use of story trees in certain kinds of story-generation programs and the 'Choose Your Own Adventure' series of children's paperbacks popular in the 1980s; for Oulipian experiments in this vein see Motte 1986: 156–62, Mathews and Brotchie 1998: 195–7, and on this whole complex of interactive fiction, electronic and otherwise, Gardner 1989: 97–8, Bolter 1991: 140–3, Gibson 1996: 10–12 and 275–8, Aarseth 1997, Landow 1997: 178–218. These developments have tempted some postmodernists to proclaim the imminent apocalypse of Aristotelian narrative and theory; this is wishful thinking (see Aarseth 1997 for a critique). For an attempt at an explicitly Aristotelian theory of interactive media, see Laurel 1993.

[15] Eisner 1990: 38–99; McCloud 1993: 86, 104–6.

[16] See e.g. Rimmon-Kenan 1989, Brooke-Rose 1990, and cf. the uneasy palinode on 'positivism' in Bal 1997: xii–xiv.

[17] See especially Gibson 1996; cf. O'Neill 1994 and, for an attempt at rapprochement, Fludernik 1996.

French-inspired, remain suspicious of any abstractions from the text that put theoretical formalisations above what is actually there on the page or screen. Texts, and only texts, are real; content, meaning, communication are artifacts of reading, and exist only in the mental representations of the individual reader. It may conceivably be acceptable to distinguish the *object* of representation (story) from the medium (text), because a story can be argued to have a sort of objective existence as what Popper has called a 'world 3 object': a construct (such as 'five', 'genetics', or 'the eighteenth century') located purely in the world of ideas that is nevertheless shared by a group of individuals.[18] But to introduce a further level of abstraction (narrative) *between* the two seems both unnecessary and illegitimate. This is why a majority of theorists have treated narrative and text as identical, or even argued (against onion-layer models of hierarchical phantom strata) for a different kind of distinction altogether – between 'narrative' and 'narration', the narrative text and the voices that produce it.[19]

Part of the problem is that narratologists have been wary of claiming that what they are describing is a *cognitive schema*: a description of how narrative is processed, represented, and comprehended by its consumers.[20] In the weakest version, 'story' (and 'narrative', if distinguished further from the text itself) are simply constructs of the critic: they are descriptive tools we find convenient in the analysis of narrative texts, but their use is justified only by that convenience. De Jong puts it concisely: 'For matters of analysis it is useful to "pull out" (distinguish between) the three layers, but what we have, in fact, is only the text. It is through the text that we approach the story, through text and story, the fabula.'[21] This is over-cautious. It seems plain that both 'story' and 'narrative' *must* exist as something more than artifacts of the critic; indeed, I am not sure that a sensible line can be drawn between the cognitive manipulations performed on a text by critics on the one hand and any other kind of reader on the other. There is a better case: that 'story' and 'narrative', while clearly abstractions from the text, are abstractions *by the reader*, constructed in the course of the normal cognitive process of reading fiction.

To appreciate this, think about our everyday experience of reading a story. As we read on in real time, each successive word (or other sign) is being semantically decoded and added to a running sum of narrative

[18] Popper and Eccles 1977: 38ff.; Popper 1994.
[19] In such a model, the three terms 'story', 'narrative', and 'narration' are best pictured as vertices of a triangular interrelationship, rather than the successive onion-layers of a stratified model represented by 'story | narrative | text' (cf. Bal 1977: 6). But see Genette 1983: 14–15.   [20] The exception is Branigan 1992 (esp. 86–7).
[21] De Jong 1987a: 32 – using Bal's terminology of 'story' for what I call 'narrative', and 'fabula' for my 'story'.

information about the story as a whole. Yet this process, if we are truly gripped by the narrative, will be quite unconscious:[22] we think of ourselves as being 'in the middle of' the story, as if the story itself were unfolding in a real-time analogue to the time spanned by our reading. In reality, of course, we are not 'in' the story at all: we are sitting in a living-room chair or a darkened theatre, our attention absorbed in a mental universe conjured out of a stream of processed signs. The illusion of temporal succession within that universe is purely an analogue, constructed from the linear succession of signs. What we really have is a mental marker of the point in the story that the main sequential narrative has reached, at the point in the text to which we have so far read. And that marker is itself a construct, born of the most powerful and ancient of all narrative conventions: that the linear sequence of the text mimics the unfolding of the story in time.

But this illusory experience of living the story in time is not the *only* thing that is going on dynamically as we read. All the while, we are simultaneously building up a mental model of the story *as a whole*. And unlike the first model, this image of the story is *timeless*: it includes everything that 'has happened' and a good deal that 'is going to happen'. At the point we have reached in our journey through the text, there are still large areas of the map that are blurred or blank. We know some, but not all, of the events already 'past' – who found the body, perhaps, but not yet who committed the murder. We have an idea of some of the things that must still happen: the murderer unmasked, the lovers united, the survivors assigned their just deserts. But we do not yet know how these things are going to happen, or for certain that they can be guaranteed to happen at all. This narrative model does not develop in the timelike way that the text does – as if a curtain were rolling back and exposing everything to view an inch at a time. Rather, its linear development is *holographic*: from an initial blur to increasing focus and clarity. From the start of our reading, it is a *total* picture of the story, with successive details filled in as we go along. It is finally complete only when the story is 'over' – that is, when we read the last word of the text.

Now, clearly the differences between these two developing narrative models at a given point in our reading may be enormous. At the beginning of *Odyssey* v, for instance, our picture of the story *as a timeless whole* already includes the fairly certain details that Odysseus starts out from Troy with his full complement of crewmates, and finally kills the suitors, reclaims Penelope, and lives happily ever after in Ithaca. But our map of the situation *in time* has Odysseus trapped, alone and resourceless, on

---

[22] On the 'reading trance' see Nell 1988.

Calypso's island, unaware that the situation in Ithaca even exists[23] – let alone how he can possibly redeem it on his unaided own. The parts of the story that explain how Odysseus got from Troy to Ogygia, and how he will return from Ogygia to Ithaca and revenge, are left deliberately and tantalisingly blank.[24]

And I want to suggest two things about this abstractive aspect to the way we read narrative. First, the *tension* between our twin internal models of the story is the source of the dynamic and affective element in plot. What we, as readers, want is for our temporal and atemporal models of the story to coincide; and all the while we read, we are actively on the lookout for ways in which they will ultimately converge. Secondly, by controlling the flow of information about the story, the narrative text can to a large extent *control* the way those models, and thus the disparities between them, are constructed in the act of reading.[25] Take these two points together, and it follows that our desire for harmony between our two dissonant and incomplete story models makes us vulnerable to *sustained and purposeful affective manipulation*. It is this, I would argue, that accounts for the power of plot.

Clearly we may not, and probably will not, be conscious of the detailed workings of this process as we read. On the contrary, many texts find it in their interest to remind us of it as little as possible. But at a higher, simplified level of description the three terms 'text', 'narrative', and 'story' do precisely distinguish the stages we are aware of in the act of reading fiction. We can see, obviously, that what we are reading is a text, a mere optical array of printed words or projected images whose resemblance to the structure of our own experience of the world is purely conventional. But we are also required to posit, as a *sine qua non* of the narrative transaction, that there is, somehow and somewhere, inside or beyond that text, a story: a set of events which *do* conform to the shape and texture of real life. Its people are members of our own species, its world obeys the same or similar physical laws, and it unspools in a time with the same flow and structure as our own. At the same time, however, we sense that something intervenes between that world and its embodying words: that our access to the story is being gatekept by a ghostly appa-

---

[23] We will later learn that in fact he has apparently been informed of the situation on his visit to the underworld (XI.115–17). But this is certainly not the picture we have at the start of v.   [24] Sternberg 1978: 56–89.
[25] The idea that texts can do anything whatever to determine the way they are read is still abhorrent in some quarters (e.g. Fish 1989: 68–86). But it is clear from recent studies of linearity and its hypertextual alternatives that there are kinds of determinacy in inflexibly sequential texts that do not operate in hyperfiction; see Aarseth 1994, and for an attempt at empirical testing Hanauer 1998. *Re*-reading is a more complex but not qualitatively different case: see Prieto-Pablos 1998, and the essays in Galef 1998.

ratus of voices, vantages, and filters that is also being constructed from the text simultaneously with the story, and yet is not reducible to a part of either.

To see the importance of this for a model of plot, consider an analogy. When we watch a film or a television programme, we are processing not one narrative track but two. There is the visual text on the screen, and there is the soundtrack coming at us out of the speakers. They have been separately assembled, often by different people, and lovingly pasted together to create the impression of unity, but it is our 'reading' of the film that actually connects and collates the two. Without our being consciously aware of it, the sounds may be directing us to impose a meaning on the images that goes far beyond the literal content of what we see. And this is how the 'narrative' level functions in plotting. The screen image is the story, the necessary core of any fictional text. But as we read the text, we are also half-consciously picking up a commentary on it. Along with the story, the text dubs on top of it a stream of narrative metadata that guide the reader to assemble, and continuously to update, a sophisticated internal picture of the story as a whole. This stream can be sifted for nuggets of undigested story information that simply need to be inserted at the appropriate point in the model. But much of it arrives in *code*, and needs to be run through a translator before it can be used.

So what we are fed as we read the text is in actually three things. First, there are the raw *sequential* data of story: 'She entered the room. The telephone rang.' These we use as our axis of internal orientation, our index of where we 'are' in the time of the tale. Second, there are *non-sequential* facts, whether purely narratorial ('This was to be their last evening together') or tied to the simulated mental processes of viewpoint ('It dawned on him that the woman at the bar was Juliette, whom he had last seen six years ago in Vienna'). This second stream of information feeds directly into our holographic story-model. And finally, and most subtly, there are coded *rules* about the universe of the story, from which we can ourselves deduce further conclusions about missing elements of the global model ('She knew that Peter was not the kind of man who breaks a promise given in good faith').

All the while we read, then, we abstract. Along with the timelike stream of story information, we are also absorbing a series of clues, pointers, and hints about the shape of the story as a whole: as Chekhov famously counselled Shchukin, 'if in the first chapter you say that a gun hung on the wall, in the second or third chapter it must without fail be discharged'.[26] And in our private screening-room, as we unspool the text and run it

[26] Kotelianksy 1927: 23.

through our mental projector, a specialised lens filters the different-wave-length signals that emerge into a triptych of juxtaposed images. The main panel, obviously, is our cinema screen proper, on which is projected a vivid moving image of the story unfolding in time. It looks real enough, but we should stress again it is only a projected image. We see only what the camera intends us to see, through a carefully framed moving window on the imaginary world. And even the semblance of time is a technical sleight. If we think about what we are seeing, we will realise that the flow of story time is being subtly edited throughout; and if we slow the projection mechanism down and examine it closely, we will see that what looks on the surface like real movement is just an optical trick conjured up by a machine-gun barrage of snapshots, a procession of tiny marching frames of information.

But to the side of this screen is a second, less turbulent panel. This wing of the triptych is more like a blackboard, and on it is a set of notes and diagrams of the rules that govern the story universe. There is a sketch map of the fictional world, roughly jotted with arrows and x-marks; a cast list of characters, with thumbnail annotations of their essential qualities and importance; and a table of rules explaining which events and story states are permitted, and which forbidden. Unlike the first panel, the contents of this board are only intermittently updated. There was a flurry of writing in the early stages, but most of the notes are soon finished in draft and only require an occasional confirming tick. But just now and again, a subtitle will appear on the central screen with an important update or correction. It will be labelled clearly enough for readers to chalk it up in the correct place on the board without taking their eyes off the screen. (It might say something like 'Moral rules/14(c)/update: to 'violence is not permitted to succeed as a strategy of response' append 'except where the response is to a prior act of actual or intended violence from the rival party'.')

The third panel is different again. It is a partly-finished jigsaw picture of the story as a whole. The lower parts are gradually filling up in an orderly sequence, left to right and one layer at a time, but even here a few strategic blank areas may still be waiting to be tiled. The borders are mostly in place, and some areas of the upper picture are beginning to take tentative shape – especially at the top, where already a patch of colour on the border seems to match a number of still unplaced pieces. There will be patches of partly connected fragments still looking for a place, and scatters of pieces loosely laid in the regions where they seem to belong. From time to time, a note on the blackboard will point to where pieces connect. But the placing of pieces is only complete when a particular section of the image turns up on the adjacent screen; and sometimes the screen will abruptly reveal that what we thought all along was a piece of sky was actually a part of one of the characters' coats.

In many kinds of storytelling, these flanking panels are at least as important as the main screen. They may even be more important: in detective fiction, the reader is unabashedly challenged to complete the jigsaw against the textual clock. But however it is used, the dynamic relationship between this detachedly global and achronic model of the story on the one hand, and our involved illusion of experiencing the story in time on the other, is one of the most powerful instruments of narrative art. In immersive reading, the timeless part of our narrative model may easily become invisible to our conscious attention, and we may seem to translate the linear text directly into a series of linear events in time. But whether at a conscious level or a subliminal, we are performing two higher-level cognitive operations all the time we read. First, we are making a constant series of checks and comparisons between our timelike and our timeless models of the story. And second, we are continuously refining the hologram by *extrapolation* – inductively and deductively projecting conclusions about the story from the narrative rules supplied.

Now, this process of extrapolation is ultimately made possible by a property of narrative whose implications for plotting are central to my model. *In the coding of a story into a narrative text, the universe of the story is necessarily presented as a closed system.* The *degree* of closure will vary widely, according to the needs of the particular text. But the *levels* on which such closure operates are more or less constant across all genres, modes, and cultures of narrative, because they are intrinsic to the narrative process itself. First and most obviously, the universe of the story is closed in *time*. All stories have to end, for the simple reason that all *texts* are finite.[27] The *quality* of the closure may vary considerably from the Aristotelian sense of 'end' as the terminus of a self-contained causal chain. Some stories may apparently 'just stop' – though even that is a sign that a narrative pattern of some kind has been completed, albeit perhaps a pattern consciously antagonistic to classical ideas of plotting.

But stories are closed in other ways as well. To varying degrees, for instance, they are also closed in *space*. One of the most strictly closed in this respect is classical New Comedy and its derivatives, where all the story is tied directly or indirectly to a single outdoor street-scene. There

---

[27] There are, of course, novelty examples of stories that do not, in fact, terminate in the ordinary sense – either by going into loops, or by ending in the narrative equivalent of an infinite series, or by closing the whole internal timeline of the story into a circle. A minimal example is John Barth's 'Frame-tale' from *Lost in the funhouse* (1968), an infinite sentence composed of ten words looped on to a Moebius band. But such recursive gimmicks are still in an acceptable sense endings – points in the story beyond which nothing new occurs.

are forms, such as film and the novel, that may seem at a first glance not to be closed at all. But even here the very finite nature of the text forces some kind of limit on the range of locations used. There is not an infinite expanse of *narrative* space available, even if the *story* space available is, theoretically, boundless; even if a novel invoked a new location in every sentence, it would only get through a few thousand. And in practice, the internal logic of the story world is bound to enforce much tighter spatial limits than these. As a maximum, all stories – science fiction, obviously, excepted – are confined to the surface of the Earth or its close proximity, and the great majority to a fairly narrow range of that surface. What is more, in any story certain locations will be unavoidably more *important* than others, exerting strong pressure on the narrative to *structure* the story space in a significant way. In some forms – Greek tragedy, for example – this structural significance is very overt and insistent. In others, such as the first half of the *Odyssey*, it may seem to be scarcely there at all. Yet in fact, as will later be argued, the *Odyssey* is one of the most coherently spatialised narratives in literature – albeit in an adventurous and unexpected way, of great significance for later plot technique.

Thirdly, all stories have a necessarily finite *cast*. A great many stories go much further, and limit the main action of a story to the experience of one single lead player and a highly selected supporting cast who interact with that lead. Characters are assigned varying degrees of significance in the narrative: one hero or heroine, a handful of second-circle speaking parts, and a faceless outer throng of extras. Furthermore, the range of possible *behaviours* of characters in the first two circles is tightly determined by their 'characterisation' (a famous problem term we shall consider further below); and those in the third circle, being purely functional and instrumental, are more restricted yet.

But quite apart from these more concrete-seeming limitations on the range and structure of story, there are in all story universes further rules of a less tangible and more purely narrative kind. These rules restrict the operation of *causality* in the story universe, by excluding certain theoretical possibilities from narrative consideration – even when they may be more 'realistic' than what actually happens. It is never, for instance, an option in the *Odyssey* for Penelope to die in the measles epidemic of 1216 BC. *Why* this is impossible is not instantly easy to say, let alone how the reader comes to know it. Indeed, it is precisely questions of this kind that existing theories of plot seem unable to address. But classical narrative is permeated by such restrictions on the real-world structure of causality; and the next chapter makes a first attempt to analyse their operation. The development of a workable framework for such rules is, I will argue, an achievement specific to archaic and classical Greece, and is one of the most remarkable, if least remarked, legacies of ancient poetry to European culture.

Now, this narrative presentation of a story universe as a closed system seems to a large extent a 'natural' metaphor, in the sense that it presses into service a cognitive mechanism we use instinctively from infancy onwards in structuring our experience of the real world. We may believe that our view of the outer universe is fully open and unrestricted, but the very way we process experience guarantees that it is not. We centre *history* on the span between our individual birth and death, and our lives on the gliding bead of present time that forms a moving boundary between memory and desire, the ineradicable past and the infinitely possible future. Our subjective *map* of the world is limited in detail to a tiny handful of familiar or important locations, with the conceptual topography reflecting our personal priorities in the organisation of individual spatial experience.[28] Our mental *directory* of the human species has large entries for persons known to us from close acquaintance, while the volumes for (say) Gabon or Sarawak may be almost entirely empty, save for a few blurred video stills pasted in from half-remembered documentaries. And even our perception of what can and cannot *happen*, particularly to ourselves, is tightly restricted by a model built up from experience and imagination – though it may of course be surprised now and again by the more fertile inventiveness of the world outside our heads.

And cognitive science recognises that these strategies of selection and rule-making are central to the intertwined processes of learning and memory.[29] In both, we make implicit decisions about the relevance of information: what needs to be retained, what can be painlessly ignored. In both, we look for general principles that can help us package and retrieve complex data as structures rather than as disorderly heaps of mental lumber. Some of these organising principles reflect rules that exist in nature: ice is cold, things fall downwards, stones do not talk. Others are local and conventional assumptions: fairytales end happily, there are six balls in an over, men with sooty faces and lamps on their helmets are miners.

It seems very likely, then, that what storytelling does is to hijack a set of existing mechanisms we use for structuring the external world, and to harness them in building *artificial* universes inside our heads. If we accept this, we must surely also accept that this machinery is not ideally described by a linguistic model. Because of the seminal influence of linguistics on both structuralist theory and cognitive science, most attempts at a formal model of plot, in either field, have based their formal structure

---

[28] See e.g. Gould and White 1986; Downs and Stea 1977.
[29] For a lucid interdisciplinary survey of relevant work see now Emmott 1997.

on language systems. But few would now claim that these models have been outstandingly successful in any of their main declared aims – in generating story texts, in explaining how story texts are processed and remembered by readers, or even in providing a sufficiently powerful and flexible descriptive vocabulary for the analysis and classification of narrative forms. The failure of the story-grammar model is symptomatic. There seems no reason to suppose that the way we construct models of the universe is any any useful sense syntagmatic – that the structure of cause and effect, for instance, is comprehended by some kind of 'grammar of events'. This is not to dispute that linguistic structures are involved at the surface level of processing, the translation of textual signs into narrative code. But for the kind of complex, multi-chambered machinery I have suggested is involved in the deeper cognitive operation of decoding narrative into story, it is hard to see how a linguistic model could be made to work.

So is there a ready-made alternative? One influential movement in cognitive science has sometimes seemed to offer one. In the seventies and early eighties, a number of workers in the cognitive field became interested in the detailed parallels between the human modelling of reality and of fiction. The Yale group, in particular, led by Schank and Abelson, showed that fairly simple and unitary models could simultaneously represent the way stories are remembered, the way narrative texts are understood during reading, and the way real-life situations are addressed from a repertoire of experience. In particular, Abelson's idea of 'scripts', sets of articulable rules akin to Bartlett's 'schemas' and Goffman's 'frames' that describe what is and is not expected to happen in a given situation, has drawn considerable interest from narratologists, as well as sparking some of the most successful attempts to create and understand narrative texts by computer.[30]

Yet the long-term prospects for the script model do not look inspiring. Though quite wieldy for analysing very limited repertoires of behaviour and narrative types, it has proved hard, perhaps impossible, to reduce to any widely generalisable formal principles. The Yale school's most successful experiment in narrative modelling, Meehan's TALE-SPIN program, succeeds despite rather than because of its Schankian trappings (which in any case are fairly superficial). Its most impressive innovation is less the goal-centred, problem-solving approach it takes to story situations than its view of stories as tightly inventoried pocket *universes*, whose inhabitants negotiate a sophisticated three-way exchange between what they know, what they have, and what they need.

[30] Meehan 1976; Schank and Abelson 1977; Wilensky 1982. For scripts in narratology see especially Herman 1997.

And this kind of *world-based* schema has had a considerable boost in recent years from an important movement in narrative semiotics itself. The impetus comes from an application of possible-worlds semantics to the theory of fiction, seeking to understand narrativity in terms of the way fictional universes are constructed as a constellation of *embedded modal worlds*.[31] In this model, fiction is a Schrödinger's cattery of virtual states of affairs desired, permitted, expected, and believed that exist within the consciousness of characters, and which the reader perceives as a suspension of possible realities out of which the actual storyline crystallises along the thread of narrative time. It is a powerful and sophisticated model, for which ambitious claims have been made; but I admit to some reservations about its completeness as a description of how narrative modalities are constructed, as well as over its wieldiness as a tool for the practical analysis of texts. In particular, and in common with Meehan's TALE-SPIN, it seems too centred on *characters* to be able to deal easily with those important constraints on the narrative world that originate outside its inhabitants.

There are signs, however, that a fourth, related model is beginning to emerge, especially among those narratologists who have taken an interest in the *dynamic* structure of such fictional worlds as they modulate between their successive states.[32] It is a model, moreover, that has the double advantage of being both a *natural* metaphor and (in notable contrast to linguistic structures) a *vernacular* one that turns up across all cultures. In this model, narrative worlds are structurally homologous with a second, very familiar type of world-3 universe, whose structure and operation we learn to understand almost as early in life as we learn to make sense of stories. Like the worlds of stories, this second type of model universe is also highly abstract and artificial, yet fully communicable through a variety of textual signs. It is what – despite Wittgenstein – we continue to find it convenient to call a *game*.[33]

Games share several striking properties with the universes of fiction. Both are closed, but in a configuration that is essentially dynamic rather than static: they cannot exist without development in time from one state

[31] Dolozel 1976ab, 1979, 1988, 1989, 1998; Eco 1979, 1989; Maitre 1983; Pavel 1985, 1986, 1989; Currie 1990; Gerrig 1993; Ronen 1990ab, 1994; Semino 1997; and especially Ryan 1985, 1991, 1992b, 1995.
[32] See especially Pavel 1985, Ryan 1985; to distinguish my own somewhat different approach, I have borrowed from Ryan's paper the term 'narrative universe' for the more widely-used 'fictional world'.
[33] I use this term in a hard rather than a soft sense. 'Most of the uses of "game" in recent literary discourse seem sadly invertebrate ... The ideas of games advanced by some literary scholars should convince readers that they could never have played even a very simple game' (Wilson 1990: 79 – the standard work on the term's many uses and abuses in literary theory).

to a different one. The contents and articulation of both can be formally described, though such a description is always complete in the case of a game and always approximate for a story world. Most intriguingly, both consciously emulate, albeit to varying degrees of explicitness and detail, the structure of the actual universe outside.[34] Yet neither is straightforwardly a *representation* of anything: it is a self-standing symbolic system whose mimesis of reality is incidental to its formal operation. The rules of Monopoly, for instance, are independent of the game's metaphoric mimesis of the world of real estate – just as Propp recognised that narrative functions can be abstracted from their subjects and still preserve their structural identity.[35]

Without insisting on the point – I know of no empirical studies to back it up – I would suggest that these homologies between the two different kinds of model universe may be more than coincidental:[36] that narrative universes and games are different cultural artifacts of a common underlying cognitive apparatus, originally evolved to interpret real-world experience into an intelligible system of mental representations. This might explain why games and stories seem so often to merge in such a wide range of cultural domains, from children's role-play to the narrative puzzles of detective fiction and story-driven multimedia games.

I should, however, make it clear that my use of this convenient cognitive metaphor makes no claims whatever on the *mathematical* notion of games. Fictional worlds are like some games in some respects, but these are not generally the mathematical ones of von Neumann's 'game theory' proper.[37] One can imagine other, equally pseudo-formal metaphors, but the game is such an accessible, vernacular concept that it stands out as far the most useful analogic tool for uncovering the internal machinery of

[34] The variation is much wider for games, even within a single limited class. Among board games, for instance, *go* is amimetic, chess is metonymic, Monopoly metaphoric. There are even games (field sports, for example) that use real-world constituents, such as human agents, as the elements of their model universes; such games might be construed as an equivalent to the narrative mode of drama.

[35] As an undergraduate I used to play a version of Monopoly that substituted Cambridge Colleges for the streets, courts for houses and chapels for hotels, with the academic metaphor waggishly extended to every space on the board and every card in the stacks. The rules remained as ever: the pleasure was purely in the novelty of their metaphoric expression.

[36] For chessplay as a vehicle for the study of larger cognitive processes see especially Saariluoma 1995.

[37] Pavel 1985: 14 credits his model to 'notions derived from game-theory', but I can see little direct debt beyond the very broad terminology of 'moves'. The remarkable Romanian school of 'mathematical poetics' led by Solomon Marcus has made a number of attempts to apply the mathematics of games to the poetics of theatrical plotting; some of the results can be judged in English in a special issue of *Poetics* (6.3, 1977: articles by Lalu, Teodorescu-Brînzeu, and Steriadi-Bogdan). For an attempt to develop a game-theoretical model of *author–reader* interactions, see Bruss 1977 and Davey 1984.

plot. Its use in narrative theory has been relatively limited, Pavel 1985 being the outstanding instance to date; but as the next chapter explains in detail, I want to press the metaphor much further, and to use terms like 'move' in a somewhat different sense.

This way of talking about the structure of narrative worlds – by exploiting their formal resemblance to the structure of games – is the final element in the definition of plot I want to propose here. *Plot*, I suggest, *is the affective predetermination of a reader's dynamic modelling of a story, through its encoding in the structure of a gamelike narrative universe and the communication of that structure through the linear datastream of a text. In a classical plot, this narrative universe is strongly closed, privileging the values of economy, amplitude, and transparency.*

Leaving the second sentence for Chapter 4 to amplify, let me briefly explain how the first is intended to draw the threads of this chapter together. The 'coding' of story into narrative typically gives it the form of a timelike stream of story events – but with a crucial editorial overlay of viewpoint and narration, in which certain events and editorial comments are flagged with labels identifying their role in the game structure. Filtered off and decoded, these labels carry a wide assortment of meta-narrative mottoes that tell us what story information, explicit or inferred, to place where in our jigsaw synopsis of the story as a whole. 'This character is a player; you must retain an interest in the fulfilment of her goals. That character is not; he is simply a functional instrument in the fulfilment of others' story goals.' Or: 'This episode demonstrates a rule of play; it will be invoked in a parallel episode later in the narrative.' Or again: 'These events continue to have consequences, but off the field of play. This character will not appear on the board again.' Or: 'This tension must be resolved as a part of the endgame. The resolution will be complete when such-and-such conditions are satisfied.'[38]

Plot, then, is something texts do inside our heads in the action of reading. They take advantage of the different simultaneous levels of

[38] Like Long 1976: 20, I am mixing metaphors here: normally we have pieces on a board and players on a pitch. But they are formally equivalent, at least for my purposes. My particular species of the genus 'game' is a multiplayer board-game (a card- or word-game may be mathematically quite similar, but is useless for my analogy) of strategy (rather than chance), in which each player takes part as an individual (not as a member of a team) and is represented by a single moving piece on the board (so that there is formal identity between 'players' and 'pieces'). Only a few games actually fit this model in every respect, though one large family is the role-playing adventure games of the *Dungeons & Dragons* type that became popular in the 1970s. Particularly significant is the fact that these games require an entire narrative universe to be laboriously set up *ad hoc* for every game, resulting in a considerable secondary market in ready-made modules, the more elaborate of which can impart a strong storylike directional push to the course of play: more evidence for the close formal and cultural relationship between narrative and games, as the traditional space between them becomes ever more colonised.

mental machinery we use in processing fiction from text into narrative into story: superimposing a system of gamelike narrative rules on the structure of a fictional world, and then feeding us, bit by bit, information about the progress and the overall shape of that game that deliberately encourages tension between our simultaneous, interdependent, yet contrastive models of the story-in-time and the story-as-a-whole. It is a rearguard action fought by texts against the power of the reader and their own openness and indeterminacy – an attempt to seize control of the cognitive activity of reading, by playing directly to the mental structures we use for our construction of experience. And it is a property specific to *fictional texts* because its operation depends essentially on coding a constructed universe (a fictional world) in linear form (a text).

I want to make some fairly strong claims for this view of plot, in response to the challenges raised in Chapter 1. First, it preserves the traditional centrality of the notion of *causality*, because what game rules do is precisely to define the causal machinery of their universe. It is thus a model that draws a solid rather than a dotted line between causal links and other kinds of structurally significant patterning (formal or textual correspondences, thematic development, etc.) that may shape the reader's expectation of narrative outcome – *except* where such patterning is argued or implied to be itself the result of a supernatural causality.[39] Second, it offers a compact solution to the problem of *narrativity*: a 'tellable' story is one that allows the story world to be constructed as a minimal game of sufficient complexity to set up affective dislocation between the reader's diachronic and synchronic models of the story, while untellable stories fail to allow an adequate game structure to be read from the story text. And finally, and of special value for my purposes, the game model is *descriptively* powerful. In particular, it allows narrated and dramatic forms to be discussed according to a shared scheme of common elements, and thus for epic, drama, and the novel to be treated as a historical continuum – in short, for a history of narrative to begin to look writable.

Ultimately, these claims stand or fall on the use to be got from the narrative-universe model – specifically, on the merits of the game analogy as a general vocabulary of description for what I see as the most important narrative structures in the dynamics of plot. In the next chapter, I outline the main terms of this vocabulary in detail, and describe how I see its ele-

---

[39] In contrast to some models, for example, it *excludes* techniques such as ring-composition, verbal patterning, book-division and book-structure, and paratextual allusion to other narrative templates – elements closely implicated in the formation of narrative expectation, yet which significantly would *not* be covered by the kinds of vernacular usage and understanding of 'plot' from which we began.

ments as functioning in practice. Then in Chapter 4 I try to define the specialised version of this system I call *classical* plotting; and in the transitional Chapter 5 pass from theory to history, briefly reviewing the main rivals to this system as they emerge in the literature of archaic and classical Greece.

3   The narrative universe

In this chapter, I want to use the vocabulary of games to set out an elementary system of terms and categories for discussing the structure of narrative worlds, and to give a brief account of what I see as their general range of functions in plotting as defined at the end of the previous chapter. The resilience of the game analogy makes it possible, I think, to get away with a reasonably parsimonious lexicon of basic terms and types. They fall into three groups. First, there is the *shape* of the total narrative universe in time (the narrative 'clock') and in space (the 'board'). Second, there is the human *population* of that universe: the 'players', or characters, and the 'moves' they are empowered to make. Finally, there is the framework of external *rules* that they play by, and particularly the 'endgame' conditions that must be satisfied to complete the closure of narrative in story time.

1   The clock

When I say the game of plot is played to a *narrative* clock, I mean one that registers the difference between what we might call 'story time' and 'text time'. *Story time* is the absolute chronology of the story universe, and (barring a few science-fictional exceptions) it obeys the rules of real-world temporality – with an irreversible arrow of causality and entropy, and (if we are allowed to overlook relativistic effects) a fixed rate of universal flow. *Text time* is likewise absolute and, under normal conditions, unidirectional: it is measured by the yardage of physical signs from which the text is constructed, irrespective of the pace or sequence of their processing by a reader.[1] In contrast to both, the *narrative time* measured by the game clock is entirely fluid: it can start, stop, run faster or slower, suspend

---

[1] In the case of film, this is in any case constant, at twenty-four frames per second; while in live performance text time *is* real time. But I want to make the point that text time is measured by the number of signs elapsed, not by the rate at which they are consumed. Halfway through a book is still halfway no matter how long it takes to get there in real-time reading.

movement, or reset to an earlier or later date. In some cases, it can even run backwards.

What the clock specifically records is the passage of *primary narrative*.[2] By *primary* narrative I mean the top level of the story's narrating, as opposed to subsidiary narratives that are reported within it. In *Odyssey* IV, for example, Menelaus' speech in primary narrative embraces the *secondary* narrative of his own wanderings, which in turn contains the *tertiary* narrative of Proteus' prophecy. John Barth's 'Menelaiad', a *jeu d'esprit* much savoured by narratologists, contrives to extend the nesting to a septenary level of embedding; but the record still seems to belong to Antonius Diogenes' *Fantastic adventures beyond Thule* as known from Photius' summary, in which Antonius apparently reported to Faustinus (1) Balagrus' transcription (2) of Erasinides' written record (3) ?of Cymbas' dictated reproduction (4)? of Dinias' narrative (5) of Dercyllis' account (6) of Astraeus' version (7) of Philotis' story (8) of Mnesarchus and Pythagoras (9). In these two cases the top level of narration is a document rather than an extended narrative, but there is still an implicit primary-narrative situation in the world of the document's existence and transmission to the reader.

This 'primary' narrative consists of the part or parts of the story which the reader is invited to experience analogically in time. For that reason, it normally keeps to a sequential, timelike structure, with only minimal anachronies and embedding. The one widely tolerated exception to this principle is the special case of simultaneous story events in different locations – which cannot be simultaneously reported in a unilinear text, and so from the *Iliad* onwards use a 'meanwhile . . .' pattern of successively narrated segments. Otherwise, when any other kind of flashback or flashforward needs to be embedded in the primary narrative level, the classical solution is to disguise the narratorial intrusion, by hinting that the embedded narrative is at least partly a secondary report, the thoughts of a viewpoint character transcribed. We meet this, for instance, in the most famous ancient case, the tale of Odysseus' scar – which pause-buttons the narrative of the hero's recognition by Eurycleia at the precise moment when memory of the scar flashes into Odysseus' thoughts.[3]

The narrative clock serves six main functions. It marks the start and finish of primary narrative, and the boundaries between successive phases

[2] I use this term to simplify the subtle but inelegant Genettian terminology of 'diegetic levels'. See Genette 1980: 227–31.
[3] *Odyssey* XIX.390–470. As a general rule, primary narrative is modally more straightforward than secondary – which can embrace lies and half-lies, imperfect memories, errors, as well as predictively imperfect vows, wishes, prophecies, and the like. Only 'unreliable' narrators, such as the narrator of Lucian's *True history*, confound the modality of primary narrative.

of play. It also helps us keep track of the story as we read, by measuring its elapse, timing its flow, and locating episodes relative to one another in story chronology. To recast this in plot terms, it feeds into our narrative model a beginning, an end, and an internal temporal structure, as well as helping us in various ways to label the pieces of our story jigsaw with the appropriate absolute dates. Let us look more closely at each of these functions in turn.

(i) To begin with beginnings, the narrative clock is set running not when the story starts, but when the *primary narrative* opens. This cannot be earlier than the beginning of the story, but it can be a good deal later. Both the Homeric epics begin nine years into a ten-year story, and at points cast their narrative net still farther back. In fact, it can often be quite difficult to determine where exactly a *story* begins. Aristotle's helpful-sounding suggestion that a 'beginning' should be an event that is not the result of an earlier event is, taken literally, an absurdity; apart from the cosmological big bang, there is no such thing. Where does the story of the *Iliad* begin? – with the plague? the rape of Helen? *gemino ab ovo*? with the birth of Achilles? the birth of Thetis? the birth of Zeus? No wonder that the poet felt it best to refer this question to the divine wisdom of the Muse; for the Muse's secret is that primary narrative can begin absolutely anywhere. Secondary narrative, unlike primary, is unbounded, so that all relevant backstory can always (given sufficient ingenuity) be embedded in the primary narrative at the most appropriate points.

(ii) We might imagine *endings* worked in a similar way, but in fact they are far more constrained. For one thing, it is not possible simply to trust in the Muse and stick the narrative pin blindfold in the graph of story time, because the end of primary narrative has normally to do double duty as the end of story. Any protrusion of story beyond the temporal limit of primary narrative has to be either dismissed as of no narrative interest (happy-ever-after endings, for instance) or somehow embedded in secondary narrative. This is not quite as impractical as it sounds, because a common endgame pattern in classical plotting is to establish a set of programmed consequences as part of the rule-system, and then to terminate primary narrative at the point where the conditions are satisfied. (Once we know that, if the hero kills the dragon, he will marry the princess, inherit the throne, and live to a happy old age, the credits can come up the moment the dragon is dispatched.) But it is still difficult to embed more than a very general and narratively uninteresting series of moves and positions in this way. The *Odyssey* tries, through Tiresias' prophecy, to do more, but modern taste finds the effect rather odd.

Secondly, one advantage to beginnings is that they do not have to be signalled in advance. But endings, by their nature, loom on the far horizon throughout our narrative journey. It is, of course, perfectly *possible* for the narrative clock to be stopped as simply and as arbitrarily as it began. Many narratives do this, merely ending at a point of adequate closure without any prior advertisement to the reader (unless of course we can see the end coming in textual time – by counting the pages left, or by looking up the start of the next programme). But if the *anticipation* of an ending is to feed into our narrative model, we need to know *in advance* when the clock is going to be stopped – to have, as it were, an alarm set.

This can be done in one of two ways. The easier is simply to incorporate an absolute temporal *deadline* into the narrative: a point where the curtain will ring down after a specified elapse of playing time, irrespective of the state of the game at that moment. In such cases, obviously, the reader's uncertainty over how the game will end is shifted from *when* to *how*. Not surprisingly, it is a device used much more in modern narrative than in ancient, where the accurate measurement of instantaneous absolute time was technologically impractical. Nevertheless, we do find sunrise and sunset occasionally used as temporal markers in drama – such as the deadlines set for financial transactions in Roman comedy, which in any case correspond by convention to the span of the play.

The alternative, and far the commoner technique in classical plotting, is to make the deadline not absolute but *conditional*. In this variation, the game will terminate not at a fixed point in time, but if and when a certain set of conditions are fulfilled: when Penelope's web is finished, say, or Telemachus reaches manhood, or when it is determined whether Odysseus is dead or alive. Because such convergences are a product not of temporality as such but rather of the operation of local narrative *rules*, I reserve such *endgame* configurations for discussion below.

(iii) Both techniques of ending can of course be used *within* the narrative, to section it off into more-or-less closed *subgames* or episodes (like the 'levels' common in the structure of computer games). In the first type, a narrative whistle can blow at a prearranged *time*, signalling players to move to their starting positions for the next phase of the game – perhaps taking with them whatever transferable advantage they may have gathered in the first stage of play. In *Iliad* IX–X, for instance, the anticipated resumption of fighting the following morning spurs the Greeks to try and better their positional advantage during the normally inactive period of dusk to dawn: first by enticing Achilles back to active play, and, failing that, by stealing a march on the Trojan strategists. Alternatively, a certain set of *conditions* may need to be met before a required phase of the game may be started: thus Odysseus has to contrive a way back to Ithaca before he can even begin to address the problem of the suitors.

(iv) It can help the plot in a number of ways to keep track of the span of story time *elapsed* in primary narrative. First, it contributes to the sense of *verisimilitude*. A narrative is more seductive if we can picture not just *where* we 'are' in the story, but *when*: what time of day it is, where the sun is, the temperature, the quality of the light. Secondly, in a narrative where story time is clearly structured into a regular cycle of *routine*, a sense of time elapsed can help us to anticipate both the quantity and the nature of the action remaining in an episode. If the hero's daily routine is to work nine to five, and the narrative clock currently shows noon, we can reasonably expect the next five hours of story to deal with events in the workplace. Finally (though this will not always fall within the narrowly causalistic definition of plot adopted here), temporal patterning can be used in a purely *formal* way, as a grid on to which our model of the story can be structurally mapped. If we know the story is three days long, for example, we will naturally look for, and if necessary impose, certain kinds of formal pattern in the action of those three days: beginning, middle, end (ABC); echoes between the events of days 1 and 3 (ABA'); and parallels between the three days (AA'A'). But we cannot do this without a sense of the particular timing of particular actions on their own respective days.

(v) The relationship between the *rates of flow* of story and textual time has been much analysed in narratology. Sometimes, as in direct speech, the two may synchronise word-for-word; at other times the narrative may speed or slow, jump or freeze. Bal (1985: 71–7, 1997: 102–11) arranges these different options into a particularly elegant fivefold classification of narrative tempi, in descending order of textual speed relative to story.[4] First, there is *ellipsis*, where a story event is jumped instantaneously over without any narration at all. Second and third, we have the familiar notions of *summary* (where an event is reported in passing outline, but without full dramatic details) and *scene* (where the narrative sets out illusionistically to evoke the event's actual occurrence and duration in story time). Fourth is Chatman's *stretch* (Bal's *slowdown*), where the narration of an event in story time takes so long as to evoke a sense of slow motion. We meet this frequently, for instance, in Homeric descriptions of woundings: a bravura variation is the improbable penetration of Menelaus' spear through Paris's armour and tunic in the split second before he dodges (*Iliad* III.357–60). And finally, there is *pause*, where a single time-frozen image occupies the narrative, as frequently in passages of static description or analysis.

A couple of points are worth noting on this. First, the availability of tempi depends on the narrative mode. Narrated literature and film have

[4] Following Genette's fourfold division (1980: 95); a similar, but less logically ordered, list in Chatman 1978: 68–75.

access to all five, though film has to use special techniques to approximate summary (through voiceover, montage, or fast motion). But drama is limited to two primary-narrative tempi, scene and ellipsis – the latter very rarely used in ancient drama outside Aristophanes, except for the special case of trilogic intervals in Aeschylus. Secondly, narrative tempo correlates inversely with story detail: the faster the pace, the less significant detail can be included. This frustrating paradox forces storytellers into some difficult decisions: do they build up to a climax by *accelerando*, or by increasing textural richness and density? The *Odyssey* actually tries out both, opting for retardation in XIII–XXII and acceleration in XXIV, though most readers feel little doubt which is the more successful technique in its context.[5]

(vi) Finally, the presence of a reliable narrative clock allows the reader to construct an orderly and consistent model of the story in time from what may be a radically *dislocated* narrative sequence. Temporal markers allow us to datestamp the individual fragments of action. When we slot them into our story jigsaw, we can see that certain events turn out to be simultaneous, or linked in a sequence of previously unnoticed cause and effect. We can see where a storyline has a crucial gap, and what kind of information is needed to fill it. So long as the story information we are supplied is flagged with a sufficient marker of its place in the story chronology, there need be no close relationship at all between the timeline of the story and the sequence of bits in the text: the narrative is free to dictate its story to the reader in whatever order has the desired hermeneutic effect. If this means telling the story backwards, or inside-out, or even with the absolute story chronology obliterated entirely, plot has the power to do all three. All it needs to do is to display, or choose not to display, the narrative clock. The *Odyssey* is clearly intoxicated with its discovery of this device's versatility; its bravura showcase of the narrative tricks made possible becomes a *de facto* handbook for all future users.

2   The board

If the role of time in narrative has been well discussed and understood, the importance of *space* has been comparatively neglected. Its narrative manipulation has three main functions: to *limit*, to *structure*, and to *reify* the reader's modelling of the story. First, by setting spatial *boundaries* to the story, the sphere of the action is made finite. Certain story possibilities are ruled artificially out: in a country-house murder, the killer is likely to

[5] 'Our poet, who has proceeded hitherto with dignified step at moderate pace, suddenly indulges in a moment of leap-frog followed by a gallop for the goal . . . the story rushes spasmodically and deviously to its lame conclusion' (Page 1955: 112–13).

be apprehended within the grounds rather than (as might seem more 'realistic') in Paraguay. Second, the *shape* of the board offers a guide both to the shape of the narrative and to the structure of relationships within it. The action, for example, of Golding's *Rites of passage* trilogy is mapped around three strongly-defined spatial structures: the internal divisions of the ship itself; the relation between the ship's island community and the hostile sea outside; and the voyage from familiar England to alien antipodes upon which the ship is bound. And third, the setting of action in specific, strongly evoked *places* is a major device in fleshing out the story with a convincing pretence of reality – of seducing the reader's assent to the fake tangibility of a wholly imaginary world.

Before we look at these three themes in more detail, two passing definitions may be helpful. I use the term *location* to mean a spatial area of the narrative board narrow enough for everyone in it to communicate freely. As a rule of thumb, a location will extend as far as a character in it can comfortably see and hear. In visual media there is a further constraint: the location has to occupy such space as the *audience* can actually see. In theatre, where the visible space is of constant size, there is little flexibility; in film or comics, which allow varying degrees of longshot or closeup, the limits of location are simply set by the widest shot available. Following from this, I define a *scene* as a *series of events occupying the same location without narrative interruption*.[6] The action may of course revisit the same location many times over: much of the action of *Citizen Kane* takes place in Kane's newspaper office, but on different dates as much as years apart. Or a single continuous story scene may be fragmented by *narrative* interruptions: the characters stay put and the action continues, but the narrative cuts away elsewhere and later returns.

First, then, *boundaries*. The simplest kind of spatial closure is what is traditionally termed 'unity of place', where *all* the events of the story happen in the same location. In the strictest sense, this is extremely rare.[7] It is certainly not classical. What we usually mean when we speak of unity of place is more like unity of *primary-narrative* place. Everything that is presented to the reader directly is tied to a single location; but important events in the *story* still take place 'offstage', and are simply *reported* to us, at one remove, through explicit or implicit recounting in the onstage

---

[6] A drawback of this definition, of course, is that the term becomes unusable for rigidly illusionistic theatre, such as classical New Comedy, where the whole narrative necessarily occupies the same location. I therefore avoid the term 'scene' in such drama ('episode', as defined on p. 68 in the next chapter, serving in its traditional place).

[7] One example might be R. Crumb's single-page strip 'A short history of America', whose successive panels show the same scene gradually transformed from wilderness to slum by human encroachment. Perhaps significantly, though, this is a story without characters in any ordinary sense.

action. Far from the whole story's unfolding in the same location, it is only the *telling* of such stories that is spatially bound. In fact, their narrative has positively to persuade us that we are looking through a fixed window at a world that extends in time and space *beyond* the limits of our restricted view. The world of primary narrative is rarely self-contained, except in certain kinds of postclassical experiment.[8]

So it is important to distinguish between the spatial limits of the story and those of the primary narrative. A story confined by strict unities of time and space at the narrative surface (a dramatic monologue, say) may invoke far broader limits to its actual world of events. Aeschylus' *Persians* and *Agamemnon* each observe the unities of time and space in primary narrative, but use reported offstage action, reminiscence, and prophecy to tell a story extending over generations and continents with an effective cast in the hundreds of thousands.

As a general rule, the narrower the story universe, the tighter the plot. A severely limited board obviously narrows the range of possible moves and outcomes, and is therefore an instrument of strongly closed, classical plotting. But there is a dilemma here: clearly if the board shrinks so tight that the action can hardly move at all, the possibilities for complex, expansive narrative are severely restricted. Thus Carl Schenkel's 1984 film *Abwärts* (*Out of order*), which takes place almost entirely among four characters trapped in a lift, is a self-consciously paradoxical exercise in perverse virtuosity – deliberately straitjacketing the most spatially open of modern narrative forms with preposterously claustrophobic story conditions.

Despite this, there are some narrative forms that do depend for their essential interest on tightly constricted story environments. Significantly, they tend to be either rather brief texts in themselves, or local episodes embedded in more diffuse and open tales. A well-known genre example is the locked-room mystery, in which the reader is challenged by the narrative to come up with a model of how a major story event (traditionally a murder) outside the primary narrative could have been brought about in the sealed and inventoried story environment of a single room.[9]

Classical narrative's traditional solution to the dilemma is the one first developed in the *Odyssey*. The borders of a story universe do not have to be constant; they can expand and contract in the course of play. In a large-scale narrative, this raises the attractive possibility of *funnelling* the story from a wide open to a tightly closed field of play. Thus the world of the

[8] It is often the case, for example, in short animated films. Svankmajer's *Dimensions of dialogue*, for instance, presents a series of three such universes, each populated by a single pair of disembodied heads that interact according to a different set of severely restrictive rules.   [9] See Adey 1991, which gives away the solutions to over 2,000 such stories.

Odyssey opens out early on to what is arguably the widest compass in classical fiction – land and sea, Greece and Egypt, the real world and the fabulous, earth and heaven, life and death – yet there are early signals that the real locus of the action is in Ithaca, and specifically in the *megaron* (hall) of the palace; and over the second half of the poem the essential action and players are progressively assembled, and at last literally sealed, in the single location where the endgame is due to be played.[10]

This has proved an enormously popular and powerful solution, for two reasons. First, it gives large-scale narrative a strong directional movement, a sense of forward thrust and destination. As such it marries particularly well with the classical element of *endgame* discussed below. Second, it allows the storyteller to have his narrative cake and eat it – to paint on a huge canvas, but with all the classical control of a set-bound endgame. Not surprisingly, then, it remains a mainstream structural technique in modern-day classical storytelling – particularly in Hollywood film, where even the most exotic and diffuse spectaculars often move to an endgame assembling all the key players on a single soundstage (as invariably in the Superman, Conan, and Indiana Jones cycles, for instance).

From the external boundaries of fictional space, we turn to its internal *structure*, which can articulate a number of valuable narrative ideas. First, as we saw in the discussion of location and scene above, the assignment of particular sections of the story to specific locations is an important device in narrative *phrasing*. One of the strongest ways of defining an episodic unit within a narrative series is to announce and establish a location at the outset ('The appearance of the little sitting-room as they entered, was tranquillity itself . . .'[11]), and close by cutting away to a different location or a different narrative mode. On a larger scale, the story as a whole may be structured around a series of successive locations, of which only the last is signposted as the site of the endgame: this, once again, is the Odyssean solution. Spatial movement is a valuable resource in large-scale narrative's constant need to episodise[12] – a strong reason for the popularity of journeys and quests as a large-scale narrative structure.

On a smaller scale, divisions of space within narrative help to determine the grouping and sequence of *interactions* between characters. Only characters occupying the same location may interact directly; the conquest of separation in space is an important prerequisite to the confrontation or union of key players and pieces. Sometimes this can result in the field of play's being zoned into sectors, as (again) in the *Odyssey*, with the exit from one set of story boundaries placing the character at the entrance to the next traversible narrative field: a pattern most apparent in adventure

[10] See below, pp. 95–6.   [11] Jane Austen, *Emma*. Vol. II, Chapter 10.
[12] See below, pp. 68–9.

and computer games, especially of the 'platform' variety. The progress of a character across a board towards a specified goal can thus serve as a running index of the progress of the story towards its endgame.

Perhaps most important of all, the internal structure of narrative space may code information about the *structure of relationships* between players. In particular, spatial structure offers a ready-made matrix for differentials and spheres of *power*. A character's authority and competence within a narrative environment will generally be bounded by obvious spatial limits: the home, the workplace, the legal community. Thus one very familiar story pattern is the transfer of a focal character from a position of security to one of vulnerability, by translocation from the home domain to the domain of an antagonist (from the Shire, say, to Mordor) – where the hero has to overturn the natural pattern of dominance in a critical endgame confrontation. So the space of the story can very often serve as a map of its world's configurations of power, with the movements of the characters over the board reflecting shifts in those configurations as the story progresses in time. We shall see a great deal of this technique in later chapters.

The third function suggested above for the narrative structuring of story space is simple *verisimilitude*. Space, and its contents, are the most vivid evocation of the actual experience of a substantial world. This is all the more important when it is far easier for texts to evoke synthetically the experiences of time, thought, and feeling than the experience of the senses. Not all narrative media, of course, have to synthesise. Some (theatre, film) can construct illusionistic sights and sounds with relative ease; others can manage sight but not sound (comics), or sound without sight (radio). Even so, few narratives have direct access to the reader's senses of taste, touch or smell;[13] and some, such as the novel, have access to none.[14]

So the sense of space is vitally important in narrative's attempt to seduce the willing suspension of disbelief. The visual sense is, generally, the easiest to evoke in textual signs; and what we see in the world of experience

[13] Few, but not none: John Waters' film *Polyester*, for example, issues the audience with scratch-and-sniff cards, with ten numbered panels cued by signals onscreen; while some varieties of theme-park ride aim at an elementary form of tactile, or at least physically experienced, narrative.

[14] It is striking how much easier even the one- or two-sense media are to process than the comparatively demanding reading of literary narrative; and that literary non-fiction is significantly easier to read than fiction written at the same linguistic level. Fiction, unlike most non-fiction, asks the reader to construct a full sensory model of a non-existent universe on the basis of purely analogous signs on the page. It is not surprising that readers also find a collection of short stories, where this process has to begin afresh every few pages, harder going than novels, where the model can be carried over and incrementally modified across the whole text.

at any moment is, by definition, a location, connected to other locations by a mental map. At minimum, a narrative that wants to be classically 'transparent' – to entice the reader into surrender to the illusion that the experience of the text is the unmediated experience of story – needs to evoke this kind of spatial sense. Any additional polyaesthetic textures – sound, smell, sensation – will naturally add flesh and substance to the sense of location. And the more specific and evocative these aspects of narrative environment, the more powerfully the reader's consciousness is sucked into its own creation, its own constructed model of the story world.

3   Players and moves

Not all the inhabitants of a story universe are players in its narrative game. The characters in a story world divide into stars and walk-ons: full players, and comparatively faceless and incidental extras. The status of 'player' hangs above all on whether the reader is invited to feel an interest in the character's ultimate fate. Other factors tend to correlate with this: players usually have a participant role in the endgame, and they will also tend to be the human focus for whatever moral, intellectual, and emotional complexities engage us in the narrative. But Aristotle was probably right to argue that these last are not in themselves essentially part of *plot*, and in classical narrative at least – the only sort he recognised – are technically secondary to it. Looked at purely in plot terms, the reason certain characters' internal sub-worlds of experience, thought, and emotion are more fully evoked than others' is simply that it tempts the reader to make an affective investment in modelling those characters' motivation and narrative goals.

There is a repertoire of devices for flagging characters as players or extras. Two very simple ones are *speech* and *naming*: players are both assigned a personal label and allowed to express their inner worlds, while extras are denied one or both of these claims to distinctive identity. Thus a character such as the nurse in Euripides' *Hippolytus* may speak more lines of dialogue than some of the named players, but because she is unnamed we do not feel a sense of loose-endedness when she fades from the action and her fate is left unresolved. Though an impressive and memorable *character*, she is not flagged as a player whose final fate need interest us.

Above all, though, it is the use of *point of view*[15] that labels a character as

---

[15] Like Chatman 1978: 151–61 (cf. 1986, 1990: 139–60), Lanser 1981, and Ehrlich 1990, I use this more traditional and inclusive term to subsume Genette's 'focalisation' – whose proper usage, albeit disputed (Genette 1988: 72–3; Jahn 1996), is confined to the spoken and written word, though Branigan 1992: 100–7 makes a case for applying its distinctive nuances to cinema (and reserves 'point of view' for a more generalised effect: 115). In the text I generally favour the more compact and syntactically flexible form 'viewpoint'.

a player. To be allowed, even momentarily, inside the head of a character in the story generally establishes that character as a player, not an extra. This is, at least, a rule much more commonly broken by inept narratives than by accomplished ones, and the reason for it lies in an important fact of narrative economy. A restricted character viewpoint (what Genette calls 'internal focalisation', and Bal 'character-bound focalisation') is not simply a narrative window on the story in the way that quasi-objective reporting ('external focalisation') straightforwardly is. Each character has a private, internal model of the story universe, which will derive from his or her own individual experience of that world. For that reason, it may differ in many essentials from the reader's model: often the reader will have been told things the character has not, and sometimes the character may be in possession of information that is, for the time being, withheld from the reader. And to complicate the picture further, each character will have his or her own model of all the *other* characters' models, which again may differ sharply on crucial points.

The *reader's* model of the story, reconstituted from the narrative, must somehow include *all* of these secondary models of the story. 'Aha,' we think: 'A thinks that B thinks that A thinks X. But we know that B knows that A knows Y . . .' This is a hugely cumbersome process. If the plot is not to become cluttered with endless third- and fourth-order models of models of models, the reader needs to be assured that only a handful of the inhabitants of the story-world 'matter'. The comfortable maximum in a complex classical plot – a Feydeau farce, say – is around twelve. Characters beyond this limit must in practice either be little more than extras or remain confined to segregated episodes.

The differentiation of these secondary story-worlds, the second- and higher-order internal models of the story, is an important resource of irony and complexity in classical narrative. But the players in a story have a double function. As well as being *witnesses* to the story, they are also its *agents*. They provide a point of view, mediating the events to the reader, but they also act, creating the events within the story world. Some players may, of course, do one without the other: many narratives use a main viewpoint character detached from the main strand of the action, a reporter or bystander rather than an full participant, while some key players (such as the main antagonist) may in practice be little used for viewpointing lest the reader see too many sides of the issue. Dr Watson only occasionally helps with the solution; Professor Moriarty is never allowed to speak his case to the reader.

There is, of course, a famous system for classifying players, or more precisely game roles, according to this active side of their narrative function. Greimas's grouping of Souriau's six principal dramatic functions into three pairs of 'actants' (subject/object, helper/opponent, sender/receiver) provides an extraordinarily elegant model, powerful yet satisfyingly minimal, for the description of role structures within a narrative state.[16] Some of the finest work done anywhere with this model has been in the classical field, and specifically in the study of New Comedy.[17] Nevertheless, it is less a model of individual or collective character than of *narrative transactions*: a kind of circuit diagram showing paths of transmission for the particular goal-currency (money, sex, power, or whatever) local to that narrative universe. It is thus extremely valuable as a system for summarising game states and their transformations, but of no use at all in analysing the *internal* structure of individual character.

For this 'actorial' structure, however, Greimas himself proposed a separate, tripartite model of exemplary clarity and strength, which I adapt here with a few tacit modifications.[18] Whatever the intricacies of thought and feeling involved, a character's actions are ultimately determined by just three modal variables: *motive, knowledge,* and *power*. Motive determines what a character wants; knowledge identifies the available manifestations of that desire; power defines the character's practical ability to achieve it. This in turn allows us to put forward a general model for story movement: what, in the game metaphor, we can call a definition of the *move*.

(i) *Motive*. Players need goals. These may be overt (known to both character and reader), suppressed (known to the character, but deliberately withheld from the reader in narrative), or implicit (not consciously known to the character, but apparent to the reader as a necessary and appropriate outcome). Some general goals are more or less universal: survival, justice, power, pleasure, security. Thus the generic happy ending is the one where the hero escapes from perilous odds (survival), punishes the villain (justice), inherits the throne (power), marries the heroine (pleasure), and lives happily ever after (security).

But characters' goals can also be determined locally, either by cultural context or by particular narrative needs. Under the former heading, for instance, money has not in all times and places been as prominent a goal as it is in modern popular fiction of the capitalist West. Under the second, goals can be specified *ad hoc* in particular stories: if Henry's burning ambition is to ride in a fire-engine, the reader must be prepared to see the fulfilment of that goal as a satisfactory outcome to Henry's personal story.

---

[16] Greimas 1966: 129ff., 1983: 49–66 (English version in 1987: 106–20). Brief definitions of these six terms may be found in the glossary.   [17] Bettini 1982; Wiles 1991.

[18] These mainly affect Greimas's category of *vouloir*, which I have relabelled 'motive' and contaminated with the idea of 'goals'; see Bal 1985: 33. Meehan's TALE-SPIN program independently uses a remarkably similar template in defining its (admittedly rather rudimentary) characters.

Some characters may have goals the reader wishes to see *frustrated*. Fairly obviously, this tends to be the case when their fulfilment interferes with the goals of a character in whom the reader has invested a deeper sympathetic commitment. Where different characters' goals do compete, as they generally will in any story with an element of conflict, the reader is prompted to deduce from wider narrative rules which goals will be allowed to succeed and which must fail. The verdict is steered by a mixture of narrative and judgemental cues. For instance, closer narrative identification with particular characters (through extensive use of their personal viewpoint on the story, and alignment of their goals with values ideologised by the text or its milieu) will tend to engage the reader's preferential sympathy. At the same time, we will be comparing the different conceivable endgames for overall quality of closure: looking for an outcome that best satisfies the ideological and metaphysical *rules* established for the story world as a whole.

Finally, a host of internal personality factors may combine to promote or inhibit the character's will to *proceed* towards his goal, and the route selected to reach it. This is what we normally understand by 'characterisation' in its widest sense: the moral, intellectual, and emotional qualities that influence the decision-making process. In general, though, these qualities will be of *plot* interest only in so far as they influence the *execution* of the character's goals. (They may be of considerable *human* interest, but that is only incidentally a factor in plotting – mainly by securing the reader's engagement with the inner lives of the characters.)

(ii) *Knowledge*. Characters may, in the early stages, need to acquire information before their goals are correctly perceived, or realistically approachable. The information may or may not be currently known to the reader, and often (in tales of detection, for example) is revealed to viewpoint character and reader at the same narrative moment. Such information can be anything relevant to the current game state: first-order information about the location, identity, and function of essential players or props; second-order information about other characters' internal game models; third- or higher-order information about other characters' models of the character's own game model, and so forth.

This makes it sound as if the reader's model of the story world quickly disappears into endless recursion. If our model includes every character's model of every other character's model, and every character's model of all those other models, and all the models of models of models, *ad infinitum* . . . where does the modelling stop?[19] But stop it does, and at a relatively shallow depth of embedding, owing to a simple but essential difference

[19] A fascinating empirical study of this problem now in Graesser et al. 1999.

between narrative universes and real ones: in the closed system of a narrative universe, *information about the state of the system is a thermodynamic quantity.* The total information content of a narrative universe cannot be added to or reduced, but only *redistributed* among elements of the system; and that redistribution will always be in the direction of increased *entropy*, the more even distribution of information amongst players in the game. Truth will always out: unequal distribution of information among characters is an unstable configuration, and (a vital rule of farce) the more dissonant the variant models of reality the more unstable the barrier between them. False (that is, 'negative') information can of course be introduced locally, just as a local temperature difference can be introduced in a thermodynamic system. But both come at the cost of greater instability in the system as a whole, and in the long term the spread of information must grow more homogeneous, not less.

In practical terms, this means that in narrative we are only required to note *dissonances* among the embedded models of the story: what Ryan (1980) terms the 'principle of minimal departure'. The default is that everyone knows everything we do; we are only required to register the exceptions. So in a classic cross-purposes, A may not be aware of fact p; B may not be aware that A is unaware; A may not know that B is unaware of A's belief; etc., apparently without limit. But in fact there are only three actual beliefs here: 'p', 'not-p', and the meta-belief 'he thinks what I think'.[20] Furthermore, the higher-order the dissonance, the *more* unstable it is – one reason why plots dependent on third- or higher-order misapprehensions are so comparatively scarce.

(iii) *Power.* Characters may have the motivation and the necessary knowledge, but still be barred from effective action by outside circumstances – their position, as it were, in the present structure of the game. They may simply be in the wrong place; or they may lack an essential prop, such as a weapon or tool; or they may be subject to another player's will rather than their own. On his first appearance in the *Odyssey*, the hero suffers from all three: he is stranded on Ogygia, without the ship he needs to take him to Ithaca, and unable to make a move until Calypso formally releases him. All these are cases of a lack of harnessable *power* – 'harnessable', because Odysseus is not short of moral, personal, and supernatural dynamisms; his problem lies in converting these into a form in which they can be useful in the present situation (such as a boat, provisions, directions, wind, and permission to leave).

[20] This is easier to show formally in the game-state notation used in Chapters 8–10:

p | A:-p B:p | B:A:p A:B:-p | B:A:B:p . . .

collapses to 'p | A:-p B:p' plus the rule 'X:Y: = X: '. (For an explanation of this notation, see n. 22 below.)

We should note that the three components of character are not functionally of a kind. The motivational element is to a large extent an *intrinsic*
determinant of action, part of the fixed structure of personality we call
'character'. It may be redefined or modified in the course of play, but such
changes (a character 'developing') tend to be gradual, selective, and
involuntary. Moreover, much of what we think of as transformation in a
character's motivation may more accurately be changes in their knowledge or competence: adjustments to the current goals made as a result not
of inner personality changes but of new understanding of the external
story universe, or changes in the character's freedom to act. By contrast,
the other two factors are circumstantial, externally imposed, and constantly subject to immediate and voluntary adjustment.

This adjustment is what I define as a *move*: a *change in the game state*
produced by a *finite and legal manoeuvre* on the part of a single player. In
the game of story, this manoeuvre can change one or both of two game
values: the distribution of *information* (knowledge and belief) or the distribution of *power*. Any difference between any two characters in either or
both of these domains establishes the potential for a move. When the
move is made, the potential is wholly or partly discharged, and the game
state redrawn with a new distribution of the relevant value. By no means
all actions in a story qualify as moves: brushing one's teeth, for instance,
rarely increases knowledge, and only very slightly alters one's practical
capabilities. If the game state is not measurably changed, the action is not
perceived as a move – though that does not of course mean it has no plot
function. (It may send other kinds of narrative signal to the reader, such
as marking a note of time or place, or preparing the ground for a future
move.)

(i) *Moves of communication (c-moves)*. In any story where different characters' model of the game state differs (in the simplest case, by one character's knowing something another does not) there is a potential channel
for information flow. The information does not *have* to be released, and if
it is it need not be true. The contents of a communicative move can carry
any of a range of modal values: absolute truth or falsehood, subjective
belief or disbelief.[21] A character may, for instance, report an absolute fact
in the personal belief that it is a lie. The character told it may then reject
the truth of the statement, while accepting that the first character believes
it. When multiple-order, multimodal gradations of story information are

[21] The possible-worlds model additionally allows for the categories of will and power to be
treated as modal worlds in the subjectivity of characters: an elegant approach, though
perhaps only suitable for subliterary degrees of narrative complexity. See above, p. 31
n. 31.

concerned, c-moves can be extremely complex. But they are, in principle, reducible to formal terms by presenting all the c-moves in propositional statements.[22]

(ii) *Moves of power* (*p-moves*). In a similar way to c-moves, p-moves are enabled by any potential difference in the circumstantial capacity of characters to act. The difference may be between individual characters in confrontation: one may have a gun while the other is unarmed, in which case the p-move could involve firing the gun, fighting for possession of the gun, or compulsion of a further p- or c-move at gunpoint. Or the difference may be between a desired and an achievable state of affairs: Cinderella may want to go to the ball but lack transport and costume, in which case the p-move involves the gift of the missing means from an outside source. The two categories are not as dissimilar as they appear: both involve access to goals or subgoals, which may be competitively sought by more than one character, or may simply require adjustments to the present power-balance before the goals can be approached from the current game state.

P-moves are subject to one vitally important constraint, imposed by the nature of narrative power itself. Like games, narrative universes are constructed as a *closed system*. Within that system, narrative power is effectively *conserved*: it cannot be created, destroyed, or even transferred between players in the course of the game, but only converted into differently harnessable forms. When characters seem to acquire power, we understand them to be in fact actualising a narrative potential they have been carrying in a different form: informational, positional, instrumental, social, intellectual, moral, even supernatural. When characters seem to surrender power, they are simply translating it back from a kinetic

---

[22] See Ryan 1985 for a good system. In Chapters 8–10 I use a loose formal shorthand for game states according to which 'A:x' means 'A knows or believes x is the subject of a local narrative function' (such as 'being in my house', 'being alive', or if x is a further proposition, 'being true'; occasionally a plus or minus sign is used to assign an affirmative or negative value to a function that recurs in several propositions); 'A(x)' means 'A is the subject of a local narrative function of which x is the object'; 'A,B' means 'A and B are paired in the same grammatical role in a local narrative function'; and a space or vertical bar (|) marks off separate but simultaneous components of the same game state. Second- and higher-order embedding is indicated by simple left-to-right concatenation. Thus if the local function is 'loves', the game state

A(B) C(D) BD(C) | BC:A(C) BA:C(A) | C:B:C(D)

describes a situation in which A loves B who instead loves C, who instead loves and is loved by D. But B and C both labour under the impression that A actually loves C, and B and A both think that C loves A. C, however, supposes that what B imagines is that C loves D – as is indeed the case. If this sounds an impossible brain-twister in its bare skeleton, it does not particularly strike us so in the form of *Twelfth Night* v.i.158–65; and New Comic plots are often far more convoluted than this.

to a potential form; and even when one character succeeds in eliminating another from the game, he does not actually absorb the defeated character's narrative power. Quite the reverse: sometimes it remains residually behind in a different form, continuing to work against the victor's goals as if its wielder were still active.

This deep underlying notion of narrative power, and the principle of its conservation in the reader's construction of the narrative universe and its closure, is easy to undervalue, precisely because its actual manifestations are so fluidly defined. Indeed, a major resource of flexibility in plotting is the particular choice of qualities or commodities registered locally, generically, or culturally as forms of narrative power. *Information* is itself the most important: the farmer who knows where the treasure is buried has a huge narrative advantage over the king who does not. Prometheus has a narrative edge over his antagonist even in bondage and torture, because he knows how Zeus may be overthrown and Zeus does not. The leakage of that secret seems to transfer power from Prometheus to Zeus, but what has really happened is that the difference in potential has shifted from knowledge to *moral* power. Prometheus is already overwhelmingly in credit in the moral balance-sheet, and the loss of his informational edge translates, through Zeus's escalation of his punishment, into a further difference in moral potential that has finally to be resolved. Information, in fact, is simply a storable and portable form of narrative power. Thus the c-move is really a special case of the p-move.

But there are endless other guises in which potential narrative energy can be stored for later conversion to kinetic forms. *Intellectual* power, for example, makes one character more likely than another to put two and two together – to connect up individual pieces of information into a larger whole that can be converted into action. Other kinds of power are extrinsic, though still inalienable: *positional* power, for instance, depends on a character's placement relative to his goal in the narrative topography of the board. They need not be adjacent: there merely has to exist a narrative route, invisible or inaccessible to other players, leading more directly to the goal. (The route into Mordor via Minas Morgul may look on the map like the long way round, but it actually passes through fewer narrative quicksands.) *Instrumental* power is concentrated in the form of props: one ring to rule them all, conferring such unrivalled narrative power on its owner that it has to be destroyed and its vast narrative energy dissipated by conversion to unharnessable forms. *Social* power makes it more likely that neighbouring players – friends, family, community, allies – will add their power to yours in pursuit of the same goals: Sauron may be individually more powerful than any other player in the game, but unlike the members of the Fellowship he is perilously short of friends.

More subtly, power can reside on a narrative *metalevel* to the story proper. Thus *moral* power, a versatile catch-all, places a character in what in the metaphysical topography of narrative is literally the moral high ground. In the end, the heroes win (if they do) because they live in a story universe where good has an intrinsic narrative advantage over evil, of a kind that is not merely thematic but actually *causative*. Such a causality can often be articulated in terms of supernatural agencies: the presence in the narrative universe of an explicit or implicit higher plane of intelligence, which may guarantee the causal force of ideological advantage by allying its own strength to that of the players in just the same way as ordinary mortal characters can. We shall have more to say about such narrative *control levels* below.

Thus the moves in a narrative game, the transformations of narrative power within the system, are much more tightly controlled than we might imagine. In any plot, the final game state will already be potentially present in the initial configuration of board and players. Its unpredictability will depend not on any transfer of power in the course of play, but simply in the conversion of narrative energy from one form (perhaps overlooked by the reader) to another. The forms in which this energy can exist, the 'exchange rate' between one currency and another, and the entropic direction of such transformations in the game as a whole are all determined by the game's global narrative *rules*. To these we now turn.

4   Rules and endgames

The clock, board, and players define between them the contents of a narrative universe, but they do not in themselves determine the actual course of play – the sequence of moves that assembles into a finished story. Two last conditions need to be established: what kinds of move the players are *allowed*, either collectively or as individuals; and how the game must *end*. These values are set by a local system of overall narrative *rules*, whose function can be summed up as defining the *logic of causality* in the world of the story. More specifically, they define modifications to the operation of 'natural' causality – the set of default rules that are understood to govern action and consequence in the real world. In a grammatical model, they would be the syntactic rules that prescribe how the narrative 'nouns' (players) and 'verbs' (moves) can combine to produce 'speakable' (affective or tellable) 'sentences' (stories).[23] But they are far easier to understand and formulate in a game model, because it preserves the *worldlike* structure that we use (I argue) to apprehend fictional systems.

[23] I here summarise the set of analogies proposed by Egan 1977–8, rather than any of the formal story grammars referred to on p. 11 n. 19.

Narrative rule-systems need not be defined *de novo* in every text. One of the distinctive qualities of *genre* is that it allows a common rule-system to be assumed across a whole corpus of texts. A reader familiar with a system of genre conventions will not need to have the rulebook spelled out within any particular text, any more than Italian-speakers need to consult a grammar every time they engage in conversation. But for this very reason all narratives *must* import some artificial rules of causality – of what the reader is entitled to expect of the story events, and what we can afford to exclude from the world of possibility. In theory, there seems no reason for a narrative universe to be entirely 'realistic', to avoid any modification to real-world causality; in practice, however, this is impossible. There is no such thing as a narrative innocent of genre. Even the *anti-roman* cannot shake off three millennia of narrative heritage; the closest, perhaps, we can get is those few isolated works like *Gilgamesh* or the *Iliad* for which no prior generic context happens to be extant.

The most helpful way to define particular rule-systems, then, will usually be through the study of genre. But we can note a few of the broader ways in which narrative systems can modify natural causality. The simplest is to introduce at *story* level a system of explicitly paranormal causality: magic, invented laws of nature, and so forth. This is the pattern of folktale and fantasy – though to use it classically, the narrative must establish a set of strict (if necessarily somewhat arbitrary) rules for its management. Even irrational forces need rational structure: we would need to know which characters have access to what forces and powers, what limits exist to their operation.

Most rule-systems, though, work by superimposing *narrative* restrictions on the causality of the story universe. The commonest type simply streamlines the story movement by labelling certain game patterns as narratively impossible – even though they may in terms of story causality seem perfectly 'realistic'. Some exclusions of this kind have become so widespread in Western storytelling as to be almost cultural universals. (Heroines preserve their virtue; knockout blows to the head do not cause brain damage; etc.) But often the exclusions need no more complicated motive than to insulate the game structure against disruptive turbulence. In classical plots, for instance, problems that need solving turn out to be soluble; lead players as a rule are not removed arbitrarily from the board by random accident; power does not leak suddenly out of the system. Thus Penelope is not, after all, struck down in the third year of the war; Odysseus does not suffer a fatal mishap with a javelin at the Phaeacian games; the suitors do not come down in a mass with food poisoning on the day of the showdown.

More elaborately yet, the narrative can impose some form of

metaphysical *teleology of value* – according to which some ideologically charged statuses or behaviours are understood to translate (normally via explicit or implicit supernatural enforcement) into potential narrative energy. Though it is a simplification to say so, the *Iliad* and *Odyssey* can be seen as the paradigms of the two commonest species of this genus: the *elitist*, which places members of a particular social group (usually aristocratic) on a narrative pedestal; and the *moralist*, according to which the righteous are consistently rewarded and the wicked taught an appropriate lesson. (There are, of course, narrative worlds in which it is the other way round.)

There is grave danger, however, that such imposed causalities may interfere with pressures – particularly strong in classical narratives, for reasons discussed in the next chapter – to narrative transparency and suspension of disbelief. It is a paradox of classical narrative that, on the one hand, well-made plots have to tamper drastically with the natural workings of causality; and yet the further the story moves from real-world causality – from 'likelihood' or 'naturalism' – the less likely the reader is to acquiesce in it. One question that the reader may understandably ask is: why is this fictional world different in kind from my own? What enforces the working of all these narrative rules, whether moral or magical or simply a sense of inevitability and purpose in story direction? Are not these rules the inept impositions of an author seeking artificial control over his subcreation?

One versatile bypass for these tricky questions is the incorporation into the story world's metaphysical structure of what we may term a *control level*: an intelligent, purposive force or player-set that directs and manipulates the board-level, terrestrial action. The earliest, and still archetypical, agents of control in fiction are the epic gods. But the supervisory intelligence need not be different in metaphysical kind from the players, and there can be advantages to leaving its status somewhat ambiguous.

This supervisory plane of the narrative universe is set apart from the main action by three essential features. First, its effect on the story proper is *unilateral*: it directs events without being itself affected by them. Second, its workings are *screened* from the players' full knowledge. If the controllers' activities are made explicit at all, it is directly to the reader through the omniscient voice of an external viewpoint. Finally, at least in classical narrative, the control level itself is *rule-bound*: there are limits prescribed, implicit or overt, to the kind of interference in the action the controller is allowed.

These are the constants; there is much variation within them. One degree of freedom is the extent to which the control level is made articulate to the reader. The Homeric Olympians mark one extreme, where the controllers are given names, intelligible forms and personalities, a native habitat, and a carefully circumscribed range of attributes and interventionary powers. At the same time, their operations are fundamentally inscrutable to the players, except in a very selective and limited way.[24]

As an attempt explicitly to rationalise the unabashedly irrational, there is little if anything in later fiction to match this. But fifth-century tragedy is already experimenting sporadically with an alternative, in which the activities of the same Olympians is still taken for granted but allowed to remain inscrutable to the audience as well as the characters. Story can still be patterned by structures *suggestive of* a controlling supernatural intelligence: curses, moral syllogisms, the manipulation of seeming chance events. Where story input from the control level is overt, it consists of information only – an oracle, prophecy, or omen, rather than a personal and physical epiphany. Aristotle and his New Comic inheritors liked this Sophoclean variation, which managed to avoid dogmatic assertions about the unknowable, yet still to allow the audience to extrapolate from the artificialities of narrative closure to the workings of a rational metaphysics (rather than to the crude machineries of a human author).

In general, though, even such a model of an *implicit* control level becomes hard to sustain outside a theistic world-model. It is not impossible: information leakage, at least, from an implied control level is occasionally tolerated as an *ad hoc* device. It may be that a mysterious gypsy woman mutters cryptic plot hints at the hero; or a character credited with uncanny secular expertise or insight may simply offer startling predictions about a future turn of events. In such cases, there will be a narrative signal of the information source's authority, but no analysis of the basis of their uncanny expertise. But it remains a device to which sophisticated readers are all too alert, and quickly earns scorn if overused.

So an alternative widely preferred in modern fiction is to *secularise* the control level altogether, displacing the epic gods with modern forces that govern players' lives in a similar way: historical determinism, perhaps, or faceless bureaucracy, or (especially) the unseen world of elite power and wealth. Criminal masterminds, Kafkaesque organisations, political conspiracies, corporate power-games – these are the standard forms of control-level plotting in the materialistic world of twentieth-century fiction, and it is symptomatic of that world that it favours a post-romantic story pattern in which the control level is confronted and defeated by its own puppets.

Though a modern variation, this type highlights a persistent hazard of the use of control levels in story universes. Free will is essential to narrative interest. If the players' moves are heavily manipulated by external forces, the internal operation of will, knowledge, and power becomes irrelevant or positively obstructive. There is a large repertoire of standard escapes from this dilemma, all variously effective fudges. The most straightforward is to *limit* the input from controlling influences in frequency, extent, or both. For the Homeric gods, this works well; but a problem with the divine is that gods are generally imagined to be omnipotent and omniscient, so it is not surprising that this recourse provokes early theological controversy.

Alternatively, the narrative viewpoint on the action may be closely tied to the human plane. The players' free will is then technically an illusion, but as the reader is given little opportunity to view the action from the controller's perspective the problem is covered up much of the time. The difficulty of this approach lies in answering, or else submerging, the question of why the players are needed at all. If the controllers have full power to manipulate the board in whatever way they wish, the presence of tension and imbalance in the game state is hard to explain in the first place.

There is, however, a second danger to narrative credibility here. The operation of a control level faces the constant danger of being construed as a mask for the *author*. Aristotle's contempt for the Euripidean *deus ex machina* centres on just such a violation of the transparency principle discussed in the next chapter. A sudden intervention from a celestial controller whose rationale has been nowhere suggested is equivalent to a fat envelope landing with a thud on the characters' doormat, stamped 'author's instructions: follow at once'. The modern solution mentioned above, in which the players revolt and the control level is eventually assimilated into the board, has not generally been an available option; so that the only realistic recourse for classical fiction has tended to be to confine the control level by strict rules (usually self-imposed) of its own. In later chapters, we can examine this in detail.

But why should narrative need artificial causalities in the first place? Ultimately because fictional worlds differ from real ones in one crucial respect: fictions *end*. Aristotle was the first to argue that the causal line of a story should be *closed* – should have, in his much-abused phrase, 'a beginning, a middle, and an end'. But in real life, closed chains of cause and effect – 'stories' – are not a widespread phenomenon. Even if we limit discussion to the life of the individual, the only natural causal boundaries are birth and death, neither of which (for different reasons) offers much intrinsic scope as a central plot event. At best, an individual life story can offer a convenient set of ultimate narrative horizons to some kinds of story world. But difficulties arise in narratives that prefer a narrower timespan, or a plurality of alternating leads – let alone those works of fiction, from Aeschylus' Theban trilogy to the novels of James Michener, that extend far *beyond* the individual lifetime to span generations or even centuries.

Aristotle gave intense thought to this problem of causal completion. To follow a single character's total experience from birth to death, he argued, was not a helpful recourse. Rather the storyteller should look for a structure of events which have some internal causal completeness *qua* events: the wrath of Achilles, the return of Odysseus. In fact, as we have already seen, this is a chimera. Neither of the epic plots singled out by Aristotle for approval is causally self-contained. Quite the reverse: both poems go out of their way to embed the overt story in a more extensive and less narratable wider story (the Trojan war, its shadow on the lives of the survivors) of which the present tale is somehow a microcosmic version. Key events in the logic of both plots are assumed, but not yet fulfilled, at the end of each poem: the death of Achilles, the sack of Troy; Odysseus' appeasement of Posidon. As should be clear by now, the closure of plot is simply a *narrative device*: a bold distortion of the natural logic of real-life causality. What happens is simply that the reader's model of the unfolding story is programmed with a set of *output conditions*. When these conditions have been met, the story is deemed to have ended satisfactorily.

But that is not to say that the structure of what we think of as 'endings' is arbitrary. The output conditions nearly always involve the *fulfilment of goals* assigned to one central character or group (the 'hero'). It is also conventional for those goals' fulfilment to place the story universe in a *steady state* of unlimited duration, in which the chief tensions and imbalances in the story are repaired and the reader's sense of the proper place of things prevails. Greeks were of course well aware that to mistake narrative for life, and apply this model of closure to the real world, was a silly deceit. 'Call no man happy till he is dead': the Sophoclean platitude articulates an uncomfortable awareness that in real life stories do not terminate in a happy-everafter stable state. But this does not in practice prevent us from viewing the future in terms of short-range goals, and their attainment as the moment when everything comes vaguely right. Classical fiction simply takes this goal-based life-model and treats it as conventionally true.

In a well-made classical plot, the terms of the ending will be established early in the narrative. Some of these terms will be explicit, or nearly so: the goals the leading players need fulfilled, for example. But others will be more subtly defined and signalled in the narrative rules and structure: the place and time of the closure, the participants in it, the final sequence of moves that deliver the goods promised. It is this final sequence that I call *endgame*, and in classical narrative it is perhaps the most important structural principle of all.

The canonical endgame consists of a structured sequence of closing moves, usually confrontational, in a single location and with all the chief surviving players involved, in which the terms of the resolution are fulfilled in a rapid series of strongly rule-bound events. The dynamic effect of those events will be the *final actualisation of stored narrative power*: the final share-out of information, the final translation of narrative potential into kinetic forms, the final resolution of differences in personal narrative power between players; above all, the final discharge, among main viewpoint characters, of *emotional* potential that has been built up by the resolution postponed. This last is of particular importance: a good ending needs to deliver some kind of emotional buzz to the reader, and the traditional means of delivery is a viewpointed discharge of pleasure or pain in the experience of one or more lead players.

The endgame's input and output are generally signalled long in advance, by any or all of a number of different means. Some are internally explicit: oaths, prophecy, challenges, compacts issued among characters within the story world. Others are editorial: narrative anticipations, patterns of structure and timing, the accumulation of moral or emotional potentials of the kind just mentioned. In whatever case, the more strongly rule-bound a narrative world, the clearer the foreshadowing of endgame will tend to be. But what remains suppressed until the endgame is actually narrated is the precise nature and sequence of the moves themselves. In the classical model, the reader is actually teased to speculate beforehand how the known rules of engagement can produce the outcome required. The art of the endgame often therefore lies in surprising the reader with an unexpected but legitimate application of the rules – what Aristotle called 'things happening because of one another but contrary to expectation'.[25]

So plot presents its reader with a hermeneutic challenge akin to a chess problem. Given a finite board, of a certain structure, populated by a family of pieces with distinctive individual ways of moving, and a further set of overall rules defining game states which can and cannot arise: how can a particular future state of play be legally derived from the present one? The essential difference, of course, is that narrative universes occupy a place in the hierarchy of complex systems considerably closer to the actual space-time universe than to a round of nine men's morris. If narrative universes do nevertheless share some formal properties with games, it is because both draw on a common cognitive apparatus for analysing and representing causality. We read stories in the same way as we read the world; and Chapters 5–10 will argue that it is from classical antiquity that we have learned our distinctively Western narrative ABC.

[25] *Poetics* 9.1452a4.

4   The classical plot

Let us recap. Plot is a way of coding worlds into games and games into serial arrays of narrative bits. Two things particularly determine how a reader will shape and order an internal model of the story assembled as the text unfolds: the choice and sequence of the textual bits themselves, and the contents and rules of the narrative universe they describe. And all through this readerly process of piecing the story back together, two different but simultaneous pictures of the story are being built up in the reader's mind: an inside, timelike view of the events as they unfold one after another, and an outside, timeless overview of the shape of the story as a whole. The art of plotting lies in keeping these two pictures interestingly different until the final pieces are in place and they fuse into one; while its science lies in taking advantage of the cognitive structures readers can be expected to use in converting a text into the vivid conceptual experience of an imaginary world. In the last two chapters, we have looked at these aspects in turn.

It remains to expand the second term in my title. I use the word *classical* in its regular ahistorical sense to mean a way of doing things that, while not mandatory, is sufficiently paradigmatic for it to be either consciously accepted or deliberately rejected; a way, moreover, enshrined in certain canonical exemplars at the source and centre of the genre or tradition; and which, while perhaps obsolete in practice, is still perceived as a mainstream, orthodox, accepted way to proceed. It also tends to imply a positive acceptance of formal artifice, rather than an attitude of indifference or open rejection.

For us, the idea of a 'classical' way of doing plot is defined above all by *Poetics* 7–14. But these chapters need to be viewed as an articulately theorised, though partisan, distillation of a inherited narrative *practice*. Aristotle's own direct influence on literary practice (as opposed to the legacy of his variously careful or careless abusers, amongst whom Horace is hardly the first, and Castelvetro – or Robert McKee – far from the last) is surprisingly hard to estimate, especially with the loss of so much Hellenistic narrative literature. Within a generation, to be sure, the rules he formulated found, in Attic New Comedy, their supreme ancient articulation. But the *ideas* that define classical plotting were around long before Aristotle, and were available to Greek readers in much more immediately accessible forms. The roots lie in the Homeric epics, but their extension to widespread narrative practice is a specific legacy of early Attic tragedy. The extant plays show that the evolution of a classical type was by no means a straightforward, inevitable, unilinear, or unresisted progression. But by 406 BC we can at least see that some lines of experiment had been permanently abandoned, and others increasingly pursued, in a way that clearly agrees with much of Aristotle's prescription – even granted that that prescription was a highly personal and selective view, both of the full range of possibilities and of actual practice. Aristotle's was, of course, a personality more than usually comfortable with formal abstractions, fascinated with the intellectual modelling of causality, and aesthetically excited by an elegantly close relationship between function and form. But these emphases in his model do not, I think, undermine his analysis as a generally fair description of what had evolved.

Aristotle wanted three things from an ideal plot: two explicit, one repeatedly taken for granted. First, its story should stand as a organic *whole*, a single self-contained causal chain – closed at beginning and end, and bound together internally by links of probable and necessary consequence. Second, the story should sit within certain broad limits of *scale*. At minimum, he suggested, there should be room for one major reversal of fortune; as an upper bound, the plot must remain apprehensible as a whole. Within these limits, the more action the better, so long as the law is not infringed. And finally, Aristotle had a horror of gaps in the scenery. Any *breach* of the story world's naturalistic causality, let alone any explicit acknowledgement of the artifices of storytelling, meant the collapse of the whole narrative edifice, and the exposure of the shamefaced author lurking behind. These three principles – we can call them *economy*, *amplitude*, and *transparency* – are really three facets of one: that the narrative universe, the game structure the narrative imposes on the world of its story, should be *strongly closed*. 'Economy' describes the *quality* of the story's internal narrative closure, the way its elements bind together; 'amplitude' is its *quantitative* structure, the scale and shape of the story as a whole; and 'transparency' is its *external* closure to narrative forces beyond the boundaries of the story world. In the rest of this chapter, I try to explain how and why these principles work.

1   Economy

Classical plots are narrative systems that *minimise redundancy*, or maximise the ratio of functionality to content in the narrative information presented to the reader. In other words, as much as possible of the contents of a story world should play an essential role in the narrative game: Chekhov's gun on the wall is there to be fired. The story's narrative limits in time and space should therefore be as tight as the game structure allows; the cast of players should be defined early, retained throughout, and fully required by the move-structure; and all moves should both conform to established rules and advance the action towards the endgame, which itself should be built entirely from elements already clearly planted in the narrative.

In its extreme formulation, the economy principle demands that *everything* in the story should be part of the plot: 'the parts of the action should be organised in such a way that its wholeness is dislocated and disturbed if any part is transplanted or removed' (*Poetics* 8.1451a32–5). This is not in itself a very practical recipe, if the implication is that every word of dialogue, every movement or gesture by a character, must advance the plot – nudge the balance of information and power a little further in the direction of entropy. Clearly everything in the text communicates information of *some* relevance to the plot, however small and indirect. If one character says 'good morning' rather than 'hello' to another, that tells us something subtle (if not always of crucial importance) about the relations assumed between the speaker and the addressee. If the narrator observes that a room is empty, we ask who or what might have been expected to be in it, and when, and why. It is part of the compact between text and reader that *everything* is significant, even when it seems least so. All the while we read, we are writing private *S/Z*s (Barthes 1973) in our mind, pouncing ruthlessly on each single hermeneutic bit of textual data. But the fact that everything is significant does not mean that it is all *equally* significant, or significant in the same ways. On the contrary: in the previous chapters, I have tried to argue that the process we call 'plot' takes it for granted that readers can and will filter many different kinds and degrees of narrative information out of what looks for all the world like an undifferentiated stream of textual bits. And I have suggested that one of the most important mental filters in the experience of plot is the narrative apparatus I call *game structure*, which we use to identify the functional relations between elements in the story universe.

So it is in the interests of effective plot economy for narratives to mark a strong distinction between what we have been calling *moves*, sharp changes to the game's balance of knowledge or power, and the kind of incidental pottering that produces only gradual and incremental shifts. As we saw in the last chapter (p. 51), not everything that happens in a narrative will be read as a move. In fact, most of the everyday business of story is not. Rather, it is concerned with either exploring the *consequences* of earlier moves, or setting up the arrangements for the next. All the walking down streets, thinking things over, and swapping one-liners have less to do with plot than with the exploitation of plot states for other, often more valued, narrative ends. Moves need to be spaced; the players need to breathe. Even in the densest plotting, the reader needs to be able to *anticipate* an affective release of information or power through a phase of accumulation and tension; and to give its affective discharge time to settle, as reader and players alike take in the implications of the new game state. There is much more to storytelling than plot, and even the most classically economical narratives proceed in spaced jumps rather than a constant juddering scrape. It is perfectly possible for a work to be exquisitely well-made without very many things actually happening. Greek tragedy itself is a trove of interesting examples.[1] In practice, even in a tightly economical plot genre such as farce, some lines are there not to direct the action but to raise a laugh – to exploit the situation, rather than to transform it.

This is not to say that plot is inactive beneath the scale of the move. Between moves, there still operates a kind of *microplotting* of reaction and motivation, which serves not to alter the power balance in the game as a whole but to preserve a naturalistic causal texture. It is important, as Aristotle tries to drum in, for moves to succeed one another in a probable and necessary way. If a character needs to say 'I am your long-lost daughter', the dialogue to which that forms the climax needs to be composed so as to establish a plausible context for the revelation to emerge. The sequence of natural causality has to be mimicked at all levels of the story; a character should never, as Aristotle put it, 'say what the author wants, instead of what the plot wants'.[2]

In general, though, the greater the functional economy of equipment and moves, the more tightly plotted a work of fiction will seem. In film, especially, the pressure to narrative economy is intense, resulting in a hugely elaborate repertoire of conventional closures and shorthands: deadlines, tokens, stratagems and capers that in another medium would seem absurdly contrived.[3] Even so, complex characters and relationships can often only be accommodated in a hundred-page filmscript if the main developments are already set up before the narrative opens.[4] Old flames,

---

[1] Aristotle noted that less tended to happen in the plots of early tragedy than in the mature drama of the later fifth century (*Poetics* 4.1449a28, 6.1450a35–8). But even such a comparatively late work as *Philoctetes* boasts a plot of few moves and only three effective players, yet of very great narrative density and economy.
[2] *Poetics* 16.1454b34–5 (on Orestes' half of the recognition in *IT*).
[3] 'Movie budgets make it impossible for any film to contain unnecessary characters . . . Sophisticated viewers can use this law to deduce the identity of a person being kept secret by the movie's plot' (Ebert 1994: 60).
[4] On the implications for myth and fiction in the theatre see Chapters 8–9 below.

old wounds, and protagonists with obscurely complex pasts have always been abnormally popular with screenwriters, not merely because they are so often scripting for middle-aged stars. These sackloads of backstory are a ruse for pushing as much as possible of the story outside the expensive and limited borders of primary narrative. Only the fulcrum of their story is actually narrated; the extensive set-up is taken as read at the point where the narrative opens, and conveyed by a mix of genre assumptions and minimal glosses in the text.

It is important to understand that the principle of economy applies to the narrative level, not to the story: not to the material constituents of the story world as such, but to the *information* about them placed in the reader's domain. As a result, in a strongly classical fictional form such as film that combines high narrative economy with low narratorial presence, this economy of narrative information can itself feed into the reader's plot model as a *metanarrative* rule in itself. Thus, in film dialogue, we accept that everything is a Chekhovian gun: if information is supplied, it will be used (Ebert's 'Law of economy of instruction'). When John Mills, in *Ice cold in Alex*, gives a detailed lecture on precisely why the Depression route is far too dangerous to be an option, we immediately know that that is precisely the route the party will be forced to take. Conversely, loose ends are intolerable: if a piece of what looks like crucial game information has been planted in our narrative model but turns out *not* to be functional, we feel cheated or surprised in a way we probably would not in a novel.

2 Amplitude

Classical plots are best appreciated at length. A joke or a cartoon strip can be just as tightly constructed as a film, and usually needs to be even more so. But Aristotle was not interested in miniaturism. For him, plotting was most impressive – indeed, was only interesting at all – as a property of ambitious, large-scale narratives. Looking over his shoulder at the corpus of Greek literature available, we can see something very like a classical plot system at work in the fable, or in the longer *Homeric hymns*. But these forms, like most small-scale narrative species, were beneath his attention. For Aristotle, at least, the general rule of amplitude was clear: 'the bigger something is, the more attractive, up to the limit where it ceases to be intelligible as a whole' (8.1451a10–11). This important Aristotelian notion of a narrative's μέγεθος[5] needs some slight rewriting. I should prefer to define it as the *quantity of narrative in a given text* – in effect, the number of *moves* in its plotgame. This is not, strictly speaking, the same

[5] Literally, 'bigness'. I adopt Hubbard's translation over the more usual, but too neutral, 'size'. Μέγεθος is for Aristotle a weighted, judgementally positive term.

thing as text length – though Aristotle himself not unreasonably takes it for granted that the two will normally be equivalent, and in one passage has to tack on a codicil clause to deal with the exception.[6]

The more action there is in a narrative, Aristotle felt, the more ambitious and satisfying it will be. In itself, there is nothing particularly difficult in this. If a story has no ambitions to tight plotting, there is no effective ceiling on its size; it can ramble harmlessly along like a soap-opera, from one arbitrary episode to another, without much worrying about going back to clear up its narrative litter. But in *classical* plotting, there is a catch. For the reader who has to make sense of the game structure *as a whole*, more action also means more work. The art of amplitude in classical plotting lies, therefore, in reconciling the competing claims of amplitude and economy: in constructing large-scale narrative that nevertheless preserves an economical and intelligible game structure. To make things harder still, Aristotle was aware that the amplitude of a narrative would be further constrained by three things: the conventional or intrinsic limits of the *form*; the particular text's overall narrative *density*; and the nature of the actual *moves* involved.

First, Aristotle recognised that different narrative forms have to live with restrictions to their narrative amplitude. Epic has more intrinsic plot room than drama, for example; Aristotle speaks with scorn of poets – apparently including even the distinguished Agathon – who try to pack epic plots into tragic dramas (18.1456a15–19). To try and tell the whole story of the Trojan War in a tragedy, or for that matter in any practical narrative form, would lead to one of three absurdities. Either the play would go on for weeks, or it would rattle through the action too fast to follow, or it would leave out so much of the story as to make nonsense of the attempt. Even epic is advised to steer clear of stories on this scale. As Aristotle was careful to spell out, such limits of form may not always lie essentially in the nature of the medium. Tragedies, for instance, have a particular slot to fill in the festival programme, setting a clear upper bound to their duration in performance. But it is only a conventional limit. If the regulations demanded a hundred tragedies a festival, they would obviously have to be much shorter.[7] There are also, however, *absolute* limits of form, determined ultimately by the capacity of the reader's cognitive machinery: our memory, our attention span, how much active

---

[6] 'Another astonishing thing about Homer, compared with other epic poets, is that he did *not* try to write the whole story of the war, even though it did have a beginning and an end; because its plot would have been too big and impossible to grasp as a whole – or, if it *were* kept to a reasonable (text) length, it would have become tangled in its own variety' (23.1459a30–4; cf. 18.1456a10–19).

[7] 9.1451a6–9 (accepting Janko's defence of the transmitted text).

information we can hold in our mind at one time. It is these limits, as Aristotle saw, that restrict the narrative amplitude even of forms like the epic where no conventional limit exists.

This general insight has not been invalidated by the invention of narrative forms and media that Aristotle could never have imagined. If anything, the distinction he drew between drama and epic has become sharper and more generalisable, as both our narrative media and our ways of reading have evolved. There is still a basic divide between the real-time narratives of drama and film, played straight through once only in a single session at a tempo outside the reader's control, and written forms such as the novel that can be readily suspended and resumed, revisited and reread. Aristotle was not prescribing for quarter-million-word potboilers that can be gobbled up silently on a train journey; but their invention, far from rendering his model obsolete, simply raises new challenges for the rule of amplitude, of classical plotting on a scale beyond Aristotle's conception. Nor is it completely absurd to make comparisons between the narrative amplitudes of (say) novels and films, even though the kinds of information they can convey are so different. True, a film can describe a scene in a twenty-fourth of a second, while a novel can use thousands of words and still achieve only a partial approximation. But in practice there can be no serious doubt that a feature film is far more restrictive of plot than a novel. The script of a film, which must contain all the plot information that needs to be put across on screen, is rarely as much as half the wordage of a novel; and adapting a novel to film generally involves extreme selectivity and condensation, while film novelisations usually have to pad heavily with new matter.

Secondly, even within a single genre particular texts can vary considerably in narrative *density*. Aristotle recognises this, in admitting at least the theoretical possibility of a tragedy that dramatised the whole of the *Iliad*, or an epic that recounted the entire Trojan War.[8] It is also implicit in his famous passage on the relative numbers of potential plots for tragedy contained in Homeric and Cyclic epic: 'from the *Iliad* and *Odyssey* one or at best two tragedies could be derived, but many could be made from the *Cypria* or the *Little Iliad*'.[9] What we know of their length and content confirms that the Cyclic poems evidently proceeded at a far more rapid narrative tempo – ran through far more moves, we might crudely say, per hundred lines – than do the *Iliad* and *Odyssey*.[10] At the other extreme, Aristotle observes that early tragedies were comparatively lacking in

---

[8] Above, n. 6.
[9] §23.1459b2–5. A dutiful addendum, part or all of which has its editorial defenders, follows in the manuscripts, listing 'more than eight' (in fact ten) actual titles drawn from the *Little Iliad*.   [10] See further below, pp. 80–1.

incident[11] – a judgement that does seem borne out by the earliest extant, Aeschylus' *Persians* and *Seven aganist Thebes*.

Finally, the nature of the *moves* involved will clearly play a part in deciding their number and spacing. Characters can lie to one another as long as invention holds out, but they can only once discover they are brother and sister. There are really two rather different kinds of constraint here. First, the available narrative *power* will be finite, and the longer the game the more carefully it must be made to stretch. A short plot can use up its narrative potential in a few brisk moves; a long one has to be careful to keep some in reserve. In the first-draft screenplay of *Monty Python and the Holy Grail*, the grail was found lying in the grass a few feet away within moments of the announcement of the quest. The joke, of course, is that the whole narrative potential of the quest is absurdly dissipated in a single bathetic move; but for that precise reason the scene could hardly be allowed to survive into the film that was made. More subtly, some moves use up more of the reader's cognitive *capacity* than others, and too many such moves can overload our processing power. Thus c-moves, on the whole, are harder to keep track of than p-moves, because of the multiple levels of embedding and recursion demanded in the reader's model; and the higher-order the c-move, the more mind-twisting the demands on the reader. What makes convoluted cross-purposes so hard to sustain is the need to model the different game maps inside different characters' heads, perhaps extending to maps of maps of maps. By contrast, straightforward powerplays such as battle scenes may be heaped up for as long as the players have the narrative power to fuel them.

The constraints on narrative amplitude, then, are considerable. But Aristotle has usually been felt right to argue that a classical plot is nevertheless more satisfying if it can sustain the principle of narrative economy on the largest scale available – in effect, to build the most capacious narrative universe permitted by the form. The challenges, and the repertoire of classical techniques evolved to meet them, fall into three main areas: *variety, sense of direction*, and above all *pacing*.

(i) The problem of maintaining *variety* in large-scale classical narrative is addressed by the subdivision of the plot into *episodes*, each with its own internal gamelike closure.[12] An episode is marked by a short, self-contained causal chain leading to its own endgame, the output from which then becomes input to the main plot. It is commonly segregated off from the framing action by the 'scening' device of establishing a new location as the episode begins; or by the introduction of new and local players or rules at a stage in the narrative when the main game elements are already

---

[11] Above, n. 1.   [12] See above, p. 39.

established. There will usually be an introductory signal (such as the framing of a plan or a set of instructions) to explain how the episode inserts in the main strand: whether it moves the plot as a whole towards or away from the endgame, what local characters or equipment will be output to the main plot, and so forth.

Episodes can slot together in a number of ways. The simplest just strings them end-to-end along a single thread of internal story chronology. But assembling episodes into a coherent overall structure need not require rectilinear continuity to be preserved. There may, for instance, be multiple narrative lines, perhaps viewpointed through different players, which *converge* on a common endgame: so, most famously, in the *Odyssey*, where the Telemachus and Odysseus plotlines meet only in book xv. Or the episodes may be temporally *embedded* in the main plot, as flashbacks or other secondary narratives. The *Odyssey*, again, is especially rich in these: apart from the great flashback of IX–XII, we also have extensive use of false tales, bardic performances, mythological examples, prophecies and omens, and narratorial similes. Some of these, such as the versions of the tale of Agamemnon, connect up into an embedded series in their own right, causally detached from the main plot but intimately linked to its rule-system.

(ii) Nevertheless, within this diversity of texture, the reader must be kept aware of a guiding unity. This *sense of direction* in classical narrative is one of its most characteristic qualities. In all plot, the reader is encouraged to anticipate possible local outcomes to a move or a game segment before it is recounted. But in classical plots the reader usually has a long-term prospect of the *ultimate* destination of the narrative, and the terms on which this endgame will be played.

Sustaining this sense of direction in a long or complex narrative poses a considerable technical challenge. It is not generally enough to signal on the first page that the lovers will marry, and spend all but the last ensuring that they do not. The intervening episodes need to be linked by some internal plot logic of their own that will keep the game moving, rather than just stalled between far-distant moves. But the stronger that sense of local, episodic closure, the greater the risk that the reader will lose sight of, or interest in, the endgame – which has, for reasons considered further below, to carry the strongest narrative punch of all. The challenge, then, is thus to preserve this double perspective on the plot, the local and the global: to *reconcile* variety with economy. The crude solution would be to insert regular and laborious reminders of destination explicitly into the narrative, either from the lips of the characters or, if desperate, in the narrator's voice. Less clumsy, but limiting in other ways, is to resort to a very streamlined game structure – such as a journey or quest – whose narrative trajectory is so simple and unilinear that the multiplication of episodes reinforces rather than obscures the sense of final destination. Such plots, however, risk lapsing into a mode of picaresque aimlessness, multiplying episodes at whim simply to fill up the available narrative space.

A far more versatile solution than either of these is to use some form of narrative *shorthand* to collapse the complexities of long-term game structure into a readily grasped local subgoal – in effect, to package the required narrative power into an economical *token* or object of local pursuit (what Hitchcock whimsically christened 'the MacGuffin'). Such tokens serve as the material or human embodiments, within the world of the story, of the narrative power needed to fulfil the players' goals – in effect, a shorthand for the endgame itself, or at any rate for entry to it. The pursuit of the token then takes over in the narrative from the often complex set of goals it empowers: 'saving the world' is compressed down into 'recovering the microfilm', 'achieving wealth, happiness, and a stable lifestyle' into 'finding the treasure map', and so on more or less *ad lib*.

Clearly, plot tokens come in many narrative guises. They can be things or people – and if the latter, players or extras. The goals they enable can be local to an episode, or final to the whole narrative. Their narrative power can reside in the operation of 'natural' causality (in the case of an incriminating love-letter, say, or a stolen nuclear device), or be defined *ad hoc* within the local rules of the story universe ('One ring to rule them all'). They can be ends in themselves (such as an object of desire), or merely the instrumental means to an end. At one end of the range, there are mere props – a sword, a vehicle, a telephone – instrumental in the fulfilment of short-term goals. These may, if access is problematic, be tokens, but normally they are unemphasised and unsurprising fixtures of the story environment. At the other extreme, there are what we might call plot *vouchers*: specialised items serving one specific function in the story world and of use only in accessing that function – proving identity, perhaps, or blowing up Manhattan. They may be cashed in only once, whether in the endgame or in an episode en route to the endgame. Very bad plots, particularly in superhero comics or the interminable fantasy-novel polylogies so popular since the 1980s, develop a series of shamelessly *ad hoc* plot vouchers into a kind of collect-the-coupons plotting, where players have to charge around the board assembling a requisite quota of otherwise otiose *objets d'art* for no better reason than that the local narrative rules have defined them as needful.[13] They are, as Aristotle might have put it, 'manufactured by the author, and therefore inept'.[14]

(iii) *Pace* presents problems of a different kind. In a classical narrative,

---

[13] Langford 1997.   [14] 16.1454b30–1 (on bungled recognitions).

the endgame will often be visible in outline to the reader as soon as the story components are laid out (or even before, if there are strong genre conventions about the kind of resolution expected). The narrative has then to satisfy two difficult and seemingly irreconcilable demands. First, it has to *delay* the anticipated endgame by interposing other material that will carry the reader's interest just as well. But at the same time it has to ensure that the endgame is the most *affective* point of the narrative, justifying both the reader's anticipation and the author's postponement. It is hard, in fact, to think of a single more insistent rule of classical narrative than that of the grand finale. Endings are massively important in narrative structure, and the more so the greater the amplitude of the narrative text. In popular film, especially, where classical plotting is *de rigueur*, the endgame has not only to satisfy the already stringent plot brief of resolving the crisis, but to do so with a massive discharge of dramatic energy in the form of emotion, violence, spectacle, or ideally all three. And it has to do this in a way that still manages to catch the audience by surprise in some essential way: some twist in expectation, perfectly within the rules, that places the last bits of jigsaw in a way that only seems obvious with hindsight.

There are three essential qualities required of classical pacing, beginning with *escalation*. A well-paced plot will be phased into a series of episodes of *rising affective intensity*, with the strongest discharge of energy at the end and the other main punches spaced out in roughly ascending order through the text. There is some flexibility in the early stages, but the timing of the final blows can be critical – particularly in the use of multiple or decoy endings, and in the placement of the final resolution relative to the end of the text. We tend nowadays, with our tastes shaped by the dominance of classical cinema in our narrative culture, to feel that a false ending is most effective if the true resolution follows immediately upon our recovery from the decoy; and that the true ending must not only raise the pitch of the false one, but come as close as possible to the end of the text, with perhaps a single-scene aftermath, epilogue, or summary to review the resulting final game state. Intriguingly, however, this preference does not seem to emerge in ancient narrative until Roman comedy and the Greek novel. Both the Homeric epics and New Comedy prefer the second ending (Hector's ransom, the Laertes episode, Menander's fifth acts) to be quieter and less overtly dramatic, and to be more widely spaced from its precursor than modern taste comfortably accepts.

This introduces a second principle of classical pacing: the need to *target* releases of narrative energy. Episodes should ideally discharge their affective potential at a point, not over half an acre of text. A sharp, sudden release of plot momentum is more effective than a graduated series of smaller moves. Aristotle noted two forms of this targeted, instantaneous discharge of narrative power: ἀναγνώρισις, 'recognition', is an abrupt redistribution of information, an extreme and climactic instance of what I have been calling a c-move, while περιπέτεια, 'upset', is a similarly sudden and violent p- or c-move that overturns the game state's configurations of power – in Aristotle's words, 'a reversal of the direction of events' (11.1452a22–3). Aristotle felt that an ideal plot should be built round one central upset of this kind, and that it should be a simultaneous release of information *and* power: 'recognition is best when it coincides with upset, as happens in the *Oedipus*' (11.1452a32–3). But the principle is a very broad one, and can operate on the local scale of scene and episode as usefully as on the macroscale of the narrative as a whole. In fact, the smaller the narrative unit, the more acute the need for targeting. In jokes, anecdotes, and synopses, the most effective textual structure is that which releases as much as possible of the accumulated narrative potential as late as possible and in the fewest possible words. Indeed, we call this device a 'punchline' precisely because it seems to deliver the full affective energy of the narrative at a point.

The third and final principle of pacing in large-scale classical narrative is *suspense*. If a strong sense of direction is established across otherwise diverse episodes, the reader will constantly be comparing an internal jigsaw model of the plot against the verified story data as it becomes available. The purpose of suspense is quite straightforward: to focus the reader's attention on certain *blanks* in the emerging picture, and then to retard the release of those pieces until the latest possible stage in the narrative.

There are, in practice, three general ways this can be done. The most straightforward is what we think of as a *cliffhanger* – a simple *postponement* of the final move of a game or episode at a point where that series seems close to resolution (and perhaps the direction of the resolution is still in doubt). It is a technique that can turn up on any or all of the three reading levels. Thus a *story* break simply postpones the expected resolution in internal time: the lady is tied to the tracks, but the train is not due for another hour. The pieces are in position, and the outcome already determined, but the final move of the series is delayed in story time by a missing (but expected) game element. By contrast, a *narrative* break interrupts or delays the *recounting* of story. Such a break may be a narratorial digression, a sudden jump backwards or forwards in story time, a cut to a different story strand, or a simple retardation of narrative pace. And finally, a *textual* break interposes a physical division in the text. It may be a purely conventional division, such as the end of a chapter – though in such cases the function of the cliffhanger is less to retard narrative than to keep the reader hooked by suppressing a convenient pause. But it may be a material break in the text that the reader has to endure or repair with effort. Such a break may be temporal, such as the end of an instalment in serial publication; here the reader has no option but to wait for the next chapter to appear. Alternatively, it may be a discontinuity in the physical text, such as a break between volumes (as a cliffhanger device, apparently an innovation of the Greek novelists). Even a foresighted reader who has laid up all the parts in advance will have to suspend his reading and take down the next from his shelf: a small but effective investment of time and commitment.

Alternatively and more subtly, the information may be withheld from the reader not by postponement but by *concealment* behind the screens either of viewpoint or of narration. In the former case, a restricted character viewpoint may block out information the reader is aware must exist somewhere in the narrative world. The viewpoint character may not himself know the murderer's identity, or that a murder has taken place, or even that there *is* something he does not know. And even if the viewpoint consciousness, whether personal or more generally omniscient, holds the information somewhere, it may still be tacitly or overtly withheld by the *narrator* – on the pretext that it is still in the future, or locked up in a character's head to which access is currently unavailable, or simply inappropriate to the reader's needs at this point.

Most sophisticated of all, the narrative can resort to deliberate *misdirection*: placing the relevant pieces on the board, but flagged with narrative labels that tempt the unwary reader to misplace them in the process of extrapolative modelling. Actual misrepresentation is not, under the normal conventions of the narrative transaction, an option, except in those special cases where the narrative situation itself is opened up to interrogation by establishing the narrator as 'unreliable' – as lying, or deluded, or incompetently articulate. But it is possible, particularly at the viewpoint level, for significant narrative information to be *left out*, and the holes filled unobtrusively in (the *Roger Ackroyd* solution); or for information to be misleadingly *flagged* with a narrative function other than, or additional to, the one it actually serves; or for fallacious lines of *reasoning* to appear in the internal plot models of characters with whom the reader is encouraged to agree.

3   Transparency

The final duty of a classical plot is to erase all palpable trace of its own existence. Author, text, reader have to sink beneath the surface of conscious attention, along with the whole elaborate system of narrative modelling and decoding that connects them. Only the story, or the reader's internal model of the story, is left. Fiction and reality swap cognitive places for the duration: the story, and only the story, becomes the real world, and any worlds outside it are suspended. In reality, of course, every work of fiction is a nest of worlds that have to be peeled away if the innermost sphere, the world of the story itself, is to be fully exposed. This *story world* is included and enclosed within a *narrative world* of game functions and rules, a set of tools for modelling the story's narrative structure. And this narrative universe is itself enclosed by the top-level world of the *text*: a world that also contains the text's author, its reader, and the whole environment in which reading takes place. Yet classical plot encourages the reader to disregard the mediating elements of narrative and text, and treat our own experience of the text in time as a direct analogue of the players' experience of the story. Both T-world and N-world must fade to perfect invisibility if the S-world is to establish total occupation of the reader's conscious experience. As we have seen, however, 'reading for the plot' is anything but a simple activity. When the reader is most immersed in the text is where the cognitive acrobatics are most frenetic. In effect, readers who lose themselves in a book have erected a screen between their conscious mind and all the mechanisms they are using to decode the story – as well as the external environment in which they and the book exist.

The audiovisual media of fiction have a distinct edge over the merely verbal here, in two respects. First, they are already more illusionistic: instead of an anthropomorphic narrator mediating the narrative to the audience, we have as Aristotle put it 'all the storytellers doing the business themselves' (3.1448a23–4). And secondly, these media can nowadays be served up to their consumers in the semiotically sterile surroundings of a darkened theatre, offering the minimum distraction in the form of alternative objects for the reader's attention, and with the order and pace of narration removed from the reader's control. But even in film and theatre transparency is not automatic. It can be broken, of course, by any reference to the outside world: to the audience and their context, or to the film as film. Such moments of opacity, where suddenly we focus on the glass in the window rather than the view beyond it, are generally termed 'breaches of illusion'. Being difficult to avoid, they are usually purposely chosen, and are widely used in both naïve, subclassical storytelling and in self-reflexive and postmodern modes. So ingrained, in fact, is the classical model in our Western fictional heritage that we take illusionism for granted as the norm, and see lapses from it as a sign of either primitive artlessness or high sophistication. It takes some effort of imagination to grasp that the presence of author and audience in the narrative act is the normal and desirable mode for any storytelling that seeks, as part of its function, to involve and confirm the communicants in the social performance. It is the historical impact of the Greek invention of illusionism that has twisted our perspective round the other way.

Still, there are subtler and less readily avoided ways to infringe the transparency rule even *within* the textual microcosm. Not only must the N- and T-worlds be screened off from explicit reference; but the entire contents of the reader's thought-balloon world has to be disguised as part of the story. Transparency is shattered if readers once think out loud in their skull: 'ah, this is a narrative rule', or 'this will be used in the ending', or worst of all 'this has been put here by the author'. Authors – not the real author, but a phantom figure projected by the reader – lose their invisibility as soon as their traces leave a noticeable imprint on the narrative. Aristotle, for one, was almost allergically sensitive to such spoor – which attract attention whenever the internal story flow of cause and effect breaks down, and particularly when decisive moves are inadequately motivated in the story's own terms. 'The resolution of plots should emerge from the plot itself, and not from supernatural flim-flam' (15.1454a37–b1); 'he comes right out and says what the author wants, not what the plot wants' (16.1454b34–5). Needless narratorial intrusions can have the same effect: 'the author should speak *qua* author as little as possible, because when he does that he stops being an artist' (24.1460a7–8).

So it is not enough simply for explicit references to the N- and T-worlds to be suppressed. The reader has also to be insulated against any shocks to the cognitive machinery that might ripple the surface or cloud the waters beneath. For this to be possible, everything that comes between the reader and the story has to be camouflaged as *internal* features of the fictional universe. The whole *narrative* overlay – the game structure, the narrative codes and signals that sustain it, the editorial tucks and snips of time and voice – needs to be disguised as natural outgrowths of causality and viewpoint. The signs that make the *text*, whether words or images, are passed off wherever possible as the players' own words, or as hidden-camera photographs of the story as it goes about its business. The *author* wears the mask of a control-level presence built into the story universe; while the *reader's* window on the story world is an invisible fourth wall, of which the natives remain imperviously unaware.

Two specific rules are vital to preserving this forest of camouflage. First, *all game states must be output from previous game states*. It is not enough for a move to be legal within the known rules and to involve only those game elements already established. It must also be *generated* by the application of existing rules to those existing elements. If it is not, the reader's default assumption will be that the author has lost control of his story and has input a move while the program is running.

Aristotle's somewhat cryptic term for such perceived inputs is ἀπὸ μηχανῆς, more familiarly Latinised as *ex machina*. Aristotle seems to be fusing a broad and a narrow sense of the Greek word here. Μηχανή means 'contrivance', but the 'machine' was also the technical name for a stage crane used in Aristotle's day for end-of-play divine epiphanies; and Euripides, especially, had been fond of using such epiphanies to bring the action to an abrupt and complete close where human events had reached an impasse. In the otherwise exquisitely plotted *Iphigenia in Tauris*, for instance, the heroes have devised an elaborate scheme to secure from their barbarian captors a chance of escape, a ship to escape in, the statue token they need to take with them, and the guarantee that the guards will be looking the other way. All goes to plan, and the threesome are sailing off to Greece and safety, when without warning the wind changes direction and blows them straight back into the harbour and the waiting hands of the irate and heavily armed barbarians. Cue Athene ἀπὸ μηχανῆς to impose a truce, prompting the audience – and Aristotle, who liked the play – to ponder why the goddess (if available as a game element) chose not to intervene *before* the arbitrarily frustrated escape plan.

Why Euripides thought such endings desirable, and even (as here) preferable, is a question beyond the scope of this book.[15] But it was Aristotle's taste rather than Euripides' that prevailed in the later tradition, and especially in New Comedy. The *deus ex machina* well illustrates the hazards of an imperfectly rule-bound control level within the story, and the temptation for the reader to see the agent of control as merely a convenient mask for the author. Significantly, later fiction is generally much stricter about the rules governing control-level inputs: either the putative control level is segregated entirely from story view (as in New Comedy, where the divine inputs are camouflaged as chance events, and the god is only briefly seen even by the audience), or else the machinations of divinity are fussily rule-bound and articulate (as in the *Aeneid*, a somewhat unique case).

But extraneous story inputs, disruptive of transparency, need not emanate from a supernatural control level at all. It is enough for the move to involve game elements or rules that have not been previously established as part of the story *données*. The transparency of a murder mystery, for instance, would be broken if an anonymous tip-off, never identified, supplied a missing clue – we would, in fact, positively expect the informant to be exposed as one of the players. (In *Jagged edge*, the audience is prompted to grasp that the first resolution is false by the metanarrative fact that the source of the helpful anonymous notes has still not been

---

[15] A fine recent treatment in Dunn 1996: 26–44 (rightly stressing the influence of the end of the *Odyssey*).

identified.) But if the input seems to originate from outside the system entirely, the Aristotelian reader concludes by default that the author is the source. It need not, as in the last example, be an input of information. In fact, the commonest infraction of the transparency rule is probably that involving an unexplained input of power – the obtrusive use of *coincidence*. The hero sets out to comb the world for his nemesis, and five minutes later bumps into him in the neighbourhood shop; the villain suffers a fatal heart attack at the moment he is about to deal the hero's death blow. Coincidence can, of course, be a powerful and positive classical plot device if used in the appropriate way – particularly to suggest the operation of an unseen and unspecified control level *within* the story world, as in Aristotle's example of the murderers killed by the collapse of their victim's statue (9.1452a7–9). It can be used ironically, particularly in comic and postmodern narrative, to evoke a fantastic world-view in which events follow a preposterous logic of their own. And it can be put to work more sparingly at crucial moments to suggest a realistic interference by chance in the best-laid human schemes: the gun jams, the power is cut off, a police car happens to be passing. But these cases all use coincidence to imply an underlying causality. Detached from such implications, coincidence becomes an obtrusion of the author.

This is where the second rule comes in: *all moves must be seeded in the narrative before they are required*. Motivation must be *ante eventum*; it is no good, in the film version of *The Poseidon adventure*, for Shelley Winters to turn out to be a former swimming champion at precisely the moment when the only escape is for one of the survivors to swim through a flooded passage. The gun must be on the wall, not stashed away in a drawer to be produced where needed. The only exception, perhaps, is where the initial *post eventum* emergence of a game element sets it up in advance for future, more significant use. ('Lucky I always carry that knife in my boot. You never know when it might come in useful.')

It is, of course, perfectly legitimate for a move to catch the reader *deliberately* by surprise, by producing a game element overlooked or misleadingly filed on its first appearance. There is, indeed, an art in placing elements on the board without signalling their function to the reader. An early instance is the fig tree in *Odyssey* xii, introduced as an apparently casual touch of scene-setting detail, and passed over in innocent silence in the first Charybdis encounter, but eventually to prove the life-saving *sine qua non* on the surprise second visit at the book's end. As a general principle, misdirection of this kind works best when *viewpointed* – if the character from whose perspective we experience the story overlooks, forgets, or misfiles an item of data, the reader is allowed to do the same. But clearly it is less acceptable for a viewpoint figure to suppress, in recounting his experience of events, something he would have been aware of at the time.

In general, the seeding of moves is effective in proportion to the narrative interval between seed and fruit. If a character is an expert swordsman, it is not much use to establish this for the first time on the page before he has to fight a duel – unless, of course, the character is one of those heroic omnicompetents who is constantly coming up with surprising expertise. Such late seeding dents transparency by producing an impression of *ad hoc* improvisation, by an author only barely in control of his narrative.

But it needs stressing again that the reader's glimpses of an author at all such moments are themselves merely a projection from reading the text. The *real* author's compositional activity may bear scant resemblance to that foisted on his stand-in by the reader, which by default assumes a speechlike linear composition of both text and story in real time. In *actual* composition, the seeding of moves may be quite accidental and retrospective, resolving story dilemmas on the spot by the opportunistic exploitation of game elements already in place. Yet the very reason why real-world authors are limited at such moments of improvisation to what is already on the board is that the move has to *seem* to have been planned all along. It is enough for the process of composition to kick over its traces, leaving the plot to *appear* conceived and executed as a whole. In the end, of course, the reader can never be wholly unaware of a text in his hand, and the ghost of an author behind it. But the classical author must remain, as purely as possible, a construct projected by the text, ideally exhibiting a godlike coupling of invisibility with omnicompetence. The reward for the real author, if transparency is successfully preserved and the reader sees the narrative as a perfectly programmed machine, is considerable: to be worshipped as the infinite disembodied intelligence most real-world storytellers would so dearly love to be. No wonder classical plotting has survived so well.

5 Unclassical plots

The narrative productions of the Graeco-Roman world, if not quite *innombrables*, are enormously diverse. A catalogue by extant genre alone would have to include epic, hymn, lyric, narrative elegy and iambus; tragedy, comedy, satyr-play, and mime; history, biography, philosophy, oratory, fable, novel; and a host of variously experimental crossbreeds between. Every one of these forms has left its own distinctive print on the narrative traditions of the West. This book is concerned with one historical strand out of many: the set of narrative values I have labelled 'classical plotting', and whose characteristics I have tried to describe in the preceding chapters.

Part II will argue that this paradigm's historical evolution, though it runs across generic boundaries, is the specific product of a handful of narrative genres, and indeed of a narrow band of the spectrum within each: Homeric epic, fifth-century tragedy, Graeco-Roman New Comedy, and the Greek love-novel. While the classical paradigm may well owe much of its historical resilience to its peculiarly efficient use of our innate cognitive apparatus for narrative processing, its original rise is tied to a series of unabashed cultural accidents in the Greek world over the half-millennium from 750 to 250 BC. Principal among these are: the existence and early canonisation of the *Iliad* and *Odyssey*; the invention of Attic drama, and the canonisation of three fifth-century tragedians; the late emergence of prose and of literary fiction; the peculiar relationship between Attic tragedy and comedy; and the closing of the Alexandrian literary canon by Aristophanes of Byzantium. These claims are for later chapters to pursue and, I hope, to justify.

The business of this chapter, however, is to map the omissions – and, in doing so, to sketch the emergence of some of the principal long-term rivals to the classical plot paradigm. Some forms appear in this inventory simply because, though classically ordered by the standards of their time, their innovations (if any) do not appear to influence the traditions of later classical practice. Others offer a genuine alternative to the classical paradigm, a way of organising narrative that does not privilege the classical economics of closure, or which operates on a scale below the high classical genres, or which openly and integrally proclaims its own narrative situation; while others again deliberately reject or subvert the norms of classical plotting for ironic, polemical, or experimental ends of their own.

The story, briefly told, is this. For inaccessible reasons, the Homeric poems seem to represent the final creative flowering of their tradition just as Greek narrative emerges to literary view. The archaic successor genres, both within and without the hexameter epic tradition, experimented with modifications to the Homeric paradigm: a rival 'lyric' model of the relationship between narrated and narrating worlds, and new degrees of fictionality to colonise the space between the contemporary world of poet and audience and the world of heroic myth. The rise of drama transformed this scene by offering (i) in tragedy, a revised paradigm of classical Homeric plotting tailored to the new mode of drama; (ii) in comedy and mime, theatrical rivals to tragedy in the same mode, but defined by their freedom to resist tragedy's fetishisation of Homeric narrative values. At the same time, prose narrative genres emerged that drew on Homeric plotting for a rhetoric of causality in genres which laid claim to factual truth, and which together instigated a notion of prose narrative that for Aristotle was antithetical to his classical poetics of verse. But the canonisation of the Homeric model and its tragic successor in Aristotle and the generation of his students, including the heyday of Greek New Comedy, became the basis for a concerted programme of resistance by Callimachus and his generation, whose rival neo-archaic values were to dominate the narrative poetry of the Hellenistic and Roman worlds.

1   Cyclic epic

What we can reconstruct of the character and reputation of post-Homeric epic suggests a narrative paradigm quite different from the *Hymns* and, surprisingly, from the *Iliad* and *Odyssey*. Many of these later poems, along with the longer *Iliad* and *Odyssey*, coalesced into the first encylopaedic compilation of Greek myth: the so-called 'Epic Cycle' of a dozen or more individual poems, spanning the history of the world from its creation to the generation after the Trojan war. The perception of fundamental narratological differences between Homeric and 'cyclic' epic seems to have been a factor in the crystallisation of an idea of 'Homer', both as an author and as an ideal of classical narrative values.

Aristotle's verdict on these sub-Homeric epics was dismissive: in emphatic contrast to the *Iliad* and *Odyssey*, they lacked any sense of wholeness or causal connection.[1] They sought unity in a series of poorly connected events strung loosely around a single character, or a period of time, or a sprawling and structureless episodic process.[2] Modern study of the fragments and testimonia for these mostly vanished texts seems if anything to reinforce this verdict. To judge from their known length and content, the cyclic poems seem to have scanned through their material at a relentless fast-forward; and there is much to suggest that the material itself was far less coherently rulebound than the worlds of the *Iliad* and *Odyssey*. The interest of the cyclic poems for later writers was mainly as a mythological quarry for story material and, at least in tragedy, an occasional anti-Homeric paradigm of narrative values; but after Aristotle's time their currency fell steeply, though for reasons not necessarily attributable to the *Poetics*. Narratological innovation and influence in the post-Homeric tradition seems concentrated instead in the peripheral epic genres – and increasingly in genres outside the hexameter tradition altogether.

2 The narrative hymn[3]

The seven longer *Homeric Hymns* at the front of the mediaeval compilation are the earliest in date and the fullest in narrative content. All embed a continuous mythological narrative within a standard hymnic frame in honour of the divine figure who becomes the protagonist in the narrative core. The frame is minimal, compared with the scale of the text; the author and audience are not asserted; and though the narrative serves an ostensibly panegyric and illustrative function within the hymnic frame, this thematic orientation is loosely pursued and in practice hardly interferes with the self-sufficiency of the central narrative section.

Despite wide variations in length, quality, and narrative ambition, the long hymns as a group clearly subscribe to a Homeric rather than a Cyclic or a Hesiodic narrative paradigm. The *Hymn* – more probably two *Hymns* – *to Apollo* is the exception, with its loose episodic structure and curt narrative style. But the major *Hymns* to Demeter, Hermes, Aphrodite, and (on a smaller scale) Dionysus are strongly Homeric, and specifically Odyssean, in narrative technique, with closed casts, articulate rules, foreshadowing of endgame, and a deft control of pace, scene, and viewpoint. Particularly strong in these respects is the short seventh *Hymn*, to

---

[1] *Poetics* 8.1451a16–29, 23.1459a29–b7; see especially Griffin 1977 and Herington 1985: 130–6; a misplaced attempt at resistance in Nagy 1990: 70–9.
[2] There is a textual problem at 1459b1, but if any of the words are genuine this seems to be approximately the sense.
[3] A concise survey with bibliography now in Clay 1997.

Dionysus – with its tightly-defined board and cast (the ship and its crew), articulation of moral rules and signalling of endgame (by the helmsman), and subtle viewpointing camerawork throughout in the selection and sequence of details. Even the much longer and more episodic *Demeter*, the least immediately classical of the four, is structured and told with a consistent signalling of narrative closure and goals.

Yet the influence of these remarkable texts on the development of classical plotting is historically negligible – even though two, *Demeter* and *Aphrodite*, rank easily among the greatest narrative poems in the language. They were not much read, and (Sophocles' *Trackers* and the *Hymns* of Callimachus apart) very little imitated. Within the tradition of Homeric narrativity, their innovation was to devise a classical template for plots with divine protagonists – a challenging brief, as such players would seem in principle to be unlimited in competence, and therefore impossible subjects for the restricted, rulebound moves of Homeric plotting. The bold solution was to make the core of the story an imposition of *limits* on the divinity's knowledge or power (conflict with other gods, temporary subjection to mortals), and the conquest by the divinity of those limits. But this theme depends on a distinctively archaic view of the status and knowability of the divine, and it is striking that narratives with a divine rather than human centre henceforward virtually vanish from the classical tradition. Significantly, it is the latest of the four (*Hermes*) that treats its players with ironic lightness, discards the theme of dangerous leakages across the boundary between mortal and divine – and alone of the set is reworked in a later classical medium.

3   Early didactic and catalogue poetry

Hesiodic narrative, in contrast, is a bewilderingly different experience from that of the epics, to which the poems otherwise seem so close (in date, language, and compositional techniques). Terms like 'primitive', 'archaic', 'naïve' pepper the language of Hesiodic criticism: there are sequential narrative lines, but little sense of structure or direction; there are defined scenes and even speeches, but these are invariably bald, brief, and by Homeric standards perfunctory; there are variations of narrative pace and of detail, but the former often seem haphazard and the latter never approach the circumstantiality of Homer. The paradox, in fact, of such catalogue poetry as the Hesiodic *Theogony* and *Ehoiai* and the Homeric catalogue of ships and pageant of heroines, is the presentation of uniquely dense story content in a form that makes only minimal claim to narrative status. Only the genealogical *Theogony* and its lost, much longer, sequel the *Ehoiai* attempt any continuous internal story chronology; while their siblings are thematically organised anthologies of causally disjunct names or summaries. Their narrative legacy, which is considerable but indirect, is as a paradigm of encyclopaedic polymyth, a literature of meta-narrative commentary on the vastness, variety, and productive coherence of the mythological corpus.

The culmination of this tradition is the *Works and days*, which, like its many successors and offshoots in the epic subgenre nowadays termed 'didactic', is only sporadically a narrative text at all. Rather, narrative fragments are embedded *ad hoc* in a wider argumentative frame, to support or illuminate the strongly personalised didactic content. As a use for narrative, this is revolutionary: the *Works and days* is, as the *CHCL* writers put it (100), 'the first attempt in western literature to compose a large-scale work without the armature of a given narrative line'. As already in *Theogony*, the narratorial voice claims an explicit identity and narratee, and personalises the narrative content with a strong (quasi-)autobiographical imprint of individual outlook and experience: a momentous innovation, and the beginning of archaic poetry's long and seminal exploration of resilient alternatives to Homeric epic's cult of transparency and the self-erasing poet. This personalised hexameter poetry had its own tradition in the archaic period and beyond; but the most far-reaching experiments lay in genres outside the epic tradition altogether.

4 Lyric, elegy, iambus

The non-hexameter genres of archaic poetry form a cluster of complex interrelations, reflected in the frequent modern extension of the label 'lyric' (strictly, any solo and choral verse performed to string accompaniment) to include the closely related traditions of archaic solo verse and song in spoken iambic and pipe-accompanied elegiac metres. In particular, there are cross-border patterns in the use of *narrative* across these diverse forms and genres that justify their treatment here as a single category, and together help to define the significance of 'lyric' as a key generic marker in Western poetics; for it was in these archaic Greek genres that three developments combined to forge the most potent and durable rival system of narrative values to the classical model pioneered in the Homeric epics.

First, lyric narrative generally rejects the pursuit of transparency. A defining feature of lyric is its freedom to acknowledge the moment of performance, the audience, text and author – though with many degrees of creative disingenuousness that can heavily fictionalise all of these. In the supreme vehicle of lyric narrativity, the Pindaric epinician, this oscillation into and out of myth is one of the chief articulations of its vision. The

Pindaric victory-song collapses time: the victor, the hero of the present day, breaks through at the moment of triumph from mortal time to divine eternity, to the dreamtime of myth and the immortality of song. The song affirms this annihilation of temporality by repeated, narratologically violent jumps not just within the chronology of story, but also from the story-world to the textual present. For ideological as well as technical reasons, this radical dismemberment of epic narrativity left little direct legacy of emulation; but this poetry rated highly in the ancient canon, and its drastically un-Homeric approach to narrative was always present to view.

A second, closely related general feature of lyric narrative is that its narrative compass is restricted and subordinate. Most lyric texts are very short in comparison with epic; they therefore have far less text in which to tell their stories. The regular solution is to recount a myth by selection and allusion within a non-narrative frame – which may be personal, gnomic, panegyric, cultic, or even (as frequently in Pindar) a second, embedding narrative. But because the frame itself is necessarily more closely bound to the performance situation, the myth then occupies a subordinate role, generally paradigmatic or exploratory of themes in the frame. Details of the myth are selected and highlighted to reflect this strictly functional and subordinate use. Events may be alluded to without being fully told, or in an order determined by external thematic function rather than internal story chronology. A widespread device is a pattern of synopsis and selection: first the myth is summarised in outline, and then one or more scenes are singled out for fuller recounting.

This is not, however, a role filled uniquely by narrative. In the poetry of Sappho, especially, we find a quasi-autobiographical dramatic frame mediated by movement into and out of an imaginative annexe to the outward situation.[4] This slide into fantasy encourages reading as stream-of-consciousness association, arising from the subjective meditation of the author-figure. But precisely because the transition is one of subjective association, many other kinds of imaginative overflow may serve in place of myth: memory, simile, description, daydream, didacticism, self-analysis or confession. In lyric, narrative is rarely self-sufficient or self-contained: rather, it is part of a larger process dictated by non-narrative elements in the text. The one striking exception, the long mythological lyric of Stesichorus, seems rather to mimic the epic in mode and dimension; what we have of these strange and exhilarating texts does not seem to suggest any radical modification to the narrative ambitions and idioms of contemporary epic.[5] But the other lyric genres complete the dethrone-

4   See e.g. Bagg 1964: 51.   5   See especially Burnett 1988.

ment of narrative by asserting their ultimate freedom to dispense with narrative altogether.

Finally, while the content of lyric narrative still draws from the epic stock – that common heritage of archaic story material that Herington (1985) memorably termed 'the forest of myths' – the prominence of the narrating moment in the lyric narrative situation allows movement away from the distanced world of myth into historical, contemporary, or personal milieux. Both the narrative content and the narrating voices of lyric borrow freely from the post-mythological world, moving closer along both axes in the direction of what we (though not the ancient world) would call 'fiction'.[6] Although 'pure' fiction, in the sense of narrated events in unmediated voices that make no claim ever to have happened, has to wait for the birth of comedy, it is a point of some importance for the history of Greek narrative that our dividing line between fiction and fact was neither explicit nor rigidly applied by the Greeks themselves; on the contrary, it was constantly and inventively being blurred. Myth and history, for instance, were not clearly separated categories, even in the chronological sense; and as early as the proem to Hesiod's *Theogony*, the worlds of imagination and life were liable to merge without any special embarrassment or warning. First-person narrative, especially, was a creative battleground between the poet outside the text and the poet within, the author as author and the author as projection of the text. We tend, perhaps too readily, to say that Hesiod and Sappho are writing 'fiction' when they describe face-to-face epiphanies and dialogue with gods, but 'fact' when they sing of winning tripods in poetry contests or losing lovers to men. The texts, at least, make no distinction.

5   Fable

A second locus of the fictional experiment was this elusive but persistent subliterary tradition, an archaic narrative type that lacked autonomous literary form until the first prose collections in the early Hellenistic period, though we have a reasonable impression of its mainstream 'Aesopic' variety.[7] Of considerable interest as an early attempt at minimal rule-bound narrative, it has attracted special attention in empirical discourse studies,[8] in part arising out of its earlier appeal to AI researchers as the leading candidate for a fully programmable narrative genre. Meehan's 'Aesop-fable generator' in TALE-SPIN mode 3 works by starting with a

---

[6] This is a theoretical and historical minefield, but see especially Rösler 1980, Bowie 1993, Finkelberg 1998, with further discussion in Lowe (forthcoming).
[7] A comprehensive survey now in van Dijk 1997.
[8] See e.g. Dorfman and Brewer 1994.

moral that the fable has to demonstrate, breaking it down into a set of goals, strategies, and outcomes which the program can understand, and constructing a story universe whose characters and setting are determined entirely by those elements. Thus in TALE-SPIN's version of 'The Fox and the Crow', the programmer breaks down the moral 'Never trust flatterers' into three necessary story elements that are then fed to the program to work on: a character who flatters and is trusted, a character who is flattered and trusts, and a reward for the first character at the expense of the second. The program then constructs the most economical possible story that can accommodate these three desiderata: in this case a two-character story with a single, jointly pursued reward, won by the fox through a strategy of flattery and deception.

Considering its limits, this is not a bad model for fable plotting. The story elements are specifically chosen to work out a moral syllogism, through a functionally minimal tale of conflicting goals and rewards. Animal characters are especially well suited for this purpose, bringing with them ready-made, stereotypically simple goals and competence relationships. But narrative obtrudes on story in a very unclassical way: the reader accepts that the story exists for the sake of the narrative rules it demonstrates, whereas in the classical model the rules are understood (rightly or wrongly) as merely a means to the intelligibility of the story. The TALE-SPIN model's limitations as a general model for narrative are largely those of the fable genre itself: its bijou scale, insistent thematic pointedness, and restricted subject matter. But as a popular subliterary paradigm of strongly-functional narrative economy, operating with stories that need not be known beforehand, it offered an early model for 'pure' fiction that seems to have been one of the formative influences on comedy. As such, it bridges the gap between the counter-classical experiments of the archaic period, which define themselves by distinction from Homer, and those of the classical period, whose baseline is increasingly Attic tragedy, and which fall into two groups: the dramatic genres of comedy and mime, and the narrated prose genres of history and oratory – with the dialogue straddling the boundary between.

6   Old Comedy[9]

In the extant dramatic traditions of the ancient world, Aristophanic comedy stands in striking isolation. Its tragic contemporary and its New

---

[9] The traditional division of Attic comedy into three historical periods is ingrained but misleading; it would be more accurate to think of 'Old' and 'Middle' Comedy as one seamless phase of constant, energetic innovation and development that comes to an abrupt, mysterious, and fossilising halt in about 320 BC.

Comic posterity share a common language of theatrical and narrative convention: they are Homerically plotted, illusionistic and naturalistic, strict in their observance of causality, transparency, the intelligibility of character and the functional economy of action. Old Comedy, for reasons not yet understood, is none of these things. It respects no consistency of space, time, causal logic, dramatic illusion, or human psychology. That is not to say that it rejects these classical shibboleths out of hand – simply that it abides by them when convenient, and annihilates them without qualm when it is not.

This is not an environment in which Homeric narrative values can easily thrive. The rules and boundaries of play shift unpredictably; players softly and suddenly vanish from the board; few moves can be anticipated causally from the outcome of earlier moves. Nevertheless, Aristophanes' plays do have a powerful plot poetics of their own; it is simply not a poetics that makes a fetish of causality. Aristophanic narrative is organised around a fertile, flexible combination of formal and thematic principles, to which the logic of cause and effect comes a very poor third. Unlike tragedy, Old Comedy has a rich dramatic vocabulary of traditional formal elements that structure story in familiar and predictable ways. Some are more or less guaranteed to turn up in their regular place and sequence (prologue, *parodos*, *parabasis*, final *komos*); others are optional and available at need (*agon*, musical syzygy, and the regrettably nameless pattern of a series of rapid, physical scenes involving a series of new characters played by the second and/or third actors in successive confrontations with the lead). All of these exert their own tidal pull on the shape and pace of the action, raising well-defined audience expectations within seconds of being activated – the length of an episode, its output, the initial and eventual relation between its players. At the same time, however, and closer to fable than tragedy, Aristophanic plotting is strongly driven by theme. The prologue formally establishes a situational premise – itself generally a fantastic modification of the natural order, a state of affairs that could never arise in nature. A lead player is singled out and labelled with story goals tied to the consequences of that premise; antagonistic players or forces are marshalled; and the resulting clash of goals pursues a thematic thought-experiment through a dramatic dialectic of personal confrontation, with a series of formally patterned episodes leading at last to an endgame of triumph and celebration.

This is a powerful and attractive alternative to the classical system of directing expectation. But the neighbouring tragic model is already exerting pressure in Aristophanes' time. The plays of the middle period (*Birds*, *Lysistrata*, *Thesmophoriazusae*, *Frogs*) show an increasing tendency to closed casts, coherent use of space, early signalling of endgame, and continuity of story goals across the *parabasis*; while the late plays *Ecclesiazusae* and *Plutus*, though apparently retrograde in some of these respects, testify to a reduction in some of the more fantastic elements in fifth-century comedy, though perhaps as much for budgetary as for dramatic reasons. And one of Old Comedy's subversions of the classical plot paradigm will paradoxically determine the future of that paradigm itself: comedy is the first overt literary fiction to abandon the use of myth, previously the canonical source of story material for any fiction acknowledging itself as such. For the history of plot, this is a crucial move. Despite the versatility and creative flexibility of myth in fifth-century tragedy, as a source of story it brought with it severe difficulties for classical narrative.[10] For classical plotting to manipulate its own reading most fully, not just the narrative packaging but the story content – characters, environment – had to be open to creation *ex nihilo*. Old Comedy did not, of course, shun myth altogether, though we happen to have lost all of Aristophanes' known fully mythological plays. But the fact it could make up its stories at will may have been one of the reasons that comedy embarked on a new lease of creativity at exactly the time that tragedy passed into decline.

7   Mime

This is an impossible subject. The term *mimos* is first used by Aristotle, of the prose sketches of Sophron and Xenarchus in the previous century. We do not know how these connect historically with other early manifestations of Syracusan and Tarentine popular drama, such as the verse comedies of Epicharmus, the soft-porn mythological cabaret in Xenophon's *Symposium*, the *hilarotragoediae* of Rhinthon and his school, or the so-called *phlyax* farces that used to be identified with the last. If our Athenocentric perspective on fifth- and fourth-century Greece were replaced with an equally Syracosiocentric view, we would no doubt be just as puzzled by the relations between tragedy, comedy, satyr-play, and the Platonic dialogue. As it stands, our earliest usable evidence is the third-century poetic pseudomimes of Theocritus and Herodas, already coloured by Hellenistic anti-classicism – which may have turned to the mime as a subliterary alternative to the restrictive Aristotelian high genres. Our only preserved scripts for performed mime are the papyrus mime texts of Imperial date, precarious witness for the pre-Roman period. The nature of Sophron's influence, if any, on Plato's dialogues remains an engaging speculation.[11]

[10] See below, pp. 159, 188–9.
[11] Haslam 1972 (earlier discussions are obsolete); Clay 1994: 32–7.

What little we can divine of the character of mime suggests the story content was slight, and the plot content less. The main narrative interest of the literary mimes of Herodas and Theocritus lies rather in their signalling of action through dialogue alone, unsupported by either third-person narration or visual amplification of the verbal text. How new this was is difficult to say; by comparison the Socratic dialogue, our only earlier unperformed narratorless narrative, makes comparatively little use of implied action and setting. But presumably these writers' educated consumers were well practised by this time in the private reading of play scripts, originally intended for performance but still packed with dialogue indications of action, so the technique is not entirely novel.

Otherwise, mainstream mime seems to have set more store by sophisticated naturalistic observation of character, behaviour, and dialogue than by the programmed manipulation of reader modelling of story. Length may have been a limiting factor here: mimes seem commonly to have observed unity of time and place, but in very short texts, often restricting story in effect to a single dialogue scene. This allows for a certain limited progression of goals, such as a process of persuasion or seduction, but little in the way of complex patterning of moves; and for Hellenistic and Roman Callimacheans the genre (if it merits the term) seems to have been valued as a model of anti-Aristotelian narrative values in the mode of drama. By contrast, the major prose genres which grew in the fifth century out of the Ionian treatise made ambitious use of Homeric narrative architectures to interrogate the notion of causality in narratives outside the domain of poetic fiction altogether.

8   History

For Aristotle, as for us, history is the enemy of fiction; the two kinds of narrative pursue irreconcilable ends. The historian's truths are particular, not general: 'what Alcibiades, for instance, did or what happened to him'.[12] And the historian's material controls his narrative art, instead of the other way about: 'in histories it is necessary to give a report of a single period, not of a unified action'.[13] The historian's task is to chronicle what actually happened, not to seduce us with plausible accounts of what we know did not.

But Aristotle appreciated poetry better than he did historiography, and particularly Greek historiography. History is a discourse of causality and explanation, not a dispassionate chronicle of 'whatever was the case in that period about one man or more'. The very act of narrative itself

[12] *Poetics* 9.1451b11.   [13] *Poetics* 23.1459a22–3.

requires the historian to select, interpret, and suggest causal connections between the events chosen for report. For just this reason, narrative is regarded with some suspicion in current historiographic theory, one important strand of which approaches narrative history as fundamentally a mode of rhetoric.[14] At the very least, a *narrative* model of history cannot help assigning to events a value, significance, and sequence – none of them easy properties to define or defend objectively.

Even so, modern readers are puzzled and embarrassed by some quirks of ancient historiography that seem unduly provocative of such border agreements as exist between fact and fiction. Most notorious is the unquestioned and persistent use of direct speech, when a transcript of the original words could not possibly have been available. We also chide Herodotus for his cheerful inclusion of preposterous anecdote and folk-tale, Thucydides for his disingenuous tragedising, Xenophon for his woeful unconcern with documentary accuracy. All three, to say nothing of their successors, can be caught red-handed massaging intractable historical truth into higher, and often more Aristotelian, dramatic truth.

All this has a common source: the pioneer historians modelled their narrative art unabashedly on epic, and particularly on the *Iliad*.[15] This was no artistic subterfuge, but a matter of plain necessity. The epic was the only repertoire then in existence of techniques for narrative composition on such a scale. It was, by modern standards, an eccentric model for historical narrative, with its strongly closural plot economy, sophisticated internal viewpoint, and largely invisible narratorial presence. It was, in fact, a narrative paradigm evolved specifically to give plausible substance to events the audience knew to be imaginary. And by accepting *faute de mieux* the narrative principles of epic, Greek history committed itself to a dramatic, vivid, eyewitness approach to historical reportage at odds with its rhetoric of objectivity.

There were, nevertheless, two particular attractions of the Homeric model for the founders of historiography. One was openly intertextual: Herodotus was possessed by the exuberant vision that the events of living memory, the birth-pangs of his contemporary world, were an epic tale fully worthy to rival Homer's, with dazzling deeds, continents in conflict, and the destiny of nations in the balance. Thucydides, completely infected by Herodotus' epic vision despite a very different outlook both on history and, not irrelevantly, on the *Iliad*, took the conceit a final step further. For Thucydides, he and his readers were *living* an epic. The

---

[14] Bibliography begins with White 1973: 1–38, 1978, 1987; for ancient historiographers' responses see Momigliano 1981, Woodman 1988 (esp. 197–212), and especially Hornblower 1994, Rood 1998.

[15] Strasburger 1972; see now Shrimpton 1997 (esp. 21–2, 98–9), Nielsen 1997: 27–36.

greatest epic plot in human memory was neither the Trojan nor the Persian wars, but the experience of his own generation; and it was moreover an *Iliad* in the original minor key of suffering and tragedy, stripped of Herodotus' comfortably Odyssean moral and patriotic reharmonising.

But a subtler, perhaps more insidious, attraction of the Homeric narrative model was precisely that it *did* offer a readymade framework for interpretation and judgement, allowing the historian of the Persian or Peloponnesian wars to draw on the narrative devices of epic to reveal intelligible coherence and closure in impossibly complex events. There would be, if not a strict division into players and extras, at least an Iliadic ranking of pieces by levels of significance: key players, given a significant share of the action and dialogue; a ring of supporting players, recurrently named and involved in the action; and an outer circle of the anonymous multitude, impelling the action only as a collective will. There would be a beginning and end to the chain of story, not just a march of middles – even though defining a beginning was evidently a laborious process when denied the epic recourse to the judgement of a Muse, while all three of the extant monumental historians are beaten by the challenge of ending. And above all, there would be rules of causality: moral, political, religious, military, in varying proportion according to the personality of the work, but rules nevertheless that explain why the story as a whole has the causal shape that it does. Thus the spell of narrative history is the spell of Homeric plotting itself: the epic fiction that events on a scale of nations and generations are perceptible as a unified causal whole. Nor was history itself the only emergent prose genre to appropriate a Homeric narrative poetics to impose a rhetoric of causality on the disarray of real events.

9   Oratory

The use of narrative in forensic (and to a much lesser extent, political and epideictic) oratory is unlike any other literary application. The story it tells is neither historian's truth nor poet's fiction, but an *agonistic* version of the truth competing openly for credence. Defendant and plaintiff will normally have conflicting accounts of a set of real-life events, only one at most of which can be fully correct. The orator's task is to convince the audience, by narrative means alone, that his version rather than his opponent's is the true one. The task of this narrative is to establish the truth of story.

How is this achieved? There are two main tactics, the choice dictated by the circumstances of the case. It may be that there is substantial agreement between parties on the facts of story, with only their legal interpretation in dispute. This is the case in the (fictitious) *Tetralogies* of Antiphon, where the reader has to judge, for example, whether a javelin-thrower is guilty of murder if a fellow athlete wanders fatally into the path of his cast. Here the reader has to decide whether a story conforms to a specified narrative rule, in this case the legal definition of murder; and the story is subjected to rival narrative interpretations to argue the competing claims of the case.

Alternatively, the legal issue may be clear-cut, and the judgement depend on the reconstruction of what happened. Here a notorious difference exists between ancient and modern legal procedure. Documentary, circumstantial, and corroborative evidence (such as oaths, witnesses, material proofs, testimony from tortured slaves) are all of secondary weight in Athenian courts. In an oral culture, seemingly straightforward events can be reported in bafflingly different versions. Though we only have speeches preserved from one side of each real-life case extant, we can sometimes get a glimpse of the scale of the problem from references in the preserved speeches to the opponent's version. In Lysias I, whose core is the famous narrative of the speaker's apprehension of the adulterous Eratosthenes *in delicto* with the speaker's wife, it emerges that the prosecution asserts that the victim was abducted in the street or even from sanctuary at an altar, not (as is necessary to sustain the legal defence) caught and executed in the speaker's bedroom in front of a party of witnesses.

Both of these types attempt to manipulate the reader's internal model of events. But the first directs attention less to the story itself than to its fit with a set of given narrative rules: the relevant laws in the Attic code. The reader is invited, not to reconstruct the story from the narrative, but to assess its conformity to a given narrative pattern. That invitation will be only partly couched in narrative terms. To be sure, the story will normally be told in a way that accentuates details that fit the legal model, while suppressing those that do not. But there will also be an appeal to purely analytic discourse: both the story and the relevant laws themselves will be subjected to rational, casuistic interpretation.

By contrast, the second type of forensic narrative depends much more closely on the mechanisms of plot. This narrative uses the techniques of fiction to evoke the impression of fact: the story, not the narrative, is what the reader is openly challenged to judge, and as with classical plotting the narrative overlay exists only to enhance the verisimilitude of the story. So the story is packaged in the way that makes best use of the reader's existing models for comparison: assumptions about human nature, stereotypical patterns of events, 'realistic' uses of incidental narrative detail. Motivation, in particular, is subjected to exhaustive narrative scrutiny, as the reader is invited to judge which of two alternative motives best explains a given action, or which of two actions would have been more likely given a specified background of motivation.

Notwithstanding the central focus on causality and narrative rules, this is a use of narrative that shares more with a lyric than a Homeric model. Narrative content is subordinated to narrating situation; narrator and audience are strongly acknowledged throughout, and a Lysias will actively tailor his material to the persona of his real-life client. Other kinds of discourse frame and bolster the narrative core: in the canonical arrangement, the narrative section is prefaced with an argumentative exordium, and then followed by a more analytic dissection of the proofs before the final summing-up. Finally, it is only incidentally part of the orator's art to phase the release of information to his audience: the advantages of laying the full case early before the audience generally outweigh the possible dramatic pay-off available from more conventional use of suspense and surprise, though Lysias especially is not averse to such techniques in the deployment of circumstantial detail. Such harnessing of narrative closure to forensic or persuasive ends is taken still further by the third major prose genre to emerge in the classical period.

10   The dialogue[16]

Its origins are contested, and seem diverse;[17] apparent influences include sophistic oratory, the Syracusan mime, agonistic dialogue in Attic drama, and *oratio recta* debates in fifth-century historians. Plato and Xenophon did not invent the form; our earliest example of dialectic in a dramatised and historicised dialogue form is the Melian debate in Thucydides V, a work unlikely to postdate the death of Socrates, so the form seems to have been established before its uptake by the Socratics. Aristotle, who would have known, attributed the earliest *Socratic* dialogues to an otherwise enigmatic Alexamenus, and pre-Socratic dialogues were claimed for Zeno of Elea.[18]

As a narrative form, the philosophical dialogue may seem somewhat limited, but two formal innovations deserve remark. First, it is the earliest extant literature to convey narrative chiefly or exclusively through direct speech, with only the attributions of speaker left to a narratorial voice. Unlike the drama, which was written to be performed with an accompanying visual text also composed by the poet, the dialogues of Plato and Xenophon were not (to our knowledge) acted out, and thus have to

---

16 On the issues sketched here see especially the chapters by Frede, Kosman, and Halperin in Klagge and Smith 1992.
17 Hirzel 1895 i.2–67 remains an invaluable survey; latest discussion in Clay 1994.
18 Athenaeus XI.505c = Aristotle, fr. 72 R. (from the lost dialogue *On poets*).

convey the whole burden of information about setting, characters, and non-verbal actions through the use of dialogue alone. In practice, these resources are only occasionally used, and generally only at the scene-setting beginnings of the dialogue. The most memorable dramatic episodes in Plato and Xenophon come in the externally narrated passages of mixed-mode dialogues: the end of the *Phaedo*, the incidental action of each writer's *Symposium*. But since the focus of interest is the dialectical content rather than the outward events that frame it, there is little scope and less interest in giving those events a programmed structure.

At the same time, the dialogue is the boldest product yet of the continuing Greek experiment with historical fiction. Xenophon's *Cyropaedia* would take the foisting of imaginary actions and speeches on historical characters a stage further than either philosophy or history had yet gone; but the achievement of the Socratic literature should not be underestimated either. Actual historical events (Socrates' trial, Agathon's victory) become the frames for blatantly fictitious conversation and, in the case of Plato's *Symposium*, incidental action. In the historians, the speeches are auxiliary to the historical frame; in the dialogue, the priority is reversed. But Plato goes further, and on occasion allows historical verisimilitude and fictional self-consciousness to clash in ironic conflict. Two notorious cases are the *Menexenus* and *Symposium*, which use Russian-doll stacks of nested reporting to make mischief with chronology and narrative distance. In the first, a pastiche funeral oration on the war dead of 386 is put into the mouth of Socrates (d. 399), who claims it was composed by Aspasia (disappears from history 429). In the second, the most historically vivid, specific, star-studded, and circumstantial of the dialogues in both setting and narration is reported as Apollodorus' second remembered account of Aristodemus' account of the party, told many years on and including further levels of nesting within the dialogue (Aristophanes' unattributed just-so story, Socrates' report of his lengthy and abstruse conversation with Diotima).[19] These ironic games with narrative framing and distance mark the emergence of a powerful counter-classical narrative type. Its calculated deconstruction of transparency and illusion is an early link in a literary chain leading eventually to the fully self-conscious fiction of Lucian's *True history*, which nudges the reader with explicit jokes about its own fictionality.

All the same, in a curious way many of Plato's dialogues (in contrast to Xenophon's) *do* have something sufficiently akin to a classical plot structure to test the notion of plot itself. There is a closed list of speakers, fol-

[19] See Halperin 1992.

lowing the contemporary theatrical norm of one clear protagonist and one or more successive secondary roles in tension with him. Characterisation and the motivation of speech are explored with considerable dexterity, including a naturalistic attention to verbal idiosyncrasy and detail: Plato's dialogues are the closest attempt before New Comedy to capture the cadences of everyday Attic conversation. Above all, the text constantly invites the reader to develop an internal model of how the argument will proceed, and even (in early dialogues) an outline of the aporistic endgame, as players compete to persuade interlocutor, reader, or both of the superiority of their argument, and the reader projects and anticipates the course of play.

And yet, is this 'plot'? Has the *Ion*, say, a 'story'? Does anything 'happen'? Yes, in the sense that the state of relations between two players changes dynamically through a series of communicative acts. No, in the sense that none of the moves involves an exchange of information about events in the world of action. There are, of course, many kinds of plot in which nothing happens outside the heads of the characters: where all moves are c-moves, and the only elements of the game state to alter are modalised states of perception internal to the players' private mental universes. But there is always some outside event or action to which the exchange of views ultimately connects, and without which the discussion would be senseless. In the *Ion*, the outward events mentioned (such as Ion's rhapsodic performances) are *not* the ultimate topic of discussion – though it is part of the dialogue's elaborate comedy that Ion persists in believing that they are. Rather, it is the status of modal worlds themselves that is under discussion: the nature of states such as belief, knowledge, and so forth, irrespective of what the belief or knowledge is about. Even in the *Phaedo*, the death-cell setting is a narrative convenience: the arguments for immortality gain point and poignancy from their frame, but they could equally have been set on a sunny afternoon in Piraeus in 420.

I would therefore claim the Platonic dialogue as an exemplary case of something it might be useful to term *quasiplotting*: the development of plot*like* structures and reader response in non-narrative texts. In some respects, of course, Plato's dialogues *are* narratives: they make a pretence, at least, to be records of real words spoken by real characters in real settings. But most of the structural dynamics would be equally apparent if the arguments alone were presented, stripped of these dramatising elements, in a continuous, impersonal tract.

The structural rules applied to this particular quasiplotting are the rules not of narrative, but of *dialectic*. We can see which way the argument will go through our grasp of reasoned argument: a flaw spotted in the case

put by Socrates' opponent, say, or a conclusion beginning to be glimpsed
in a series of analogies. Dialectic has, if anything, an even more rigorous
and comprehensible formal substructure than narrative plotting, and it
was Plato's achievement to grasp that this structure itself could be dramatic, especially when imposed on an authentically plotlike universe of
seemingly autonomous figures in a landscape. It could generate, as plot
does, a convincing impression of character, through the emotional and
intellectual responses of speakers to propositions (rather than, as is more
general in narrative plotting, to events). It could establish a plotlike sense
of potential and discharge, using dialectical rather than performative
competence as its currency. Thus the reader is expected to anticipate
arguments that Socrates is capable of producing, and to match what is
actually said against this model. If the dialectical discharge is delayed, the
effect will be a plotlike impression of postponed resolution, or humour, or
both. Dialectic can thus mimic the powerful plot techniques of suspense
and dramatic irony. And finally, the dialogue can reproduce the *negen-
tropic* movement of plot, the sense of emerging order from problematic
chaos, by a similar mix of generic stereotyping and *ad hoc* signalling.
Generically, the reader of an early dialogue will know that Socrates must
triumph, that claims to knowledge must be overthrown, that a general
acknowledgement of *aporia* is the likely outcome; while in any particular
case, the reader will be encouraged to pigeonhole certain speakers or
views as constructive, others as marked for varying degrees of demolition.

   This use of argumentative closure as an artistic device is not new; it is as
old, in one form, as the Homeric speech, which frequently postpones an
anticipated argument for irony or suspense. But what Plato did was to
substitute, as the core of an overtly dramatic medium, this dialectical
system of structuring argument for the regular narrative system of structuring story. This was not simply a packaging ploy, a smear of honey on
the lip of the Lucretian cup. By exploiting the structural analogy between
narrative and dialectic, Plato set out to show that philosophy could be as
dramatic as storytelling. All the same, it was not a lead that was widely or
successfully followed. Of Aristotle's lost exoteric dialogues we cannot
write; while Cicero's dialogues are often finely tuned works of historical
re-creation, but neither their dramatic nor their intellectual qualities are
impressive. The radical features of Platonic quasiplotting are never again
so deliberately or deftly exploited, and even the ironic undermining of
narrative transparency takes a long time to re-emerge in open literary
practice.

11   Hellenistic developments

The *Poetics* marks a turning-point, though its initial impact may have been indirect.[20] By the generation of Callimachus there existed a consensus notion, however tacit, of the differentiation between high and low poetic genres, with epic and tragedy on one side of the divide, and lyric, comedy, and the rest implicitly marooned on the other. This was not Aristotle's own conception: the overwhelming concentration in our *Poetics* on epic and tragedy is partly a historical legacy of the debate Aristotle inherited from Plato and the sophists before him, and partly a corollary of his own somewhat idiosyncratic view of the essence of poetry. Epic and tragedy had already emerged by the end of the fifth century as the twin foci of critical discussion of the function and value of art in general – epic because it was already canonical, tragedy because it was contemporary, and both together because their common core of mythological narrative made for obvious correlations and comparisons. And in any case, Aristotle was personally fascinated by these genres because they were the most ambitious manifestations of narrative *fiction* – a topic which so dominates his literary interests that he comes close on occasion to wanting it synonymous with 'poetry'.

All the same, it is hard not to see Aristotle and his school as at least partly responsible for the newly emergent notion of a classical canon within the poetic genres. For Plato, the next orbit out from Homer is still occupied by Hesiod and Pindar; for Aristotle, it is filled exclusively by tragedy, and this is the model that the rest of antiquity inherits. Certainly the most vibrant literary art of the following generation – the first generation of the vastly expanded Hellenic cultural ambit – shows Aristotelian narrative principles triumphant on the Attic stage. By the time Alexandria rose to challenge Athens for the cultural crown of Hellas, there was certainly something in place to react against.

However we analyse it, the new poetics of Callimachus and his adherents was the first overt rejection of a dominant literary culture.[21] The Aristotelian genres were looked on with suspicion (by Callimachus) or a sense of positive mischief (by Apollonius and, perhaps, Lycophron and the Pleiad). They turned instead to archaic or subliterary forms (didactic,

---

[20] It is unclear how widely the esoteric treatises were read outside the Peripatos in the two centuries before their publication by Andronicus; or how much of the substance of the *Poetics* was accessible in exoteric works by Aristotle himself (such as the dialogue *On poets*) and his successors, in particular Theophrastus.

[21] Cameron 1995 challenges Callimachus' alleged hostility to epic, but cannot so easily dispose of Callimachus' rejection of Aristotelian narrativity. As Cameron himself demonstrates, the insinuation of the poet's voice into the narrative world is a cornerstone of Callimachean poetics.

epigram, iambus, mime); and against the classical view of the seriousness and social utility of art they advanced an aesthetic of sophisticated hedonism, mixing technical experiment, romantic realism, scholarly erudition and wit to challenge categories and disarm prim preconceptions of the rules permitting poetry to work.

In third-century narrative, the Aristotelian rules snap like straws. Organic wholeness of action is disdained: even mythological narratives in epic metre become a tapestry of episodes (in the *Argonautica*) or an Ames room of skewed proportions and perspectives (in the *Hecale*). Amplitude is rejected, by limiting the scale of narrative to the episode, scene, or vignette (Theocritus, Herodas, the individual *Aetia*); or else varied at whim, with the *Hecale* thrusting incidentals to the narrative foreground and major action offstage. Action begins and ends in mid-air, especially in Theocritus; and the causal sequence of narrated actions is deliberately fragmentary and disjunct. Where classical narrative manipulates expectation to make narrative predictable, Callimachean narrative seeks the pleasure of the unexpected. Transparency is mocked; the author obtrudes by constantly outwitting the reader's attempts to second-guess him. But this is far from a destructive or incoherent approach to narrative poetics. To judge from the more ambitious and extensive narrative works surviving in this mode – the *Argonautica*, Catullus 63 and 64, Virgil's Aristaeus epyllion, the *Metamorphoses* – the effect is rather to shift complexity away from plot to other areas of the reader's involvement with text. Unity is determined not by story content itself so much as by the complex structures of language, theme, and voice that are laid over it.

Three general principles emerge in the treatment of plot by this two-tongue, three-century literary countercurrent stretching from Callimachus to Ovid. First, in the new poetics, myth is dead. It can no longer be creatively reshaped with free invention; nobody takes it seriously any more; and in any case everybody knows all the stories in all the established versions, which by now are anyway fossilised. None of these propositions is true, and all of them are blatantly disregarded by major writers somewhere; yet they are central to the new compact between text and reader. The Alexandrian or neoteric reader is credited by the text with an encyclopaedic knowledge of all myth; he can no longer be surprised, so that even if by any chance the reader is classically manipulated by a story he does not know, the pretence has to be maintained that he knows it already. One consequence is that myth is now narrated more *lyrically* than epically, alluded to within a situational frame rather than recounted at length by a ghostly, anonymous narrator.

Second, and relatedly, if a text wants to follow a more classical mode of plotting, directing the reader's modelling of story by releasing story data we do not yet possess in a programmed and structurally organisable way, the story has to be drawn from a source other than myth: from personal experience, or from free invention. There are not, it is fair to say, many stories told in literature from Theocritus to Silius that depend essentially for their effect on the reader's not knowing the outcome until it is told. New Comedy, Greek and Roman, is the one substantial exception; only with the advent of the novel are its lessons applied outside the comic drama. Otherwise, we have a handful of the more dramatic Augustan elegies; narrative satires from Lucilius and Horace; and a number of historical or mythological stories that are either so obscure that they can genuinely be told as if fresh (such as Parthenius' *Poignant romances*), or so muddied with variants that the reader frankly has no idea what particular ragout will in the event be served up (as in the case of the *Aeneid*).

Third, any antagonism that Callimachus may have seen between his own and the classical canons of genre and narrative was not perceived by all, even most, of his heirs. Epic and tragedy flourished in Alexandria; a generation later, they were the first Greek genres to be naturalised into Latin; and there was scarcely a generation in the half-millennium following when one or the other was not at least toyed with by one or more of the literary lions of the age. If the 'Aristotelian' principles of classical plotting went underground, it was less from any ignorance or rejection of Peripatetic narratology than from a dearth of suitable genre material. Only comedy had successfully made the transition from myth to historical or contemporary fiction in a classical form, and by 100 BC it was moribund in both languages. Epic and tragedy, meanwhile, which balked at lowering their traditional themes to the plane of contemporary fiction, were still struggling to reinvent themselves around the inherited mythical or historical subjects. It would take a revolution from outside the literary mainstream altogether to take classical plotting across this last creative barrier, and refashion it one last time in what ironically was to prove the most historically durable of all its ancient modes.

Part II

The Classical Plots

6   Epic myth I: *Iliad*

The historical shape of European literature owes much to the fact that it begins from a singularity. No literary text earlier than the *Iliad* was known in antiquity; yet for a millennium Homer was the unattainable summit of the cultural canon, casting an enveloping shadow over all literary production. No other literary tradition erupts out of vacuum in this way, and we still do not really know why it happened with the Greeks. We can piece together much more than they could of the preliterate development of the oral tradition from which the epics emerged; and we can hazard a guess that the manner of their emergence had something to do with the unusual historical conditions of the Greek rediscovery of writing, and something to do with the eighth-century social changes bound up with the 'rise of the polis'. But current views on why the *Iliad* and *Odyssey* were so different from everything else that emerged from the same tradition; on why there were two monumental epics, rather than one or many; on how and when they were composed on such a scale, and how and when they came to exist in writing – all these, like faith in a personal Homer, remain articles of belief rather than investigable hypotheses.

The historical impact, at least, is clear enough. The only emulator successfully to challenge the *Iliad*'s supremacy as a model of how narrative should be done was the *Odyssey*, apparently a generation or so later. Yet despite its higher technical ambitions and accomplishment, even this did not knock the *Iliad* off its paradigmatic perch. What it did instead was to bequeath to later narrative systems a *dual* template: a pair of fundamentally distinct narrative key signatures, one minor and one major, between which all subsequent Western classical narrative would be required to choose or compromise. That the twin models were read as complementary rather than contradictory is with hindsight hardly surprising, since the *Odyssey* passionately endorses the *Iliad*'s fundamental narrative values even while competing with them almost point-for-point in the manner of their expression. Thus the idea of a classical way of plotting is already there in the first documented act of ancient reading, the *Odyssey*'s reading of the *Iliad*; and the development of such plotting through all its ancient transformations is in effect simply a series of applications, extensions, and refinements of techniques prototyped in these epics.

The *Iliad*'s principal narrative legacy is its paradigmatic combination of classical economy, amplitude, and transparency: the articulation of a vast story, in a very long text, through a narrative universe that nevertheless achieves virtuosically tight gamelike closure. The mere demonstration that such a combination was attainable, and could carry immense affective power, more than compensated in influence for the poem's narratological archaisms and technical deficiencies by the standards of the mature classical model – many of which were in any case made good in the *Odyssey*. But the *Iliad*'s example went far beyond this, in further demonstrating that a closed narrative system of articulate global rules could constitute a compelling description of human experience *in general* – even if the particular description advanced in the *Iliad*, the narrative worldview Aristotle called 'tragic', arguably owes its central place in Western culture to a far from inevitable accident of narrative history.

We take so much of this Homeric narrative legacy for granted that it is only when we encounter its great non-Western counterparts – the *Mahabharata*, say, or the *Romance of the three kingdoms* – that we can see how seminal its plot ideas have been for all that came after.[1] For Aristotle, who had the advantage of the Cyclic poems to compare, the impact of the revolution was much more directly visible – drawing from him a language of enthusiasm unparalleled elsewhere in his entire writing.[2] Weaned on the *Iliad* and its uncountable factual and fictional descendants, we do not think of war as a particularly intractable narrative subject; yet the technical challenge is perhaps greater than for any other major literary theme. Unfolded from its delicate narrative packaging, the *Iliad*'s story would be a shapeless sprawl. Even if we admit only those merely terrestrial events and places *absolutely indispensable* for understanding the plot, it ranges over two continents in space and ten years in time. If we also let in the more incidental material of anecdotal and exemplary flashbacks, the human action extends back at least a further two or three generations, and the Olympian action far beyond. And the cast is colossal: the Greek char-

---

[1] Miner 1990: 135–212 attempts to show what a synthesis of narrative poetics East and West might look like, but the great work here remains to be done.

[2] 'Sometimes one thing just follows another in temporal succession, without any common end being involved; and most epic poets write like this. But a further astonishing (θεσπέσιος, an Aristotelian *hapax*) thing, besides those already mentioned, about Homer compared with the rest is that he did *not* compose a poem about the whole war . . . Instead, he extracts a single part and uses many of the others as episodes – interspersing his narrative, for instance, with the Catalogue of Ships and other episodes. Everyone else, such as the poets of the *Cypria* and *Little Iliad*, wrote epics about one man, or one period, or one action with many parts' (23: 1459a30–b2; for the omitted part see p. 66 n. 6 above).

acters around 100,000, the Trojans approaching 10,000, with the Asian allies sufficient to balance the odds.[3]

The daring, and uniqueness, of the *Iliad*'s solution to the sheer scale of its story material was impressed on Aristotle especially by the comparison with the other Cyclic poems on the war.[4] Aristotle took it as self-evident that the *story* of the *Iliad* – as opposed to its primary narrative – was not the wrath of Achilles, but just what its title claimed: the Trojan saga as a whole. Yet scarcely any of that story is directly told. In particular, two key events, essential to the completion of the poem's story, are still in the future as the primary narrative closes: the death of Achilles, and the sack of Troy and death of Priam. There is, in fact, no more than a vague scattering of hints as to how and when these outcomes will follow causally from the point where our narrative ends. Nevertheless, the narrative frame has been tightly packed with an extensive apparatus of flashbacks and foreshadowings to establish that this seven-week episode late in the career of Achilles is microcosmic of the ten-year intercontinental war as a whole. Few works of fiction have ever dared to trim so much story so savagely down to fit such a ruthlessly Procrustean narrative frame. It is not surprising that the technique impressed the ancient world, and especially its dramatists, as compulsively imitable and inexhaustibly rich. In the rest of this chapter, I try to describe how this radical system of economies works.

The *Iliad*'s most celebrated narrative economy lies in its structuring of *time*. The continuous action notionally spans fifty days; but in narrative terms, as Table 1 shows, this figure is rather misleading. The first and last books each include two nine-day intervals during which a prevailing *status quo* is summarised, formulaically, in a single line as springboard for a tenth- or twelfth-day transformation of the impasse. From the night of Agamemnon's dream at the start of book II to the end of the funeral games in XXIII is a mere eight days; and of these the last two are entirely occupied with the local events of XXIII, the funeral and games, while the two days of the truce in VII make up barely a hundred lines together. Approximately 85% of the poem – the section framed, in one of a number of famous concentric closures between the start and end of the poem, by the portentous dreams of Agamemnon and Achilles – takes place on four days and the intervening nights, with only a perfunctory and narratively accelerated suspension at VII.381–482.

As has long been recognised, these four days' fighting map the main phases of the poem's narrative movement.[5] Day 22, the day on which Achilles is absent from the narrative, is framed by a pair of formal duels

---

[3] Visser 1997: 356–7.   [4] See pp. 80–1 above, and Taplin 1986: 51–7.
[5] Earlier discussions now displaced by the exemplary treatment in Taplin 1992: 14–22.

Table 1. *Chronology of the* Iliad*

Days	No.	Events	Reference	Lines
1–9	9	plague	I.8–53	46
10	1	assembly; return of Chryseis; gods in Aethiopia	I.54–476	423
11	1	return from Chryse	I.477–87	11
12–20	9	Achilles sulks	I.488–92	5
21	1	council of gods (+ night)	I.493–II.47	166
22	1	fighting	II.48–VII.380	3,653
23	1	truce	VII.381–432	52
24	1	funeral	VII.433–82	50
25	1	fighting (+ night)	VIII.1–X.579	1,857
26	1	fighting (+ night)	XI.1–XVIII.616	5,667
27	1	fighting (+ night)	XIX.1–XXIII.108	2,161
28	1	funeral	XXIII.109–225	117
29	1	games	XXIII.226–XXIV.21	693
30–38	9	mutilation of corpse	XXIV.22–30	9
39	1	ransom (+ night)	XXIV.31–694	664
40–48	9	truce	XXIV.695–784	90
49	1	funeral	XXIV.785–8	4
50	1	burial	XXIV.788–804	17
				15,685

*Cf. Hellwig 1964: 40, Taplin 1992: 14–19.

and a pair of negotiated truces aimed unsuccessfully at prematurely ending the war. Through a series of programmatic set-pieces we are introduced to the scale and issues of the conflict; the main players on each side in earth and heaven; and the principal narrative rules delimiting the outcome. This strictly introductory phase of the narrative is set off, by its confinement in a single day and by the suspensions of time and fighting in book VII, from the three-day nucleus of the plot: day 25, on which the tide turns to the Trojans; day 26, the high-water mark of Trojan success, and the crisis of Patroclus that turns the tide back; day 27, the re-entry of Achilles and the final annihilation of Trojan hope with the killing of Hector.

Within this overall narrative time-structure, several specific techniques have been spectacularly influential on classical plotting in general. One, clearly, is the remarkable *elasticity* of story time in Homeric narrative. Not only are all five rates of narrative flow (ellipsis, summary, scene, stretch, pause) already fully exploited in the *Iliad*'s fine-scale narrative;[6] but they are matched by a careful control of *large-scale* pace and duration. Significant moves are narrated not just with the more lavish and involving dramatic detail that a flexible narrative tempo allows, but with *neighbouring* events also retarded and elaborated to make room for ambitious effects of anticipation or response. One technique, for example, almost overused in the *Iliad* is to foreshadow an event as chronologically imminent, and then to delay its occurrence for several books by the massive elaboration of routine intervening action that at another time in the story would go unreported. Thus the Greek reverse is promised at I.524 but not begun until VIII.72; Hector's advance to the ships, Patroclus' death, and Achilles' return promised as a block at VIII.473–6, but only fulfilled, piece-meal, in XV, XVI, and XIX. Chronologically, the intervals are insignificant; the retardation is an artifact of deliberately increased narrative detail.

A second, closely related, general technique in the *Iliad*'s plotting of time is the structural use of *routine*: the establishment, in the early stages of the narrative, of a regular rhythm of events, usually quotidian, which continues through much or all of the subsequent action. In the *Iliad*, the routine is the inflexible daily programme of fighting first demonstrated in full for the (narratively) long day 22 – although it has apparently been operating since at least day 12. The pattern runs: dawn (II.49f,. VIII.1, XI.1, XIX.1–2); breakfast (II.398–431, VIII.53, X.578, XX.156ff.) and arming (II.42–6, VIII.54–7, XI.15–44, XIX.356–XX.3); Greek advance and Trojan sally into plain (II.441–III.14, VIII.58–63, XI.47–71, XX.31–40); fighting to sunset (VII.282, VIII.485, XVIII.239–42); withdrawal of armies to camp and city (VII.306–12, XXII.606–11 and XXIII.1–3); supper (VII.313–22, VIII.545–550 and IX.88–91, XVIII.315, XXIII.29–56); night watches and sleep (VII.380, VIII.553–65 and IX.558–668 with 713–X.2, XVIII.299, XXIII.58). Councils and/or assemblies are optional at mealtimes (II.50–397, VII.323–79, VIII.489–52 and IX.9–79 with 92–181, XVIII.245–313,

[6] See above, p. 40. Richardson 1990: 20–1 argues there is no ellipsis in Homer, on the grounds that action in the unnarrated passages is at least accounted for, even if not explicitly: 'The Homeric passages that come closest to being true ellipses are those where night falls and a new day dawns immediately, but even here the characters are said to be doing something – lying down, spending the night, sailing, plotting, sleeping.' This spoils a good point by overstatement. At XXIV.787, for instance, the Trojans ignite Hector's pyre shortly after dawn on day 49; then in the next line day 50 breaks, and we find the Trojans assembling again round the still-burning pyre. (When did they leave? Where were they during the night?) An even more violent narrative jump-cut is VII.433, where the Trojans and Greeks return to base, apparently in mid-morning, with their gathered dead, and abruptly we find ourselves with the Greeks at their pyre in the following foredawn. Kirk *ad loc.* calls attention to 'the failure to suggest nightfall (either directly, or by the mention of an evening meal or going to sleep)'.

XIX.42–276). Once the outline is established, it becomes possible to vary the way elements in the sequence are presented: an individual warrior's arming implying similar action throughout both camps, or one side's evening routine narrated with the tacit understanding that the pattern is paralleled in the other camp. Naturally the routine is not followed during truces, or on days such as 1–10 and 28–39 where one side is too weakened or demoralised to fight. But these days are given comparatively little narrative space, and the poem deliberately concentrates plot events into days when the normal routine does hold.

This kind of narrative 'rhythm track' is valuable to plotting in four ways. First, it gives the reader a ready index of the *passage* of story time, and thus of the changing relationship between the pace of story and narrative – as with the gruelling narrative elongation of the fighting hours on the critical day 26. Second, it offers a regular *sequence* of daily actions that can themselves become the basis of significant plot moves: the rhythm can be dramatically varied, broken, or simply brought to the foreground of importance. On the night following day 26, for instance, the Greek watch is replaced by a wake for Patroclus (XVIII.314–55), while the advance to battle on day 27 is boldly transplanted to heaven as the first stage of the theomachy. On day 27 the Trojan withdrawal dramatically precedes and isolates the duel with Hector, and his killing, uniquely, ends the day's warfare *before* the sunset (which is therefore not recorded). On day 25, the Trojans' unusual field camp in the plain charges the normally innocuous evening routine of supper, watches, and sleep with tension, as well as supplying the material for a spectacular episode (the Doloneia). Even the routine event of breakfast finds itself significantly in the foreground on day 27, when Achilles tries and fails to impose his own programme of fast and vengeance on the rest of the army. Thirdly, the existence of a regular cycle of routine is an important device in reader *anticipation* of future story events. Thus on day 25, through his ban on divine assistance and his assurance of Trojan success (VIII.10ff., 68–77), Zeus gives the reader an authoritative promise of what will have happened by that day's sunset; and the long night following that sunset draws sustained tension from the certainty that battle will resume with the dawn, however unwelcome that prospect to the beleaguered Greeks. And, finally, the incorporation into the cycle of a phase in which plot moves are normally excluded – in this case, obviously, sleep – allows the story a regular element of *closure* that divides the narrative into discrete segments of relatively self-contained action. Iliadic nights are (the Doloneia pointedly apart) times of reflection and deliberation rather than action, a phase in the cycle when the board may be studied between moves. The fall of dark signals a closure of action and a shift to reaction. There may, of course, be times when it becomes desirable for the narrative to minimise the sense of closure to sustain tension – which is why the crucial night VIII.485–X.579 is occupied with continuous scene-by-scene action from dusk to dawn. The *Odyssey*, as we shall see, has learned much from its predecessor's use of bedtime and dawn to phrase its story into episodes, and in Attic tragedy and New Comedy the frame becomes almost standard.

A third, especially powerful and influential, technique in the *Iliad*'s plotting of time is the restriction of primary narrative to the few days of *crisis* – in effect, the endgame of a much larger story invoked entirely by secondary report and allusion. Greek poets regularly found themselves faced with the problem of identifying a beginning and end in a story excerpted from myth, where the audience would be well aware of other events in the lives of the characters and their families that could in principle extend the chain of story indefinitely into past and future. As noted in Chapter 3 (p. 38), some such self-consciousness is evident in the epic poet's conventional surrender of this initiative to the Muse. The *Iliad*'s solution, enthusiastically seized on by the *Odyssey* and tragedians, was to begin as close as practical to the point of crisis, and to end as soon as the lines of sequel seem determined.

As Aristotle saw, however, this need not exclude the overt narration of episodes *outside* that primary time-frame. One regular Iliadic device, noted by Aristotle, does disappear from the classical repertory with the *Odyssey*: the notorious use of anachronism, transplanting to the tenth year of the war episodes that would more naturally sit in the first.[7] (Aristotle mentions the Catalogue; the Homeric scholia, with less justice, add the Teichoscopy.[8]) But the *Odyssey* does enthusiastically take over the *Iliad*'s abundant range of *embedding* techniques – which translate temporally distant story events into *secondary* narratives, related either by the epic narrator or (preferentially for classical transparency) by the players. Essential events in the *Iliad*'s past so treated include Achilles' parting from Peleus (IX.252–9), the complex raiding expedition in which Chryseis and Briseis were captured and Briseis' and Andromache's kin massacred (I.366, II.690–1, VI.416–24, XIX.291–6), and Calchas' prophecies on the duration and outcome of the war (II.301–29).

---

[7] Above, n. 2. See Bergren 1979 for a good discussion of the poetics of this device.

[8] Why, it was already being obtusely asked in Aristotle's time (fr. 147 R.), does Priam wait until year 10 to ask Helen to identify the Greek commanders from the wall? Partly, no doubt, because there has never been a formal duel, involving Paris, close to the wall. *Helen's* presence on the battlement is clearly abnormal, requiring supernatural prompting and psychological manipulation. The Trojan elders' famous reaction underlines their surprise at this event. More importantly yet, Priam's speech to Helen at III.162–70 is anything but an innocent request for information: it is a delicate rejection of the hostile judgement passed in the elders' speech (compare especially 164–5 with 159–60).

More daringly still, the narrative *breaks off* before the resumption of battle on day 51, the death of Achilles, and the final Greek victory. These events are not merely understood by reader and players alike as inevitable (XXIV.667; XXII.356–60, etc.[9]; XV.69–71, etc.[10]); they are events with which the involved players have already made their peace by the end of our poem. As Macleod remarks, 'one could imagine an epic like the *Iliad* which ended with the sack of Troy or the death of Achilles'.[11] That our *Iliad* consciously and artistically rejects these options is not merely a daring flirtation with the reader's expectation, but a vigorous assertion by the poet of what is to become the classical principle of narrative economy.

Finally, the device of embedded anachronies also allows the plot a further manipulative hold over the reader's story model: the choice of *when* to report crucial story material that happens to lie outside the narrated timespan. The more information is excluded from the overt temporal frame, the freer the poet is to release that material to the reader at a moment of calculated narrative impact. We *could* have been told of the famous choice of Achilles (IX.410–16) in book I, but it would seriously have interfered with the psychological and thematic economy of the quarrel. In book IX, however, it becomes central to the analysis of Achilles' dilemma, as he has to make a long-postponed decisive choice, against an immediate deadline, between the two available positive and final actions (to sail home, or to rejoin the battle).[12]

It will be noted that the above discussion makes no mention of what many would feel to be the *Iliad*'s most significant structural device: the use of narrative time to structural effect in a purely *formal* way, by the establishment of artificial patterns of symmetry and closure in the arrangement of events. A famous instance is the elaborate mirror symmetry between the first and last books: the ten- and twelve-day suspensions in each are part of a wider pattern of correspondence taking in the two initiatives from Apollo, the complementary scenes between Thetis, Achilles, and Zeus, and the symmetrical restitutions of children to suppliant fathers.[13] Patternings of this kind continue to dominate or monopol-

---

[9] See Duckworth 1933: 29.   [10] Duckworth 1933: 30–2.
[11] 1982: 27; cf. Morrison 1992: 90–3.
[12] For analyst critics, the question does not arise, since the two passages can be claimed to belong to different putative strata of composition. But in discussing the *Iliad*'s influence one is obliged to adopt an agnostic *de facto* unitarianism irrespective of personal methodological inclinations. Similar issues arise, but more acutely, for the case of Roman comedy; see p. 207 n. 25.
[13] Whitman 1958: 259–60; Macleod 1982: 32–5; Stanley 1993: 241–4 (with further references). In fact, the whole temporal structure of the *Iliad* is elaborately chiastic. The central day 26, the turning-point of the war, is far the longest in narrative duration, and occupies a middle position between the two days of tide-turning either side. Only the long introductory action of day 22 disrupts the concentric structure, and this itself is framed by a pair of set-piece formal duels in III and VII.

ise discussions of Homeric 'structure'; but it is important to stress again that, while such structures clearly do encourage the reader to anticipate the closure of large-scale patterns in the narrative, they are no part of the poetics of classical plotting. Indeed, it is moot whether these non-causal devices for the structural shaping of readers' narrative expectations really qualify as 'plot' at all in any vernacularly understood sense; and in many works in 'classical' narrative attire – from the pseudo-Senecan *Octavia*[14] to the films of Peter Greenaway – such a formalistic approach to temporal structure can be directly at odds with more classical principles of plotting.

All the temporal devices surveyed here help the reader to construct, from what presents itself as a purely linear narration of events, an increasingly confident global model of the shape and structure of the story as a whole. At the same time, however, we should also recognise that there are some familiar later tricks with narrative time that the *Iliad* fails to exploit. For one, despite the specific discussion of the date of Troy's fall in book II, and despite some detailed foretelling of the local action of specific days, there is no early sense of *deadline*, of the overall duration of the story ahead. Nor is there much sense of the *passage* of time during battle, the stretch of story between the narrative 'now' and the coming sunset. The few and formulaic references to times of day in the battle books if anything confound rather than clarify the reader's sense of duration.[15] But these may not be oversights. To an extent, these particular structural needs are articulated not by time but by other kinds of narrative pattern: especially, the plotting of story in *space*.

If the *Iliad*, despite looseness and longueurs in the narrative of fighting, is already boldly economical in the handling of time, its treatment of space is almost ruthlessly so. As with its temporal compass, the *Iliad*'s potentially vast field of play is laid out so as to subordinate its more scattered story locations to a single main arena, with the narrative purposefully patterned around the natural topography of that primary space. The narrative space of the *Iliad* is essentially a single straight line.[16] At the eastern end is the city of Troy, protected from assault by its impregnable walls. Beyond the walls lies the great no-man's-land of the river plain; beyond that, the Greek fortifications built in VII, and beyond these the Greek camp and ships. Behind these is the ocean, and far behind that the distant, remembered homeland to which they can only return when the war is completed. A Greek victory requires penetration of the walls of Troy itself; a Trojan victory needs either a Greek withdrawal to the sea and home, or a penetration of the Nestorian defences followed by

---

[14] Herington 1961: 22.   [15] VIII.66–8, XI.84–90, XVI.776–9.
[16] See especially Taplin 1986: 55–7, Scully 1990: 41–5.

massacre and destruction of their means of escape. In the poem, therefore, the progress of that war is mapped out in the changing tidemarks of
battle along the axis from city to beach. Whichever side makes the necessary breakthrough will win the war.

As the poem opens, however, the war is in stalemate. Neither side has
succeeded in pressing its attack beyond the plain; now, with the withdrawal of Achilles, the advantage starts to fluctuate dramatically. First, in
II, the Greeks come close to spontaneous retreat to the ships and home.
This threat averted, the two sides join in an inconclusive day's fighting,
before Zeus suspends his help to the Greek cause and in VIII the tide of
war spectacularly turns. By the end of the book the Trojans possess the
plain, and the Greeks are besieged; next, after various fluctuations, the
Trojans strike through the Greek defences in XII, and reach the limit of
their advance with the burning of the first ship in XVI. But Patroclus drives
them back again, eventually carrying the battle as far as the walls of Troy
itself, before being blocked by Apollo and destroyed at the limit of his
success. Hector fails to regain the advantage; it is under the walls that he is
killed by Achilles, and now the plain is in effective Greek control. But the
final twist is the defenceless Priam's voluntary journey across the whole
narrative domain – from the safe ground of Troy to the opposite end of
the narrative world, Achilles' shelter by the ships. Thus the final com-
munion of victor and victim is powerfully expressed by the cancellation of
the symbolic distance the narrative has established between them.

This spatial plan may seem a rather obvious arrangement, given the
subject matter. But it is surprising how little the battlefield space is used
with any comparable clarity and simplicity in other ancient fictional narratives of warfare. Virgil, for one, favours a much less closed and more
topographically diffuse arena in *Aeneid* II and IX–XII alike;[17] the same goes
for Tryphiodorus and Quintus Smyrnaeus, as well (so far as can be
divined) as for the lost cyclic epics dealing with the war. Ironically, it is a
historian, Livy, who regularly delivers the strongest sense of invented narrative topography among Latin writers; and not until Heliodorus is there
anything comparable in Greek to the *Iliad*'s unilinear clarity of epic space.

Some subtler tricks of economy deserve mention here. First, the spatial
and temporal boundaries are *interdependent*. This close-locked struggle in
the plain is local to the time of primary narrative, this fifty-day span in the
final months of the war. It is by no means typical of the war as a whole:
there have, for instance, been frequent Greek raiding expeditions around
the neighbouring territories, so that for the heroes at least the siege has
been at best intermittent.[18] Yet of all the directly narrated action of the

---

[17] Willcock 1983.   [18] See especially Jones 1995.

poem, only one human episode is sited 'off the board': the expedition to Chryse under Odysseus in the first book. This seems more than acciden- tal. Odysseus' return has the effect of closing the door to the wider world, sealing the rest of the poem in the grim, claustrophobic world of camp, city, and warplain. In contrast, the cyclic poems dealing with the war seem to have opened the action out considerably.

Secondly, even within the topography of the city, plain, and seashore, much that could have been structurally developed has been left purposely neutral to keep the lines of the narrative map clean. The various rivers, the surrounding hills, the famous springs mentioned once *ad hoc* in XXII could all have been charged with general spatial significance in the narra- tive: in fact they are barely acknowledged. It is possible, by ingenious col- lation of the relevant passages, to draw up a map of the order of the Greek ships along the beach;[19] but the poem, though apparently clear on the point, chooses to dismiss the issue from the reader's consciousness. On the other hand, it is (rather surprisingly) *not* possible to draw up a street plan of the city of Troy, despite the repeated use of a few key locations such as the Scaean battlement (III.149ff., 384ff., VI.392ff., XXI.525–35, XXII.462–515), the house of Hector (VI.370ff., 497ff., XXII.440–62), and Helen's bedroom (III.125ff., 382, 423ff., VI.321ff.). The dominant, purely linear, spatial structure has to stand clear and uncluttered for the ebb and flow of narrative advantage from Greek to Trojan to Greek to retain its clarity.

This does not, of course, preclude the narrative use of individual story locations, especially behind the Greek and Trojan lines, for *scening* pur- poses. The narrative versatility of a well-defined story topography is mas- terfully displayed in the account of the assault on the Greek camp in XI–XVI: a dazzlingly intricate multi-stranded stretch of simultaneous, sus- pensefully intercut actions in carefully distinguished locations. First, there is the thick of the battle, the Trojan attack on the Greek defences, at one stage elaborately divided by the poet into five separate points of assault. (In fact he cuts back and forth between three: XII.120–74 and 181–83, 251–64 and 439–71, 292–350 and 373–429.) Next, there is the action behind the lines, as Patroclus travels from Achilles' compound (XI.598–615) to Nestor's (XI.617–803, with a follow-up at XIV.1–132) to Eurypylus' (XI.841–7, XV.390–405) to Achilles' (XVI.2–100, 124–54, 220–56) and finally out to battle (XVI.256ff.). And finally, there is the divine counterplot centred on Mount Ida (XIV.283–353, XV.4–79, 151–69). Thus the cuts between these three braided plotlines deftly exploit the established story topography to distinguish narrative zones of

---

[19] Willcock 1984: 225.

action, abeyance, and supervision respectively in what on the story level would be an undifferentiated and simultaneous matrix of events.

The third strand here exemplifies one vital exception to the spatial closures and structure discussed so far: they do not bind the *gods*, whose native space is not merely separate from but inaccessible to the human characters. When not out of range on Olympus or the bottom of the ocean, they perch on the summits of neighbouring mountains for an appropriately chessboard perspective on the human scene. Only when certain of them choose to intervene directly in the war do the Iliadic gods share the board with the mortal heroes, and even there they generally elude detection. But this spatial segregation is at least as much a sign of *narrative* difference as of metaphysical. Because the gods serve as the storyworld's *control level*, their line of movement from sky to earth to deep lies *perpendicular* to the land–sea axis of the mortal narrative. Their perspective on the story is thus tellingly parallel to the reader's, in its panoramic view of the action in space and its holographic model of the story in time.[20]

In its *internal* structure, however, the divine space of the *Iliad* is if anything even more tightly bound and determined by narrative codes than is its human domain. There are four degrees of divine involvement with the action, and all but the last are associated with separate story locations on their vertical axis of place. The most intimate is personal *intervention* in the battle, where the gods descend to share the board on the players' own level. One tier removed from this is *observation*, where individual gods position themselves on an elevated and inaccessible part of the board, generally a mountain-top, to supervise the battle with a view to swift intervention if required. Further removed yet is *detachment*, where the gods remain in their native habitat (generally Olympus, but the ocean for Thetis and Posidon) and may not attend consistently to the human action below, though they remain within reach of human prayer and sacrifice. Finally, they are subject at rare intervals to individual or collective *removal*. In the epics, the convention is to pack them off for an extended sabbatical in Aethiopia, though a more fragile equivalent is achieved by Hera's narcosis of Zeus in XIV. As with the voyage to Chryse, there may be some purpose in the placing of the Aethiopian sojourn in the introductory stages: the gods' return effectively closes the narrative door on any further absenteeism from the field of play for the duration of the remaining story.

The challenges to the *Iliad*'s pursuit of narrative economy in the plotting of time and space are even more urgently echoed in the economy of

[20] Lowe 1996: 524.

players. It is vital for the very feasibility of plotting that the *Iliad* should somehow restrict, and categorise by plot function, the hundreds of thousands of participants in the story. Here one vital implicit narrative rule of the *Iliad* – though pointedly not of the *Odyssey* – is that *only the aristocracy can be players*. No common soldier, subject to another's authority, is given either name or voice in the poem. The one possible, but very disputed, exception is Thersites, who lacks patronymic and clan identity, and finds his application for the status of player roundly rejected; the reasons, however, appear to be narrative rather than sociological.[21] A handful of slave women are named (III.144, IX.664–8), but only as adjuncts to their aristocratic owners, and only two ever speak: Andromache's anonymous housekeeper (VI.382–9), and the aristocratic Briseis (XIX.287–300).

There is, of course, a roster of active players on either side incorporated early in the text, in the form of the Greek and Trojan catalogues in book II. In practice, however, the catalogues contribute little (apart from the size of contingents and incidental remarks such as II.768–70) to cue the reader on which names belong to the inner circle of players; and its recourse to a major narratorial intrusion in the poet's voice limits its influence on later narrative to self-conscious *hommage*. Far more specific is the Teichoscopy in book III, which singles out five names from the Greek catalogue for special narrative interest, while also complying with the rule of transparency by embedding the exposition in a more or less naturalistic dramatic frame. Even so, the list is not the one we might expect: Agamemnon, Menelaus, Odysseus, Ajax, Idomeneus, but not Diomedes, Nestor, or Patroclus and Achilles. Both episodes, in fact, are additional to requirement. Readers of the *Iliad* have their list of Greek players drawn up well before the catalogue and Teichoscopy; and the names have been flagged in the narrative for insertion on that list by a system of eminently – and influentially – classical cues.

The principal such cues involve the use of *direct speech*. Speech gives a character's inner life a voice, and in the Homeric epics, which avoid extensive narratorial use of indirect discourse and psychological commentary, it is the *only* device allowing the reader any deep access to that inner life. No character of significance to the plot of the *Iliad*, no character whose private experience invites more than momentary reader interest (as for example in a necrology), is denied a speech. The nearest exception is the poignantly absent Peleus – who does in fact have a speech quoted by Odysseus at IX.254–8. The striking difference even a single brief speaking scene can make is highlighted in the narrative difference between the faceless, passive Chryseis, a mere token in the game, and the otherwise parallel Briseis – whose status as a minor player, the Greek mirror-image of Andromache, is memorably impressed by her solitary speech in XIX.[22]

But not all names who speak are equally and automatically players, as Table 2 documents. There are seventy-seven speaking characters in the *Iliad*, not counting the occasional speeches ascribed anonymously to undifferentiated groups (e.g. III.154–5, 297): 28 Greeks, 28 Trojans and allies, 19 gods, one neutral (Chryses), and one horse. But the great majority of these are excluded from the inner narrative circle by one of three circumstances: the *quantity* and *placement* of their speeches, and the functional *niche* the characters occupy in the narrative.

First, fewer than half of the speaking characters speak in more than one book, and almost a third are represented by a single speech. In general, as might be expected, the importance of a character to the narrative is proportionate to both the number of lines spoken and the number of speeches quoted. (The two correlate closely except for the unique case of Phoenix, whose one speech is the longest in the poem. Counting speeches yields the order Achilles, Hector, Agamemnon, Zeus, Nestor, Hera, Diomedes, Odysseus, Priam, Menelaus; if we count lines the order becomes Achilles, Hector, Nestor, Agamemnon, Odysseus, Zeus, Diomedes, Hera, Priam, Phoenix, with the 'wordier' characters like Nestor and Odysseus promoted a couple of places and the more succinct immortals correspondingly down.) Already some banding is evident, with Achilles far ahead of the pack despite his absence from half the books of the poem; a broad group of Hector, Agamemnon, Nestor, Odysseus, Zeus in the 300–530-line range; and the closer trio Diomedes, Hera, Priam in the 200–250 range before a further marked gap below which the frequency and quantity lists diverge. As a rough rule, we could say the *frequency* of speeches indexes a character's importance in plot, while their *length* is more a measure of their reactive and psychological interest – most clearly in the case of Andromache, whose speeches are few but emotionally rich.

Second, the poem is careful to *introduce* the key players early on: certainly before the implementation of Zeus's design on day 25, which marks the move in book VIII from preliminaries to main plot, and ideally in the first available scene. For Greek characters, this is the sequence of five assemblies and councils in book I. Of the leading Greek players only three have their voice delayed: Diomedes, whose *aristeia* will in any case be the centrepiece of the programmatic battle narrative in III–VII; Ajax, whose purely martial (rather than strategy-making) importance is strongly

[22] See de Jong 1987b: 110–13.

Table 2. *Speakers and speeches in the* Iliad

	Speaker	Speeches	Lines	Avg.	First	Longest
Greeks	Achilles	87	965	11.1	I	122
	Agamemnon	43	445	10.4	I	67
	Ajax	17	129	7.6	VII	19
	Ajax II	3	24	8	XIII	9
	Alcimedon*	1	5	5	XVII	5
	Antilochus	5	35	7	XVIII	14
	Automedon*	4	22	5.5	XVII	8
	Briseis*	1	14	14	XIX	14
	Calchas*	2	19	8.5	I	9
	Cebriones*	1	8	8	XI	8
	Diomedes	27	239	8.9	IV	23
	Epeius*	1	9	9	XXIII	9
	Eurypylus*	2	19	9.5	XI	14
	Idomeneus	12	115	9.6	IV	20
	Menelaus	22	152	6.9	III	16
	Menestheus*	1	8	8	XII	8
	Meriones	5	23	4.6	XIII	7
	Nestor	31	489	15.8	I	148
	Odysseus	26	342	13.2	I	82
	Patroclus	11	83	7.6	XI	15
	Peneleus*	1	5	5	XIV	5
	Phoenix*	1	172	172	IX	172
	Sthenelus*	2	15	7.5	IV	8
	Talthybius*	1	4	4	IV	4
	Teucer	2	11	5.5	VIII	7
	Thersites*	1	18	18	II	18
	Thoas*	1	14	14	XV	14
	Thootes*	1	10	10	XII	10
	Tlepolemus*	1	14	14	V	14
Trojans & allies	Acamas*	1	5	5	XIV	5
	Aeneas	6	104	17.3	V	59
	Agenor*	2	15	7.5	XXI	8
	Andromache	4	102	25.5	VI	38
	Antenor*	2	25	12.5	III	21
	Asius*	1	10	10	XII	10
	Asteropaeus*	1	8	8	XXI	8
	Cassandra*	1	3	3	XXIV	3
	Deiphobus*	2	8	4	XIII	5
	Dolon*	5	51	10.2	X	19
	Euphorbus*	2	15	7.5	XVII	9
	Glaucus	4	117	29.3	VI	67
	Hector	50	530	10.6	III	45
	Hecuba	6	63	10.5	VI	16
	Helen	7	78	11.1	III	15
	Helenus*	2	32	16	VI	25

Table 2. (*cont.*)

	Speaker	Speeches	Lines	Avg.	First	Longest
	housekeeper*	1	8	8	VI	8
	Idaeus	4	30	7.5	III	14
	Lycaon*	1	13	13	XXI	13
	Pandarus*	4	51	12.8	V	37
	Paris	7	62	8.9	III	17
	Pisander & Hippolochus*	1	5	5	XI	5
	Priam	25	213	8.5	III	39
	Polydamas	4	90	22.5	XII	30
	Sarpedon	7	70	10	V	21
	Socus*	1	4	4	XI	4
	Theano*	1	6	6	VI	6
Gods	Aphrodite	7	26	3.7	III	5
	Apollo	18	111	6.2	IV	22
	Ares	4	32	8	V	16
	Artemis*	2	8	4	XXI	6
	Athene	20	159	8	I	23
	Charis*	2	4	2	XVIII	3
	Dione*	2	36	18	V	34
	dream*	1	12	12	II	12
	Hephaestus	5	45	9	I	16
	Hera	29	238	8.2	I	18
	Hermes	8	81	10.1	XXI	15
	Hypnos*	3	30	10	XIV	20
	Iris	13	103	7.9	II	17
	Poseidon	16	158	9.9	VII	30
	Scamander*	5	40	8	XXI	16
	Themis*	1	2	2	XV	2
	Thetis	13	116	8.9	I	33
	Zeus	37	337	9.1	I	29
Others	Chryses*	3	17	5.7	I	6
	Xanthus*	1	10	10	XIX	10
	anonymi	10	38	3.8	II	6
		666	**6,729**	**10.1**		

* = speeches confined to a single book.

trailed at II.768–70; and Patroclus, a deliberately late entrant present and addressed in I, but who speaks only on the day of his *aristeia* and death. For Trojans, the equivalent occasion is the truce in book III, with only Hecuba and Andromache held off till the second montage of city scenes in VI; and for gods, the divine scenes at the end of I – again with those figures involved in battle rather than deliberation introduced *ad hoc* and piecemeal in IV–VII. (Apollo does not speak until IV, but he has already been thrust to prominence by his role in the plague at 1.8ff.)

So the early attribution of numerous and substantial speeches to a character is one important way of flagging that character's proportionate *significance* in the plot. (Frequent naming, obviously, is another.) But we need also to be able early on to mark individual players' *function* in the plot: the matrix of motive, knowledge, and power that determines each character's capacity to contribute to and profit from moves in the story. It is here, in the poem's remarkable rapprochement between functional clarity and human complexity in the play of goals and moves, that we approach both the nucleus of its plotting and the central engine of its meaning and resonance.

Combatant characters in the *Iliad* appear to assume a consensual but inexplicit matrix of common goals that we sometimes incautiously call a, or the, 'heroic code'. It is traditional to discuss this ideological system, if such it is, as a social rather than a narrative phenomenon; but it is a system optimised for the *Iliad*'s particular kind of move-structure, and there is something to be said for considering its narrative functionality as in some ways anterior to its historical or quasi-historical status as a machinery of value.

The central principle of Iliadic society is *reciprocity* – between men and men, men and gods, individuals and groups. Every commodity of value is drawn into this system of barter, including many to which no absolute value can easily be assigned: survival, κλέος (glory), dependants.[23] Achilles' μῆνις (wrath), flagged by the poem's first word as its central subject, means in plot terms precisely a refusal to play by everyone else's rules of reciprocity, a recalculation of the exchange rate between different narrative values, and is thus the mechanism behind the threatened breakdown of the tacit system of reciprocities itself, whose existence depends on a kind of consensual illusion.

The spine of the *Iliad*'s plot is thus a series of failed reciprocities, or incommensurate exchanges, within this system (what Murnaghan 1997: 39 calls 'the equation of unequal things'): a series of moves of a single type, the exchange of valued commodities between three main agents (Table 3). The principal exchanged commodities are Briseis; military control of the Trojan plain; Patroclus; and Hector. While the first two of these end up where they started, and Agamemnon ends up cost-neutral, Achilles has exchanged Patroclus for Hector with Priam's Trojans, and

---

[23] This is the model canonised by Lévi-Strauss 1949 (building on Mauss 1925), who already notes that exchange in primitive societies 'embraces material objects, social values and women' (1969: 62) – commodities that tend to differentiate into distinct systems of exchange as a society evolves.

Table 3. *Incommensurate exchanges in the* Iliad

	exchange		Agamemnon	Achilles	Trojans
0.	Chr:	Ag → Chryses	−Chryseis		
1.	Br:	Ach → Ag	−Chr, +Briseis	−Br	
2.	p:	Ag → Tro	−Chr, +Br, −p	−Br	+p
3.	p:	Tro → Ag	−Chr, +Br	−Br	
4.	Patr:	Ach → Tro	−Chr, +Br	−Br, −Patroclus	+Patr
5.	Br:	Ag → Ach	−Chr	−Patr	+Patr
6.	Hec:	Tro → Ach	−Chr	−Patr, +Hector	+Patr, −Hec

each side feels it has the worse of the deal. What makes this set of transactions so subtle and complex is that none of the commodities are remotely equivalent, two of the players are supposed to be on the same side, and each values the exchanged objects differently. The lesson of the *Iliad*, which Achilles has already learned by the time of his great speech in IX, is that life cannot be calculated in systemic terms, however indispensable the pretence may be to the continued functioning of social practices. Thus Achilles' own final ransoming of Hector's corpse back to Priam in exchange for material goods is a symbolic rather than functional exchange, marking Achilles' return to the system of reciprocity even while he recognises it as nothing more than a social myth.

Nevertheless, most players behave *as though the system worked*. The famous speech of Sarpedon at XII.310–28, usually felt to express the consensual version of the warrior ideology, claims a compact of reciprocity between the aristocrat and his people: they award him material and social honour in return for his pre-eminent place in battle. Personal excellence is demonstrated by effectiveness in public combat – facing as many major enemies as possible, and ideally killing them rather than being killed, though personal survival is a lower priority than discharge of public obligation to fight, particularly in individual duels. It is taken for granted by all that the side that collectively discharges these obligations best will eventually, gods willing, win the war. (In the *Odyssey*, of course, we learn that the war is finally won by a quite different set of strategic priorities; but that is the *Odyssey*.)

From the outset, however, the case of Achilles is special in two respects, which together explain why he of all players should be the locus of the poem's problematisation of its consensual system of value. First, and the overt cause of the quarrel in I, the system places Achilles (as the principal fighter) and Agamemnon (as supreme commander) on a collision course. Achilles is discharging his own side of the contract by putting his life on the line and making the most impressive individual contribution to the war. But Agamemnon's status as commander-in-chief pre-empts Achilles' claim to proportionate reward. Secondly, it swiftly emerges that Achilles uniquely holds *knowledge* that marks him off from the other players. He alone knows that, for him, early death is not a risk but a certainty (1.416), or at most that he has a choice between ignominious longevity and glorious demise (IX.410–16). The only contractual return for his continued fighting (that is, inevitably, for his death) is the honour due his pre-eminence as a warrior. Once this honour has been challenged and hijacked by Agamemnon, Achilles can no longer be won back to the original contract, however generous the terms. It requires the substitution of a wholly new goal, the avenging of Patroclus, to induce him to press forward to his death: a commodity to which Achilles can assign a subjective value commensurate with, and so exchangeable for, his own life.

Significantly, aside from this special case of prophetic foreknowledge the *Iliad* does not use differences in characters' game *knowledge* as a major plot effect. There are a few points, such as the news of Patroclus' and Hector's deaths, where the slow transit of information about events on the battlefield to the home zone of camp or city is exploited *ad hoc* for local suspense. But generally the *Iliad*'s is not a plot about the ironies of information distribution. In particular, in striking contrast to some later retellings, it avoids any development of the mistaken-identity device hinted at in XI.797–8 and XVI.41.[24] It will be left for the *Odyssey* to excavate the full range of narrative possibilities here.

In contrast, the plot factor of *power* is most carefully used in the differentiation of players. First, characters divide cleanly into combatants and dependants (Greek prisoners; Trojan elders, women and children). The small but vital group of *dependants* is barred from influencing plot physically, though as the sixth and final books movingly demonstrate they may still possess *persuasive* competence through their moral, intellectual, and emotional capabilities. The *combatants* themselves are ranked in a rough pecking order by prowess, the order established mainly in I–VII by a mixture of direct confrontations, individual demonstrations, and narratorial comment. The order approximately runs: Achilles; Ajax; Agamemnon and Diomedes; Hector, Idomeneus and Odysseus; Menelaus and others; Paris. From the duel in VII, for instance, we learn that Hector is more than a match for Menelaus (105), but himself outclassed by Ajax (179, 216–18, 312) and also at a natural disadvantage to Diomedes and Agamemnon (179–80). And from II.768–9 we know that

---

[24] At XVI.280–2 the Trojans take Patroclus for Achilles; at 423–5 Sarpedon expresses uncertainty over the mystery warrior's identity; at 543 Glaucus knows it is Patroclus.

Ajax himself ranks second after Achilles (who is effectively vulnerable only from gods: XXI.278, cf. XIX.417, XXII.359–60). Even the support of a god at no point actually displaces a warrior from his relative ranking. Thus during Hector's *aristeia* not just Achilles but also Diomedes, Agamemnon, and Odysseus are judiciously removed from the running, recovering only in time to compete in XXIII.

This ranking by prowess is vital to the reader's extrapolation of story. Mismatched encounters on the battlefield are a familiar dramatic device, but the poem is parsimonious with the deaths of heroes. Only three characters who speak in more than one book are killed in the course of the narrative: Sarpedon, Patroclus, and Hector, all at carefully telegraphed turning-points in the story. The default rule is that both combatants will survive the encounter, teasing the reader to guess in advance what inventive twist of plot will save Paris from Menelaus, Aeneas and Glaucus from Diomedes, Hector from Ajax, Aeneas and (in XX) Hector from Achilles. More crucially, it is a foregone assumption from early in the poem that if Hector duels with Achilles he must die; Zeus's promise at XV.68 merely confirms that such a duel will in fact take place. And finally, the drama of XXIV lies in the unique confrontation of the leading combatant with the leading dependant, a face-off between the martial might of Achilles and the moral and human strength of Priam. Priam's victory thus becomes a triumph of one kind of narrative power over another: the final displacement of violence by humanity.

It should be clear by now that the plot of the *Iliad* depends on a tightly *rule-bound* narrative, in ways that often smudge the distinction between causal and merely formal kinds of patterning. On the small scale, there are elaborate formal patterns structuring the otherwise chaotic business of warfare: the exchange of spears preceding hand-to-hand sword-fighting, the moment of vulnerability when a victor tries to strip or retrieve the body of a victim. The literature on 'type-scenes' is full of such instances, though more as an issue in compositional than in narrative poetics.[25] To pick two well-known broad illustrations, individual *combats* follow a fairly restrictive set of conventional patterns both in their telegraphing (the first to cast spear is regularly the ultimate loser) and their dovetailing (third parties become involved for revenge, opportunism, or interest in the corpse); while *wounds* are, for reasons of purest narrative utility, either instantly fatal or wholly curable. The poem has no functional use for either slow death (the special case of death speeches excepted) or permanent disability, because the outcome of plot moves needs to be immediate and decisive. A player is removed from the board

[25] Gainsford 1999 takes this issue by the scruff.

temporarily, finally and completely, or not at all: these are the only outcomes of real narrative significance.

This rule-boundness extends to the plotting of larger episodes, and
usually establishes three things: the local player set, the range of permis-
sible moves, and the significant available outcomes. The duels in III and
VII are exemplary cases, with the conditions of combat explicit in the
terms of the truce. (Much rides on each, but both ingeniously fail to
provide for the actual outcome. In particular, the bizarre upshot of the
duel between Menelaus and Paris serves as a springboard for subsequent
action by problematising the status and conditions of the truce agreed.)

But terms are set also for episodes of all-out combat: the range and
extent of divine interference, the immediate military objectives on either
side, the strategies to be followed, the principal figures on whom the effort
depends. For these purposes the most important device is formal *councils*,
where the state of play is regularly reviewed and the next moves deliberated by the players themselves, on earth and in Olympus. Even in pitched
battle, where formal gatherings are obviously excluded, there may be
scenes of *ad hoc* deliberation to define the options at a local juncture in the
narrative. There is even one character on either side, Nestor and
Polydamas, to specialise in these scenes of strategic counsel in the mid-
stream of battle. Finally, even an individual player may be presented in
narrative with a choice of alternative moves – a device ubiquitous in the
Odyssey – or with an authoritative warning of consequences to a specific
action. We do not need to know the basis for Achilles' warning to
Patroclus (XVI.87–96), not to pursue the Trojans back to the city, to
appreciate that this is a boundary condition of the following narrative,
marking a point of no return for Patroclus' advance.

At the highest level are rules determining the shape of the narrative as a
whole. Some are implicit: for instance, that major heroes will generally
not meet in face-to-face combat, despite all natural pressure to the contrary, and if they do we can assume the duel will be aborted unless we are
explicitly warned otherwise. Again, the whole narrative logic of the
poem's plotting asks the reader to accept that only *military* action will
decide the war's outcome; it cannot be settled by negotiated terms, as signalled strongly by the failures in III and VII. Even divine intervention has
strict limits outside those imposed *ad hoc* in particular books: death is
final, miracles are limited to healing and teleportation, and gods may not
kill mortals themselves except by collaboration with another mortal. In a
weaker sense, of course, implied plot rules of this kind permeate the
poem. *Any* repeated pattern in the narrative or its textual expression
invites the reader to keep it on file as a template for further incidents.
Many such structures are only plot*like*, in the sense that they do program

the reader's expectation of action, but in purely formal ways unrelated to the operation of story cause and effect. A prominent case is the famous 'three times . . . but the fourth' formula at v.436–9, xvi.702–6 and 784–7, xx.445–7 (cf. xxii.165 with 208). It is hardly that there is an inbuilt physical law of the story universe that no inconclusive action may be repeated more than three times. Rather, this is a purely formal narrative pattern to signal to the reader that here is a series of repeatedly frustrated human attempts to be followed by a divine breach of the deadlock.

But undoubtedly the most important and influential devices used by the *Iliad* to impose rules on its story are the constraints explicit in the narrative itself. There are three species: *narratorial* commentary, usually brief anticipations of later events; the much more numerous and elaborate *control-level* statements articulated within the story by the gods and their agents; and the more frangible conditions imposed by the human *players* themselves.[26]

In classical storytelling generally, the overt statement of narrative rules by an external narrator is discouraged, violating as it does the principle of transparency. (The case is different for a narrator who is also an inhabitant of the story universe. Here transparency is preserved by the pretence that the narrator is reporting his personal, viewpointed knowledge *qua* character, not his omniscient knowledge *qua* author.) The one tolerated exception is due to the precedent of the Homeric epics themselves: a past-tense narrator is allowed limited *foreshadowing* of future events in his own voice, because it can be construed as narratorial hindsight rather than as authorial *control* of the story itself.

In Homer, such *narratorial* foreshadowing is very strictly limited in timespan, content, and range. The commonest is the νήπιος-statement type (first at ii.38–40), where the narrator appends an ironic aside to a report of a character's hope, advising the reader that the hope will prove ill-founded. More generally, we find occasional short-term anticipations of characters' deaths in the early stages of their fatal combat encounter. But long-range foreshadowing is rare in the *Iliad*, and where it comes it is usually deliberately incomplete. Thus i.1–7 is reasonably detailed on the events of book i (the quarrel and wrath), but purposely vague on the aftermath: many Greeks died (when? how? why?), and the plan of Zeus (what plan?) was fulfilled (how? when? by whom?). At ii.694 we are told Achilles was 'soon to rise up again', but not how soon, why, or with what consequences. At xi.604 Patroclus exits from the hut to hear Achilles' assessment of the battle as 'the beginning of his doom' – a teasingly cryptic remark, when all Patroclus is called on to do here is visit Nestor

[26] Duckworth 1933: 6–20.

and report back on the identity of his wounded companion. (In the event, it is Nestor who will raise the fatal suggestion that Patroclus enter the fighting in Achilles' place.)

More detailed foreshadowing, and the more general articulation of narrative rules, is above all the job of the gods. But as we saw in Chapter 3, there are threats as well as advantages to classical transparency and economy in this kind of narrative *control level* to the story world. On the one hand, the narrative has to preserve at least the narrative illusion of free will on the part of the players; on the other, the operations of the narrative supervisors must not seem so arbitrary and *ad hoc* as to be merely a mask for the author. Yet the Iliadic gods are, in principle at least, omniscient, omnipotent, and individually committed to irreconcilably different ends. How can their impact on the story be kept under coherent narrative control?

The *Iliad*'s solution is remarkably elegant, though it does involve complications of theology that have not recommended it to later classical fiction. In the *Iliad*, there is a hierarchy both of knowledge and of power *within* the Olympian family, with Zeus in principle holding ultimate control of both. Yet Zeus does not always choose fully to exercise this control, in practice allowing subordinate powers to improvise within the established limits of his asserted will. Thus, for a start, not everything that happens in the *Iliad* is predetermined, let alone known to all the divine characters. The *Iliad*'s concept of fate is notoriously ambiguous, but there is nothing actually inconsistent with the idea that all predestined and foreknown actions in the human world of the *Iliad* are the result of policy decisions, past and present, by Zeus himself.[27] This is not accidental. It is extremely convenient for the poem's narrative economy if the reader can at least assume that Zeus is both the ultimate source of information about the future, and the authority for its fulfilment.

At the outset of the poem, relatively little of the events to come is in the public domain. From 1.416 we know that Achilles is destined to a short life (this from Thetis, who evidently has it from Zeus); from II.324–9, that Zeus intends Troy to fall in the tenth year. It is during the narrative of the first book (505–30) that Zeus, in deference to Thetis, inserts the codicil that he will support the Trojans until Achilles receives the honour due him. Not until xv.63–71 is the plan amplified to include the killings of Sarpedon by Patroclus, Patroclus by Hector, and Hector by Achilles; and the ransom of Hector by Priam is not added until xxiv.75–6. Nothing more is said of how, and precisely when, Troy will fall; and the network of

[27] 'In Homeric athanatology "Fate" is not a metaphysical power separate from Zeus' (Taplin 1992: 141 n. 20). On the productive ambiguities of the 'plan of Zeus' (1.5) see especially Lynn-George 1988: 37–41, Murnaghan 1997.

prophecies about Achilles' death at the hands of Paris and Apollo avoids any direct attribution to Zeus altogether.[28]

Otherwise, Zeus's edicts reported in the poem are directed not to the foreshadowing of endgame, but to the restriction of divine interference in the story, which the poem is at pains throughout to limit by strict and explicit rules. The first day's fighting (day 22) is, significantly, the only one where the gods are free from general restrictions on involvement, and to an extent its function is to show why on other days the gods are barred from full intervention. Over and over, the gods threaten to hijack control of the story. Even Diomedes is directed closely by Athene: only he is allowed to see the gods in the battle, and he is permitted to attack only two. By contrast, the second day's battle (day 25) begins with Zeus's restraining order on divine intervention of any kind, an order rescinded formally only on the decisive day 27 (xx.23–5). On the intervening day 26, Hera and Posidon are able to defy the edict temporarily, but only to see their efforts frustrated when Zeus awakens, recalls Posidon, and author- ises Apollo to support the Trojans. And in the Theomachy of xx, despite Zeus's mandate to intervene freely, the partisan gods decide in practice on a voluntary code of their own, refraining from more than limited involvement (134–55). Only in the final duel in xxii is free divine support for both sides restored, and the poignant effect is significantly to deny Hector the dignity of free will and a fair fight in the hour of his death. Throughout the poem, therefore, the power and understanding of the controllers are themselves rigidly controlled, by the higher narrative authority personified in Zeus. What is more, because Zeus (as a matter of policy, or if we prefer of narrative convenience) will not descend to the battlefield in person, the injection of divinely held information nearly always involves a formal change of scene from earth to heaven – even in the limited case of comments on the granting or refusal of prayers. The result is that the human story and the divine rule-making are in practice widely segregated in narrative, preserving still further the integrity of story causality.

Human rule-making, by contrast, is by its very nature vulnerable and provisional. Indeed, this is more often than not its narrative function: to assert conditions to the story that may or may not be fulfilled. Often, in fact, the narrator will comment ironically on the futility of a hope, promise, or prayer immediately it is quoted. But there are limited ways in which the players themselves can determine at least some of the local rules of story. One is by consensus, as with the terms of the truces in iii, vii, and xxiv – though it is far from clear how Achilles is able to give surety

[28] xviii.95–6, xix.416–17, xxi.277–8, xxii.359–60, xxiv.85–6.

for the Greeks as a whole. Another is by the statement of enforceable will: orders supported by formal authority, promises within the character's power to deliver. Finally, even necessarily unenforceable pledges can be effectively sealed by strong formal declarations such as oaths, investing the promise with such a strong personal commitment to its fulfilment as in practice to guarantee to the reader that it will come true.

Such is the case, for instance, with Achilles' oath at 1.239–44. Achilles has no way of actually knowing that the Greeks will be massacred by Hector, who might (did it not lie outside the implicit rules of permitted action) suffer an unfortunate domestic accident in Andromache's kitchen that same evening. But it does establish firm rules for Achilles' own involvement in the fighting: his return is subsequent and conditional on the prior suffering and repentance of the Greeks. The fulfilment of those conditions in ways unforeseen, indeed utterly undesired, by their maker is one of the central ironic ideas in the poem, and a supreme confirmation of the epic's distinctive worldview, the prototype of that we call 'tragic'. None of the rule-makers, on earth or in heaven, takes pleasure from the execution of his plans. Even Zeus cannot simultaneously satisfy his obligations to Hera, Thetis, and Sarpedon, or his moral roles as avenger on the one hand of ξενία violated by Paris, and as patron on the other of the consistently pious Priam. In the minor key of Iliadic plotting, everyone is a victim. Of the leading players, it is Achilles who takes the longest to learn this truth about the rules that write the story of his life, and by implication of our own; and only when he does is the plot complete.

So far as we can judge, in fact, the *Iliad* is the ultimate source of what will prove one of the most persistent ideas in Western literature: that *life itself is plotted*, determined by a relatively tight and comprehensible system of narrative rules. In learning and applying the rules that allow us to respond to a particular narrative, by engaging actively in the modelling and extrapolation of story, we submit to an education in the human predicament at large. Thus the most persuasive narrative systems are capable of actually reversing the cognitive relationship between our reading of fiction and our reading of life. Instead of merely importing our understanding of the outer world to help us make sense of a fictional world, we re-export the fictional world's rules to the world of experience. Yes, we say: that way of seeing the world 'fits'. The paradox of the *Iliad*'s achievement is to design a story world in which violent death is the central reality of daily experience, and then use it to frame a worldview of compelling humanity and sensitivity. And central to this achievement is the subjection of a vast, intrinsically shapeless story and cast to strict *narrative* closure in space, time, and causality, making graspable sense of a seemingly limitless world. In the global game-patterns of experience it demonstrates, the episode of the wrath of Achilles can be easily understood as paradigmatic of the war as a whole; and the war, by a ready extension, of all our lives.

As suggested at the beginning of this chapter, the particular narrative game-shapes proposed by the *Iliad* and *Odyssey* have a far more than merely technical legacy. They are the twin paradigms for the worldviews of ancient narrative. All classical fiction is modelled on one or other of these types; and the division between them, though early and repeatedly traversed, remains one of the most fundamental shaping forces in the history of European narrative art. (Surprisingly, the distinction was not felt, or at any rate not articulated, by Aristotle, though he is largely responsible for some of its vocabulary of terms.) In the *Iliad*'s 'tragic' or *minor* plot key, the story universe and the rules that shape it elude the control, though not necessarily the comprehension, of the board-level (as against control-level) players. To put it another way, it presents a universe dominated by loss, where human weakness leads inevitably to failure and the frustration of personal goals. By contrast, in the Odyssean or *major* key, the story universe is to a limited but crucial extent accessible to player control, through a careful understanding of its narrative rules and the systematic (if not always conscious) choice of goals and strategies consistent with those rules. This is the mode of comedy and romance, and historically the more popular and prevalent: we shall examine its beginnings in the next chapter, and its further development principally in Chapters 9 and 10.

In itself, however, and despite all, the *Iliad* remains an incomplete template for the fully classical plot system. For all its strong sense of causal unity and closure overall, its internal episodic structure is notoriously loose, particularly in the books where Achilles is involved only by his absence. The signalling of endgame, too, is comparatively weak: there is little early sense of Achilles and Hector as main antagonists, and none of Achilles and Priam as narratively linked figures – though we may well feel that this avoidance of insistent telegraphing is a strength, particularly for the elegiac XXIV following and completing the false close of XXII. Its particular use of the story's polytheistic control level is prodigal and, in terms of economy of narrative function, unwieldy; while there is hardly any exploration of the potent classical device of the c-move, or indeed any of the traditional complications of plotting deriving from the uneven distribution of information among the players. The *Iliad* is supremely, as Weil's famous title recognises, the poem of power – in narrative terms as much as any other. And yet, astonishingly, the other half of the classical paradigm finds its authoritative lexicon only a generation later, in the text that more than any single other has defined the canons of European narrative.

7   Epic myth II: *Odyssey*

A generation ago, it hardly seemed controversial to declare that 'western literature has been more influenced by the Bible than by any other book'.[1] Yet already this is looking less true, and perhaps it never was. In the forms and media of popular fiction, at least, the pagan influence of the *Odyssey* has always been incomparably more alive. Now, as the traditional borders between high and low culture seem to be opening permanently to traffic, that persistent influence is more visible than ever.

This tyranny of the *Odyssey* over the forms of Western narrative has two quite separate causes. First, like the *Iliad* but immeasurably more so, the poem has been the historical template for a general narrative system of remarkable versatility and strength: the system that in the last chapter I termed plotting in the *major* key, as opposed to the minor or tragic mode of the *Iliad*. Throughout history, this has been the more popular key for narrative composition – largely, no doubt, because one of its defining characteristics is the happy ending, something already noticed by Aristotle (*Poetics* 13.1453a30–5) as more attractive to groundling taste than the more emotionally challenging resolutions he preferred.

Even more importantly, though, the *Odyssey* is the most encyclopaedic *compendium* of technical plot devices in the whole of ancient storytelling, and one of the most dazzling displays of narrative fireworks anywhere in literature. Of classical writers, only Terence and Heliodorus approach the *Odyssey*'s sheer joy in plotting, its exuberant passion for bravura narrative acrobatics. An astonishing number of the poem's structural inventions number among the most imitated, and still unexhausted, inspirations in the art of fiction.

Remarkably, the *Odyssey* seems at first sight openly to reject most of the radical plot techniques pioneered by the *Iliad*. The earlier epic had ingeniously exploited the physical and human limitations of its battlefield setting to bind a sprawling, untellable story to a strict narrative frame. Thus the narrative universe is limited in space to the disputed territory

[1] Frye 1957: 14.

between the Greek ships and Trojan city; the narrative time compressed to the few critical days when the outcome of the war is finally determined; the players limited to that narrow segment of the warrior class on whom the fates of all depend; and the rules of narrative engagement are the rules of heroic warfare, stylised and conventionalised to a point but still generally naturalistic in the kind of causality they assume.

And at first sight, the *Odyssey* seems to throw all this away. By comparison with the narrow universe of the *Iliad*, the world of the *Odyssey* is vastly opened out. Spatially, its terrestrial action spans not a square mile of battlefield but the whole of the Mediterranean, known and imagined, from Egypt and Crete to the sunless rim of earth. Temporally, a similar span of primary narrative time (forty days as against the *Iliad*'s fifty) has to find room for nine years' worth of fully reported secondary action. Socially, the cast of Odyssean players seems determined to span the spectrum: from kings in their palaces to slaves at the pigpen, goddesses on magical islands to dogs mooching on dungheaps. And the range of action admissible in this narrative world is immeasurably wider than the *Iliad*'s – both in itself, and in the causal rules that shape it. This is a world where heroes not only wage aristocratic feats of arms with their peers, but just as vitally battle with man-eating monsters, canoodle with goddesses, conjure shades, and wrestle with beggars for the prize of a haggis. It is a world whose natural law is not of spear and sinew only, but of magic wands and herbs, necromantic rites, mind-altering drugs, and assorted supernatural transformations. It seems in short, an unbounded story universe apparently beyond the rule of narrative law.

In fact, the reverse is true. The *Odyssey* is able to open up its storyworld precisely because it has devised a narrative system powerful enough to contain it. It demonstrates for all time that an arbitrarily open story universe can accommodate a *narrative world-structure* that is fully and classically closed. The techniques that make this possible lie especially in areas of plotting left relatively unexplored by the *Iliad*: in particular, the arts of endgame, c-moves, and global narrative rule-making. But the poem has also learned and applied much from the *Iliad*'s general ambitions of narrative closure and the particular technical devices coined to achieve them: its flagging of players, its machinery of foreshadowing and control, its episodic segmentation and closure, and above all its plotting of narrative space and time. All these are pursued by the *Odyssey* with a relentless virtuosity that at every turn seems bent on exploring technique to the borders of paradox and beyond.

Nowhere is this more evident than in the treatment of *time*. Comparison of Table 4 with the equivalent *Iliad* chronology (above, p. 106) reveals a

Table 4. *Primary chronology of the* Odyssey*

Days	No.	Events	Reference	Lines
I	I	Council of gods; Athene to Ithaca	I.11–444	434
2	I	Ithacan assembly; Telemachus sails (night)	II.1–434	434
3	I	Telemachus in Pylos	III.1–403	403
4	I	Telemachus to Pherae	III.404–90	87
5	I	Telemachus to Sparta	III.491–IV.305	312
6	I	Menelaus' story; ambush set	IV.306–847	542
7	I	Council of gods; Hermes to Calypso	V.1–227	227
8–11	4	Odysseus builds boat	V.228–62	35
12–28	17	Odysseus at sea	V.263–78	16
29	I	Posidon's storm	V.279–387	9
30–31	2	Odysseus drifts to Scheria	V.388–493	106
32	I	Odysseus to Alcinous	VI.1–VII.347	678
33	I	Phaeacian entertainments; Odysseus' story	VIII.1–XIII.17	2,836
34	I	Odysseus to Ithaca	XIII.18–92	75
35	I	Odysseus to Eumaeus; Telemachus to Pherae	XIII.93–XV.188	1,069
36	I	Telemachus to Ithaca	XV.189–494	306
37	I	Telemachus to Eumaeus	XV.495–XVI.481	544
38	I	Odysseus to palace	XVII.1–XX.90	1,728
39	I	Massacre of suitors	XX.91–XXIII.346	1,585
40	I	Laertes; suitors' kin	XXIII.347–XXIV.548	574
				12,000

* Ap. Stanford 1959: x–xii.

number of immediate differences. First, though the timespan is shorter, the action is more diffused over more days; there is not the *Iliad*'s concentrated economy of timescale, with each main act compressed into a single elongated day. As a result, the only Odyssean day to take up as much text as the four great Iliadic days of battle is the special case of day 33, with its immense embedded secondary narrative. Secondly, significant temporal elisions, such as occur in the first and last books of the *Iliad*, are both less and more abundant in the *Odyssey*: less, in that the only substantial such elapse in the *primary* narrative is the fraught voyage from Ogygia to Scheria in v, but more in that they figure prominently in the *secondary* narrative of IX–XII (Table 5). Finally, the elaborate concentricities of time and action, such a striking pattern in the *Iliad*'s structure, are hardly evident, despite such ingenious attempts as Whitman's analysis of VIII (1958: 289).

And yet, the temporal structure of the *Odyssey* is tightly controlled, and (unlike the *Iliad*) controlled far more by internal plot dynamics than by

Table 5. *Secondary chronology of* Odyssey *IX–XII**

Duration	Events	Reference
?	Troy to Ismarus	IX.39–61
?	Ismarus to storm landfall	IX.62–73
2 days	waiting out storm	IX.74–5
?	to Malea & Cythera	IX.76–81
9 days	Cythera to Lotophagi	IX.82–104
?	Lotophagi to Cyclopes	IX.105–51
1 day	feasting on island	IX.152–69
3 days	in Polyphemus' cave	IX.170–59
?	Cyclopes to Aeolia	IX.560–X.1
1 month	with Aeolus	X.1–27
10 days	Aeolia to Ithaca	X.28–46
?	Ithaca to Aeolia	X.47–79
7 days	Aeolia to Laestrygonia	X.80–132
?	Laestrygonia to Aeaea	X.133–141
3 days	Aeaea: mourning & feasting	X.142–186
1 day	confrontation with Circe	X.187–466
1 year	guesting with Circe	X.467–540
?	Aeaea to underworld	X.541–XI.22
1 'day'	in underworld	XI.23–638
?	return to Aeaea	XI.639–XII.7
1 day	with Circe	XII.8–141
1 day?	Sirens, Scylla, Thrinacia	XII.142–315
1 month	on Thrinacia	XII.315–398
1 day	Thrinacia to storm	XII.399–425
1 day	shipwreck to Charybdis	XII.426–446
10 days	Charybdis to Ogygia	XII.447–50

* Cf. Hellwig 1964: 51.

mere superimposed formal architecture. The poem falls, of course, into two very distinctive halves: the diffuse, centrifugal I–XII and the tight, centripetal XIII–XXIV. In the first, space, time, and narrative continuity are all extravagantly fragmented. The three storylines of Telemachus, Penelope, and Odysseus diverge in space; and the narrative falls into three clear movements, with increasingly open time structures and increasingly complex narrative shapes. In the Telemachy (I–IV, 6 days), the narrative tracks Telemachus continuously from Ithaca to Sparta, culminating in the great secondary narrative of Menelaus' Egyptian adventure and fateful homecoming, with a final narrative jump back to Ithaca and the suspended ambush. Next, in the Phaeacis of V–VIII (27 days), it is

Odysseus who is tracked, but this time with temporal elisions, much more elastic pacing, and a virtuoso narrative detour in the first part of VI. The space of this story is wholly fabulous, and full of exotic inventions; the more-or-less even temporal rhythm of the Telemachy gives way to a progressively more detailed and retarded day-by-day movement; and the eighth book brims with elaborate secondary narratives, all three of Demodocus' songs ironically reflecting in different ways on the primary moment of performance. Finally, in the Apologoi of IX–XII, we enter a first-person secondary narrative spanning at least sixteen months and a vast oceanful of real and imagined places, peppered with chronological ellipses and elisions, and liberally planted with tertiary narratives such as prophecies, forewarnings, and the lavish variorum anthology in XI. Yet at the same time, the *primary* narrative has reached its greatest density and retardation, as this entire vast monologue sprawls over a single late evening.

In the second half, the Ithacan *Odyssey* proper, the narrative flow is very different and, with qualifications, rather more Iliadic. Where the primary narrative alone of I.I–XIII.92 (the moment of Odysseus' arrival on Ithaca, and a popular alternative division between the two *Odyssey*s in modern times) takes up almost five weeks, from Odysseus' awakening on Ithaca to the Alexandrian *telos* at XXIII.293 is a mere five days.[2] As a necessary correlate, the days themselves become longer and more crowded with event; the pace becomes ever more leisurely, with the two final palace days stretching over three books each. There is also a much more structured sense of the *passage* of time, with the daily routine of work, meals, and bed used as in the *Iliad* to measure the narrative pace against an underlying metronomic story rhythm.

What is going on here? For many readers, the slackening pace of the Ithacan books has seemed a sign of failing narrative momentum – even of

---

[2] Most editors prefer six, with Athene's visit to Telemachus at XV.1ff. following chronologically on the end of XIV rather than the end of XIII, and a missing day with Eumaeus passed over in silence at the Ithacan end. But (*pace* Hoekstra *ad loc.* and Olson 1995: 96–7, *q.v.* for earlier discussions) the poem does seem concerned to evade this implication. The anticipated dawn-formula is suppressed in the Ithacan action of day 35, allowing us if we wish to imagine the conversation between Odysseus and Athene in XIII taking place in the halflight before dawn, immediately subsequent to which she visits Telemachus in sleep at Sparta. It would be misguided to fuss over this unduly, but the unusual retroversion at XV.1 does have a parallel in the much bolder Phaeacian anachrony at XIII.125–87; and to modern taste, at least, the temporal ambiguities of XIII if anything enhance its pervasive sense of liminality and mystery. Clearly I do not share the old view that the *Odyssey*'s sense of chronology is *purely* 'qualitative' (Bassett 1938: 33, Thornton 1962 *passim*), and that glaring illogicalities of time-scheme are comfortably tolerated; cf. Bergren 1979, Apthorp 1980, and Olson 1995: 91–119 for more balanced views.

intentional padding, as a later poet struggles to emulate the scale and detail of the *Iliad*.[3] Such a view seems fundamentally to mistake both the artistry of this section of the epic and the design of the *Odyssey* as a whole. Appreciation of the *Odyssey* has been dogged by our perverse modern tendency to see the poem's secondary narrative as primary, and vice versa – as if IX–XII are the 'essential' *Odyssey*, and the remaining twenty books mere narrative appendages. In this reading, the Ithacan crisis of XXI–II is anticlimactic, overshadowed by the adventures of the Cyclops, Circe, and the dead; while most modern reworkings and retellings severely abridge or even delete the events of XIV–XX altogether.

It should not need saying that such a view gives a bizarre distortion of the *Odyssey* we actually possess. As Aristotle, along with most ancient readers, took for granted,[4] the Ithacan *Odyssey* is the narrative hub; the Telemachy, Phaeacis, and Apologoi are satellite narratives, their function preparatory and preliminary. This is not to deny the integrity of the first twelve books: merely to restore the primacy of the last twelve in the poem's total design. The change of temporal rhythm in XIII is one of several signals that the narrative is entering a more sustained, concentrated, and decisive phase. Divided storylines begin once more to converge; the net of action draws tighter in space and time; the environment of story becomes more circumstantially realistic; new goals are set, new tactics deliberated, new forms of divine control introduced; and dialogue interaction becomes fuller, to manage the far richer human texture of these intricately psychological books.

The *Odyssey*, in fact, has discovered a narrative principle only haphazardly exploited in the *Iliad*: that slowing the pace can actually increase the narrative momentum. As the crisis approaches, the quality of time changes. Small events become significant – a word over dinner, a look exchanged – as the forward pressure of events inexorably accumulates, only rarely and weakly suspended in sleep.[5] It is not simply that tension is raised by the postponement of anticipated action: the rise in narrative density makes room for further layers of drama and complexity on the microscale.

[3] Kirk 1962: 357–61; cf. Griffin 1980b: 49 ('The reader feels at times that bulk is being sought for its own sake'), and for a rebuttal Rutherford 1992: 9–16.

[4] 17.1455b17–23; see above, p. 4. Of sixteen references to the *Odyssey* in the *Poetics*, only one is to an event in the first half of the poem (16.1455a2–4, to Odysseus' weeping at Demodocus' Trojan song). Otherwise, there are three lines quoted to illustrate figures of speech, and one discussion of an event which does *not* happen (25.1461b4: why Telemachus does not visit Icarius in the Peloponnese). Aristotle shows no interest at all in the modern nucleus, the adventures of IX–XII.

[5] Significantly, though both Odysseus and Penelope do sleep on the eve of the crisis, the *narrative* cuts boldly back and forth between their waking hours, so as to span the night without the familiar pause.

This long-term plotting of story in time is closely supported by the *Odyssey*'s remarkable use of narrative *space*. Like its predecessor, the *Odyssey* finds an ingenious match between the narrative form of its storyline and the space in which the events take place. But the *Odyssey*'s is a far more daring spatial metaphor, and both its story topography and its narrative symbolism are far more elaborately extended. If the *Iliad* is a battlefield, the *Odyssey* is an archipelago: built of a string of island episodes, each with its own closed internal topography, and cut off from communication with its neighbours by the sundering sea, Posidon's elemental domain, a place without rules or landmarks, defying human certainty and control.

There are fifteen such narrative islands beaded out along the storyline: Ithaca, Pylos, Sparta, Ogygia, Scheria; the lands of the Cicones, Lotus-Eaters, Cyclopes, and Aeolus; Laestrygonia, Aeaea, the underworld, the Sirens' isle, Scylla and Charybdis, and Thrinacia. Not all, of course, are necessarily literal islands. The journey from Pylos to Sparta even lies overland. But there are excellent narrative reasons for this exception. First, the marine leg of Telemachus' journey, from Ithaca to Pylos and back again, *is* subject to all the perils and uncertainties of the sea. But the road from Pylos to Pherae and Sparta is pointedly free from threat; Telemachus' traversal of it is in fact a sign of his acceptance into the heroic community of Peloponnesian ξένοι linking Nestor, Diocles, and Menelaus. Secondly, the exceptional ease of passage between Pylos and Sparta locates Sparta as a virtual narrative suburb of Pylos – where Telemachus has left his ship, and to which he is therefore bound to retrace tracks en route to Ithaca (evading, somehow, the social perils of Nestor's all-too-leisurely hospitality).

Within the archipelago, individual islands have their own *internal* narrative contours – at least where this is useful to the plot. Generally they follow the recurrent pattern of a simple linear route from beach or harbour to homestead, city, or palace: thus the further Odysseus and his men advance inland, the further they move from the security of their ships into the ambivalent power of the natives. (In the penultimate variation, Odysseus' inland pilgrimage on Thrinacia ironically results in doom back at the ships.) Functional variations on this map usually serve a special purpose in the episode's local narrative topography: the offshore island where the rest of the fleet can moor immune from the non-seafaring Cyclops; the fatal topography of the Laestrygonian harbour; the Scherian river-mouth permitting a variety of activities essential to the plot, including swimmer access from the sea, laundering, loss of handball, and bathing.

The narrative archipelago's *overall* layout is still more artfully defined. Ithaca, literally an island, is in plot terms the narrative mainland. Over half the poem is set there, and from an early stage all plotlines can be seen to converge there – specifically, in the *megaron* of the Ithacan palace. The island's landmarks are all sites of specialised narrative function: the harbour for public access to the wider world; the cave of the nymphs for back-door arrival, security and concealment, and the interface of human and divine; the agora for collective community involvement, Eumaeus' hut as an antechamber to the disorderly kingdom itself, and Laertes' estate as a segregated episode of aftermath and finalities, outside and independent of the narrower terms of the palace endgame.

Even the palace itself has a complex internal plan – notoriously obscure in its physical layout, but a lucid model of *narrative* architecture. The main set is the *megaron*, the heart of palace life. It is here that the struggle for control of Odysseus' identity is played out: in the suitors' incessant feasting on Odysseus' meat, in the interactions between Penelope and the suitors, in the ever more perilous confrontations with Telemachus, and finally in the armed combat to the death. House, household, property, mistress, kingship: the five objects of the suitors' aspiration, five challenges to Odysseus' hold on his identity, are all assimilated in the space of the king's feast-hall. Here the endgame *action* of XXII is literally sealed, by closure and control of all the narrative entrances; and here too the story *knowledge* of Odysseus' return and vengeance is sealed, overnight at least, by the ruse at XXIII.130ff.

From this main arena a cluster of satellite stages lead off, connected by tightly defined gangways of narrative linkage. The most important is Penelope's quarters, her private space as woman and queen, inaccessible to any but permitted servants and legitimate family. Its landmark is her bed, symbol of the suspended marriage that defines her own threatened identity, and site of the weeping and dreams to which she retreats most deeply and alone. Other bedrooms serve more local, but no less personal, functions as private narrative space: Telemachus' room in I and XIX, framing his own peregrinations and return; Odysseus' oak-tree bedroom extending this function to furnish his final proof of identity, and complementing the *megaron* as the destination of his private (as opposed to his public) quest. Even the most architecturally incomprehensible detail, the storeroom of XXII, makes precise narrative sense in its context as a repository of plot instruments, imperfectly sealed against infiltration by guile.[6]

---

[6] Again the *narrative* topography is as clear as the story topography is obscure. Melanthius' downfall is triggered by his own incompetent plotting: in going back for a second haul he fails to realise that the informational advantage has shifted in his *enemies'* favour, since his trick is exposed as soon as the first suitors arm. This shift in the balance of knowledge transforms the storeroom from a repository of power to a lethal trap.

All the decisive action is initiated in Ithaca, and to Ithaca all the lead players must finally return, after their various tours round the outlying narrative islands. But these islands themselves are laid out on a sophisticated narrative map. Real placenames lie within access of normal sail: Pylos, the Cicones (from Troy), the suitors' neighbouring islands. But fabulous places lie at a geographical and narrative remove, marked off from the map of the known world by the narrative dislocations of storm or sleep. Thus between the Cicones and Lotus-Eaters a storm intervenes to blow Odysseus' fleet out of the Aegean into islands of fantasy: a narrative boundary he can only recross under supernatural authority and propulsion. Odysseus' first attempted return to the known world and Ithaca in x is miraculously steered by Aeolus' magic wind – and reversed by his other winds when Odysseus falls untimely asleep. His second attempt, Circe's route from Aeaea to Ithaca via Thrinacia, is aborted by a second storm, again sweeping the hero to unknown parts – this time, Ogygia. His departure thence for Ithaca (as he and Calypso both think, though we have Zeus's promise that Scheria is a planned stopover) is driven by Calypso's kindly wind, and broken by Posidon's storm; and his final, successful voyage from utopian Scheria to craggy Ithaca takes place under the uncanny propulsion of the sentient Phaeacian ships, and the distancing narrative cover of darkness and sleep.

Most important (and influential) of all, the *Odyssey*'s action is purposefully *funnelled* in a consistent spatial direction. From the Ithacan books I–II, with ample signals that here we must ultimately return, the action opens out to span first the Peloponnese, then the unknown lands where Odysseus himself is still removed. In the embedded narrative of IX–XII the compass widens further, reaching its fullest extent at the midpoint of the text. But in the second half the elastic links that tie the various characters to the Ithacan endgame begin systematically to contract – drawing first Odysseus, then Telemachus to the coast of Ithaca, to Eumaeus, and finally to the palace itself where the crisis is preparing. This tightening of the spatial net, already influential on the dynamics of space in ancient drama and novels (especially Heliodorus), has become still more canonical in film plotting. It allows complex, open stories to be organised into successive narrative *phases*: in the first the players have to win access to the area of the board where the endgame is within reach, and only then can the decisive moves be played out.

So much for the shape of the Odyssey's narrative world; what of its human inhabitants? In *defining* its player set, the *Odyssey* for once faces considerably less difficulty than the *Iliad*, thanks to the easier design of its story. But the challenges are not yet negligible, and are ingeniously met. We know, of course, from the poem's first word that this is a narrative with a solo central character, but naturally there are other characters than Odysseus of concern to the plot. The *Odyssey*'s solution is a straightforward but influential refinement of an Iliadic idea: the first two scenes in heaven and in Ithaca introduce *all and only the characters decisively involved in the endgame.* The suitors, shrewdly, are reduced for now to a collective, with only Antinous and Eurymachus individualised as spokesmen. (In the later books, where there is more leisure for it, we will be allowed to meet a few others – notably the pious Amphinomus, whose introduction complicates the moral chiaroscuro and is therefore put back to a more appropriate moment. But the use of a collective characterisation and identity for a large, undifferentiated group is a powerful technique of narrative economy, and is substantially retained throughout the poem.)

Two corollaries deserve note here. First, any character introduced *after* the first day's action is of secondary interest to the plot. In Ithaca, this includes not only the Ithacan nobles of II and the perpetually offstage Laertes, all of whom are in abeyance till XXIV, but also such later entrants as Eumaeus and Philoetius, Melanthius and Melantho, whose status and participation in the final books are strictly subordinate to the lead players'. Of characters encountered outside Ithaca, only Odysseus himself has an endgame role. In fact, only Odysseus and Telemachus are at all empowered to cross episodic boundaries in the archipelago of plot. Otherwise, it is a ground rule that all players such as Calypso, Nausicaa, Alcinous, Polyphemus, and Circe are confined in the plot to their own narrative islands.

Second, the rule of introductions applies to the *divine* cast as well as the human. The *Odyssey* has greatly simplified the control-level structure of the *Iliad*, selecting three divine players to perform the three required roles in plot. Athene helps; Posidon opposes; Zeus mediates and if necessary overrules: these three Olympian agents, and only these, are assigned narrative portfolios in the opening council. The only other Olympian active in the poem is Hermes, whose purely ancillary function as messenger is also introduced (1.38–43) and immediately confirmed (84–7). Other gods, such as Ino–Leucothea and Hyperion, play strictly local and subordinate roles, while the terrestrial deities such as Calypso, Circe, and Scylla are not involved in the councils of control at all. Most of the Iliadic gods do not even appear, and the structure of the pantheon has been stripped to its minimum functional narrative core.

Among other benefits, this allows the *Odyssey* to deal much more elegantly with the problems of faction and authority raised by the abundant, partisan gods of the *Iliad*. In the *Odyssey*, there are only three effective divine players, and as agents of plot their motive, knowledge, and power are scrupulously defined in each case. In practice, only two of the three are fully important; as it turns out, there are virtually no significant differences in the distribution of *knowledge* among the divine players, whether of present or future game states.[7]

Posidon's rules of engagement are spelled out with singular clarity at 1.75: he will not kill Odysseus, but forces him to wander far from home. This is in punishment for Odysseus' blinding of Polyphemus, and we later learn the precise terms of the wounded Cyclops' granted prayer (IX.530–5): if Odysseus is already fated to reach Ithaca alive, let him come late, miserable, and alone, on a foreign ship, to find trouble at home. Posidon's interference, as already underlined at 1.21, will cease if and when Odysseus reaches Ithaca; and we learn in V that Odysseus is in practice safe from further action by Posidon once he reaches the *Phaeacian* coast, since Odysseus' home-coming is guaranteed by destiny from that point on (V.288–90). Posidon therefore pointedly exits from the poem at V.380–1, returning in XIII only to discharge his residual frustration on the Phaeacian navigators for abusing his favour in the service of his enemies – by which time his final appeasement has already been guaranteed by Tiresias' instructions (XI.121–37, their fulfilment promised at XXIII.248–84). There is no justification for the view that the theme of Posidon's wrath is mishandled or incompetently dropped from the story: the terminus of the wrath is meticulously defined from the outset.

Athene's aims are of course to fulfil Odysseus' personal goals of home-coming, vengeance, and prosperity, as well as to enhance the qualities and reputation of his son. But her power of intervention is inhibited in several ways. Outranked by Posidon, she cannot challenge his will or actions directly (VI.329–31, XIII.341–3). The celestial rivalry thus expresses and extends the poem's terrestrial theme of intelligence as a form of power. Athene is unable to outplay, or even to confront, Posidon in a face-to-face power-play: what she can do is to outwit him, turning an intangible advantage in knowledge into a practical advantage in the game. When Posidon is active in the story, however, Athene has no choice but to retire, as she scrupulously explains in answer to Odysseus' complaint at XIII.312–43. She is happy to steal a march during Posidon's temporary absence from the board (1.23–5, 48ff.), only to withdraw again when he returns in V; and it is only when Odysseus reaches Ithaca that she is free to involve herself fully in his cause.

Even that involvement is itself limited, however, by the nature of Athene's patronage. Athene values Odysseus for his resourcefulness of mind and body (see e.g. XIII.330–2, XXII.236–8); her strategy therefore is to use these, rather than her own powers, to determine the outcome.

---

[7] The one crucial exception is Posidon's absence in I–V.281, allowing a vital and irreversible move to take place behind his back.

Despite repeated pledges of support, her actual role in the Ithacan endgame is surprisingly limited: it is confined to Odysseus' supernatural disguise, the suggestion he visit Eumaeus, deflecting the suitors' spears in XXII, and some minor if pervasive psychological prompting all round. By contrast, all the planning and execution of the vengeance on the suitors is presented as the work of Odysseus' unaided intellect and prowess.

This is not accidental. The *Odyssey* wants as far as possible to *suppress* the overtly supernaturalist Iliadic metaplot, in favour of a more subtle, less directly visible machinery of control. This control is seen not in the openly miraculous manipulation of causality, but in the implicit demonstration of guaranteed narrative rules. In the *Odyssey*, these rules are above all *moral* rules, and their sole and sufficient enforcer is *Zeus*. Even though, as in the *Iliad*, the hand of Zeus is nowhere directly visible in the terrestrial action, the figure of Zeus lends authority to the moral sanctions accepted as part of the structure of cause and effect. For much of the time, including the whole of the Ithacan *Odyssey*, his interests run closely parallel with Athene's. But he is capable of endorsing other divine interests, including those of Posidon and Hyperion, when wider moral principles run counter to personal patronage.

The power and historical influence of this narrative conception can hardly be overstated. The spatio-temporal inventions discussed above certainly help the *Odyssey* to impose narrative closure on an open story universe. But more important still is the subjection of that entire universe to a set of *global rules of moral behaviour*, enforced, by the controlling intelligence of Zeus, as a principle of cause and effect as natural and binding as physical law. The principle is articulated by Zeus in the poem's first speech (1.32–4): mortals blame the gods, saying their sufferings come from us, but in fact they earn excess misery by their own transgressions. What is more (37), the gods ensure human responsibility by warning of the sin and its consequences in time to allow the perpetrator an escape. Inexorably, wilful transgression by mortals brings first a warning and then, if the warning is unheeded, disaster. And though Zeus's words in 34 allow room in principle for the unshakeable Greek conviction that some residue of suffering *is* unmerited, in practice the poem pursues the stronger implication that all suffering incurred by the players is the result of transgression by those players or their immediate kin.

What needs to be defined, however, is the rule-structure that determines what *constitutes* a transgression. Here, once again, the *Odyssey* is uncannily forthright and articulate, presenting its audience with a series of deft illustrations and analyses to establish the ground rules early on. Zeus's chosen illustration is the recurrent exemplum of Aegisthus, whose career of crime and punishment is a template for that of the suitors: warned against usurpation, murder, and designs on the queen, on pain of vengeance from a revenant son (1.39–41). This and other secondary narratives repeatedly define the schedule of crimes and penalties applicable in the primary narrative. Reminders can come from unexpected quarters: in the theologically frivolous *fabliau* of Ares and Aphrodite, for instance, another adulterer is brought unhappily to book, and the moral is drawn, 'Ill deeds never prosper; swift after all is outrun by slow' (Shewring's rendering of VIII.329). Even the gods, in other words, are subject to the three great Odyssean principles that will become virtual constants of the rule-system of classical narrative: that crime brings inevitable punishment, brain is intrinsically stronger than brawn, and trespass on another's sexual property is an invariably fatal violation.

As regularly in Greek thought, the fundamental category of offence is transgression of the legitimate boundary of respect between men and gods. The *Odyssey* is obsessively fussy about this boundary, even in quite casual interactions. Relentless ingenuity, for example, is spent on the principle that gods and their actions can only be successfully opposed by other gods – not by the unaided power of mortals. Whenever Odysseus faces a threat from a divine antagonist, he has to find another god from somewhere to assist with an injection of either power or information – as Ino against Posidon, Hermes against Circe and Calypso, Circe against Sirens and Scylla. More importantly, however, any mortal contempt for divine status or authority – including the civilised codes of ξενία and human respect that are enforced by divine sanction – invariably brings retribution, whether on the ogre Polyphemus, the beggar Irus, or even (in his blasphemous final outburst to the blinded giant) Odysseus himself.

So the supernatural world of the *Odyssey* is a carefully regulated one. Not only the individual divine supervisors, but the whole metaphysical framework of action and result follow a strict code established in the first book and repeatedly enforced in the episodes and the embedded narratives that follow. When Odysseus eventually reaches Ithaca, all the leading players find themselves for the first time together in the same zone of the board – so that the stage is set for a final, decisive test of the plot rules Odysseus and the reader have learned in the earlier books. In this sense, I–XII are a series of episodic *rehearsals* for the Ithacan endgame: training players and readers alike in the laws of the Odyssean universe, so as to be able to engage fully in the intricate process of plotting and anticipating the denouement.

To a great extent, the narrative roles of the human players themselves are straightforwardly defined in terms of these moral laws. Odysseus' desire, spelled out as early as 1.13, is for two things: νόστος (home-coming) and γυνή (wife). The overwhelming legitimacy and reasonable-ness of these goals is underlined by his explicit rejection of the more metaphysically perilous alternative offered by Calypso (v.206–24). Against this, the suitors' crime, as defined by Odysseus himself at XXII.35–41 immediately prior to executing sentence, is to assert illegiti-mate claims to his *oikos* ('estate': he means property, household, and palace, along with the roots of individual identity) and wife, in defiance of the moral judgement (*nemesis*) of all gods and men. The *social* technical-ities of the suitors' ambitions and claim on Penelope have been much debated,[8] but in *narrative* terms they are straightforward enough: an attempt to dispossess the absent Odysseus of all but one of the Ithacan goals of his return – wife, son, house, household, property, kingship. Only father Laertes, less vulnerable and less of a chattel than the rest, escapes the suitors' attention, thanks to his judicious prior removal from their sphere of action. The poem has clearly thought hard about, and finally rejected, a role for Laertes in the palace situation. His withdrawal not only disencumbers the game of a morally and strategically uncomfortable complication, but cleverly locates the zenith of emotion in the reunion with Penelope, with Laertes held in judicious reserve for an epilogue.

To heighten these moral antitheses in narrative role, the suitors are systematically presented as transgressors of *all* the other values the poem and its gods hold dear – scorning the rights of guests, strangers, and beggars, insulting the authority of elders and prophets, and plotting cold-blooded murder against an unsuspecting minor. Even so, they are repeat-edly presented, by increasingly frequent and direct warnings both human and supernatural, with a generous chance to escape retribution. That to a man they pass the chance up – even the sympathetic Amphinomus resumes his seat after Odysseus' moving appeal – is a sign not of limited moral awareness or competence, neither of which would offer a legitimate narrative reason for their slaughter, but of flawed moral will, which does.

This articulation of large-scale action around a precise moral syllogism of action and consequence is one of the *Odyssey*'s most enduring legacies to narrative art. It has become the canonical model of happy endings: virtue is rewarded, vice punished in appropriate measure, according to whether the characters' motivating desires conform to or flout the story-world's moral codes. But scarcely less influential has been the *Odyssey*'s plotting of the other two dimensions of difference between players – in particular, the axis of *knowledge*, and its new relationship to the axis of power.

[8] Recent discussions, with complementary approaches and bibliography, in West 1988: 58–9, Katz 1991: 170–2, Thalmann 1998 (esp. 180–2).

Quite unlike the *Iliad*, the *Odyssey* begins from a plot configuration based on vast inequalities in the distribution of game knowledge among players. Nobody but Odysseus and the gods knows whether he is alive or dead; Odysseus knows nothing up-to-date of events in Ithaca, whether Penelope is loyal, whether Laertes and Telemachus are alive. Such information as he has is nine years old, and unmentioned outside XI.[9] Over the course of the poem, these imbalances of information will need to be adjusted – preferably, for classical reasons, in moments of sudden and climactic *recognition*.

In the event, and for sound narrative reasons, the hero is hardly ever recogniser, always recognisee. Only limited use is made of Odysseus' own ignorance of crucial game information. He is at his weakest on first arrival in unfamiliar narrative environments, new islands in the plot archipelago. Even so, all but two of these are narrated in the first person, with liberal illumination from hindsight; so that in effect we are still positioned to follow his deductions from a vantage of superior knowledge. The exceptions, where the reader does arrive first, are significantly the first and last in the narrative sequence: the climactic landfalls on Scheria and Ithaca, the programmatic and the final test-demonstrations of the hero's deductive and communicative skills.

Consider the first of these: VI.119ff., where Odysseus is awakened by female shrieking and deliberates its implications. The reader, who has spent the book so far on an elaborate narrative detour following Athene to town and Nausicaa back to the beach, knows precisely the source and significance of the sound, and the (in fact favourable) answer to Odysseus' lugubrious question 'Where am I, and are the inhabitants friendly?'[10] But Odysseus, crawling nude and bedraggled from under a bush to find himself face to face with a startled gaggle of aristocratic virgins, has a second or two of story time (eked out by the narrative clock as the wry simile 130–6) to divine at sight what the reader has been told over a hundred lines. Impressively, he manages to deduce from this momentary glance that Nausicaa is indeed human (150–2 is astute blarney: 153ff. would hardly be addressed to one suspected of actual divinity), lives in town (178) with parents and brothers (154–5) but thinks obsessively on marriage (158–9, 180ff.), likes dancing (157), and is here on laundry business (179). Our astonishment at Odysseus' prodigies of detection is kept within plausible bounds only by our acceptance of all this information as effectively already in the public narrative domain.

---

[9] There is a famous anachronism here, since the suitors began their infestations long after the notional date of the interview with Tiresias when Odysseus learned of them. At XIII.383 he expresses surprise at Athene's report.

[10] Lines 119–21 recur with similar ironic effect on his awakening in Ithaca, XIII.200–2.

Even so, the scene further establishes Odysseus as a figure gifted with heroic powers of intellect and observation: not the sort of man whom relevant information easily eludes.

In practice, however, there is far more dramatic scope in the flow of information *from* Odysseus rather than *to* him, for two good narrative reasons. Firstly, there are many more characters involved, allowing the same information to be reused over and over in different player combinations. The secret of Odysseus' identity, for instance, yields seven separate scenes of recognition: with Telemachus, Argus, Eurycleia, Eumaeus and Philoetius, suitors, Penelope, and Laertes. Indeed, the contrasting revelatory techniques of these scenes – planned or accidental, verified by outward signs or inner information – have been a comprehensive model for such scenes in later plotting. Aristotle, who saw the seminal role of the *Odyssey* here, was inspired to suggest his famous typology of recognition techniques, ranked in order of sophistication (or classicality): from *ad hoc* improvisations of birthmark or blurting to processes of syllogistic reasoning by character and reader from established story premises.[11]

Second, the *Odyssey* is fully aware of the plot principle that information is a latent form of narrative *power*. Unlike the *Iliad*, which expresses power in relentlessly actualised and physical terms, the *Odyssey* repeatedly asserts the value of communication, and its refusal, as forces in the configuration of power relationships. Straightforward contests of undisguised physical power, the bread and butter of Iliadic plotting, are virtually non-existent in the *Odyssey*. Even the studiedly Iliadic combat in XXII gives more weight to strategic advantage than is ever the case in the *Iliad*. In the *Odyssey*, in fact, physical and communicative skills regularly find themselves contrasted or even conflicting, to the former's invariable detriment: so with the ruse of Hephaestus in Demodocus' song, with the Cyclops, and with the numerous moments in the palace books where the abused Odysseus has to make an active choice between physical retaliation and strategic silence. A favourite situation type (Nausicaa, the Cyclops, revenge on the suitors at odds of 108:1) places Odysseus in a critical confrontation where he has been systematically stripped of harnessable physical power, obliging him to improvise a narrative advantage from the resources of his naked wits.

And because this use of communication as power is so strongly tied to the figure of Odysseus himself, in practice it is not in the narrative interest to subject him to shocks of discovery comparable to those he visits on others. Rather, his information-gathering (especially in VI-VIII and

---

[11] *Poetics* 16.1454b19–55a21. Aristotle fails to make it explicit that his fundamental objection is to scenes where the process is *under the recognisee's control* – a situation of considerable affective power, but of negligible plot complexity.

XIV–XIX) is methodical and controlled, in notable contrast to other characters with less sense of the currency value of information. As a key article by Rutherford (1986) has shown, the events of IX–XII educate Odysseus progressively into a strategy of careful economy with the truth, which will serve him well in Ithaca. The one mortal player with comparable resources of intellectual and communicative skill is, of course, Penelope – whose rounds against the suitors demonstrate a similar scope for informational advantage to defend a game position under apparently overwhelming attack. Tellingly, therefore, the poem's dramatic climax is not the decisive confrontation of brain against brawn in XXII, but the unique brain-against-brain confrontation of these well-matched arch-communicators in XXIII.

Not only, however, can plot knowledge be withheld and released: it can also in the *Odyssey* be *falsified*, allowing the further complication of erroneous as well as incomplete models of the game state by individual characters. In contrast to the *Iliad*, whose only pathological liars are gods, there is a great deal of lying in the *Odyssey* – so much, that it has sometimes been seen as an ethically neutral activity.[12] The result of this proliferation of false stories, especially in the Ithacan books, is an intricate web of *modalities*, with different characters' internal models of the game state ironically juxtaposed for the reader.

A single illustration will indicate the range and complexity of effects available. There is little in ancient narrative – outside Plato, there is nothing – to match the modal acrobatics of XIV.462–506, where Odysseus (as beggar) spins Eumaeus a yarn about Odysseus at Troy.[13] Eumaeus, who has survived Odysseus' extended mind-games in this book remarkably well, is aware that the story is not the drunken boast it claims, but a tribute to *Odysseus* at the narrator's expense; that it is, moreover, not true; and that its subtext ('lend me a cloak') is its true speech-act function. What *we* hear, however, is far more complex even than this: we hear a fivefold nest of concentric falsehoods, a dream within a lie within a lie within a masquerade within a fiction (Figure 1). At the top level (1), the

---

[12] In fact, it is bound by a subtle but consistent code of practice violated only in the problematic Laertes scene. There is a clear distinction between mere *suppressio veri* and the active propagation of falsehood. The former is widely tolerated: it is taken for granted in both poems that all characters hold things back, even characters as close as Odysseus and Penelope or Nausicaa and Alcinous. But deliberate lying is only permissible down either a social or a moral gradient unrecognised by the victim. Thus Odysseus may comfortably lie to Polyphemus, Eumaeus and the suitors, but not to Nausicaa, Alcinous (barring the benign improvisation at 304–7), or – to judge from his reluctance at XIX.107–22, 165–71 – to Penelope. Equally, the suitors' hypocrisy to Penelope is repellent at XVI.448.

[13] Kirk 1962: 360 singles this speech out as 'one of the poorest digressions in the whole poem'; for more sympathetic discussions see Goldhill 1991: 41–2; Pratt 1993: 89; Segal 1994: 155–6, 178; Olson 1995: 131–3.

poet is singing us, the audience, a third-person tale about Odysseus. Within that tale (2), Odysseus is playing a first-person role to Eumaeus, with the outer world as unseen audience. In that role (3), he tells his audience of herdsmen a tale about Odysseus at Troy, disguising its first-person relationship to its subject by placing the narrator elsewhere in the recounted story. In that story (4) Odysseus reports an invented dream to a two-tiered audience, composed of the beggar-to-be (who is aware of the lie) and Thoas and the other scouts (who are not); and in the dream itself (5), a god gives Odysseus a message. As Eumaeus sees, there is a clear vertical symmetry between the narrative situations in levels 3 and 4: in both the act of lying yields the beggar/Odysseus a cloak from the audience. Eumaeus thinks he has cleverly broken the intended symmetry by surrendering the cloak of his own will, instead of by being taken in. In fact, in so doing he falls victim to the higher-level fiction (2) – and even completes the symmetry, by ensuring that the dupe on both levels passes the cloak to the narrator of the next level up (Thoas to the beggar, Eumaeus to Odysseus).

Astonishingly, *every one* of these narrative levels harbours an epistemological ambiguity. First the poet (1) introduces the episode by spelling out in his own narratorial voice Odysseus' true intentions (459–61), inviting us to read the subtextual game being played out beneath the surface of the words. Next (2), as XIV as a whole has demonstrated, Eumaeus accepts the beggar is a beggar, but is aware that at least some of what he says is invention – how much, he is not yet certain. The Trojan tale (3) is misleadingly framed as a heroic reminiscence; Eumaeus has to register the discrepancy between frame and picture, and understand that it should be resolved by discarding the frame. In (4), the narrated viewpoint is a privileged one: having eavesdropped on the earlier conversation between the I-character and Odysseus, we are once again aware that the immediate audience is being hoodwinked and the real purpose of the report connects, in ways not yet apparent, to the goal defined by its narrative context. Finally, Homeric dreams (5) are, in any case, notoriously unreliable; this one, even if it were (a) real and (b) correctly interpreted, could easily emanate from the gate of ivory.

The narrative legacy of such passages is profound, and goes far beyond the mere proliferation of embedded story models. Not only the *quantity* of these interior subworlds but their *quality* is essential to the operations of plotting. As the latest wave of Odyssean criticism has highlighted,[14] the *Odyssey* revels in this kind of indeterminacy of embedded worlds. The reader is actively invited to construct the modal contents of the players'

---

[14] Goldhill 1991: 1–68, Peradotto 1990, Katz 1991, Felson-Rubin 1993; Doherty 1995.

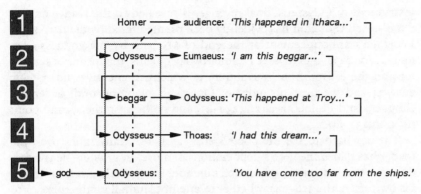

Figure 1. The cloak tale

minds – their beliefs, intentions, desires – from their outward behaviour and speech; yet on entry to their heads finds sometimes little more than a hall of mirrors. Like real people, the *Odyssey*'s players can seem undecided about what they think or want, and only the most impervious literalist would try to explain away every single case as compositional irregularities. Beliefs and wants are not always simple, unambivalent things; real people contradict themselves without any help from neoanalytic conflation. And the *Odyssey* likes to exploit this tension between the closed and the open, the determinate and the unresolved – between the reader's desire for a world of closure, certainty, resolution, and the unfinishedness of people and events in real life. The poem knows that its readers will try to construct a determinate model of everything in the story, and it plots its narrative matrix of possibilities accordingly. But to keep us working, it refuses the certainty of closure, at least for so long as the book remains open. In making sense of a narrative world as a universe of latent possibilities, the reader is constantly choosing his or her own adventure from the garden of forking pathways in the text. Some will be confirmed in subsequent narrative, many more discarded, and others still perhaps left open at the story's end.

As a purely psychological device, this active encouragement of reading between the lines is not alien to the *Iliad*, though there is a good deal more of it in the *Odyssey*.[15] What is new in the *Odyssey*, however, is its deliberate and dynamic use in plotting. As the *Odyssey* unfolds, the hermeneutic demands on the reader are carefully *increased*, until eventually we are excluded even from the hero's own processes of thought. In a daring and massively influential narrative *coup*, the stratagem of the bow, chief

---

[15] Griffin 1980a: 50–80 is the *locus classicus*.

instrument of Odysseus' final revenge, is revealed to the reader only at
XXI.4 – even though it has evidently been premeditated by the hero since
Penelope's announcement at the end of XIX, and by the goddess even
longer. At XX.38–43 Odysseus frames two problems, the means of slaughter and the escape from retribution, to which Athene gives no specific
answer; and we hear no more of Odysseus' planning until he enlists
Eumaeus and Philoetius at XXI.230–41, and nothing on the second point
till XXIII.131–40.

It is not hard to see the poem's strategy here. Many times over, the
reader has *shared* the hero's deliberations of move. In V, where he is introduced, we follow him in three such inner debates: whether to trust Ino or
his own strength (356–64), whether to attempt landfall on the rocks or to
swim further along the coast for a likelier spot (408–23), and whether to
risk exposure or wild predators in his choice of pallet (465–73). The high
occurrence of soliloquies in this book is not just dictated by the solo
action: it also serves to introduce us to the hero's strategies of choice.
Other contemplations of alternative moves occur in the encounter with
Nausicaa (VI.141–7), the Cyclops' cave (IX.299–305), the release of the
winds from Aeolus' bag (X.49–53), the sight of Circe's smoke (X.151–5),
the demurral of Eurylochus (X.438–45), and the duel with Irus
(XVIII.91–4). The regular pattern (review of two options, the second of
which is adopted) is significantly varied at the crucial XVII.235–8, where
Odysseus contemplates two forms of retaliation against Melanthius and
rejects *both* for the un-Iliadic option of suffering in silence. In addition to
all these are the many occasions where a strategic choice is presented in
the form of information or advice to or from a second party, and the innu-
merable actions for which a strategic purpose is stated or implied.

What the reader is being treated to here is an education in Odyssean
thinking, with the final exercise left for the reader to solve unprompted
from the information at Odysseus' disposal. The reward for correct inference is a satisfying anticipation of the details of endgame, our interest in
which has been systematically stimulated since the first Ithacan scene
(especially 1.163–5).[16] By observing and collating the strategic issues in
the choices listed above, for instance, the reader will grasp that the semblance of friendly help should not be trusted (Ino); that uncertain risks
are preferable to certain ones (the bush); that the more commanding
interpersonal move may not be the most effective (Nausicaa); that short-
term advantage may be longer-term suicide (Polyphemus); that surrender to circumstances is *never* an Odyssean option (the bag of winds); that
the hero's responsibility to the group outweighs his individual inclinations

---

[16] Sternberg 1978: 56–89 offers an invaluable analysis of the evolution of the reader's plot
model from clues and, equally important, gaps in the exposition of I-V.

(Circe's island); and, most difficult of all, that the heroic response may sometimes be to suppress the heroic response (Irus, Melanthius). All of these principles are later applied in decisions where the stakes are far higher: Odysseus' testing of friendly support in XIV-XIX; his choice of Scylla over Charybdis; his disguised home-coming; his concealment of the truth from Penelope; his resistance to Calypso; his rescue of the crew from Circe; and his passive response to the suitors' abuse of his beggar persona. Like Odysseus, we learn to apply the lessons of past experience to the construction of future action – with the comfortable knowledge that, unlike Odysseus', our own survival does not depend on getting it right.

Perhaps the most powerful such Odyssean exercise in plot extrapolation is the widespread technique of narrative *bricolage*, or improvisation of resources from the limited *données* of a near-empty narrative environment. A famous example is VI.128–9, where the naked and resourceless hero has the presence of mind to improvise a token attempt at clothing from the olive-bushes planted in the narrative at V.476ff. Particularly classical and satisfying in its economy is the way the bushes serve more than one plot function, having been first introduced to provide Odysseus shelter in sleep. The discharge of one function has the narrative effect of 'unflagging' the prop, disarming the reader from expecting more and other uses even though it is firmly planted in the narrative. In a similar way, we are attractively surprised by Odysseus' ingenious survival use of the Charybdis fig-tree at XII.432, when the landmark seemed originally introduced (103) purely as a topographical pointer. There is especially fine plotting in Circe's formulation of the rule (197) that Charybdis is unsurvivable, founded as it is on the premise that he approaches in a ship. As it turns out, on the return visit this premise no longer holds, and Odysseus finds an escape against all programmed expectation yet without departing from the rules as given.

Before the final battle in the megaron, the most elaborate such instance of narrative *bricolage* is the Cyclops' cave. Here, as later at the crisis, is a literally sealed story environment, with only the natural props of daily routine from which to improvise a release – and the single addition of Odysseus' super-strength wine, itself admitted for a legitimate and quite different function to that it eventually serves, laid down in the narrative well ahead of its actual broaching (IX.196–213). Otherwise, essential props are introduced casually, as naturalistic scene-setting: the sheep (237–8), fire (251), and staff (319ff.). Similarly, essential boundary conditions are set as part of the essential ethnographic background: the isolated, precommunal homesteads (so the neighbours' concern can be readily deflected by a ruse on the accusative of 'nobody'); pre-agricultural pastoralism (whence the sheep, but inexperience of wine); ignorance of seafaring (shutting off pursuit); and daily routine of penning the sheep in the cave by night, and accompanying them to pasture by day (so that the cave is empty during the day, allowing the stake to be prepared, and unblocked every morning, allowing escape). There is one weak detail (the unmotivated novelty of bringing the male animals into the cave on the fateful night), but otherwise the episode is a model for classical plot economy – as well, perhaps, as for Odysseus' own plotting of the show-down – and fully warrants the pride in it suggested by the frequent cross-references elsewhere.[17]

So information in the *Odyssey* serves three important functions largely unexploited in the *Iliad*. It leads to much greater complexity in the pro-liferation of embedded worlds; it plays a vital part in the reader's herme-neutic education; and it is the most abundant isotope of narrative *power*. Unlike the *Iliad*, in fact, the *Odyssey* begins by defining a severe imbalance of harnessable power, and challenges the reader to guess how it will finally be overcome. Despite his advantage in legitimate goals and information control, Odysseus is at a severe practical disadvantage to obtain his desires. He begins the narrative trapped by invincible supernatural power on an unknown island, lacking all friends, means, or opportunity of action. Even should he reach Ithaca, he is outnumbered a hundred to one by the suitors and much more than that by their kin, and they, not he, control the palace. As the first book reminds us, these are hefty odds, not obviously improved by sending Telemachus away to the Peloponnese. Our curiosity is invited not merely as to how Odysseus reached this unfor-tunate nadir, but far more importantly how his undoubted moral and intellectual excellences can be actualised in a form capable of overcoming the sheer physical odds stacked against him, however Iliadic his prowess.

It is these questions, more than anything, that sustain the plot's momentum as a whole. Compared with the *Iliad*, the *Odyssey* exercises far more sustained and deliberate control over its reader's modelling of *endgame*: the time, place, agents, conditions, and outcome of the final moves that will resolve the narrative tensions. As in the *Iliad*, there will in the event be three stages, defined in our texts by each of the last three books. The first and strongest discharge is in XXII, where the principal antagonists meet in open combat to the death. Cheekily, the *Odyssey* seeks to cap the *Iliad*'s one-on-one showdown by vastly increasing the odds against him: the fatalistic tone of *Iliad* XXII, where the hero's victory is never in doubt and sympathy lies more with his victim, gives way to a comforting sense of moral certainty and triumph over the odds. In both

---

[17] I.69, II.19, VI.5, VII.206, X.200, X.435, XII.209, XX.19, as well as XXIII.312.

poems, however, this resolution turns out to be false or at least incomplete: the dead have kin, whose claims must also be acknowledged and resolved in xxiv.[18] This final settlement in both cases movingly juxtaposes the hero's lost reunion with his father (allowed in the *Odyssey*, pointedly denied in the *Iliad* and surrogated instead through Priam) with the loss felt by the father(s) of his slain enemies. Again the *Odyssey* seeks to improve on the *Iliad* by multiplying numbers and satisfying the sense of justice; again we feel the humane complexities get somewhat blunted in the process. And between the xxii duel and the xxiv reconciliation is a book devoted to the hero's restoration: his status, authority, and private relationships re-established, with a curtain-call review of the players or episodes whose role in the story is done.

This pattern of close has a long influence over the Greek sense of an ending. We have already noticed (above, p. 71) the taste for placing the biggest discharge of narrative energy at the beginning, rather than the end, of the process of *lysis*; thus the lead villain Antinous is killed *first* of the suitors, not last as we would nowadays expect (and as indeed happens, for example, in the 1954 film adaptation *Ulysses*). The Roman preference, from Plautus to the *Aeneid*, is much more like the modern classical ending: loose ends are carefully tidied away beforehand, and the narrative breaks off as early as possible after the main affective release. What is still more influential, however, is the *Odyssey*'s organisation of its whole narrative *around and towards* this emerging resolution. As we saw in the last chapter, the *Iliad* does allow a picture of later events to take shape gradually as the narrative unfolds. But the *Odyssey* is far more deliberate and detailed in its mapping of the road ahead; and far more preoccupied with maximising its reader's curiosity, by selecting what information to release in what order. Even Sternberg's meticulous reading of the early exposition (cited in n. 16) and Olson's of xiii–xxi (1995: 141–60) paint only corners of this picture, so it seems worth attempting an outline here of the whole.

First, the slyly elliptical proem (1.1–10), while underlining the principle

[18] This is not to deny the disturbing problems over the poem's ending from xxiii.297, and in particular the slide into a more 'Cyclic' mode of narrative and plotting. In the kind of usefully question-begging *de facto* unitarian view taken here of the epics, the text is discussed *qua* the text the ancient world read and emulated as a unity, regardless of the complex, piecemeal, and largely irrecoverable events that led to that text's creation. But it would be cowardly to wriggle entirely off the hook. For reasons treated on these pages, it seems to me certain that the terrestrial events of xxiv, the Laertes scene and the involvement of the suitors' kin, are essential to the poem's total plot, being not only assumed but pointedly foreshadowed in the rest of the poem, and especially in the second book; but something seems to have gone strangely awry in the narrative execution. A good review of the complex literature and issues in Heubeck 1992: 342–5, to which add now Rutherford 1992: 14–16 and especially Henderson 1997.

of human responsibility for suffering, omits any mention not only of the suitors, but (as has less often been noted) of Odysseus' return. Though hinted at in the digression on his comrades' failed home-coming (5–9), it has to wait until 17 to become explicit, and even there we are only told it is imminent within a year, with Posidon still hostile. The suitors themselves are quite casually introduced, by Athene at 91–2, and though details of their uncomfortable conduct are scattered through the scene that follows it is not until Telemachus' speech at 158–68 that they are clearly identified as a problem Odysseus must confront in person. Laertes' circumstances are outlined at 188–93, but in terms indicating he will *not* be a critical component of the endgame. Athene's promise at 200–5, like all such, omits to set a precise time-limit to Odysseus' imminent homecoming; her only amplification is to signal at 266 that the suitors' punishment will be death, at Odysseus' own hands. But 295 (where Telemachus is improbably suggested as the avenger) locates the hypothetical slaughter ἐνὶ μεγάροισι τεοῖσι, 'in your palace', and the next line adds the further teaser 'by secret means or open', a formula we shall meet again.

So by the end of the first book we are already sketching in a future murderous showdown in the palace, perhaps involving guile on Odysseus' side. But we know nothing yet of when and how it will come about, or of how Odysseus found himself on Ogygia and how he will be delivered to Ithaca. The second book adds relatively little on these burning questions; craftily, it introduces instead some alarming complications. Odysseus, we learn, will have to deal not just with the suitors, but with their kin – who here ignore the warning from Telemachus and Mentor not to wash their hands of responsibility, and thereby put themselves in the firing-line for XXIV. The ruse of Penelope's weaving, too, deepens the sense of urgency: despite the careful omission of any guarantee that she would actually remarry on completion of Laertes' shroud, there is an implication of approaching deadline. Evidently the year's grace hinted at in 1.16 and 288 is far too generous, and the crisis is a matter of weeks rather than months away. Otherwise, Zeus's portent and Halitherses' authoritative exegesis confirm the prospect of massacre, but there is only one significant new detail. Halitherses' ἄγνωστον, 'incognito' (II.175), signals that Odysseus' return will indeed be secret rather than public. (But how, and with what result?) Telemachus, meanwhile, undertakes to let the outcome of his journey decide his conduct on return: if he finds Odysseus is alive, he will continue to resist the suitors; if dead, he will consent to Penelope's remarriage. Yet this, like the terms of the truce in *Iliad* III with their closely comparable role in the narrative plan, is a red herring. Though the conditions seem between them to exhaust the possibilities, neither in fact will be met, so that the consequences programmed into them become void.

Telemachus will in the event return with no certain word, and the situation will be no more resolved than ever.

No new details of the finale emerge in III-IV, though the narrative is careful to ink over the lines of our existing picture. Nestor and Menelaus both repeat the assurance of vengeance (III.216–24, IV.335–46 – the latter echoing Athene at 1.266), though Nestor plants the false clue (contradicting Halitherses' stronger prediction, if we have been alert) that Odysseus may return with an army at his back (217). The paradigmatic analogies with the Agamemnon–Aegisthus–Orestes story are pursued further, yielding an increasingly elaborate matrix of possible developments, not all by any means encouraging.[19] The strange exchange of drugged tales from Helen and Menelaus gives us some glimpses of possibly relevant Odyssean tactics (disguise and infiltration, resistance to counter-intrigue); but we have only the principle of classical economy to assure us they will actually be used, and as yet no inkling of how. The Ithacan scenes at the end of IV exclude Laertes further from consideration as an active force in the crisis, though by the same token we now expect a reunion scene at minimum. But we still know nothing of the timing or circumstances of Odysseus' return, let alone how he can contrive the promised massacre.

The first half of this question is finally answered by Zeus's edict at v.29–42 – though he artfully omits to gloss the 'sufferings' Odysseus will encounter en route (33), or to carry his projection further than the arrival in Ithaca. But we have to wait for Tiresias' predictions, amplifying the Cyclops' reference to 'trouble at home', for the next mention of Odysseus' vengeance on the suitors (XI.118–20, echoing Athene's words to Telemachus in I), and the main body of his instructions is clearly going to be hard to fulfil within what we have up to now modelled of the finale. We learn rather more from Anticleia's description of the pathetic plight of Laertes (187–96), with the urgent suggestion that Odysseus' return may be too late to prevent the old man's sharing her fate: again a promise of a Laertes scene, but of what kind and in what context is still teasingly opaque. The tale of Agamemnon returns, its exemplary status now very complex and ambiguous: we leave the underworld with an awareness more of possibilities open than of resolutions closed.

With Athene's interview in XIII, we reach a turning-point. Here at last we learn something of the strategy to come (303–10, 397–415). But it is a purposely incomplete account, raising more fresh questions than it answers old ones. We learn that the Phaeacian gifts, Odysseus' first source of anxiety on waking, will *not* be a part of the plan; that Odysseus will have

[19] Katz 1991: 29–48; Olson 1995: 24–42.

silently to endure abuse in his own palace; that he will be disguised; and that he will not go directly to the palace, but to the hitherto unmentioned Eumaeus. None of this significantly amplifies what we already know, and despite Odysseus' request that Athene should 'weave me a stratagem for revenge' (386, tr. Shewring), she in fact says nothing at all on the critical question of how the suitors can be killed. Instead, we now want to know not only the plan and timing of Odysseus' vengeance, but how and when he will even reach the palace, what kind of abuse he will suffer, how well he will sustain his disguise in the face of it, and when and how both will be thrown off. None of these questions is answered by the Eumaeus scenes, which serve rather to underline the odds Odysseus faces in the palace: the number and strength of the suitors, their violence even towards beggars, and (a new element) the hard-learned scepticism even of those loyal to Odysseus' memory. There is much sophisticated rehearsal of persona and persuasion, and the very dense texture of irony and psychological inter-play is important preparation for the intricate human detail of the palace books, but the poem still teases us with glimpses of strategies whose full articulation is withheld.

It is only in XVI, following the first of the great recognitions (itself thus marking the beginning of the final movement), that Odysseus and Telemachus analyse their prospects, and hatch their plans in detail. It is a remarkable passage, hardly less for its omissions and misdirections than for what it actually reveals. Telemachus identifies the greatest obstacle as the suitors' numbers; Odysseus nevertheless insists no further players be admitted to the conspiracy, apparently stacking the already impossible odds still further. Laertes has already been further excluded at 136–53; now Eumaeus and Penelope are named also (302–3). Since we already know that Odysseus must make himself known to both Laertes and Penelope by the end of the poem, this has the effect of splitting the pro-jected endgame into three: the suitors, Penelope, and Laertes are separate issues, and the two climactic recognitions must succeed the showdown in an order yet to be determined.

How, then, are the suitors to be overcome? Odysseus will continue to play his beggar role in the palace; Telemachus on a pretext will remove all arms from the hall, leaving a set each for Odysseus and himself; with these, they will attack the unarmed suitors in the hall itself; and Athene and Zeus will work some miracle to swing the combat in the heroes' favour (281–98). The passage has been regularly athetised since antiquity for its discrepancies with XIX.1–52 and XXII; but most of the later modifications are due to unforeseeable new factors, and the gaps in the plan here look like calculated posers. We now know that the showdown with the suitors will take place in the hall, will synchronise with Odysseus' dropping of his disguise, and will attempt to even the odds by ensuring that Odysseus and Telemachus are armed while the suitors are not. But we do not know *when* all this will happen (Athene, we are told at 281, will put it into Odysseus' mind) or how even two armed heroes can defeat the hundred-odd suitors short of a miracle (Athene and Zeus will work some magic on them, 298). These supernatural struts in the plan identify precisely those details that the narrative is saving for suspense: the timing of the final moves, and the decisive ruse. In the event, of course, no miracle is involved at either point, and it would be most out of keeping if it were. The references to supernatural input are simply a narrative flag to identify, for the reader's benefit, crucial gaps in the endgame model that will be filled in at the last possible moment.

All this planning and conspiracy, of course, has a long future in the *Odyssey*'s narrative progeny. Plots make excellent plots. If the game state can be assessed and anticipated by its own players, the move-structure becomes explicit and articulate without any violation of transparency. The one difficulty comes in sustaining suspense: if the plan we have heard expounded at length succeeds, the story is in danger of becoming *too* predictable. Surprise (ἔκπληξις) is banished if everything goes according to a pre-announced pattern. There are two solutions, equally valid, that combine to produce one of the most widespread rules in classical plotting: *if the plan is fully reported, it will fail.*[20] The only way to surprise the reader once a stratagem has been outlined in detail in the text is for something to go wrong with that stratagem; if nothing goes wrong, the only way to preserve surprise is to suppress key details of the scheme in its presentation to the reader. This is the Odyssean solution: we are *told* there is, or will be, a plan; but we are *shown* its details as and when they are individually put into effect.

Thanks to the conspiracy scene, then, we know when Odysseus and Telemachus move to the palace in XVII that all the endgame players are in position in the prescribed location. Knowing we know this, the narrative deliberately draws out the suspense. Outrage upon outrage is heaped on Odysseus by his enemies, with retaliation postponed: this further massive accumulation of narrative energy is held in readiness for its final discharge in the showdown. Because all the necessary pieces are in place, we are ready for the signal to be given at any moment; in fact the narrative is playing games with us, as we have not been told the finale will take place that day, and in the event the suitors disband for the night before Odysseus triggers the first stage of the plan, the removal of the arms, at the beginning of XIX. That tells us at last that the crisis *will* come the

---

[20] A good discussion of this principle in Ryan 1986a: 331.

following day, when the suitors return to a hall subtly refashioned as Odysseus' trap; but we still know no more than we did in XVI of how the trap will be sprung. Penelope confirms this by designating the coming day as the deadline for her own decision, and setting the contest of the bow as final determinant of her fate – both conditions with which Odysseus expresses full satisfaction. Further confirmation that the day of vengeance has indeed dawned comes throughout XX: the omen of the corn-grinder (ἤματι τῶιδε, 116), Odysseus' promise to Philoetius (σέθεν ἐνθάδ' ἐόντος, 232), and finally the narrator's own authoritative statement closing the book (τάχ' ἔμελλε, 393; closely followed by φόνου ἀρχήν, XXI.4).

As for the *manner* of the showdown, again the narrative deftly exploits the gap it has left in our story jigsaw. As already noted, we and Odysseus are told of Penelope's plans for the contest of the bow at XIX.571–87, yet only at XXI.4 do we learn for certain that it will be an instrument of power in the showdown. We, like Odysseus, have to make the connection by narrative *bricolage*: a challenge put openly in the questions framed for us in Odysseus' confession to Athene at XX.38–40. How, he asks, can I alone make a stand against the mass of suitors? And even if I do kill them, how can I get away with it? These questions, which Athene mischievously disdains to answer, are precisely the two story gaps that the plot wants to highlight as riddles to be solved in XXI-XXII and XXIV. By this stage the subsequent episodes of endgame, the recognitions with Penelope and Laertes, have fallen into place in the story model as consequent upon the slaying of the suitors – the Penelope scene clearly preceding, as she is to hand in the palace and in the primary narrative, while Laertes is still some way removed from both. There are, of course, some twists in reserve for both; but by now we are primed to expect what the poem considers it most useful for us to expect, and to keep guessing where the poem still means to surprise us.

This sustained, progressive determination of the reader's modelling of endgame over a text on the scale of the *Odyssey* is one of the most daring inventions in the history of narrative. It would be two centuries before anything detectably comparable was attempted, in a vastly different narrative mode and on a far more restricted textual scale; and it would take a full millennium before the means and the will were in place to emulate its plotting in a form and compass to rival the original. For the rest of antiquity, Homer and the *Odyssey* in particular remained the supreme textbook of plot technology, both for guiding principles and for detailed worked examples. But it might easily never have happened. That Homeric narrative ever became anything more than an isolated experiment seems entirely due to a second historical accident scarcely more explicable than the existence of the Homeric epics themselves: the invention, mass proliferation, and meteoric cultural ascendancy of Athenian tragic drama.

8   Dramatic myth: tragedy and satyr-play

The significance of early tragedy in the shaping of Western narrative taste is hard to overstate. In the archaic epic tradition, the *Iliad* and *Odyssey* were experiments without successors: not merely in their scale, but in the repertoire of techniques they devised to square the circle of strict narrative economy on a monumental scale. Some of those techniques were emulated in a narrower compass in other genres – the longer *Homeric hymns*, and perhaps the lyric narratives of Stesichorus – but it was only with Attic drama that Homeric plot values were consciously adopted and further extended in a massive and regular outflow of new texts. For Aristotle, it was tragedy even above epic that offered the definitive showcase for the kind of plot values he favoured – and especially, though by no means exclusively, the pioneer work of the fifth-century masters.

Tragedy's historical position here is due, I would argue, to a conjunction of four factors: tragedy's unusual status as an invented medium; the remarkable hegemony of myth in early Greek narrative culture; the close relationship the new narrative form seems to have sought with Homeric epic; and its unprecedented and institutionalised productivity. And the central contention of this chapter is that not only tragedy's most durable innovations in the art of plotting, but many of what we think of as the defining characteristics of fifth-century tragedy, are the product less of ritual, ideological, or sociohistorical factors than of primarily *narratological* pressures arising from these four circumstances – specifically, from the attempt to adapt what the fifth century admired in Homeric narrative to the alien medium of theatre, and from the resulting intensive exploration of the technical differences between epic and drama as carriers of narrative.

The first factor, in particular, is crucial. We far too easily underestimate the narratological novelty of tragic performance as a storytelling medium. Whatever subliterary dramatic traditions may have existed in the Greek-speaking world before 535 BC, Thespian tragedy seems to have been sufficiently different to have constituted a revolution in narrative art unparalleled before the advent of cinema. Indeed, there are suggestive similarities in the two forms' initial development and impact: the lowly,

'satyric' status of their early offerings; the mass adaptation of popular
stories from established media to new; the initial emulation of old-media
narrative techniques, gradually displaced by the invention of more appropriate devices specific to the new form; a deepening awareness of the
precise strengths and limitations of the new medium in comparison with
the old, and an increasing adroitness in the selection and tailoring of story
material to measure; the gradual evolution of a sophisticated repertoire of
semiotic codes and conventions peculiar to the invented medium; the
reciprocal influence of techniques from the new medium on latter-day
products in the old; a comparatively stable maturity achieved after a
couple of generations, after which the fundamental poetics of the new
medium is less susceptible to radical innovation.

But for the case of tragedy the relationship between old media and new
is complicated still further by the peculiar nature of its narrative inheritance. For tragedy takes over the reins of a narrative culture that privileges
the poetics of *retelling*: one in which high, serious storytelling is *de facto*
restricted to myth. Contemporary or historical subjects, such as
Phrynichus' *Sack of Miletus* and *Phoenician women*, disappeared early on;
the conceit that the struggles and achievements of the generation of
Marathon might be a worthy comparand to the age of Agamemnon seems
to have been the short-lived product of a narrow historical moment.
Wholly invented stories make just one abortive appearance at the end of
the century with Agathon's *Anthos* or *Antheus*: apparently an isolated
experiment, which itself stopped short of abandoning the heroic past as
its milieu. Contemporary fiction – entirely made-up stories in post-heroic
settings – remained the exclusive province of comedy. Even at a conservative guess, over half of the tragedians' extant plays would have climaxes
familiar enough (usually from well-known epic or earlier dramatic versions) to be predictable by the audience.[1] It is true that the extant treatments of some well-worn legends testify to considerable flexibility of
detail in the fifth century; but the flexibility is in the middle, not the end.
The kind of radical revision we meet in *Heracles* is something of an exception. It was simply not possible to present an Agamemnon who escaped
Clytemnestra's axe, or an Orestes who (in Aristotle's whimsical example)
made friends with Aegisthus and lived happily ever after.[2]

For the generations of its heyday, this was a limitation with which the

---

[1] My probably over-cautious list would run: *Persians, Seven, Agamemnon, Choephori,
Eumenides; Ajax, OT, Electra, Philoctetes; Hippolytus, Electra, Troades, Phoenissae, Bacchae,
IA, Cyclops; Rhesus.* We should remember, though, that the ancient selection, which
accounts for 24 of the extant 33, favoured the familiar over the recherché, so there is some
bias in the sample. The proportion is much lower in the Euripidean alphabeticals and, so
far as is safe to judge, the lost plays of all three.   [2] *Poetics* 13.1453a37–8.

genre was more than content to live. Myth remained an immensely powerful engine for the construction of meaning. It provided a symbolic algebra for the manipulation of communally significant categories and conflicts in narrative form; its aetiological links with the beginnings of things offered a historicising discourse in which contemporary institutions and conflicts could be collectively clarified; and at the same time it carried an inherent grandeur, authority, and claim to truth. These were important aspirations for a narrative form whose unspoken brief was to enact the ideology of the democratic polis.[3] The most important literary fact about Greek tragedy, its unparalleled semic density, is itself a close corollary of its espousal of myth – where every person, place, action, and utterance is set in a limitless web of other stories, other versions, and aetiological resonances, so that even minimal movement can send out immensely complex ripples of secondary association and meaning.[4]

More directly significant, however, for tragedy's contribution to the development of plotting are two *narratologically* striking aspects of Greek myth: its interconnectedness as story, and its transformationality as narrative. At the story level, myths are viewed not as self-sufficient modules but as *excerpts* from a collectively familiar corpus, whose global contents are familiar to the audience and part of the culture of reception. Individual stories assemble into larger constellations; beginnings and ends become arbitrary, and story composition is unusually dependent on *narrative* decisions like the opening and closing of the narrative window. And on the narrative level, still more importantly, myths are *recombinant*: predicates (narrative patterns) readily detach from their subjects (named mythological figures) and reattach themselves to others. It is not philosophically nonsensical to claim that tragic myths are literally alive, in the sense claimed by Dawkins and his successors for the notion of 'memes':[5] transmissible ideas that reproduce and evolve in the medium of culture by the rules of natural selection. In tragic plotting, as perhaps nowhere else in the history of narrative, we find the essential conditions for a process of accelerated evolution: replication with mutation by interfertilisation and recombination of genetic material; competition for resources, with improved survival rates the reward for success; and environmental pressure to reproduce prolifically.

Such recombinant fecundity is already actively encouraged in the epics by the pervasive and sophisticated use of mythological 'paradigm': the embedding in primary narrative of a secondary narrative whose event-structure suggestively parallels that of the top-level narrative even while

---

[3] So, especially, Goldhill 1988 and Seaford 1994.
[4] See Segal 1983, Calasso 1988, Buxton 1994, and especially Burian 1997.
[5] Dawkins 1989: 189–201, 322–31; Dennett 1995: 342–69; Lynch 1996.

its cast and setting are quite different, inviting the audience to abstract and compare the pure configurations of narrative form. But tragedy goes much further, using the internarrativity of myth as a machine for generating new narratives by the recycling of patterns and motifs between one story and another. Even among the extant plays, it is not uncommon to see a plot stripped down and rebuilt by its own author within the space of a few years – as Aeschylus does with *Persians* and *Agamemnon*, and Euripides with his *Heraclidae* and *Suppliants* and, especially, *Iphigenia in Tauris* and *Helen*. And an audience acclimatised to sixteen tragedies and satyr-plays a year would itself quickly assemble a vocabulary of major transferable narrative patterns and their transformational rules – which can then in its turn be taken for granted by the narrative process itself as part of the audience's toolkit for unpacking any new plots set before them.

Even the earliest tragedies surviving make this unconcealed cannibal reprocessing of earlier plot patterns a powerful resource of narrative economy and intertextual metaplotting. In *Persians*, Xerxes' invasion becomes a contemporary *Iliad*, an intercontinental epic as significant as the Trojan War itself, but one that the audience themselves have lived. Inverting the Homeric patterns of royal home-coming and court lamentation, Xerxes comes home as a failed Agamemnon, to be mourned by his court as an ignominious living Hector. In *Seven against Thebes*, an Iliadic γόος ending likewise invites parallels and contrasts with Hector, as Eteocles' open-eyed acceptance of his fate checks his Achilles and saves rather than dooms his city. In *Suppliants*, Aegyptus' Agamemnon leads an intercontinental armada to pursue his claims of sexual ownership over the chorus of fugitive Helens – who are simultaneously and paradoxically Penelopes, threatened with forced marriage to a horde of violent suitors. In *Ajax*, the hero's role modulates from Achilles to Hector, ironically collapsing the Homeric antitypes so that Ajax becomes his own worst enemy and executioner: his quarrel, alienation, and deconstruction of heroic 'codes' leading, through divine partisanship and *ate*, to his desertion of wife and son as he goes out to face his warrior's death alone, with a subsequent dispute over the proper treatment of his corpse resolved by an unexpected generosity of enemies. In *Trachiniae*, an Odyssean narrative template is similarly transformed by the fusion of antitypical roles: Deianeira is a Penelope manipulated by a conspiracy of errors into Clytemnestra, Hyllus a Telemachus turned Orestes.[6]

And by this time even the tiny corpus of extant plays is visibly beginning to recycle its *own* narratives in the same spirit of ironic recombina-

[6] Segal 1983: 183.

tion. The first part of *Agamemnon* may look like a retread of *Persians*, but this is not the real story – which is concealed, quite literally, behind closed doors until the moment when the tide of plot turns and the stage-door Charybdis disgorges its pent-up narrative burden. *Choephori* then retraces the identical narrative path from the viewpoint of conspirators rather than victims, with an increasingly insistent network of visual and situational echoes suggesting connections both thematic and, at a supernormal level, causative between successive phases of the curse. In its turn *Trachiniae*, with its bold ironic collapse of the *Odyssey*'s main plot with its own embedded inversion, alludes pervasively in staging and structure to the Aeschylean *Agamemnon*; while *Ajax* is the earliest known case of one of the most remarkable expressions of tragedy's pervasive internarrativity, a 'remake' of an earlier tragedy on the same mythological story events.[7]

But perhaps the most striking aspect of this recycling and recombination of narrative patterns is tragedy's obsessive emulation of qualities it admired in *Homeric* plotting. For in the complex of cultural developments that converged in the birth of tragedy in Pisistratean Athens, one of the most significant seems to have been the canonisation of 'Homer': the increasing perception of a qualitative difference between the *Iliad* and *Odyssey* on the one hand and the 'cyclic' epics on the other, and the reservation of the name of Homer for the two monumental epics only. And Herington (1985: 133–44) has made a powerful case for the emulation of this 'Homeric' narrative manner, as against its 'cyclic' alternative, as a guiding artistic motive in the early development of tragedy – certainly under Aeschylus, and very possibly before.

This emulation of Homer has two striking effects, with profound consequences for the future development of Greek narrative. First, simply as story matter, tragic myth itself undergoes a severe filtration. Dionysiac subjects are increasingly confined to the neighbour genre of satyr-play, while tragedy draws its myths instead from the epic corpus; and even within that corpus, the cyclic qualities of 'the comic, the fantastic, the bawdy, the annalistic, . . . the genealogical and the geographical'[8] that were still prominent ingredients in Aeschylus' lost early work have largely yielded by the end of his career to a sober Homeric naturalism, with only the persistence of such alien story motifs as kin-killing and madness to preserve the genetic memory of early tragedy's Dionysiac storylines.[9] The late, extant Aeschylus still experiments sporadically with non-mythological subjects (*Persians*), and with fantastic casts and supernatural scenarios or episodes (the Darius scene, *Eumenides*, the *Prometheus* plays true and

---

[7] The only certain remake datable earlier than *Ajax* is, intriguingly, the historical drama *Persians*.   [8] Herington 1985: 130.   [9] Seaford 1996 (building on 1994).

apocryphal); but even these traces have faded by the time of our earliest Sophocles.

Still more significant for the history of plot, however, is tragedy's emulation of Homeric *narrative* techniques, for here the process is not simply one of translation, but one of creative reinvention. Herington has already argued (1985: 125–50) that the evolution of tragedy from early Aeschylus to extant Sophocles shows tragedians gradually discovering how best to transfer certain key Homeric techniques to the new mode of drama – the relationship between tight primary and open secondary narrative, the suspenseful release of information to the narrative model, the suggestion of character behind the façade of speech. But few of the distinctively Homeric narrative devices aspired to by tragedy could be transplanted straight from the medium of epic to drama: most had to be radically adapted or reinvented to take account of the technical differences between the two narrative media. To appreciate, to explore, and to solve these differences took a long process of experiment and innovation stretched over two generations. What is astonishing, from our perspective, is that the discoveries should have been made as rapidly as they were.

Yet perhaps we should not be astonished. The sheer volume of new literary production represented by tragedy is staggering. Sophocles' lifetime output alone amounted to something in the region of ten *Iliads* – as much as the whole of Greek literature known to the Alexandrians from the period before the traditional date of Thespis' first play (535). For one of the effects of the establishment of the contest in tragedy at the City Dionysia was to institutionalise the regular production of new narrative poetry on an unprecedented and previously unimagined scale, and in a form and environment that made survival of individual works more likely than ever – whether as books, as texts memorised by citizen members of the cast, or simply in the impressions of fifteen thousand spectators. By the late fifth century, the city festivals were demanding a quota of new drama equivalent to about two new *Iliads* every year. In this unprecedented hothouse of narrative innovation, where the mythological repertoire of story material available to sustain this quota was large but still desperately finite, it is hardly surprising that experiment and invention were rapid – or that the scope for novelty was relatively early exhausted.[10] In what follows, I want to look in detail at the narrative system that emerged from this extraordinary process of discovery: at the repertoire of devices that evolved for defining the game structure of tragedy's distinctive narrative universe, and the new uses they found for the apparatus of epic plotting in a medium of far straiter narrative economy.

---

[10] Burian 1997.

Is drama narrative? Most narratologists would answer either 'of course' or 'of course not'. Hardliners would like to restrict 'narrative', and by extension 'narratology', to the media of the unadorned written word.[11] This is the case particularly for narratological systems (such as Genette's) that take terms and inspiration from linguistics, and feel uneasy about exporting such categories to textual forms that do not depend on language exclusively, primarily, or at all. Another, overlapping group feels bound by a lexical restriction of 'narrative' to the *epic* mode of telling – arguing that, by definition, a text can only be narrative if it has a narrator. This, too, is much more than a quibble over terms. There are notorious difficulties with finding equivalents outside the verbal text to some of the anchor concepts in mainstream narratology: narrators and narratees, tempo, focalisation, or point of view.

Equally, though, most semioticians of the performing arts recognise that many of the core ideas of literary narratology are clearly relevant to their own media: the *fabula/sjuzhet* distinction, the varieties of temporal order, the classification of actants and construction of actors. Film theorists, in particular, recognise an important set of analogies between the eye of the camera and the voice of the storyteller – to the extent, for example, that a term such as 'point of view' (in Henry James' day, merely a visual metaphor for a linguistic device) is nowadays *more* at home in the language of cinema than that of the novel. There is a case for claiming even that the narrator/viewpoint distinction carries over into cinema in the contrasting roles of the cinematographer (plus sound recordist) and editor – with the *framing* of shots (and selection of 'natural' soundtrack from the visible scene, together with any music or other device suggestive of an emotional perspective) conveying the sense of *viewpoint*, while the *narratorial* voice is suggested by the way in which individual shots are *assembled* (together with any voice-over or similar 'external' presence in the soundtrack). Such an equivalence is clearly implied in the occasional export of cinematic metaphors back into the discussion of verbal narration – as when we describe different kinds of linkage between successive narrative moments as a 'cut', 'zoom', 'pan', and so on.

If we allow such a system of equivalences, it becomes especially hard to draw a categorical line that includes film in the orbit of 'narrative' but

---

[11] This is, of course, a chimera; there is no such thing as a sign system composed entirely and exclusively of words. As recent work by Genette and others on the 'paratext' has stressed, even a printed book presents its text in a frame of non-verbal signs (punctuation, typography, layout, the physical structure of the volume). But it can reasonably be argued that the linguistic signs of a written, or oral, text obey a poetics abstractable from any such frame.

leaves theatre on the outside. Theatre, in this view, is simply a more restricted dialect of the same narratological language – with the camera 'viewpoint' fixed (as, indeed, it was in the early days of cinema), and the scope for editorial 'narration' limited but far from eliminated. The constraints on theatre's use of these narrative tools are less significant than the fact of their continuing functionality. In classical drama, the audience's viewpoint into the world of the story is just as controlled and contrived as it is in the novel; but it is a flat, fixed, external and impersonal fourth-wall window on the action, and any artistic *manipulation* of that viewpoint requires the action to be manoeuvred into frame rather than the frame to be redrawn around the selected action. Similarly, in strictly classical theatre the superimposition of an *external* narrative voice is not an option, but there is still a set of techniques available to approximate the narratorial function: the four fundamental dramatic choices of where to *locate* the action (and thus where to plant the narrative 'camera'); when in the story to *begin* the narrative; when to *end*; and in what form (if any) to *report* action inaccessible to the primary viewpoint (what we think of as action 'offstage'). These degrees of freedom are certainly more restricted than they are in film, in narrated storytelling, and in non-classical theatre (such as Aristophanic comedy); but the choices are there, and their consequences determine the shape of the narrative to a degree hard to parallel in other storytelling media. And I want to argue that it is above all an emerging awareness of these essential narrative differences between the modes of epic and drama that not only drives the development of tragic plotting from its beginnings to the death of Sophocles, but ultimately is responsible for the most distinctive features of tragedy's reading of the world.

Consider, first, the theatrical treatment of *time*. As already noted (pp. 40–1), drama has none of narrated fiction's scope for adjusting the relative flow of narrative time to story time. Of the five such flow rates available to epic, novel, and film, only one (scene) is normally available to the classical theatre. Ellipsis, a narrative jump ahead in story time, is widespread in later European drama but rare in Greek tragedies, though we do find it in the *Eumenides* (and occasionally in Aristophanic comedy); while summary, stretch, and pause are virtually impossible. In theatre, time runs at a fixedly literal rate, and can be arrested or accelerated only by the invocation of special conventions normally barred from tragedy. For over the lifetime of Aeschylus, tragic semiotics had made a momentous commitment – from which comedy strikingly refrained – to a principle of extreme *illusionism*: the acceptance of an absolute one-to-one mapping in time, space, and contents between the physical constituents of the performance and corresponding elements in the world of the story.[12] And tragedy's severely literal treatment of time – what a generation of theorists two millennia later would call the *unities of time and action* – has far-reaching consequences for the way it is constrained to tell its stories.

First, the story the play sets out to tell can occupy at most a day of the characters' lives. In practice, there is some slight elasticity of offstage time across the narrative punctuation of a choral ode; but even in a play such as *Heraclidae*, whose action could not conceivably take place in a single day (let alone the single hour the play takes to perform) the regular practice is to *disguise* any breach of the real-time convention, and practically all extant plays follow Aristotle's rule of thumb that the story of a tragedy should not substantially exceed 'one circuit of the sun'.[13] Tragedians do the best they can to turn the limitation to advantage: a Sophoclean trademark, for example, and perhaps the inspiration for Aristotle's remark, is explicitly to prescribe the single day as boundary to the action, as in the prophecies in *Ajax, Trachiniae,* and *Antigone*. Given the form and span of typical tragic action, it becomes almost routine to stress the proverbial motif of the sudden fragility of fortune, a single day's upheaval of a life previously thought secure. Tragedy's interest in catastrophe, and its wider reading of the world as one in which catastrophic reversals of fortune are a defining characteristic of the human condition, is a thematic response to the essentially narratological challenge of compacting epic action into real-time narration.

But the consequences run deeper even than this. Tragedy's commitment to an illusionistic treatment of time still means that stories stretching over more than a day in length (and there are few that do not) become impossible to dramatise in straight chronological order at all. Even the exemplary temporal economy of *Iliad* VIII–XXII plays over three days in story time, so that the story's diachronic narration in live performance inevitably depends on devices of narratorial summary and ellipsis inaccessible to the dramatic mode. For a while, tragedy experiments with a solution that does allow two (and precisely two) ellipses in the action: the

---

[12] *Pace* Wiles 1997, I see no opposition (unless perhaps in critical ideologies) between semiotic and realist readings of fifth-century theatre space; on the contrary, the single most important fact about the poetics of tragic space is that it is *both* highly coded *and* ruthlessly illusionistic. Where Wiles writes (165) 'We should see the space of Greek tragedy in geometric terms, as a grid upon which symbolic oppositions are organized, *rather than* in pictorial terms, as an image of the reality perceived by a single human eye', I should prefer the words I have italicised to read 'yet simultaneously'.

[13] 5.1449b13; περίοδος is apparently a twelve- rather than twenty-four-hour day: see Lucas *ad loc.* The *Eumenides* is the only extant play not to fit within a single span of daylight (apart from the *Rhesus*, a bravura experiment in night action spanning instead the period from dusk to dawn), and though mentions of dawn are quite frequent in tragic openings the endings are not usually explicit about time of day; see Arnott 1979: 395–6.

connected trilogy, which permits the three successively presented tragedies to show vital segments from a much longer story spanning days (as in
Aeschylus' lost adaptation of the *Iliad*), weeks or months (in the part-
extant Danaid trilogy), years (Euripides' Trojan trilogy), generations (the
Theban and Oresteian plays) or even centuries (if *Prometheus bound* and
Prometheus unbound were parts of the same trilogy). We do not really know
how frequent such linked trilogies were even in the lifetime of Aeschylus,
or why they fell from favour after 450.[14] But it is tempting to suppose that
one reason the trilogic experiment failed is that other, far more powerful
techniques had by now been evolved to get around the restrictions of real-
time narration.

Fundamental to these new techniques is a recognition of the increased
importance to drama of the old Homeric distinction between *primary* and
secondary narrative: in theatre, between the parts of the story that are
played out directly onstage, and the parts that are merely reported. A
play's *story* can sprawl over generations and more, just so long as its
primary narrative can be compressed into an hour or two of stage time. In
epic, the boundary between primary and secondary narrative is still soft;
in a strictly illusionistic drama, it is absolute.[15] Here as elsewhere the consequences extend to characteristic features of tragedy we would not naturally think of as narratological, as tragedy's technical fascination with the
boundary between primary and secondary narrative domains leads to a
pervasive *problematisation* of that boundary, both as a hermeneutic barrier
to the passage of information and as a thematic constructor of opposi-
tional categories of power or value.[16] In contrast to Old Comedy,
tragedy's ultra-rigid interpretation of the distinction between primary
and secondary narrative domains results in a genre which is thematically
preoccupied with the signifying boundaries, and thus with the signified
opposition, between these categories in human experience: between now
and then, here and elsewhere, public and private, signs and meanings,
and most specifically between present and past or future, mortal and
divine, community and household, the male world and the female, city
and hinterland, action and intention, word and thought.

Now, when it came to squeezing an epic myth through the needle's eye
of theatrical time, the Homeric tendency to privilege showing over telling
had already bequeathed a number of compression devices eagerly seized
on by tragedy. One key technique is to confine the primary narrative as

[14] There is no shortage of suggestions, ranging from reorganisation of the City Dionysia
programme (Webster 1965) to Sophoclean interest in the heroic individual (Knox 1964:
2–3); see the survey in Gantz 1979: 295–7.
[15] Contrast the powerful moments in Aristophanic prologues when a hitherto offstage
world erupts into primary space (*Clouds* 184, *Thesm.* 280).
[16] Cf. Kuntz 1993: 11–12, 89.

tightly as possible to the *crisis* of the story, with story material outside this primary timespan handled by naturalistically *embedded* secondary narratives in which the wider background of the war or Odysseus' wanderings are related as inserts. Homeric practice is ideally suited here for translation to the medium of theatre: as noted in Chapter 6, the epics make very little use of *narratorial* 'anachronies' (flash-backs and foreshadowings), but extensive use of embedded narratives related in direct speech by the *characters* – such as messenger speeches, prophecies and oracles, reminiscences and anecdotes, and paradigmatic or otherwise pointed examples. These devices clearly entered the tragic tradition early: all but the last are extensively used in *Persians*, the earliest tragedy extant (with the absence of mythological paradigm presumably an accident of its barbarian and historical subject matter, in view of the central use made of symbolically apt mythological inserts in the shield scene in the *Seven against Thebes* only five years later).

But already some radical modifications are emerging. Messengers, for instance, are used in Homer only to report to a character information already narrated to the audience; in tragedy, where movable viewpoint and omniscient narration are both excluded by the nature of the medium, their news is news to the audience as well. In tragedy, messengers have become not a supplement for primary action, but a richly functional *substitute*; and by 472 Aeschylus is already experimenting with a radical form of messenger tragedy in which the *entire* story is relegated to secondary narrative. In *Persians*, all significant actions are deep in the past or months in the future, and the play is organised around the gradual communicative release of story *information* to queen and court – in an almost Pindarically anachronic sequence designed to highlight the emerging moral rule-system.

Meanwhile, tragedy is already devising a number of *original* ploys to conventionalise the use of secondary times in embedded narrative, though not always without compromise to Homeric naturalism. One such device is the formal prologue, in which a god, character, or (in some Aeschylus) chorus can face, though not actually address, the audience directly through the fourth-wall window and set out the background to the primary narrative in a blow-by-blow account. Readers of all three tragedians soon notice that Sophocles already seems profoundly embarrassed by this lapse from illusionism, and in all seven extant plays prefers a naturalistic two-handed conversation on which the audience is conveniently allowed to eavesdrop; while Euripides, by contrast, is for late fifth-century tastes if anything over-fond of the opening monologue.[17] A

---

[17] Aristophanes, *Frogs* 946–7, 1198–1247.

similar device is available at least from the *Eumenides* on to sew up any
remaining unnarrated *future* action at the end of the play: the so-called
deus ex machina, where a prescient deity prophesies from on high the fates
of the surviving characters, their posterity, and the manner in which
future generations will preserve the memory of the events just told. Once
more this intrusive and prodigal device, duly derided by Aristotle, is rare
in Sophocles (extant only in *Philoctetes*), but normal in Euripides (of his
extant tragedies, only *Heraclidae*, *Troades*, and *Phoenissae* lack such a scene
entirely).

Aside from their value to narrative economy, both these devices illustrate the old epic problem of imposing a narrative *beginning and end* on a
story and characters wrenched from the seamless continuum of myth – a
task even the Homeric narrators delegate upwards to the Muse, and
which becomes harder yet for a medium forbidden the convenience of a
narratorial voice. With three of the extant Aeschylus no more than trilogic
fragments, his practice is hard to generalise, but Sophocles and Euripides,
at least, favour contrasting, characteristic solutions. Sophocles prefers
minimal exposition, naturalistically embedded in the action, and endings
with a calculated hint of openness and ambiguity: what happens to
Heracles on Mt Oeta? What final fate will the last oracle assign to
Oedipus? Is Aegisthus successfully dispatched, and what follows after? All
these are questions to which other versions of the myths offered clear
solutions, but Sophocles seems pointedly to withhold finality.[18] At the
opposite extreme, Euripides likes to extend the story fully into past and
future, albeit at an accelerated narrative rate – particularly in the numerous plays where the Euripidean plot improvises radically on more familiar
versions, pressing the poet (in Webster's phrase) to pull the story 'back on
to the mythological tramlines'.[19]

One final post-epic device for the embedding of secondary time
deserves special mention, as a conspicuous survival from the lyric origins
of tragic theatre. Though narrative is only one of its modes, the choral
interlude, with its narratological roots in the lyric rather than the epic tradition, remains the single most powerful and versatile means of embedding an anachronic secondary narrative at a chosen point in the primary
action. In all three tragedians we find choral songs used to report past
action continuous with the primary narrative of the play, as well as disjunct myths of merely thematic relevance – though it is not normally used
in post-Aeschylean tragedy as a vehicle for essential story background on
the characters we can see. And like all secondary narrative voices in
tragedy, the chorus does have the power, denied to the primary stage
action, of veering and varying the flow of narrated time. Nevertheless, the

---

[18] Roberts 1988.   [19] 1967: 252; see Dunn 1996: 64–83.

many formal disjunctures – musical, structural, stylistic, theatrical –
between the choral songs and the dialogue scenes made for discontinu-
ities in the narrative texture that would become harder to sustain in the
long term as the pressure to illusionism increased.

But whereas the epics themselves offered a range of ready-made and
extensible solutions to the problems of theatrical time, there were no such
easily transplantable devices to deal with tragedy's constrictions of narrative *space*. As remarked in Chapter 3 (pp. 42–3), the *story* of a play can
span the seas, the continents, or the gulf between earth and heaven; it is
only the space of *primary narrative* that is limited in tragedy to a single
house exterior and forecourt. Yet the challenge of compressing a plot of
tragic complexity down into these few square feet of front yard was one
for which little if any Homeric precedent existed. Both epics are clearly
aware of the value of striving for economy of locations, and the crisis of
the *Odyssey* tantalisingly showed what could be gained by enclosing a
complex action in a single set; but the particular model adopted there,
being an *indoor* scene, was ruled out once again by the tragic commitment
to illusionism, which at least from the *Oresteia* onwards made open-air
action the only option.[20]

For an outdoor people, this in itself was not catastrophic. Most public
and communal life was generally conducted out of doors anyway –
excepting a few cases like trials and council meetings, but including civic
assemblies, religious celebrations, and most male leisure pursuits.
Domestic life, and particularly that of the female, was more of a problem,
given that aristocratic women's activities were properly confined to the
home.[21] But tragedians swiftly built up an arsenal of pretexts, gratefully

[20] It is not clear to what extent pre-scenic tragedy may have experimented with indoor settings. Taplin (1972: 68–9, 1977: 103–7) argues that *Persians* 140–1 must mean that the
stage represents the interior of the council chamber, and that the setting is tacitly 'refo-
cused' for later scenes (such as the chariot entry and Darius' tomb) that clearly require an
exterior; so also for the courtroom scene in the scenic *Eumenides* (1977: 390–1). In neither
is the notional interiority made insistent. The *Iliad* trilogy, a very early work (Döhle 1967:
112–17) which remarkably does seem to have preserved unity of place throughout,
shrewdly chose Achilles' shelter as its stage location; but the fragments do not reveal
whether the action took place outside, inside, in the interior yard of *Iliad* xxiv.442 and
674, or in some shiftingly focused spatial limbo between. It would be fascinating to know
where the *Odyssey*'s climax was staged in the *Penelope* and *Ostologoi* (of unknown date): in
the hall? Penelope's quarters? The palace forecourt? Frr. 179–80 Radt apparently have
Odysseus using deictic pronouns of the bodies of the slain suitors: a prologue in the hall
following an offstage slaughter (perhaps in the previous play, or even in the ellipsis
between)? Or a finale with the suitors' kin as the bodies are brought onstage to be handed
over?

[21] This is not, as is sometimes assumed, a projection of Athenian social practice into the
world of myth. The women of the *Iliad* are normally encountered indoors, and only
brought out by special turns of circumstance; while of the many terrestrial scenes in the
Odyssey involving aristocratic or divine females other than Athene, only Calypso's beach
conversation and Nausicaa's outing take place under open sky. Penelope, Circe, Helen
and Arete are never seen out of doors at all.

seized on and expanded by New Comedy, to shepherd female characters and choruses outdoors: ceremonial duties, urgent communication with an outsider, an invalid's need for fresh air and light, and so forth. One well-recognised spin-off from these conventions is a powerful set of potential signifying oppositions between the visible outdoor world of the stage and the implicit indoor world of the *skene*: public/private, male/female, communal/domestic, open/secret.[22] The mere act of walking through a door is thus in Greek drama very often a highly symbolic act of boundary traversal. It is hardly surprising that Greek tragedy is so preoccupied with the interface between the family and the community, the tensions between the domestic and the civic life. For the most part, however, the outdoor settings give the poets noticeable embarrassment only when the source plot depends *essentially* on the primary narration of interior scenes – something that happens in only one extant play, the satyric *Cyclops*, and is addressed there with impressive if somewhat desperate ingenuity.

The real problems, rather, are twofold. First, tragic illusionism insists on *unity of location*. The last scene-change in surviving tragedy is in *Ajax*, probably a decade or less after the *Oresteia*; thereafter, even the Aeschylean and Old-Comic technique of spatial 'refocusing'[23] disappears from the tragic repertoire, restricting tragedies to a single primary-narrative location. Multiple narrative lines, whether simultaneous or successive, can now only be accommodated by (i) offstaging some events to secondary narrative, mediated back to the stage area in embedded reports; or by (ii) elaborate rotations of personnel between primary (onstage) and secondary (offstage) spaces. And since the chorus is normally onstage continuously for all but the prologue, complete discontinuity between narrative strands (with neither sub-cast aware of the other's actions) is in practice virtually impossible. Even a cursory look at the artful replotting of epic space and action in *Cyclops* and *Rhesus*, or of the different locational relationships between stage, palace, and tomb in the three Electra plays and their consequences for the plotting of on- and offstage action, gives a salutary taste of the technical challenges routinely faced by tragedians.

Again, however, the consequences extend far beyond mere narratological convenience to fundamental thematic issues of *Weltanschauung*. For one thing, there are profound implications for tragedy's presentation of the epic gods. As an essential part of the apparatus of epic, the gods are retained in tragedy (though not in all tragedies) as a narrative *control level* dictating the rules and pattern of story. But already in Homer the control

---

[22] Shaw 1975, Zeitlin 1985 (with cautions by Easterling 1987), Kuntz 1993: 87–103; and especially Padel 1990, Wiles 1997: 161–74.   [23] Dale 1956: 119, Taplin 1977: 104.

level is proving both narratologically and theologically unwieldy, and to a large extent the solutions available to the epic do not adapt well to the theatre, depending essentially as they do on multistranded narrative. Tragedy has nowhere to stage Olympian scenes; there is some attempt to retain an idea of spatial segregation, but only in the stylising device of setting metaphysically apart an area of terrestrial stage space reserved for the gods.[24] After *Eumenides* and *Prometheus*, gods do not share the stage level with mortal characters unless in mortal disguise; nor do they appear in the episodes between prologue and finale.[25] This in turn means that the gods of tragedy have little opportunity to interact with one another (*Prometheus* aside, the prologues of *Alcestis* and *Troades* are the only post-Aeschylean examples) – let alone with the mortal characters, to whom they reveal only so much as the action requires. There is nothing to compare with the relaxed, psychologically nuanced sparring of *Odyssey* XIII; and it is fair to say that, with the telling exception of the *Bacchae*'s Dionysus, no onstage god in extant tragedy makes for a conspicuously impressive or memorable *character* study.

In many plays, especially of Sophocles, the favoured solution is to remove the divine control level altogether to the domain of *secondary* narrative. Messages come from the unseen gods to the mortals onstage by the recognised routes of oracles and prophecy. Such messages still, by generic convention, carry complete authority (however this may be challenged by the players) – thus preserving their strictly narrative function as a metaphoric expression of the articulative force of the plot and its rules. But now their mediated, unaccountable, inaccessible origins push the mortal characters into speculation or outright scepticism about the inscrutable divine rationale. The Euripidean alternative, where the gods often seem to damn themselves out of their own mouths in attempting a satisfactory account of their involvement, only highlights the resistance of the divine to the kinds of intelligibility enshrined in classical narrative values. Here as elsewhere, tragedy's new way of narrating the world suggests a reading of that world qualitatively distinct from the epics': a world that problematises both the nature and the apprehensibility of the divine, just as it problematises whatever else is not directly accessible to primary perception.

But perhaps tragedy's severest challenge lies in the limited *size* of its narrative space, which rules out any direct representation of most of the types of action central to the stories of epic and myth: warfare, assemblies,

---

[24] Apparently they used the roof, or a part of it known to later authors as the θεολογεῖον; suspension in mid-air by the μηχανή was once reckoned a fourth-century novelty, but see now Newiger 1989, Mastronarde 1990, Wiles 1997: 180–6.

[25] A daring exception is *Heracles*, where the conventional practice is flagrantly breached for violent dramatic effect.

journeys, contests and celebrations, miracles and portents, and so forth. Aristophanic comedy, with its lower commitment to literalistic representation, is able to cope with the majority of these; but in tragedy all such actions, aside from the earthquakes in *Prometheus* and *Bacchae*, have to be shunted offstage. And since the staple tragic experiences of death and violence are also, for different reasons, generally excluded from the visible action, tragedy is faced with the dilemma of how to create theatre out of stories whose key incidents *cannot be shown on stage at all.*

The result is an extraordinary chamber version of epic, with plotting concentrated on the intimate, often domestic processes of decision and reaction that surround vast but largely unseen catastrophes. It is hard to exaggerate the historical importance of this emphasis. From the Greeks, we have learned that the strengths of theatrical storytelling lie precisely in accepting its limitations: in small actions rather than vast, intimacy rather than spectacle, individual rather than collective experience. Aeschylean drama still favours a kind of offstage epic, with colossal battles and casts of thousands massed in the reported domain of the offstage space. But already the primary narrative determines the outcome. The stage space, the still eye of the epic hurricane, is the centre of decision, responsibility, and response. Xerxes' invasion, the Theban civil war, the Egyptian task force to Argos, the Trojan sack: these vast events are fully programmed from the figures and space we can see, and their returning shockwaves only confirm the deterministic nature of offstage action.[26] The *decisions* are small; only the *consequences* are great. For the economy of plot, this is one of the most liberating discoveries in the history of narrative art.

And so, as with tragedy's treatment of time, the division between primary and secondary narrative space becomes thematically as well as narratologically paramount, and quickly crystallises into a matrix of powerful conventional shorthands. At least as early as the *Oresteia*, a standard set develops, consisting of a single doored structure with roof and forecourt; and an opposition is regularly assumed between the two side exits, one leading into town and the other out to the sea, fields, or wilderness beyond. Offstage locations can still be carefully plotted and evoked,

---

[26] Again the trilogic adaptations of the *Iliad* and *Odyssey* may have been seminal. The *Achilleis* dramatised the hero's decisions to let Patroclus fight, to return to the battle, and to surrender the body of Hector, but the actual combats and deaths were reported from offstage. The Odysseus trilogy, more daringly yet, seems to have offstaged not only the climactic slaughter but all of Odysseus' travels save for the underworld and Ithaca, the three plays dealing instead with the visit to the dead (where Odysseus first learns of the threat to his kingdom), the infiltration of the palace, and the resolution of the feud. We do not normally think of books XI, XIX, and XXIV as the poem's central episodes, but it is easy to see how the whole of the epic could be made implicate in these lower-key incidents and their repercussions.

through a combination of announced and reported action, character movement, and timing. In Sophocles especially, offstage locales such as Polynices' corpse, Agamemnon's tomb, and Odysseus' ship can be repeatedly visited and recalled; while late Euripides, with its increasing appetite for Aeschylean materials, becomes fascinated all over again with the possibilities of offstage mobs (Eteocles' army, the Argive assembly, the bacchants on the mountain, the army at Aulis), but now as determinants rather than determinates of the seen stage action. Even *interior* tableaux can be exposed in a limited and conventionalised way by the machinery of the *ekkyklema* – though the device is almost exclusively reserved for the production of corpses, and results in an immediate and anti-illusionistic blurring of the distinction between inside and out (permitting physical contact and verbal exchange between characters on the trolley and those notionally still outside).[27]

This fixed internal structure to tragedy's primary-narrative universe has profound implications for the art of plotting. One familiar thematic linkage between the single-house stage set and the necessarily restricted cast of players is the idea of the *oikos* or 'house' – in both the physical sense of a building and the social sense of a family group. Right from its début in the *Oresteia*, the *skene* regularly gives physical expression to the network of kinship structures that link some or all of the players into a dynastic superentity transcending the life of the individual. This surely must be one (though hardly the only) factor behind tragedy's intense preoccupation with the family, with all but three[28] of the extant tragedies plotted centrally around the fortunes of a family unit. Yet the main ideas have actually come from the *Odyssey*: close identification in the goal-structure between the building, the family, and the person; threats to the stability of the *oikos* from within (Clytemnestra) and without (Aegisthus, the suitors); infiltration of personal space as a violation of established structures of power. It may not be accidental that the first *skene* drama extant, perhaps the first ever, is a theatricalisation of the *Odyssey*'s own famous counterplot – the story that, next to Odysseus' own, embodied most clearly these narrative relationships between space, kinship, and the person.[29] In this, as in so much else, the towering influence of the *Oresteia* over later tragedy seems virtually to obliterate the memory of earlier and wider possibilities.

Meanwhile, a subtler legacy of the *Odyssey*'s endgame to tragedy is the conception of space as a network of zones of *power*. The tragic set effectively consists of four such distinct territories, each controlled by a

---

27 Taplin 1977: 442–3; Newiger 1989; Wiles 1997: 162–5.
28 *Prometheus, Philoctetes, Rhesus.* I owe this point to my student Jacquelyn Snow.
29 On these relationships in the *Odyssey* see Jones 1991: 104.

different source of narrative authority. First, there is the offstage space behind the *skene* door: this is the personal domain of the head of the *oikos*, and enemies cross the doorway at their peril. Already the *Oresteia* offers interesting plot variations by planting false models of who and where the real head of the *oikos* is: in *Agamemnon* control of the *oikos* has been surrendered to Clytemnestra by Agamemnon's absence; in *Choephori*, as in the *Odyssey*, the legitimate master wins entry by disguise, but with the new twist that his ticket of entry is the false information that the lordship has passed securely to the present occupiers. Second, there is the stage altar, the power-zone of the unseen supernatural controller; suppliants at this altar invoke the protection of the superintending deity for so long as they remain there of their own free will.[30] Third, there is the offstage space of the outside world and the forces of *political* authority that control it: a vast concentric hierarchy comprising other individual *oikoi*, the polis of their collective order, the international community of other poleis and the treaties and codes that sustain that wider Greek cosmopolis, and, beyond, the final outer circle of the barbarian other. Antagonism between the family and this wider system is a standard conflict in tragedy. And finally, there is the visible space of the stage: a neutral buffer zone between these three domains, where the familiar tragic struggle between different orders of power is regularly played out around the persons of the actors. In mapping this struggle, the locations of entrances and exits assume prime importance – with entrances suggesting a character's initial alignment, and exits the authority to which they finally submit.

This spatial arrangement has important consequences for tragedy's adaptation of the epic *endgame*. Any reader of the *Iliad* and *Odyssey* together will be struck by a close parallelism, not easily accounted for, in the structure of the two epics' resolutions. Both channel the narrative towards a two-stage endgame in which (i) the central antagonism between opposing player factions is resolved, in book XXII, in a combat to the death between a hero in search of revenge and an enemy on to whom all responsibility for the hero's grievance has by now been transferred; (ii) the conciliation, in book XXIV, of all survivors to the closure represented by this combat, in the form of a dispute over the *post mortem* rights of the victim's kin that is finally settled on divine prompting with the public agreement of all parties. The private and public conflicts are thus dealt with successively: the first stage settles the differences between individual players, and the second confirms the closure as permanent by securing the formal acquiescence, willing or reluctant, of all remaining interested parties.

---

[30] For the relationship between space and theme in suppliant plays see Rehm 1988, 1992.

This pattern is echoed pervasively in tragedy. Half of all extant tragedies culminate in revenge killings[31]; and a quarter actually end, like the *Iliad*, in scenes of funeral lament,[32] while two others (*Alcestis, Hecuba*) use funerals as false closures to the first phase of a bipartite plot, and another (*Medea*) alludes to the motif by deliberately withholding it. Disputes over unburied corpses are central to *Ajax, Antigone*, and Euripides' *Suppliants*, and the proper disposal of a hero's body is contentious in other ways in *Trachiniae* and *OC*. Some plays deliberately reproduce the two-tier Homeric endgame in a so-called 'diptych' action (*Ajax, Antigone, Alcestis, Hecuba, Heracles*), whose first phase culminates in a death and the second deals with the response of the surviving kin; while divine epiphanies impose or seal a settlement in the Danaid and Oresteian trilogies, in *Philoctetes*, and in all but a handful of the extant Euripides.[33]

But tragedy soon discovers that these Homeric story patterns need tailoring to the new demands of narrative spatiality. For one thing, the epics can take their leave of the audience with their characters snapped onstage in a final tableau; in tragedy, at least before the Roman introduction of the stage curtain, the play must signal its end by emptying the narrative space itself. As a result, a universal genre convention, of enormous value in the modelling of endgame, is that at the end of every play *all the characters leave the stage*.[34] All through the play, therefore, the audience is consciously or unconsciously asking as they process the plot: 'How and where will this character or that finally exit from the narrative?' There are only three spatial options: a character may enter the *skene*, confirming his or her tie to the set, or may leave the set for one or other offstage destination. Many plays build the whole trajectory of action towards the exit of a central character from the confining stage.[35] The escape of the Danaids from their suppliant corner to Argos; the departures of Medea, Heracles, and Ion for Athens; the surprising detention of Oedipus *Tyrannus* in the Theban palace and the teaser of where *Coloneus* will leave this earth – all these, and many others, are carefully prepared culminations of a play-long process of blocked or aborted moves towards a decisive endgame. In all such cases the final exits describe the survivors' closing position on the board: the lasting configuration of relationships that has resulted from the final adjustments of knowledge and power in the story.

This brings us, finally, to the *players* in a tragic plot, where the medium

---

[31] Aeschylus' *Suppliants* (though not until later in the trilogy), *Agamemnon, Choephori, Ajax, Trachiniae, Medea, Heraclidae, Hippolytus, Andromache, Hecuba*, both *Electra*s, *Heracles, Ion* (attempted), *Orestes, Bacchae*.

[32] *Persians, Seven, Ajax, Trachiniae, Heraclidae*, Euripides' *Suppliants, Phoenissae, Bacchae*.

[33] See above, p. 76 with n. 15.

[34] Dunn 1996: 13–25. (Sophocles' *Electra* is problematic here but not, I think, an exception to the rule.)   [35] See the discussions of *Ajax, OT, Philoctetes* and *Ion* in Taplin 1978.

imposes severe restrictions entirely unknown to the epic. First, for a complex of reasons that need not distract us here, fifth-century tragedy (and afterwards New Comedy) made a clear division between speaking and non-speaking actors, and limited the former to a maximum of three. Sixth-century tragedy, with its single solo voice responding to the chorus, would have had enormous difficulty staging Homeric scenes, and it is perhaps not surprising that epic subjects are rare among the known pre-Aeschylean titles; but the Aeschylean introduction of a second actor opened up the possibilities enormously, and the Sophoclean third brought most Homeric conversations within stageable range.[36] But even with extensive doubling the *total* number of speaking characters is limited to a tightly closed group: in extant tragedies, between three and eleven (plus chorus), of whom some will be purely reactive messengers and domestics. Here again tragedy's economy of narrative materials is considerably stricter even than Homer's – and no longer an artistic choice, but a formal necessity.[37]

Meanwhile, tragedy's elision of the narrator restricts the way in which even this reduced cast of players can be *presented* to the audience, and requires that fundamental aspects of what we understand as 'character' be permanently removed from primary-narrative view. There is no privacy, and thus no privileged access for the audience to the interior world of any character; all actions have to be performed, and all thoughts spoken aloud, in the public space of the stage. Nothing that happens on the stage is shielded from our attention, while everything that happens offstage is invisible. There are no degrees of access to a character's thoughts or actions, beyond the black-and-white choice of whether a particular speech or action takes place on- or offstage (and, if the latter, in what form it is made known onstage). Even privacy *between* characters is largely excluded: because the chorus is (with a handful of significant and necessary exceptions) always present onstage from the *parodos* to the close of the play, the only place for soliloquy or secrecy is the prologue. For some kinds of plotting, this is a considerable embarrassment: Euripides, who favours plots of intrigue, has regularly to caulk up the potential leakage of information from player to player via the chorus, by

[36] Herington 1985: 135. In some important ways, they even become *more* stageable: the polyphony of theatrical dialogue allows rapid alternation *between* voices of a kind impossible in the solo rhapsodic voice of epic – though it is a sign of tragedy's conservative adherence to Homeric models that epic *rhesis* persists as a standard dialogue structure alongside the more fluid and naturalistic *stichomythia*.

[37] Aristophanes' *Birds* is able to squeeze twenty-one characters from three actors (with only the Triballian's jabberwocking assigned to a fourth speaker), but by dint of a farcical pace and over-exploitation of convention that would be inadmissible in tragedy. (For the closest attempts see Taplin 1977: 351–3.)

swearing the chorus to silence or otherwise actively enlisting them in a partisan role of conspiracy.[38]

Again, however, the passage from epic into drama is eased by the Homeric preference for showing over telling. Already in Homer, as stressed in the last chapter, the audience regularly has to cope with characters who say one thing and mean another. Sometimes the epic narrator will help us out, by commenting on the true intention of the speech or on the thought suppressed. Yet already in Homer the gap between thought and word or deed is usually left for the audience to infer, as part of their own involvement in the plotting process. Sometimes this is easy enough; more often it is indefinitely subtle and implicit, leaving the reader teasingly uncertain how much psychological sophistication the text is inviting us to read between the lines of what the characters say.[39]

And in tragedy, this is the normal state of affairs. We sometimes catch clues from the comments of other characters, such as the watchman describing Clytemnestra's 'masculine intelligence' (*Agamemnon* 11), or Cilissa's comment on Clytemnestra's feigned grief for the supposedly dead Orestes (*Choephori* 737–41). But such comments, including the *Choephori* passage, are often themselves subjective and provisional, and in practice the tragic audience must use their Homeric skills of hearing the private thought behind the public word to make human sense of the players' motivation. In the case of the tragic chorus, the challenge can even transcend psychological modes of reading altogether, since the songs of the chorus often intersect with the context in insistently significant ways that the chorus *qua* character cannot conceivably 'intend'.[40]

---

[38] But the practice is hardly confined to him – it makes its first appearance in the historical archetype of the intrigue tragedy, Aeschylus' *Choephori*, and is adopted by Sophocles in three of the plays we have (*Trachiniae, Electra, Philoctetes*).

[39] See further Lowe 1996: 530–1.

[40] A famous case: when the chorus of Theban elders sing at *Antigone* 370–2 'Whoever shares in ignoble things for daring's sake is no citizen', they must think they are referring to Polynices, who made war on his country, and the still unidentified traitor to Creon's edict. Yet seconds later, the traitor is unmasked as Antigone: are the lines then 'about' Antigone? We inevitably think too of Creon, to whom the elders are at this stage in the play uncritically loyal. The words, especially taken with the preceding lines about 'revering the laws of the land and the sworn justice of the gods', are famously echoed in the exchange between Antigone and Creon at 449–45; but the plurality of reference in choral lyric generally makes talk of 'unwitting irony' too simple for such cases. In Pindar, the first person is often a purely conventional device, denoting not so much 'I, the performer', let alone 'I, the poet', as 'you, the audience invited to agree with the consensual judgements here expressed'. The tragic chorus inherits much of this generalising, depersonalised function from lyric, while never quite sacrificing its identity as a human component of the world of the play: rarely a player, more often an involved observer capable of giving a lyric voice to the backdrop of ideas and associations against which the audience is invited to place and respond to the story.

In plot terms, this refusal of *any* unambiguous access to the characters' thoughts means that the audience has to work much harder at constructing its own model of each player's motivation and reasoning – including that player's *own* shifting model of the plot, and of all the other players' models – from the often deceptive evidence of their public words and actions. It is hardly surprising that Aristotle had to argue hard against the notion, evidently widely voiced in his day, that tragedy was primarily about character all along. Certainly the shift from narrated to dramatic plotting throws new emphasis, away from the nakedly objective story events, and on to the complex modalities of a whole cluster of constantly shifting and interacting subjective *representations* of those events. Not all tragedies make this as central to their plotting as do *Trachiniae*, *OT*, or *Hippolytus*; but it is in the nature of drama to challenge our understanding of how people think and feel, by forcing us vividly to confront the paradoxical nature of fictional character itself. Like plot itself, 'characterisation' may rest on the rerouting of a powerful cognitive mechanism originally evolved for making successful sense of a dangerous world.[41] But fiction, and especially the narratorless fiction of drama, summons this 'intentional stance'[42] into play on an outward surface that *has no interior*: in tragedy, a literally fabricated face and a scripted mask of words, behind which lies in reality not the living inside of a human head but a second, stranger's face.[43] Here above all is the secret of tragedy's richly expanded notion of character psychology from the bare actorial matrix of motive, knowledge, and power, as the constraints of medium push it to explore the ways in which all three can be *problematised*. What we want, what we know, and what we are capable of doing all become issues where the very attempt to apply easy answers, of a kind that will reduce the universe of experience to intelligible narrative sense, exposes the confusions and complexities in the categories we try to apply.

Consider, first, tragedy's treatment of *goals*. Aristotle took it for granted that characters in tragedy, and indeed in the audience, class the rest of the human universe simply into *philoi* (friends, kin, loved ones), *echthroi* (enemies), and *medeteroi* ('neithers').[44] Most people in tragedy, as in the culture that created and consumed it, want nothing more complicated than the welfare of their *philoi* and the blight of their *echthroi*: the survival and stability of themselves and their network of associates in blood or

[41] For this evolutionary argument see e.g. Humphrey 1980.
[42] The term is Dennett's (1987, etc.).
[43] Even the *Poetics*, in canny contrast to Aristotle's usage elsewhere, effectively defines *ethos* as a property of texts, not of people (overemphases mine): 'that on the basis of which *we* say that the subjects of action are such-and-such a kind of person' (6.1450a5–6); 'that which *expresses* a choice of action (προαίρεσις)' (6.1450b8–9).
[44] 14.1453b15–17.

affection, and the blocking of their enemies' access to these goals – provided always that these states of play lie within the range permitted by larger moral, political, or supernatural codes. (Aspiring to *forbidden* goals of course triggers punishment, but in most plays this is such a morally uncontroversial process that it serves as no more than an Odyssean sense of imbalances to be finally redressed. A Lycus or Polymestor does not normally qualify for sympathetic interest.)

But from the beginning tragedy is excited by the sense of conflict or ambiguity *within* the accepted goal-structure. Who are the real *philoi*? Are our family necessarily our friends? Are our classifications immutable? Above all, what happens when goals tug in opposite directions – when harming our enemies means hurting our friends, or when the interests of one group of *philoi* conflict with another's or even one's own? Such questions originate in the dilemmas of Hector and Achilles in the *Iliad*; but tragedy is far more deliberate in their address, and makes them a central source of its human complexity. At the same time, tragedy is centrally interested in the paradoxical relationship explored in the *Iliad* between projected goals and actual consequences – where the gamestate desired by a player in motivating a sequence of moves is undercut by its unforeseen result in practice. In *Iliad* I, Agamemnon seeks to restore his standing, not to undermine it to the point where he must offer abject reparation; while Achilles fails to anticipate the price that will be paid for the restitution of his own status, and loses far more than he gains by his strategy. And from *Persians* on, nearly all tragic plots centre on intentions that *backfire* – either by banishing the very goals they were instigated to realise, or by achieving the original goal at the expense of far more devastating and undesired attendant consequences. Fully Odyssean tragedies, in which only the unambiguously wicked see their goals decisively frustrated, are in contrast very rare in the extant selection: perhaps only the barbarian plays *IT* and *Helen* exhibit the pure form, with the villainless happy end of *Ion* a striking and isolated oddity in its genre.

Equally characteristic of what we would recognise as distinctively 'tragic' plotting is tragedy's problematisation of *knowledge* states. Communication and its misuse are a central issue in the tragic universe – in part, no doubt, because they are so central to the move-structure of dramatic representation, since even p-moves in tragedy are expressed through communicative acts such as instructions or reports. But tragedy is obsessed with the ironics of knowledge that is not merely incomplete but *false*, with only *Prometheus, Heraclidae*, Euripides' *Suppliants*, and *Troades* free from the motif (since it seems to have been prominent in the missing parts of the Theban and Danaid trilogies). Part of the reason lies in tragedy's overall epistemological framework, which endorses the

Homeric world-model of a two-tier universe asymmetrical in knowledge and power – with human life poignantly confined to the inferior chamber.[45] Tragedy significantly extends this model in three ways: by exploiting the new symmetry, possible only in drama, between what Zeus does from Mount Ida and what the audience of a play does in the θέατρον or 'spectatorium'; by interpolating the chorus into the hierarchy of spectation, so that the relationship between audience and narrative is continuously mirrored *within* the world of the play; and by reifying the epistemological hierarchy in space (with θέατρον, roof or crane, ὀρχήστρα, stage, and offstage corresponding to the vistas of audience, gods, chorus, heroes, and the unseen world mediated by speech). The implication is that the chain does not stop with the audience: that our own world is the narrative product of unseen powers whose enigmatic relationship to ourselves is variously mirrored in the epic gods, in the chorus, and in the processes of play-making and play-watching.

Above all, tragedy insists on the problematical nature of *power*. In close tandem with the collisons between rival *sources* of power encouraged by the zoning of narrative space, tragedy likes to explore the interrelationships between, and the competing strengths of, different power *systems*: *nomos* against violence, religious versus secular imperatives, the individual against the group, and so forth. The default assumption seems to be that the principal codes are organised in a rough hierarchy: divine laws, communal *nomoi*, domestic *nomoi*, tyrannical legislation, force.[46] But it is rarely so linear and simple, and any search for a stable moral rule-system controlling the tragic universe is itself deferred by the elision of Homeric Olympus from primary-narrative view.

Here again the boundary between primary and secondary narrative forces a far more radical construction of these issues. In tragedy, the principal forms of Homeric p-move can *only* be carried out offstage – either because they cannot be naturalistically staged at all, or because they use up valuable stage resources (for instance, by requiring a much-needed speaking actor to lie onstage as a corpse), or because they offend against notions of propriety in heroic theatre. So with bloodshed and most forms of physical force excluded from primary action – and even the *threat* of violence diluted by the audience's awareness that the threat cannot normally be carried out while the players remain in view – the exercise of power has to find other ways of manifesting itself onstage. An important technique is the enticement of characters across a barrier of power: away from the altar, into the house of their enemy, offstage to an alien fate. Here physical abduction is very occasionally tolerated (*Heraclidae*, *OC*), but

---

[45] The rest of this paragraph condenses arguments from Lowe 1996.
[46] See Burnett 1976 (on *Heraclidae*, but with much wider application).

significantly is always thwarted. Playwrights rack their ingenuity to devise new forms of *onstage* powerplay – Euripides' hostage situations and timely rescues, Sophocles' lone rebels defying the edicts of kings. But ultimately the Aeschylean dichotomy holds: decisions onstage, implementation off.

So tragedy sets out to *recentre plot around the c-move:* the communication of fact, the propagation of falsehood, the expression of thought or intent. In tragic plotting, Orestes' actual perforation of Aegisthus becomes less interesting than his successful manoeuvring of Aegisthus into his power; the death of Laius and the copulation of son with mother signify not as acts performed, but as acts apprehended. Once again, tragedy's debt to the *Odyssey* is immense – this time, for demonstrating that the exchange rate between information and power can be as high as ingenuity allows. A single revelation can turn a tyrant into a pariah; a secret can turn a conqueror into a corpse; the right strategic decision can save or destroy a city. Deception, discovery, debate, decision, decree: these are the moves that dominate the stage action of tragedy, and as with most ways of plotting they cannot help suggesting a distinctive genre reading of the rules that make the world. The universe of fifth-century tragedy is one in which the control of information and the exercise of speech, reason, and political skills are the ultimate determinants of human events. That we may find this one of the most compelling descriptions in art of the world of actual experience should not blinker us to the fact that its adoption by Greek tragedy originates in an accident of narratological convenience.

And it is precisely in the technical tricks of communicative plotting that tragedy innovates most. The Odyssean precedents cover intentional deceptions only, and for a long time this type predominates: most barriers to information in tragedy are the result of *intrigue*, the deliberate propagation of false game models by a player seeking to adjust power balances in his or her favour. Of the twenty or so extant plays to feature intrigue plots, most pursue strictly Homeric goals: murderous revenge, escape, or (in *Rhesus*) espionage. Their epistemological structure, too, is shaped to a pair of clearly distinct Odyssean patterns: confusion of actorial *subject* (the misrepresentation of identity, as promoted by Odysseus himself) or of *predicate* (feigned intentions, knowledge, and/or power, as practised most successfully by the Odyssean Clytemnestra, attempted by Polyphemus and the suitors, and probed for by the hero himself in repeated Ithacan interviews).[47]

But tragedy extends this Homeric repertoire in a number of revolutionary ways. First, it elaborates several devices left relatively undeveloped in

---

[47] Compare the distinction between 'associative' and 'cognitive' errors in Long 1976.

epic, such as madness (realising the possibilities in Agamemnon's speech in *Iliad* XIX), false accusation and deception at a distance (both on the model of the story of Bellerophon in *Iliad* VI). Second, tragedy's widespread elision of the gods from narratives of divine delusion leads to the powerful dramatic innovation of *errors*, misunderstandings without any attributable author: in extant tragedy first fully realised in *OT*, though the true innovator here may have been Sophocles' lost, undatable *Odysseus acanthoplex* or even Aeschylus' *Oedipus*. Above all, tragedy embarks on a series of ever more ambitious experiments in the ways embedded fictions can be *concatenated*: serially (with intrigues un-Homerically failing, backfiring, or propagating further confusions beyond their instigators' control), in parallel (with two or more deceptions converging or interfering), or combinatorially (with confusions proliferating as multiple characters fall victim to different permutations of the same variables). A particularly powerful invention, though late to evolve, is *second-order* c-plotting or 'cross-purposes' – in which deviant versions of the same reality collide without either party's realising that their stories do not agree.[48]

Thus in *OT*, the c-tragedy *par excellence*, Oedipus' complex story is systematically disassembled and the pieces presented in an anachronic narrative sequence that encourages their recombination by the players into provisional stories which may be fatally false or incomplete.[49] Moreover, there is not one but a whole family of these variant private narratives at large in the play – above all Oedipus' and Jocasta's, but also Tiresias', Creon's, and the chorus's, all of which the audience has simultaneously to model and to compare. In a precursor of the New Comic device of segmented transactions, the exposure motif splits a single child of known parentage into two separate narrative identities: the child born, whose identity is known to its true parents, and the child reared, whose new identity is the property of its fosterers. These narrative roles are multiplied further by the fragmentation of the child into two further persons: the killer of Laius and the investigator into the crime, object and subject of what seemed at first an entirely separate inquiry. Eventually Oedipus learns that the role he believed he occupied, that of natural son of Polybus and Merope, does not exist, and that instead he occupies three simultaneous narrative roles of whose existence he was previously unaware: foster son of Polybus and Merope, natural son of Laius and Jocasta, and killer of Laius.

But the most striking pointer to future directions is *Ion*. Here there is a

---

[48] For worked analyses, see the discussions of *Samia* and *Epitrepontes* in Chapter 9. The one pure instance in extant tragedy is the dialogue between Clytemnestra and Achilles in *IA*; elsewhere, at least one speaker is aware that there is something the other does not know.
[49] The detail is in Vickers 1973: 501–13, with tables 502–7.

Table 6. Ion: *detectives and suspects*

		(1)	C:B	I:E	
		(2)	C:BE	I:AE	
[x =] Apollo = Creusa = Xuthus[= Y Z = Z']		(3)	C:BE	I:AE	X:C
| | | | |		(4)	C:BE	I:AE	X:D
A B C D E		(5)	C:BE	I:AD	X:D
		(6)	C:BD	I:AD	X:D
		(7)	C:B	I:AD	X:D
		(8)	C:B	I:B	X:D

similar collapse of many narrative roles into few; but there are more narrative roles to collapse, more false roles to be eliminated, and more detectives pursuing their own different versions of the investigation. What is more, the narrative roles each seeks to fill are structurally *identical*: each of the three detectives (Creusa, Ion, Xuthus) is searching for the identity and person of the players who will complete one or more missing triangles of father, mother, and child. There are, as it turns out, five such possible triangles, only one of which (we are briefed by Hermes in the prologue) is correct: Apollo, Creusa, and Ion. These five, and the versions held among the three detectives in successive steps of the inquiry, are set out in Table 6, with the various roles occupied by the critical figure of Ion marked in bold.[50]

At the start of the play, Creusa knows Apollo is the father of her lost child B, and that nobody else shares her secret; Ion knows only that he has parents, both unknown; and Xuthus that (to his best information) he has no child. As a further confusion (2), Creusa tells Ion that Apollo got a child on a mortal woman x who is *not* Creusa herself. Xuthus then reports a narrative control message from Trophonius' oracle (3), that both Xuthus and Creusa will leave the play with a child – which for the time being they take to mean one child between them, rather than a separate child each. Xuthus is then told, falsely, by the Apolline oracle (4) that the first person he meets on leaving the *skene* – in this case, Ion – is his child. Xuthus reports the god's words to Ion and both acquiesce in the new story model (5); the chorus subsequently relay it to Creusa (6). At the zenith of misapprehension, all three detectives wrongly believe that Ion is D, Xuthus' son by an unknown woman Y who cannot be Creusa. Ion additionally believes in the existence of a woman x, the mother of Apollo's child A; and that furthermore x is not Creusa, and that A now cannot be

---

[50] For the notation, see p. 55 n. 22 above. We shall see structures of this pattern, where a central bond is threatened by real or imagined rival bonds on either side, in several later comedies (*Samia, Sikyonios, Epitrepontes, Andria, Adelphoe*).

Ion himself (whose paternal identity is now accounted for). Creusa also believes in Y, but knows that X and her child A are a fiction, and that Apollo's child is actually her own B. In reality, Ion is B, not D, and Y is non-existent. In the suppliant crisis that follows the abortive murder intrigue,[51] Creusa's visual recognition of the cradle forces the instantaneous conclusion (7) that Ion and B are the same – and thus, since he cannot simultaneously be D, that her rival Y is a phantasm. Ion is readily enough persuaded that Creusa is Y, his missing mother by Xuthus, but has understandable trouble with the further claim that she is actually his mother by Apollo and that Y was a fiction of the god. This missing proof is guaranteed by Athene *ex machina* (8), leaving Xuthus to go on innocently believing in the elusive Y: a startling breach of the genre rule that none of the players should be permanently left in the dark.

These are comparatively late plays; and yet, if *Trachiniae* is as early as many now suspect,[52] the decisive innovations were astonishingly swift. The play's plotting introduces an astonishing cluster of major post-Homeric and post-Aeschylean coinages, all of them widely adopted thereafter.[53] (i) The *parallel-stranding* of onstage and offstage action is among the most complex in extant tragedy – the more so as it appears that a single, harbour *eisodos* is used for virtually all movements, with the second, Oetaean exit reserved for the final scene.[54] (ii) The reconstruction of the complex offstage story, and of the past action from which it stems, involves one of tragedy's most demanding processes of *collation* from a web of partially overlapping, and in some places apparently competing, secondary narratives – of which one in particular involves, in Lichas, (iii) tragedy's boldest-ever use of an *unreliable narrator*. (iv) The poisoned robe is a potent mechanism of *action at a distance*, allowing killer and victim to interact, without recourse to supernatural or human

---

[51] This famous Euripidean plot pattern, best known in antiquity from the probably earlier *Cresphontes*, is the one that produces Aristotle's ideal tragic crisis (*Poetics* 14.1454a4–9): an endgame where kin narrowly miss killing kin in ignorance of identity, with recognition supervening in the nick of time. Surprisingly, it is a situation extant *only* in three plays of Euripides (once each in *IT* and *Orestes*, but no fewer than three times in this play).

[52] The stoicheiometric findings of Craik and Kaferly 1987 (q.v. for earlier debate) are the closest to hard evidence so far.

[53] For what follows see especially Easterling 1981, Segal 1983, Roberts 1988, Kraus 1991, Goward 1999.

[54] Hyllus, en route from Deianeira to Heracles, actually *crosses* with Lichas' party travelling in the other direction; Lichas then returns to Heracles with the robe, and Hyllus (who has thus been crucially offstage during the Iole and robe scenes) travels back with Heracles to report the horrifying result of Lichas' arrival. As a last twist, the dying Heracles, though landing in Trachis with Hyllus, is so slowed by his condition that he arrives only after Hyllus has confronted his mother, driven her to suicide, and learned too late the truth of her intent. It is only with New Comedy that such elaborately timed and spaced movements around the secondary-narrative map become a regular feature in plotting.

co-conspirators, not merely between the stage space of Trachis and the far-offstage spaces of Pleuron and Cenaeum, but between secondary and primary narrative timeframes, and even across the boundary of death. (v) It also introduces the theatrically invaluable device of *segmented action*, in which a single act of power (Nessus' murder of Heracles) is broken into a series of moves (Nessus' instructions to Deianeira; Deianeira's steeping of the robe; Heracles' infidelity; Deianeira's recourse to the charm) whose overall effect is discharged only on the chain's completion, and is correctly diagnosed only by those who are able to reconstruct the chain in its entirety: first Zeus (in prophetic fore-knowledge), then the silent Deianeira and the chorus, then Hyllus, and finally Heracles. (vi) Deianeira's suicide pioneers Sophocles' innovative use of *domino plotting*: a single trigger event setting off a prepared chain of catastrophe, such as a cascade of sympathy suicides (most strikingly in *Antigone*'s triple suicide chain).[55] (vii) At a higher level, Deianeira's enactment of the very catastrophe she most wanted to prevent is a major refinement of the Iliadic pattern to force a direct ironic contrast between *intention and result*; while (viii) the omnipresent hidden hand of Zeus[56] is more remarkable for the fact that, for the first time, a divine controller is removed entirely from the visible cast and *mediated* to the players by oracles, oaths, and cultic ties. And all this takes place (ix) within a dense *intertextual matrix* of Homeric and Aeschylean narrative patterns that (x) closes by *resisting its own closure*, in the first of Sophocles' challenging unfinished endings.

By such a point, the tragic experiment could easily be judged already complete: 'after going through many changes,' Aristotle would baldly claim with a further century's hindsight, 'tragedy stopped, because it had attained its own nature'.[57] Certainly the narrative economics of Homeric plotting had by now been comprehensively reinvented for the new narrative mode of drama, with three decisive innovations irrevocably

---

55 Outside the source play for *Ajax*, suicide is not a device attested for Aeschylus (though it is threatened by the *Suppliants* chorus), while in Euripides it is emphatically resisted: only three in the nineteen plays, with many more where it is openly contemplated but decisively rejected. Its exploitation as a mechanism of knock-on catastrophe appears to be a Sophoclean invention.

56 'Nothing in this is not Zeus,' Hyllus charges in the final line. Zeus gave out the original prophecy at Dodona, and Zeus told Heracles in a second prophecy that he would be killed by a dead creature (Nessus); it is Zeus by whom Hyllus swears obedience to his father's final wishes (1185), and on Zeus's peak that his living pyre is sited. Heracles himself notes the convergence of separate oracles from the same divine source, as indicating a coherent if inscrutable long-term pattern (1159–73); and though there is no explicit statement, we infer that his strange dying requests may also be prompted by instruction from Zeus.   57 *Poetics* 4.1449a14–15.

established: (i) an insistence that transparency be *total*, with primary narration and explicit metatheatricality contained by the 'fourth wall'; (ii) a commitment to literalistic illusionism, resulting in a severely closed primary-narrative universe through which all story events are filtered, and whose conventional shape and articulation becomes itself an instrument of narrative form; (iii) a ready transferability of narrative patterns from one text or story to another, resulting in a loose *de facto* tolerance of narrative metarules underlying the corpus or genre as a whole. Significant consequences of these innovations included an exhaustive technical and thematic exploration of the relationship between primary and secondary action; a vast expansion of the repertoire of devices for c-plotting; and a displacement of the superhuman control level to effective virtuality.

Yet fifth-century comedy largely rejected this theatrical version of the epic narrative system, just as it rejected epic practices generally (such as the restriction of story matter to myth). Space, time, illusion, epoch, and even the natural-causality law of probable and necessary connection could be ruptured on a whim – though in Aristophanes such breaches are generally anything but whimsical, the product rather of rival dramatic imperatives that happen to override the much weaker pressures to Homeric narrative economy in the very different poetics of his chosen genre.[58] For Aristophanes, the illusionism, naturalism, and literalism that underpin tragic plotting are neither necessary nor particularly desirable narrative limits. This extraordinary coexistence of two distinct generic systems of narrative semiotics sharing exactly the same resources, audience, and festivals (perhaps on the very same day) is one of the most baffling features of fifth-century drama – as is the generic apartheid that made it an eccentric's whimsy that the same poet might be capable of both.[59]

But segregation encourages forbidden fascinations, and comedy's freedom from many of tragedy's constraints made the traffic of influence far easier in one direction than the other. No influence whatever of comedy on tragedy has yet been persuasively demonstrated; but the reverse effect was decisive for the future of both. Two innovations from which tragedy had markedly refrained were (i) to abandon its commitment to retelling and create fictional universes *ex nihilo*, making the story world entirely a creation of the narrative rather than a pre-existent given; and (ii) to operate a rigorous and explicit rule-system – such as a code of law – internal to the fictional universe itself. These absences are crucial to the dynamic tension between, on the one hand, tragedy's centripetal ten-

[58] See Lowe 1988 and above, p. 87.   [59] Plato, *Symposium* 223d.

dency to narrative and thematic closure, and on the other its centrifugal-ising deferral of finality and problematisation of narrative and cosmic value. New Comedy, however, was to take both steps, with far-reaching consequences for the long-term history of classical narrativity in the West.

9   Dramatic fiction: New Comedy

Our last play by a fifth-century dramatist is Aristophanes' *Plutus* from 388; *Rhesus* is probably a work of similar date. The next extant play is either Menander's *Dyskolos* of 316 or his *Samia* from at most five years earlier. And in the interval framed by these texts – a period longer than that spanned by our entire corpus of surviving tragedy – the form, content, and poetics of Attic comedy have been momentously transformed.

What has happened, in a nutshell, is that comedy has adopted the narrative conventions of tragedy. Literalistic unity of place, time, action; observance of real-world causality; naturalistic content and reporting of secondary action; retention of dramatic illusion – all these enjoy in New Comedy the status of narrative ground rules, assumptions the audience can take for granted in unplotting a story from its telling. And with these tragic conventions has come the whole specialised repertoire of tragic plot devices: intrigue, recognition, detection, rescue, cross-purposes, even (in Plautus, at least) revenge. Yet at the same time, and no less crucially, this reinvented comedy has retained and even reinforced two vital distinctions between Old Comedy and tragedy: it has wholly abandoned the Iliadic 'minor' narrative key and the use of myth, two tragic preserves on which Old Comedy occasionally poached.[1]

This final escape of classical narrative from myth had been a long time coming. It would be dangerous to suggest that myth was approaching a state of creative exhaustion; the vigorous persistence and popularity of new tragic writing in the fourth century, and far beyond, should warn us away from sweeping historicist assertions of decline.[2] But it would be equally dangerous to underestimate the impact on the mythological imagination of an immensely expanded canon of literary versions with classic authority. Before the fifth century, the only more-or-less inviolable myths were those told by 'Homer'. By 400, the mere existence of a version

---

[1] *Clouds*, at least in our version, is often read as a minor-key or 'dark' comedy; while around a quarter of Aristophanes' plays were mythological burlesques, though none is now extant.   [2] Easterling 1993.

of a story by Aeschylus, Sophocles, or Euripides exerted a massive gravitational tug on the direction of any subsequent treatment. It is hard not to feel that in the long term tragedy was a victim of its astonishing fifth-century fecundity and success: the emergence almost overnight of a whole new library of instant classics, numbering well into the hundreds and between them providing a model for the dramatic handling of every tractable story in the mythological heritage.[3]

At the same time, the very familiarity of mythological stories surely accelerated tragedy's extraordinary achievement in the invention and development of plot techniques, by throwing the dramatic weight away from the stories and on to their narrative packaging. The compact between genre and audience accepted that *what* was told could signify less than *how*. And the more of the story could be taken as read, the more economical the narrative line. Plays could exploit their audience's familiarity with the characters and their backgrounds to develop a kind of expositional shorthand. Everyone knows who Orestes is, and what he is famous for doing: this play is about this or that particular day in his story, when such-and-such a crisis occurs. To jettison all this in favour of free fictional creation of story and narrative alike, yet still somehow to preserve all the tightness and structural power of classical plot economics, can hardly have seemed an inviting prospect.

And in fact New Comedy does not exactly kick the addiction to the predictability of myth. What it does, rather, is to switch to a clinical substitute, replacing tragedy's dependency with equally, or even more, deterministic story material. The difference is that predictability now resides at the level not of story but of narrative, in the *generic rule-system of the corpus*. So, for example, the familiar characters of myth are replaced by equally, if differently, familiar genre types: just as in a tragedy the audience will know who Orestes is long before they meet this particular Orestes, so the Menandrean audience will know who Moschion is even though they have never met this particular character by the name. Equally, the tragic audience may not know what will happen in the early stages of this particular Orestes play, but they know that if he has returned to Argos in the opening scene and Clytemnestra is still alive, he is certain to kill her at the climax of the play. With the same confidence a comic audience knows that, if Moschion has raped a citizen virgin, the play will end with their marriage, and the gaps in the picture lie rather in the intermediate moves – in discovering *how* that marriage will eventually and inevitably take place.

Nevertheless, there is a profound shift in the *nature* of this audience foreknowledge, which takes us to the heart not only of New Comedy's

[3] Burian 1997: 205–8.

representation of the world but of the cognitive apparatus of plotting itself. The audience's knowledge of the story to come is now *extrapolated* rather than given: apart from the limited, largely redundant, predictions occasionally vouchsafed in divine prologues, the audience now knows nothing of the story to come beyond what it can project by inference from generic rules. In the Roman versions, even divine prologues decline strikingly, increasing the demands on their audiences' familiarity with genre dynamics.[4] And to support this weight of extrapolation, New Comedy operates a daring and virtually unrepeatable experiment in narrativity.

To appreciate that experiment, we need to press one stage further the game model of plot proposed in Part I. Audiences, I have argued, read plays the way chess masters read a board: as a constellation of purposeful possibilities, contours of power in time extending into past and future. An expert spectator, observing a game in progress, sees not merely a snapshot of events but a balance of advantage, stable and vulnerable positions, areas of greater and lesser dynamism or activity. Not all of the possible lines of development can be visualised in their entirety – their number is effectively infinite – but the teleology of play allows attention to concentrate on a narrow range of possible developments from any given position. And that view is hierarchical: a pawn is not *just* a pawn, but a pawn in a certain position at a certain time, and connected by a higher collectivity of purpose to the larger entity formed by all the pieces of that colour, whose behaviour is in turn shaped by interaction with its opposite-coloured counterpart.

Up to now, we have been considering kinds of plotting for which this game metaphor is at best a convenient ultra-formalism; where no 'rule' is as unbreakable as the rules of rummy or ping-pong, and the simplicities of absolute closure often seem problematised or resisted as inadequately descriptive of reality. New Comedy, however, is different: a determinedly humane, realistic narrative genre that nevertheless fully embraces the chessboard-universe way of modelling the world. New Comedy is, quite simply, the most rule-bound and programmed of all classical narrative genres. Its stories inhabit one of the narrowest universes ever created in fiction, pursuing the economy principle to a ruthless extreme that is hard to parallel anywhere in any later literature of comparable stature and ambition. Yet this is precisely the source of its enormous strength and influence, both in antiquity and far beyond, offering a way of understand-

---

[4] Divine speakers feature in 5 out of 7 of known Menandrean prologues; between 5 and 10 out of 20 in Plautus, depending on how many anonymous but omniscient speakers are counted; and 0 out of 6 in Terence, where five are nevertheless suspected to have featured a divine prologue in the source.

ing the world that ultimately rivals the tragic in power, complexity, and persuasiveness.

What New Comedy does is to propose a universe that is overwhelmingly *systemic*: a world in which individual relationships are apprehended as part of a collective process governed by precise and inviolate rules of play. Three especially significant features are: a explicit and binding procedural rule-system, enshrined in (but not reducible to) civic law; a strong generic distinction between stable and unstable gamestates; and an emphasis on the global dynamics of the system as a whole, with a sustained thematic contrast between the individualistic perspective of the characters and the systemic view available to the audience. New Comedy is the only major Western narrative form to pander in such an extreme way to our narrative appetite for systemic closure, while simultaneously professing to reproduce the essential structure of real life; and its ultra-schematic representation of its world has consequences that go far beyond mere plot economy, proposing in effect a new ideological construction of society and the person.

The essential machinery of New Comic plotting can be summarised as follows. (i) Plots are construed in terms of *transactions*, normally in persons, between households. This traffic is mapped out using a three-door expansion of tragedy's spatial shorthand of exits and entrances. (ii) Unlike in tragedy, there are global genre rules to distinguish permitted and forbidden gamestates, so that any such transaction will be recognised as stable (adoption, purchase, marriage) or unstable (abduction, embezzlement, rape). All unstable transactions must finally be replaced by stable ones, in which the consent of all parties is willingly given to a legally binding and permanent final configuration. (iii) In nearly all plays,[5] this transactional power-plot is complicated by a plotting of *information*, in which erroneous secondary models of the central transaction(s) proliferate among the characters, but finally collapse in a general recognition of the true state of affairs and universal acquiescence in a stable transactional outcome. The rest of this chapter sets out to explain these three principles in turn.

The *transactional* basis of New Comic plotting is easiest approached through its concretisation in space. As in tragedy, the spatial map of the stage universe not only supplies the narrative frame on which stories are shaped, but thereby proposes a distinctive reading of the world. But New Comedy's map is significantly different from tragedy's, its three-door

---

[5] *Dyskolos* and *Stichus* are the only extant plays in which deception or cross-purposes play no part at all; the latter's plot, however, seems to have been radically dismantled in Plautus' version.

skene the framework for a new, and vastly more complex, symbolic topography of relationships between houses. As the last chapter noted, it is a truism that already in tragedy the stage house is *oikos* as well as *domos*, a social structure as much as a material one. It is the physical abode of the collective family, and the domain of power for the *kyrios* or head of the domestic group. It is an entity in time as well as space, extending through the line of male descent back to ancestral times and forward to successive generations. It is a human organism that normally survives the death of the individual, so that already in tragedy the extinction of an *oikos* through the obliteration of its reproductive males is a catastrophe transcending the extinction of the person.

But though many tragedies use this spatial map to explore relations between individuals and *oikos*, *oikos* and community, what they cannot so easily map in a one-door set is relations between *oikos* and *oikos*.[6] It is this relationship that is central to New Comic plotting. In the systemic view presented to the audience, the plots of New Comedy are less about individuals than about houses – specifically, about the relations of power, competition and collaboration between the two or three *oikoi* represented onstage. These relations centre on the manoeuvrings of *kyrioi* and *meirakioi*, the house's supervisory ego and sexually active id, for what might be termed control of the means of reproduction. They are played out in the movements of reproductively significant persons between the power-spaces of different *oikoi*, and are resolved in the mutual acceptance of a new family configuration expressed in the legal redistribution of persons between stage houses. Often there is competing pressure towards an alternative, generically unsatisfactory, configuration, and the plot interest lies in the characters' escape from this rival pattern into one that fulfils the strict genre conditions for an acceptable settlement. The result is an image of society that views individual citizens not merely as private persons but as atoms in a dynamic matrix of *oikoi* – bonding particles exchanged by the familial superentities whose interaction comprises the systemic behaviour of the polis.

A New Comic citizen *oikos* is built from any or all of the following elements: the *geron*, a male *kyrios* of post-reproductive age; the *gyne*, his wife of similar age; one or two *meirakioi*, male heirs of marriageable age; one (rarely more than one) *parthenos*, a marriageable daughter; and a variable number of *douloi*, chattels of both sexes under the notional control of the *kyrios*. In some plays the *geron* does not figure and the *meirakios* is himself the *kyrios*; in a few the relation between *geron* and *meirakios* is adoptive;

---

[6] A second, offstage house is specifically invoked only in Euripides' *Medea* (Creon's palace) and *Electra* (the Argive palace).

and in one (*Samia*) the *geron* is still reproductively active through a *pallake* or legitimate concubine, though in the event the child does not survive. In a handful of plays (*Epitrepontes*, *Hecyra*, *Phormio*, and cf. *Amphitruo*, *Menaechmi*, *Stichus*) the *meirakios* is already married to the heroine as the narrative opens. Other types of *oikos* exist mainly as auxiliaries to or diversions from the citizen household. The most important are the houses of non-citizen sexual rivals (whether free *hetairai*, or slave *pornai*[7] in the power of a *pornoboskos*) and religious shrines (sometimes staffed by a human official in addition to the generally unseen divine occupant). None of these, however, is classed as a potential reproductive unit for plot purposes. They can give women to the citizen *oikos* as the result of recognitions, but cannot reproduce themselves.

Of the various transactional mechanisms for the reconfiguration of *oikoi*, by far the most important is the exchange of women[8] through marriage: the transfer of a bride from the house of her *kyrios* to the house of her husband. All but one[9] of the sufficiently known plays of Menander and Terence, and a majority of the extant non-Menandrean Plautus,[10] end with at least one marriage contracted or repaired. Under Attic law, for convenience assumed in comedy to extend to other poleis, these had to be legitimised by (a) citizen birth or, exceptionally, naturalisation[11] of both partners; (b) formal consent of the bride's *kyrios*. The rules of comic plotting add some purely conventional further conditions: only *meirakioi* and *parthenoi* are eligible on grounds of age, and virginity is strongly preferred in the bride – though this clause may be waived if she is deflowered before

---

[7] This is a terminology of convenience; in Greek usage, the terms overlapped, and the criterion of distinction was not slave status versus free, but range of services. 'Hetaeras who were paid by the evening must be strongly distinguished from *pornai* who were paid by the deed' (Davidson 1997: 95).

[8] The term derives from Lévi-Strauss (1949); for this traffic's role in tragedy see especially Rabinowitz 1993, Wohl 1998, and for New Comedy Rosivach 1998.

[9] The exception appears to be *Dis exapaton*, though our evidence for the ending derives of course from the Plautine *Bacchides*.

[10] There is room for a deleted final recognition and marriage (cf. *Casina* 1013–14) in most of the seven marriageless *meretrix* plays: *Asinaria* (Philaenium can be Diabolus' sister); *Mercator* (Pasicompsa can be Lysimachus' daughter); *Mostellaria* (Philematium can be Simo's daughter); *Pseudolus* (Phoenicium can be Callipho's sister); *Miles gloriosus* (Philocomasium can be Periplectomenus' daughter, and Periplectomenus Athenian). Least likely are *Bacchides* (where one sister would need to prove adopted, and be revealed as the daughter of the appropriate *senex*) and *Persa* (where Toxilus would need to prove freeborn and Lemniselenis the master's or Saturio's daughter).

[11] The Syracusan Menaechmus is adopted by a native of Epidamnus, where he marries an Epidamnian wife; at the end of the play (Plautus' quip at 1160 notwithstanding) he transplants his household to Syracuse, where we must assume his marriage will remain legal. None of these three actions would have been tolerated under Attic law; here as elsewhere the choice of non-Attic settings seems dictated by local variations in citizenship laws required by the particular plot, unless Gratwick 1993: 30 is right to suspect that in the Greek play the marriage was dissolved.

marriage by her eventual husband and admits no other sexual partner in the meantime.

Marriage is not, however, the only mechanism of adjustment available. *Adoption* allows propagation of the *oikos* without sexual reproduction, though it more commonly contributes to the story's premise than (as in *Dyskolos*) to its resolution. *Estrangement and reconciliation* between already married couples figure in *Dyskolos*, *Epitrepontes*, *Menaechmi*, and especially *Hecyra*. Such a pattern may involve competition between the claims of the married *oikos* and an extramural liaison, with the husband moving back in to signal the resolution; or there may be pressure on the wife, where the marriage is not genetically sealed by the birth of a child, to move out of the marital home and back to her father's house (*Epitrepontes*, *Stichus*, and cf. *Menaechmi*).[12] Sometimes, again, the disposal and recognition of legitimate children, whether adult or infant, is the means of the family's eventual reconstitution; in such plays as *Samia*, *Epitrepontes*, *Truculentus*, and *Andria*, the movement of babies between different houses maps out the shifting vicissitudes of their status, before finally they are readmitted to the legitimate *oikos*.

As is well known, the world of the Roman versions differs considerably from the known Menander in the kinds of structure actually built from this kit.[13] How much of this had lost Greek precedent, and how much is the result of systematic and radical intervention by the Roman adapters, is extremely difficult to assess; it may be that the overwhelming preponderance of citizen plots in Menander was less than typical of the genre as a whole. At any rate Plautine comedy, especially, is not preoccupied with affirming the family, and more often than not subverts it with *infertile* configurations even in plays where conventional endings operate. Thus one major pattern extant only in Roman plays has a free *hetaira* occupy one of the stage houses, and exercise sexual power over citizen lovers through the permission or denial of access to her door (*Bacchides*, *Truculentus*, *Menaechmi*, *Eunuchus*). In a variation, a male or female *pornoboskos* occupies the house and controls access to a slave *porne* (*Asinaria*, *Cistellaria*, *Pseudolus*, *Persa*, *Curculio*).[14] Also unique to Roman versions is

[12] *Dyskolos* is unique in that the familial *oikos* is already split into two stage houses, which the play *symbolically* merges by funnelling all the characters (including those from Sostratus' *oikos* offstage) into the neutral middle ground of the shrine of Pan; see Lowe 1987.
[13] 'The focus of the Greek material upon rape and marriage is replaced by a new focus upon prostitution' (Wiles 1989: 39).
[14] There is an obvious linkage here, reaching back to *Lysistrata*, between the house and the female body – less in any crude visual allegory of penetration than in the more important respect that a woman admitting a man to her house is a surrender of rights to her body. Note, however, an important asymmetry in the sexuality of theatre space: a woman entering a man's house is an act of sexual submission, but a man entering a woman's house is an act of power often leading to rape, and even when the woman volunteers access she is in effect consenting to the use of her body by that man.

the installation of a son's mistress in the family home itself without his father's knowledge (*Mercator, Epidicus, Heauton*) – effectively blocking the *oikos* from reproducing itself, by pairing the fertile male with a generically infertile female (a *porne* or *hetaira*), a configuration so unacceptable that in all extant cases she has to be recognised as freeborn and marriageable after all. Many of these plays turn on a dualistic opposition between familial duty and sexual pleasure, the familiar Terentian antithesis between *pietas* and *amor*, played out between the family house and that of a non-citizen sexual rival.[15]

One group particular to Plautus merits fuller comment: plays in which the citizen identity of the householder himself is threatened, undermined, or systematically degraded by exclusion from his own house, and thus from his own social identity, his position as paterfamilias, and his ownership of his own sexual property and even his own person. In Menander's *Misoumenos*, the power paradox is that the lover has voluntarily chosen to banish *himself* from his own house and his ownership of his mistress; but in Plautus, the excluded citizens are the unconsenting *victims* of a kind of rape of their social identity. In the milder cases (*Mostellaria, Trinummus*) a respected citizen returning from abroad is barred from entry to his house and, in the latter case, suffers the comic theft of his very name and identity. More disturbing are the *doppelgänger* plays in which a citizen finds himself nightmarishly dispossessed of his house, his wife, and his name by an unseen ringer. *Amphitruo* is a one-door play (the only other one is *Captivi*), entirely built around Amphitryo's frustrated attempts to pass through that door and into the arms of his wife, whose body and womb we know have already been occupied by a rival; his closing words, as he finally enters, are *ibo ad uxorem intro*, 'I will go inside to my wife.' In *Menaechmi*'s two-house version, the citizen makes a culpable confusion of sexual priorities, expressed as a choice between the house of his wife and that of his mistress. Menaechmus walks out of his own house and marriage to enter the house of his mistress, only to find himself unable to re-enter either; and as he wanders the streets, aimless and homeless, he finds his right of ownership over his very body arrogated by his wife's family, as his father-in-law's slaves try to bind him and abduct him. Yet even these victims are luckier than Pyrgopolinices in *Miles gloriosus* and Lysidamus in *Casina*, both of whom make the fatal mistake of walking out of their own house, and in the process surrendering their control of their own sexual property, to enter another's door in the mistaken belief that

---

[15] *Epitrepontes* is the only extant Greek instance. On the thematic opposition see especially the Terentian essays in Konstan 1983; it is expressed in a spatial antithesis between the house of citizen duty and the house of pleasure in all of Terence bar *Heauton*. It is not necessary for both to be onstage – though even if Bacchis' house was offstage in Terence's *Hecyra*, it may have been onstage in Apollodorus.

they are participating in an assignation – only to find that they have walked into a trap and placed their very body and masculinity in the power of their enemy, threatening Pyrgopolinices with castration and Lysidamus with buggery.

It is this typology of comic houses and their interaction that underlies New Comedy's most notorious feature, its elaborate taxonomy of individual players and goals. Characters are limited in range to a narrow repertoire of transactionally-functional types within three broad classes: family, other citizens, and chattels. All citizen family members, male and female, are banded into three discrete age-classes: the newborn, the marriageable, and the superannuable, with no points beyond or between. Non-family citizen characters likewise follow a narrow range of types: professional soldiers (in Menander sometimes family members, but never in the Roman plays), urban parasites, pimps, free *hetairai*, masterless matrons, and the occasional unattached *meirakios*, none of whom is normally permitted a legitimate marriage and *oikos*. Chattels can attach to most of the citizen characters (parasites excepted, presumably because of their limited means), but generally the only ones who can cross the border of status through emancipation are war captives and abductees, *pornai*, and (mostly in Plautus) male domestic slaves. The combination we meet in *Persa*, where a domestic slave loves a *porne* and himself supports a citizen parasite with a respectable virgin daughter, is entirely bizarre.

This highly artificial taxonomics makes clear functional sense once it is seen in terms of the systemic plotting of transactions between *oikoi*. The principal goals of New Comic leads are all forms of sexual ownership of females, with the single extant exception of *Captivi* (discussed below). The genre recognises numerous classes of sexually available female (*parthenoi, pornai, hetairai*, domestic slaves, war captives, kidnap victims), but essentially only three types of stable sexual access: marriage, chattel ownership, and long-term contractual rights. Purchasing a slave mistress and then awarding her freedom (as in *Mostellaria* and *Pseudolus*) is not distinguished as a functionally separate outcome.

The transactional focus on the citizen *oikos* means that not all male player types may compete for these rewards, and of those who can not all may succeed. *Meirakioi* usually obtain something, though not always the object of their desire: in *Truculentus* and *Heauton* a young man has to give up his pursuit of a *hetaira* and accept a citizen bride instead, while in *Perikeiromene* the feckless Moschion loses a prospective mistress but gains a sister. Married men, whether young (*Epitrepontes, Menaechmi*) or old (*Aspis, Asinaria, Aulularia, Casina, Mercator*) may not succeed with external liaisons, though an adoptive bachelor father can acquire a partner so long as there is no competing suitor (*Samia, Adelphoe*). Soldiers can love, though only in Menander do they succeed (*Misoumenos, Sikyonios,* and perhaps *Kolax*); while parasites, pimps, and (with two Plautine exceptions) slaves may not. Thus Phormio may pretend to compete for Phanium with the *adulescens* Antipho, but his real ambition (and eventual reward) is the parasite's meal ticket; Olympio can delude himself that he is a contender for Casina, but we know he is merely a surrogate for the *senex* Lysidamus, destined to share in his exposure and humiliation. Only in the anomalous *Persa* does a slave play the lover's role, and Toxilus is significantly the one comic slave whose master is barred from the play – faceless, unnamed, and banished throughout to an indeterminate 'abroad', effectively minimising Toxilus' status as a chattel.

Access to the object of desire is blocked by one or more conventional machineries of obstruction: persons, laws, or contractual requirements which place the object outside the lover's sphere of control, by the exercise of superior authority over either the lover or the beloved or both. The main types are (a) the lover's father, whose familial and financial consent must finally be won to stabilise any of the three types of liaison; (b) the beloved's *kyrios* (in the case of *parthenoi*), whose consent is required for her marriage; (c) the beloved's *pornoboskos* (in the case of *pornai*), whose chattel she is; (d) the beloved herself (in the case of free *hetairai*); (e) the legal code of the polis, defining permissible and forbidden liaisons for all members of the community; (f) the lover's wife. The first four of these are amenable to persuasion and, regularly in the Roman plays, the cash inducements of dowry (a–b), purchase (c), gift or contract (c–d). Cases (b) and (c) can be temporarily addressed by force – (b) by rape, (c) by abduction – but this is not in itself determinative, and usually modulates into a full resolution through the blocking character's acquiescence in the *fait accompli*; thus rape victims are invariably married off to their attackers, because the codes of New Comic plotting treat defloration as a contractual act establishing a family bond *de facto*, whether or not a child is in the event born. Type (e) is non-negotiable, but can be eliminated by recognition; (f) is insuperable.

Such, in outline, are the principal rules governing the elementary situations of New Comedy. But it is important to appreciate that they are not in themselves a system of plot, any more than the rules of chess are a manual of strategy. I stress this because Bettini's pioneering Greimassian 'anthropology' of the plots of Plautus, to which this chapter is centrally indebted, is actually an analysis of something rather different, though no less fundamental to the grammar of Plautine narrative. What Bettini offers is rather a structural typology of *transactional configurations* and

their transformations within the corpus.[16] There can be no doubt that
Plautine comedy, and Graeco-Roman New Comedy in general, is peculiarly constrained in this area – far more so than tragedy, for instance –
and that familiarity with the generic codes of how women and cash can be
transferred is one vital component in the decoding apparatus the narrative assumes in its audience. These codes help to define the universe in
which the story is set and the range of possible actions and outcomes
available; but they do *not* in themselves determine the moves out of which
plot is built.[17] Instead, I want to argue that the real creativity of New
Comic plotting lies precisely in the areas left open by such codes: in the
dynamic patterns of intrigue, misapprehension, and competing goals and
story-models that arise from the interaction between players.

The most important distinction to grasp here is that while the ground
rules for plotting are founded in *power* relationships, the plots themselves
are built on *communication*. Though New Comedy's underlying situations
depend on the adjustment of real or perceived imbalances of power, the
actual mechanism of adjustment around which the stories revolve almost
invariably demands the redistribution of information – normally concerning the status of one or both lovers, and the resulting interpretation of
the codes of access. Thus a slave or alien may turn out to be a citizen, and
so eligible to marry the hero; an orphan or *epikleros* may turn up a missing
kyrios; an imagined rival may turn out not to exist. The result is a genre
that completes the movement away from Iliadic power-plots towards the
plots of communication pioneered in the *Odyssey* and increasingly
favoured in fifth-century tragedy.

New Comedy is plotted almost entirely out of c-moves, no doubt in
part because comedy's genre universe excluded most of the surviving
forms in which power can be exercised in tragedy. But it is not simply that

[16] Bettini's analysis draws on Segre's quadripartite variation of the formalist model of narrative, which attempts a reconciliation of Proppian narrative grammars with both the formalist *fabula/sjuzhet* dichotomy and Barthes' overlapping *histoire/discours*. In this model,
the transformational rules of the *corpus* are a fourth and fundamental stratum underlying
story, narrative (in this terminology called 'plot', *intreccio*), and text; thus it is legitimate to
claim that these deep-structural models are the ideal destination of plot theory.
Influential in Italian theory, Segre's model has been comparatively neglected abroad,
where the tendency has been rather to treat such underlying structures as integral to the
story level itself.

[17] It cannot be overstressed that, despite the stereotypy of roles, goals, situations, and some
move-patterns, New Comedy is anything but formulaic. At most, there are clusters of
three or four plays with some significant overlap of major situational or strategic motifs.
The closest pairs are *Pseudolus* and *Curculio*, *Mercator* and *Casina*, *Heauton timorumenos*
and *Adelphoe* (Terence's prologue is an unreliable witness for *Andria* and *Perinthia*), but
there is none of the scene-by-scene parallelism we see in some tragic pairs (*Persians* and
Agamemnon, *Heraclidae* and *Suppliants*, *IT* and *Helen*) – even though the plotting prefer-
ences of the three directly extant poets are at least as distinctive as those of the three tragedians.

death, wars, miracles, and madness are generically banished from the action. The very move from prelegal to contemporary settings means that force is constrained by law – a fact of which even the aggressive individualism of Aristophanic comedy is consistently and shrewdly aware.[18] This explains why the p-moves of abduction, theft, and rape are by generic convention fundamentally unstable, and by the end of the play must either be cancelled – not even an option in rape plots – or modulate into contractual dealings sanctioned by law. The one form of comic p-move unavailable to tragedy is the cash transaction or other legal contract; otherwise, the transfer of persons is the *only* form of p-move accepted by the genre.[19]

Not all playwrights welcomed this restriction. Plautus, for whom power is an important dramatic and thematic concern, puts considerable effort into powering-up the move-structure: by favouring cash and abduction plots, by permitting limited exercise of force (normally against slaves or other low-ranking characters), and by demoting citizen transfer from its paramount status in Menander. Yet even in Plautus c-plotting dominates, and contests of power are consistently channelled into their Odyssean equivalent, intrigue.[20] There is room, in principle, for a kind of New Comic plot that revolves entirely around will, persuasion, and the removal of human obstacles by negotiation, without any recourse to misunderstanding or deceit; but it is significant that only two extant plays even approximate to this pattern.[21] As the following discussion will argue, interest centres not on the traffic in persons *per se* but on the further complications of power and perception wrought on it by the generic repertoire of available *transformations*. Some readers may find the technical detail from here to chapter-end numbing; persistence will, however, yield not only a global model for understanding New Comic plots, but the rudiments of a universal grammar of c-plotting and the elements of a formal account of 'what happens' in rigorously classical kinds of plot.

The standard New Comic transactional core involves the passage of a person from a donor to a recipient, sometimes via intermediaries, in a legally binding contract. In the case of a *nymphe*, the donor is her *kyrios*;

---

[18] There seems no instance in Aristophanes where a citizen bound by the law of the *polis* (as Dicaeopolis, Pisthetaerus, and Lysistrata are not, but Strepsiades and Philocleon are) physically abuses a free person with impunity.

[19] Lawsuits are rarely brought in the surviving plays, perhaps because they are hard to accommodate within the time-frame; *Rudens* features a trial between acts and *Phormio* a hearing before the play opens, but other legal plots prefer such measures as private justice (*Miles*), arbitration (*Epitrepontes*), and *ad hoc* assemblies (*Sikyonios*). See now Scafuro 1997 *passim*.

[20] The only Roman plays to lack a significant element of intrigue are *Cistellaria*, *Rudens* and *Stichus*; the extant Menander, however, offers *Dyskolos*, *Perikeiromene*, *Heros*, *Georgos*, *Misoumenos*.   [21] See above, n. 5.

for a *hetaira*, the donor is herself or her mother; for a *porne*, the donor is a *pornoboskos*.[22] In the first case, a dowry will normally be expected to pass with the bride (this is an issue in *Dyskolos*, *Aulularia* and *Trinummus*); in the others, cash (which is invariably lacking) will be expected to pass in the opposite direction, and the recipient's father may be a blocking character. If there is to be any tension, the donor or intermediary must be reluctant (in *nymphe* transactions), or cash lacking (in *hetaira* and *porne* transactions).

This core transaction is then subjected to any of a number of complicating transformations, which fall into two distinct layers. *P-transformations* – elaborations of the transaction itself as it develops in time – may be thought of as 'horizontal', operating in the plane of the transaction itself. *C-transformations*, however, are 'vertical', inasmuch as they superimpose on this planar transaction-map a stack of distorted copies: erroneous plot

[22] I list the ultimate source and recipient of the central transactions in the extant plays, indicating whether the object is *nymphe*, a *hetaira*, or a *porne*, and the source of cash when not the recipient. MENANDER, *Aspis*: sister$_n$ from Cleostratus to Chaereas + daughter$_n$ from Chaerestratus to Cleostratus. *Dyskolos*: daughter$_n$ from Cnemon to Sostratus + sister$_n$ from Callippides to Gorgias. *Epitrepontes*: Pamphile$_n$ from Smicrines to Charisius + Habrotonon$_h$ from Charisius to Chaerestratus. *Georgos*: sister$_n$ from Gorgias to opening speaker. *Heros*: daughter$_n$ from Laches to ?Phidias. *Misoumenos*: Crateia$_n$ from Demeas to Stratonides. *Perikeiromene*: Glycera$_n$ from Pataecus to Polemon. *Phasma*: daughter$_n$ from father to Phidias. *Plokion*: daughter$_n$ from poor father to Moschion. *Samia*: Plangon$_n$ from Niceratus to Moschion. *Sikyonios*: Philumene$_n$ from Cichesias to Stratophanes + Malthace$_h$ from Stratophanes to Theron. PLAUTUS, *Amphitruo*: Alcmena$_n$ from Amphitryo to Amphitryo. *Asinaria*: Philaenium$_m$ from Cleareta to Argyrippus (cash from Artemona). *Aulularia*: Phaedria$_n$ from Euclio to Lyconides. *Bacchides*: Samian Bacchis$_h$ from Cleomachus to Mnesilochus + Athenian Bacchis$_h$ from self to Pistoclerus (cash from Nicobulus). *Captivi*: Tyndarus from Hegio to Hegio + Philocrates from Theodoromedes to Theodoromedes. *Casina*: Casina$_n$ from Alcesimus to Euthynicus. *Cistellaria*: Selenium$_n$ from Demipho to Alcesimarchus. *Curculio*: Planesium$_n$ from Therapontigonus to Phaedromus. *Epidicus*: Telestis$_n$ from Periphanes to Stratippocles + Acropolistis$_p$ from *leno* to soldier. *Menaechmi*: meretrix$_h$ from Menaechmus to Sosicles (cash from Menaechmus) + wife$_n$ from father to Menaechmus. *Mercator*: Pasicompsa$_p$ from *leno* to Charinus (cash from Demipho). *Miles gloriosus*: Philocomasium$_m$ from *lena* to Pleusicles. *Mostellaria*: Philematium$_p$ from *leno* to Philolaches (cash from Theopropides). *Persa*: Lemniselenis$_p$ from Dordalus to Toxilus (cash from Dordalus). *Poenulus*: Adelphasium$_n$ from Hanno to Agorastocles + Anterastilis$_n$ from Hanno to Hanno. *Pseudolus*: Phoenicium$_p$ from Ballio to Calidorus (see text for cash). *Rudens*: Palaestra$_n$ from Daemones to Plesidippus + Ampelisca$_n$ from Labrax to Daemones. *Stichus*: Panegyris$_n$ from Antipho to Epignomus + Pamphila$_n$ from Antipho to Pamphilippus. *Trinummus*: daughter$_n$ from Charmides to Lysiteles. *Truculentus*: daughter$_n$ from Callicles to Diniarchus + Phronesium$_h$ from self to Strabax and Stratophanes. TERENCE, *Adelphoe*: Pamphila$_n$ from †Simulus to Aeschinus + Bacchis$_p$ from Sannio to Ctesipho (cash from Micio). *Andria*: Glycerium$_n$ from Chremes to Pamphilus + Philumena$_n$ from Chremes to Charinus. *Eunuchus*: Pamphila$_n$ from Chremes to Chaerea + Thais$_h$ from self to Phaedria & Thraso. *Heauton timorumenos*: Antiphila$_n$ from Chremes to Clinia + Bacchis$_h$ from self to Clitipho (cash from Chremes). *Hecyra*: Philumena$_n$ from Phidippus to Pamphilus. *Phormio*: Phanium$_n$ from Chremes to Antipho + Pamphila$_p$ from *leno* to Phaedria (cash from Nausistrata and Demipho).

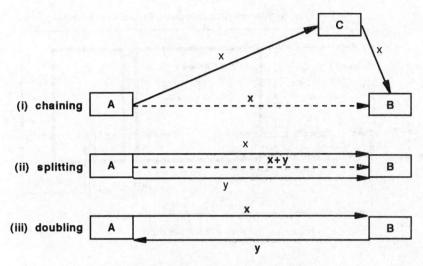

Figure 2. Transformations of the comic transaction

models, constructed by characters or audience, which may have links missing or substituted. Practically all plays plot in both dimensions, but the distinction is analytically important. All p-transformations tend to *generate* c-transformations, since some (usually all) of the characters will have a necessarily incomplete model of the total transactional structure. But these purely subtractive c-transformations can be further expanded by additive, substitutive, or combinatorial transformations of the actual move-structure in the perceptions of one or more characters.

The three elementary forms of p-transformation are diagrammed in Figure 2. Each multiplies one of the three elements of the transactional system: moves can be chained; transactions can be doubled; and objects can be split. *Move-chaining* is a purely linear complication, especially characteristic of recognition plots: segmentation of the central transaction into a sequence of transfers that needs to be traced in its entirety before the overall transaction can be correctly construed. In the tragic prototype, the infant Oedipus passes from (i) Jocasta to (ii) Laius' henchman to (iii) the shepherd to (iv) Polybus; but knowledge of the successive links is segmented among the three surviving parties, who must collate their information for Oedipus' history to be told. The longest tragic chain is Ion's, who passes from (i) Creusa to (ii) Apollo to (iii) Hermes to (iv) the Pythia to (v) Apollo to (vi) Xuthus; here the second and third links are bridged by the tokens, which prove that Creusa's child abandoned to Apollo must be the same as the Pythia's foundling.

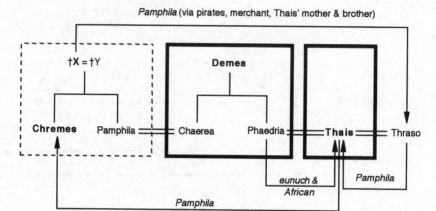

Figure 3. *Eunuchus*: houses and transactions

But comic chains are often longer still, and the detective plotting itself takes a back seat to other concerns. First, comic complications operate in more than one dimension: chaining of moves is always accompanied by either *doubling of the transaction* (where more than one transaction is running simultaneously among the same cast of participants, but along different routes) or *splitting the object* (where a single transaction divides into two or more, as a result of the fragmentation of its object into two separately transferable commodities whose transactional paths then diverge). These diverse transactions can then cross, tangle, and interfere in a multitude of fertile ways. Second, comic transactions tend to be *bidirectional*: the commodities passed *back* in the chain of exchanges can also be important for the intricate balance of advantage or obligation. And when these two principles combine in a single play, they can weave extraordinarily complex networks of asymmetrical debts and credits.

To see how this works, consider a relatively straightforward case. Figure 3 illustrates the transactional structure of Terence's *EUNUCHUS*, where the net transaction 'Chremes gives Pamphila in marriage to Chaerea' is complicated as follows. First, the transaction is *chained* into seven segments, knowledge of which is distributed among different characters. Pamphila actually passes from Chremes (her *kyrios*) to the pirates (by her original abduction) to the merchant (by sale) to Thais' mother (as a gift) to Thais' brother (by inheritance) to Thraso (by resale in Thais' absence; here the action opens) to Thais (by Thraso's gift) to Chaerea (by the rape). The missing link in Thais' reconstruction is the initial abduction, so that once Thais has tracked down Chremes she is able to legitimise Chaerea's unstable local transaction in marriage, by Chremes' consent to the net

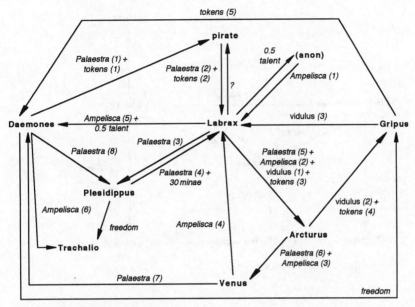

Figure 4. *Rudens*: gross

transaction constituted by the chain as a whole. But the play's central problems come from the chain's *bidirectionality*: the remarkable range of commodities for which Pamphila has been exchanged at different points in the circuit (cash, sexual favours, citizen ties, and some subtle intangibles) leaves a complex trail of reciprocal debts to be addressed by the problem ending. Meanwhile, the transaction has been *doubled* by a second transactional chain, which tangles fatally with the first: Phaedria's gifts of eunuch and Ethiopian to Thais in competition with Thraso for her favours. It is the existence of this second chain that makes the rape possible, with Chaerea's substitution of its object (in his impersonation of the eunuch) allowing infiltration of the impregnable house.

This is nevertheless a relatively compact case by comparison with a play like *RUDENS*. Figure 4 maps the full set of essential transactional links in the play and its backstory; Figure 5 deletes all intermediate links and simply presents the net donors and recipients.

The central transaction is Palaestra's passage in marriage from her father Daemones to her bridegroom Plesidippus; but this is *chained* into eight separate transactional segments by her interpolated abduction by the pirate, requiring her return to and recognition by Daemones before the marriage can considered. Her story cannot end with stage 3 (her sale to Plesidippus), because the legal and generic conditions for marriage

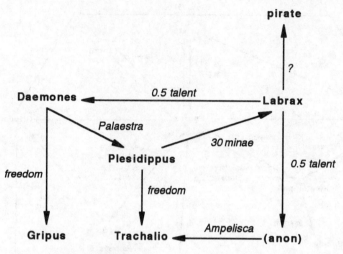

Figure 5. *Rudens*: net

have not been satisfied; thus Labrax must default and perform a second abduction, allowing the transaction to be intercepted by Arcturus and steered back to port. At this point, the transaction *splits* by separating its object into two, as Palaestra is parted from the tokens that prove her identity (and which must return with her to Daemones for her to be duly restored to him). Next, transactions *multiply*: the Palaestra transaction, already somewhat gratuitously doubled by the Ampelisca circuit, now becomes entangled with a quite separate loop involving Labrax's luggage, which carries off the tokens to Gripus instead.

And by this stage an elaborate hierarchy of *vertical* complications has developed. Only Arcturus and the audience are aware of the whole matrix, including the crucial link 'Palaestra (1)'. All other characters have their own maps, and their maps of one another's maps, in which many links are missing and some objects therefore erroneously split. Palaestra and Daemones' daughter are believed to be two different women; the identity of the *vidulus* lost by Labrax and the tokens lost by Palaestra with those found by Gripus has to be established and defended in a sequence of scenes that explore complex moral and legal questions of ownership under the rival claims of Athenian, Cyrenian, and natural law.[23] Nevertheless, *Rudens* typifies a class of plot that favours essentially horizontal complications over vertical; Labrax' initial treachery aside, there is

[23] Konstan 1983: 73–95.

no strong element of deception or cross-purposes, and the c-plotting arises entirely out of the characters' incomplete knowledge of the intricate jigsaw of transactions.

Rudens' combination of move-chaining with object-splitting is the standard template for recognition with *tokens*. In CISTELLARIA, for instance, the attainment of Alcesimarchus' desire depends on the reconstruction of the whole circuitous route of Selenium's fostering. All the stages are known to one or more characters. Demipho, Phanostrata, and Lampadio know the girl's parentage, and that she was exposed; Lampadio knows (by sight) who retrieved her; Syra and Melaenis know Syra retrieved Selenium as a foundling and gave her to Melaenis, who reared her as her daughter; Selenium herself, like Alcesimarchus and his father, knows nothing. The missing link is therefore between Lampadio, who knows the whole story up to the foundling's retrieval, and Syra, who knows the story from the retrieval onwards. The connection is made in the fragmentary part of the text, only for the proof of the whole story – the *cistella* of recognition tokens – to be mislaid at the crucial moment, so that the completion of the chain has to be played out a second time between a different pair of characters. Here, as already in *Ion*, the recognition tokens act as a marker trail for the movements of the recognisee; and their separation from their owner, the object of recognition, requires a further act of collation to re-establish the link between sign and person.

The above cases all centre on a single recognition circuit; but still more elaborate structures are possible with *doubling*, where multiple transactions are allowed to interfere with one another. CAPTIVI, for example, plays out a game of ownership between Hegio and Theodoromedes as subjects with their sons and slaves as objects (Table 7). The goal for each is to restore as closely as possible the configuration (1) that obtained before Tyndarus' abduction by Stalagmus, starting from the configuration (3) with which the play opens; and in the event the pieces are indeed restored by the endgame to their original positions. As the play opens, Hegio is two sons down and two prisoners up. At the end of the play, the balance sheet will even out by changing the two prisoners for his two sons: one by exchange, one by recognition.

It is the recognition 'Tyndarus = Paegnium' that collapses (5) to (1); but this is not a goal for which any of the characters is actively playing. Hegio merely seeks to restore configuration (2), in which one of his two sons is recovered, and is furious when the prisoners' deception turns out to generate instead the configuration (4). We know, from the prologue, that (4) is in fact fewer moves away from (1) than (2) was: Tyndarus/Paegnium is already back with his father, while Philopolemus'

Table 7. Captivi: *credits and debits*

Hegio		Theodoromedes	
1	Philopolemus		Philocrates
	Paegnium		Stalagmus
2	Philopolemus		Philocrates
	− *Paegnium*	+	Tyndarus
	− *Stalagmus*	+	Stalagmus
3	− *Philopolemus*	+	Philopolemus (via Menarchus)
	+ Philocrates	−	*Philocrates*
	+ Tyndarus		
	− *Paegnium*		
	− *Stalagmus*	+	Stalagmus
4	− *Philopolemus*	+	Philopolemus
	+ Tyndarus		Philocrates
	− *Paegnium*		
	− *Stalagmus*	+	Stalagmus
5	Philopolemus		Philocrates
	− *Paegnium*		
	+ Tyndarus		
	Stalagmus		

return is guaranteed by Philocrates' personal desire to redeem his slave. But that is not how it looks to Hegio. The central rule of exchange is that only free men can be exchanged for free; and by foolishly letting go of Philocrates, he has lost not just the one bargaining chip that could be cashed in for Philopolemus, but even the prospect of the 20-minae bail promised by 'Philocrates' should 'Tyndarus' fail to return.

As in other horizontally intricate plays, this network of exchanges raises subtle ethical questions of legality and ownership.[24] The play's moral trajectory is plotted by a repeated depression of Tyndarus' status to the benefit of other players. First, he is abducted by the runaway Stalagmus: Tyndarus loses his family, Stalagmus gains his freedom. Next, he is sold by Stalagmus to Theodoromedes: Tyndarus becomes a chattel, Stalagmus pockets the cash. Third, he is captured with Philocrates: now he is a prisoner as well as a slave, with Hegio standing to gain. Finally, he is punished for duping Hegio: Philocrates escapes scot-free, but Tyndarus is consigned to hard labour. To restore him to his native level, these four abuses have to be repaid and the profit paid back with interest. Philocrates' voluntary return redeems Tyndarus from punishment, and returns Hegio Philopolemus as well; Hegio's release of Tyndarus without

[24] Leach 1969, Dumont 1974, Konstan 1983: 57–72.

ransom sacrifices the 20 minae he originally priced for his freedom; Stalagmus' abduction by Philocrates and delivery to Hegio not only gives Tyndarus back his citizenship and family, but also transfers Tyndarus' slavery and punishment to Stalagmus himself – who, in an outcome of unparalleled darkness for comedy, departs the play under a sentence of certain torture and death (1019).

This kind of transactional maze is not, however, confined to recognition plots. We meet it especially in the cash plots so characteristic of Plautus, where two intrinsic peculiarities of monetary transactions tend especially to p-plane complexity. First, cash plots are strongly bidirectional – by definition involving *two* circuits (that of the cash and that of the commodity for which it is exchanged). As we saw in *Rudens*, these circuits need not, and usually do not, coincide. Secondly, money – unlike, say, babies – can be arbitrarily quantified, aggregated, split, or virtualised (in the form of contracts), leading to some remarkable achievements of comic accounting. There are impressive exercises in arithmetical find-the-lady in *Asinaria*, *Epidicus*, *Trinummus*, and *Phormio*, among others; but much the most elaborate comes in PSEUDOLUS, whose finances deserve analysis as the cash-plot paradigm.[25]

Phoenicium's purchase price is 20 minae. Calidorus does not have this kind of money, but Simo, Ballio, and Polymachaeroplagides all do, and Calidorus' friend Charinus can manage 5 on a short-term loan. The soldier has already paid Ballio 15 minae on deposit, and will complete the deal and take Phoenicium away on delivery of the 5-minae balance. It is this completing stage of the transaction that Pseudolus intercepts. Before he does so, however, the plot excavates a circuitous narrative canal along which the money will flow once it has been released by Pseudolus' scheme.[26] The channel is built from a pair of wagers, both for the identical sum of 20 minae.[27] First (518–56), Simo promises Pseudolus 20 minae if he can obtain Phoenicium from Ballio by the end of the play; next (1070–8), Ballio promises Simo the same sum on the same terms, but with the addition that he can also have Phoenicium gratis. (Pseudolus never finds out about this leg of the circuit – at least, not in Plautus' text.)

[25] This analysis resists the *a priori* assumption of analyst and deconstructive critics alike that the play's arithmetic cannot make sense; see Lefèvre 1998: 23–38 (with survey 12–22), and especially Lefèvre 1977, Griffith 1988, Sharrock 1996.

[26] For a similar structure based on legal rather than financial mechanisms of transfer compare *Aspis*, where the competing intrigues exploit the legal rules of ἐπιδικασία to construct rival channels of transmission along which the desired packages of women and property can legitimately pass.

[27] There is in fact a third promise, made by Pseudolus to Calidorus at 118. Strictly speaking, it is not kept: the 20 minae never pass through Calidorus' hands, and what Pseudolus actually delivers to his master is Phoenicium herself, the purchase for which the 20 minae were wanted.

Table 8. Pseudolus: *the balance sheet*

Step	Lines	mn	from → to	Polym.	Ballio	Charinus	Pseudolus	Simo
1.	53–4	15	Poly → Ball	−15	+15			
2.	734	5	Char → Pseu	−15	+15	−5	+5	
3.	1016	5	Pseu → Ball	−15	+20	−5		
4.	1163	5	Poly → Ball	−20	+25	−5		
5.	1232	20	Ball → Poly		+5	−5		
6.	1231	20	Ball → Simo		−15	−5		+20
7.	1313	20	Simo → Pseu		−15	−5	+20	
8.	733	5	Pseu → Char		−15		+15	
9.	1328–9	15	Pseu → Simo		−15			+15
10.		15	Simo → Ball					

1. Polymachaeroplagides pays Ballio 15 minae on deposit.
2. Charinus loans 5 minae to Pseudolus.
3. Via the disguised Simia, Pseudolus delivers the 5 minae borrowed from Charinus to Ballio. (At this point Ballio releases Phoenicium to Simia, who transfers her to Pseudolus, who hands her over to Calidorus.)
4. Now Harpax comes along, and pays Polymachaeroplagides' balance of 5 minae to Ballio.
5. On discovering Pseudolus' trick, Ballio is forced to return the full 20 minae to Harpax, who will return it to Polymachaeroplagides.
6. In fulfilment of his wager with Simo, Ballio now has to hand over 20 minae to Simo.
7. Simo in turn has to pay up 20 minae on his bet with Pseudolus.
8. Pseudolus has then to go through with his promise to pay Charinus back the 5 minae he loaned in step 1.
9. In the final lines, Pseudolus half-promises to hand over to Simo 'half or even more' of his spoils. A figure of 15 minae would fit this description admirably.
10. Simo can then make the transaction legally binding by paying Ballio the balance of Phoenicium's price (he already has the 5 from step 3) with the 15 minae he has just received back from Pseudolus.[28] The end result is that Ballio has paid for Phoenicium out of his own pocket. As figure 6 shows, none of the characters is now richer or poorer from the deal; but Ballio has effectively given Phoenicium away gratis, thanks to his ill-considered (but binding) wager with Simo at 1075. This line, and Pseudolus' offer of the refund to Simo, are thus essential steps to the legal conclusion of the intrigue – rather than the inconsistency or flaw that is often argued here.

---

[28] Steps 8–10 lie outside the play, and are signalled with descending degrees of definiteness. Step 8 is firmly promised; 9 is a teasing offer by a drunk; 10 is left entirely to be inferred in Plautus' version, though it is hard to imagine it was so suppressed in the Greek. But some such concluding move is demanded by convention. It is part of the generic rulebook that title to the heroine must finally be made legal, and that all financial scores must be settled: 'Theft did not entitle one, even in comedy, to retain free possession of what had been stolen' (Willcock 1987: 17).

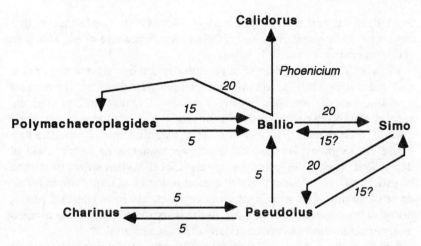

Figure 6. *Pseudolus*: where the money goes

Thus the release of Phoenicium from Ballio to Pseudolus (by whatever means) immediately triggers a two-stage flow of money to the sum of 20 minae, from Ballio to Simo to Pseudolus. By this route, the 20 minae required to buy Phoenicium becomes theoretically available from Ballio himself. The trouble is, it will only reach Pseudolus after he obtains Phoenicium. Pseudolus thus faces a paradox: Phoenicium can only be obtained by securing the money, but the money can only be obtained by securing Phoenicium. One way to do this, of course, would be by borrowing the cash short-term from a third party, paying it over to Ballio for Phoenicium, and repaying the loan with the sum received from Simo. But the only sum available on loan is the 5 minae from Charinus, meaning that the remaining 15 minae must be directed along a different route. There are thus two sums involved, the 15-minae deposit and the 5-minae 'trigger', and their movements are if anything even more complicated than is usually assumed. The full sum actually works as shown in Figure 6 and Table 8.

In itself, however, this analysis of p-transformations misses what for most readers is the vital element of *Pseudolus'* plot: the central element of *intrigue*. The plays considered up to now have favoured p-complications, with comparatively shallow overlays of misunderstanding and intrigue, and the c-complications that have arisen are mostly subtractive. But the most intricate comedies tend to plot heavily with knowledge: plots of deception, cross-purposes, and multi-layered confusion, where simultaneous variants of the same reality can collide and interfere in the rival apprehensions of the central transaction by different characters. Since the overwhelming entropic momentum of New Comic c-plotting is that 'everyone finds out everything' (*Hecyra* 867), the sense of instability in such gamestates is extremely strong.

Plots of this kind fall most strongly into Aristotelian movements of *desis* and *lysis*, complication and disentanglement. In the first, the tree of worlds puts out branches, as the versions of reality multiply; in the second, the shoots are pruned, and the rival realities collapse into a single disabused consensus. The nodes of *divergence* that characterise the first phase are moments of false inference: spontaneous or (in the case of deceptions) assisted fallacies that create a local deviant subworld in one or more characters' heads, where a transaction is misrepresented by an error of identity or a misdiagnosis of relationship. In the second phase, nodes of *convergence* allow versions of the story to be collated and merged by the mechanisms we conventionally dub 'recognition'.[29]

Now, two things make this vertical proliferation of deviant story models especially complex and dynamic. First, they can be *embedded* in an internal hierarchy of worlds, where the distribution of cognitive power is measured by the number of other subworlds each player's subworld manages to 'capture'. Pseudolus, for example, as the only character with knowledge of all the transactional segments, can assert and cash in his informational advantage over the other characters as ultimately superior power. In cases of straight deception, the deceiver's embedded story model will entirely include the deceived's – though the relationship can be inverted if (as in *Andria*) the deception leaks out to the intended dupe without the decipient's knowledge. But these embedded worlds can also be cycled in a recursive *mise en abîme* of higher-order embedding, since each character's subworld contains its own model of the world outside. And each such internal representation of the true, objective state of affairs – 'reality', as perceived from the privileged vantage-point of gods and theatre audiences – itself contains an image of the characters and their thoughts, including images of their images of reality. This mechanism underlies the effects traditionally classed as 'cross-purposes', and we shall see some instances in the plays discussed below.[30]

---

[29] In fact, however, even Aristotle's five classes of recognition can be mechanisms of divergence as easily as of convergence: even where no deception is intended, signs can be misread, confessions can be (as at *Samia* 320) ambiguously worded, information can be wrongly collated, inferences can be fallacious, and fictions can escape and proliferate by the laws of probable and necessary connection (as the deceptions in *Andria* and *Adelphoe* escape to delude members of the deceivers' own faction).

[30] By way of formal underpinning, I here append an elementary calculus of 'errors'. Errors are constituted by any departure from a default state of affairs in which nobody is mistaken about anything or anyone. In formal terms, the first-order default is X: = Y: (everyone believes the same thing); the second-order default is X:Y: = X: (everyone thinks other characters share their own beliefs); and the third-order default is X:Y:X: = X: (everyone

Second, these deviant realities can be vertically concatenated or *stacked*, as *Captivi* stacked an impersonation on a case of mistaken identity. Such multi-tiered errors are dramatically valuable in intrigue plots for their compound instability, the accumulation of vulnerable points at which the whole house of cards can collapse – as Tranio's doomed improvisations in *Mostellaria* erect ever more desperate layers of fiction on an already fragile premise, or Epidicus' virtuosic multiple identity-substitutions unravel at the detection of the first impersonation in the chain. As a broad rule, where the best p-plotting tends to explore external, societal issues of law and entitlement, c-plotting throws the spotlight on human themes: character, motive, judgement, understanding, sympathy. One important reason for this is that undetected disparities of knowledge tend to be misconstrued as disparities of will. Lateral thinking is not an instinctive human thought-pattern; the default response to aberrant behaviour in others, in theatre as in life, is to make projections about motive rather than to check for differences in versions of the underlying facts. A pattern, therefore, especially characteristic of the best Menander (*Samia, Misoumenos, Epitrepontes*) is to interpret unexplained behaviour in terms

thinks their beliefs are transparent to all other characters, and so on upwards through the higher orders, whose contents will normally be redundant). There is also a zero-order default that beliefs are correct. Thus the global default is that *everyone knows the truth and knows that everyone else knows it*:

p | A:p B:p | A:B:p B:A:p | A:B:A:p . . . (and so on recursively).

Normally, it is only necessary to record departures from these defaults. Any discrepancy between A: . . . and B: . . . chains of order n, where there is no discrepancy at order n-1, entails a statement at order n+1 to explain it. Thus intentional deception of B by A is [p | A:p B:p′ | A:B:p′] under the second-order default rule, but if the second-order statement were instead to be A:B:p, then we would have a situation of innocent error in which A remains unaware of B's mistake.

There are thus six elementary second-order patterns (omitting reciprocal permutations, and assuming the second-order default rule that B:A: = B:), of which the four common forms are:

(i) p | A:p B:p | A:B:p – the error-free default.

(ii) p | A:p B:p′ | A:B:p – A is right, B is wrong, but A is unaware of B's misapprehension.

(iii) p | A:p B:p′ | A:B:p′ – A is right, B is wrong, and A knows but does not correct this.

(iv) p | A:p′ B:p | A:B:p – an especially piquant configuration in which A is wrong, B is right, and A is aware of the discrepancy but mistakenly believes B to be the party in error (as in *The importance of being Earnest*).

I have not yet found any actual examples of (v) p | A:p′ B:p′ | A:B:p or (vi) p | A:p′ B:p′ | AB:AB:p – where A and B are both wrong, but one or both parties mistakenly believes the other to maintain something different which, as it happens, turns out to be the truth.

(Note that throughout the above 'p″' means 'p is not the case' or 'something other than p′ rather than 'not-p' or 'p is false', though in most cases they will amount to much the same. 'A: p″' would include situations in which the possibility of p has never even entered A's mind, for example because A is unaware of the existence of characters or elements essential to the very definition of the event represented by p.)

of confabulated motives rather than dark secrets, bringing concealed tensions to light in relationships previously believed secure.

MISOUMENOS, for example, is built on a complex pair of chained p-transactions, with Crateia passing from Demeas to Thrasonides to Crateia to Demeas to Thrasonides, and the sword from Demeas to his son <to another soldier?> to Thrasonides. But the play's human complexity stems from its c-plotting, which involves not only the collation of fragmented information about the chained transactions, but a double stratum of illusion, in which a false version of events has to be erroneously 'recognised', three times over, before the truth can supervene in a second recognition. None of the characters knows that Crateia's brother is alive, and Thrasonides and Demeas have not yet even 'discovered' that he is dead. First Crateia recognises her brother's sword, the night before the action starts; then Demeas, having recognised the same sword, discovers both his daughter and the apparent fate of his son; and finally Thrasonides (somehow, in a lost scene) learns the truth about Crateia's and Demeas' hitherto baffling hostility, before (or just as) all three are disabused. The sequence is brilliantly strung together through the multiple hermeneutic use made of the captured sword, the signifying token to which the structure of false inference is attached.[31]

But what lifts the play above the level of mechanical farce is the response of the characters to these unrecognised disparities of knowledge – resulting in a rich thematic exploration of the highly Menandrean paradox of women's power over their owners, and the triumph of moral and emotional forms of power over the outward forms of social and legal control. The unexplained hatred comes from Crateia, a mere chattel; Thrasonides has full freedom to force her to his will, were it not for his own feelings. Thrasonides' great opening speech underlines this extreme inversion (A9–16): 'I can sleep with the woman I love. She's in my house. I can have her. I want her, as much as any crazed lover. And I don't do it: I prefer to wander around out here in the freezing cold.' All Thrasonides' power as male, soldier, and master is cancelled by his reluctance to enforce it against Crateia's own will; and the arrival of Demeas on the scene vastly complicates the already paradoxical power game. Unlike *Perikeiromene*'s Glycera, Crateia is a war captive; Thrasonides is thus legally entitled to retain ownership, legal and sexual, even after her origi-

---

[31] Compare Therapontigonus' ring in *Curculio*, which serves no fewer than four plot functions: the proof of authority Curculio needs for his intrigue; the item the soldier bets and loses in his fateful dice game with Curculio (*anulum* in 356 seems confirmed by 610); the clue that allows Planaesium to trace her family; and the proof establishing Therapontigonus (who has inherited it from his father, who used to wear it) as the present head of the family, and thus empowering him to give his sister in marriage.

nal *kyrios*, her father, is found. But this is not the kind of ownership Thrasonides wants: he wants to marry her, something that can only be achieved by surrendering his title on her to Demeas, then receiving her *back* in marriage. Both stages of this curious transaction require the voluntary assent of both contracting males, but Demeas too is effectively bound by Crateia's will, and refuses to allow the second stage. The loss of the rest of the fourth act leaves much uncertain, but what is clear is that, when the brother was finally found alive, the decisive line was spoken by Crateia herself (439): 'Yes, Daddy, I want . . .' Five lines later, Demeas is out of the house and betrothing: the only passage in ancient literature where a woman is consulted by her *kyrios* over her willingness to marry.[32]

Perhaps the most striking case, however, is Terence's *HECYRA*, where possession of Philumena is split between three males: her father, her husband, and the rapist whose child she bears. That husband and rapist are the same man, and that therefore the conflict of ownership of Philumena's body is an illusion, is suspected not even by those who know the rape took place, since neither rapist nor victim is aware of the other's identity. The only clue is Philumena's ring, stolen in the act by Pamphilus, who gave it to his mistress Bacchis, with whom he subsequently broke. Thus the only clues to the identity of the victim (the ring) and to the identity of the rapist (possession of the ring) are doubly removed from the eyes of the only characters who can decode them, Philumena's immediate family.

But this powerplay is further complicated by a powerful set of c-transformations. Even more than usual for early Terence, the most elaborate plotting takes place inside the characters' heads, in a stack of misapprehensions. Only Philumena, her mother, and (later) Pamphilus know that Philumena was raped; only Pamphilus and Bacchis know that he committed a second (actually the same) rape. Thus there are three versions of events: (i) the official history, that Pamphilus married Philumena and fathered her child; (ii) the secret history, that Philumena was raped by someone other than Pamphilus; and (iii) the true history, that Pamphilus raped Philumena and later married her. Access to (iii) is only possible for those characters who have already advanced to (ii); yet (iii) is in fact transactionally homologous to (i) and far closer to the truth than (ii), allowing a remarkable conclusion unparalleled since Euripides' *Ion* and calling for

---

[32] Surprisingly, this includes the novels, which resort to all manner of intrigue, elopement, and oracular rigmarole to avoid the heroine's having to speak of her love to her father. Heliodorus' Charicleia is asked by both Charicles and Thyamis to agree to an arranged marriage, and in both cases gives her assent; but the whole point is that neither is her true *kyrios*, and on both occasions her consent is false.

Table 9. Hecyra: *the shifting blame*

1.		Philumena	→	Sostrata		
2.		Philumena	→	*Sostrata*	→	Philumena
3.		Pamphilus	→	*Philumena*	→	Sostrata
4.	*Myrrhina* →	Pamphilus	→	Philumena	→	Sostrata

a wry metatheatrical joke at comic convention (866–7). The only players who know the truth at the end are Pamphilus, Bacchis, Philumena, and her mother Myrrhina. Laches, Sostrata, Phidippus, and Parmeno, though all part of the story, will never apprehend it in full.

The plot is therefore constructed around a series of *pretexts* – fabricated models of motive to validate action in the eyes of characters excluded from the 'truth'.[33] These pretexts all vary a regular pattern, in which unilateral hostility is assumed between a pair of parties on either side of the marriage tie. But the identity of the guilty party (actually of course Pamphilus) shifts from one current model to the next, as somewhat inadequately shown in Table 9 (with the putative villain italicised). For us, it is precisely the psychological, ethical, and ideological complexities explored in the plot's quest for plausible motivation that makes this play so rich and unusual (and which seem to have proved too much for its first audiences).[34]

Here New Comedy's recentring of theatrical plotting around love, birth, and citizenship has an important consequence for the structure of complex c-plotting. Sex, unlike violence, is combinatorial: it requires characters to pair off. The range of possible outcomes is therefore (i) *entangled*, in that the fulfilment of some pairs entails the frustration of others; (ii) *multiplicative*, in that the number of possible pairings rises exponentially from the number of eligible partners;[35] and (iii) *volatile*, in that small changes to one element (such as the ineligibility of one particu-

[33] A Terentian trademark is this fascination with paradoxical inversions of truth and falsehood; compare the ἐπιδικασία case in *Phormio* and (especially) the dizzy games of bluff and counterbluff in *Andria*.

[34] Konstan (1983: 136) remarks of the particularly beautiful paradox sealed by Pamphilus' exit at 495: 'I like to think that it was at this point that the Roman audience deserted' (though strictly, as Gilula 1978 and Sandbach 1982 note, they did not desert, but stayed put and clamoured for the play to remove itself).

[35] For a single boy–girl pair (B, G) there are only two possible outcomes, 'boy wins girl' (B = G) and 'boy loses girl' (B ≠ G). With the introduction of a rival for the affections of one party (say B1, G, B2), the outcomes rise to three: B1 = G ≠ B2, B1 ≠ G = B2, and B1 ≠ G ≠ B2 (the fourth permutation, B1 = G = B2, being impossible under the usual rule of exclusivity, though it is permitted in Terence's *Eunuch*). But further rivals multiply the possible outcomes exponentially. A set of two boys and two girls, for example – the so-called 'double plot' favoured especially by Terence – allows seven outcomes: B1 = G1 ≠ B2 = G2

Table 10. Adelphoe: *parental versions*

0.	DMH:	Ctesipho		Bacchis		Aeschinus		Pamphila
1.	DM:	Ctesipho		Bacchis	=	Aeschinus		Pamphila
2.	M:	Ctesipho	=	Bacchis		Aeschinus		Pamphila
3.	HD:	Ctesipho		Bacchis	=	Aeschinus	=	Pamphila
4.	HM:	Ctesipho	=	Bacchis		Aeschinus	=	Pamphila
5.	D:	Ctesipho	=	Bacchis		Aeschinus	=	Pamphila

lar match) can have catastrophic consequences for the whole system. *SIK-YONIOS*, for example, revolves around a pair of mutually exclusive possible outcomes: the first desired by Moschion and already partly in place with Stratophanes' earlier liaison with Malthace, the second desired by Stratophanes, Theron, and the audience. (Thus Theron figures, correctly, that his interests coincide in obtaining Philumene for Stratophanes.)

Moschion = Philumene | Stratophanes = Malthace | Theron
Moschion | Philumene = Stratophanes | Malthace = Theron

But it is as objects of c-plotting that such combinatorial patterns come into their own. A comparatively simple case is *ADELPHOE*, where the lovers (as often in Terence) are already paired off, and the complications instead spiral out from the divergent successive models held by the three *senes* to whom they are principally narrated (see Table 10).

Each of these stages in turn generates a matrix of second-order story models, between Demea and Micio (in 2 and 4, the predicate of D:M: is erroneously identical to that of D:) and between Aeschinus and the *senes* (at 4, A:H: has predicate 3, A:M: and A:M:A: predicate 2). Most of the humour centres on Demeas' progressively dislocated internal model of the facts, and the conspiracy of repeated wool-pulling to which the rest of his family and household subscribe, ensuring that Micio is consistently the last to arrive at the truth.

More elaborate, and typical of early Terence in the density, psychological intricacy, and ironic convolutions of its c-plotting, is *ANDRIA*. Pamphilus wants to marry Glycerium, and his friend Charinus wants to

$\neq$ B1, B1 $\neq$ G1 = B2 $\neq$ G2 = B1, B1 $\neq$ G1 $\neq$ B2 = G2 $\neq$ B1, B1 = G1 $\neq$ B2 $\neq$ G2 $\neq$ B1, B1 $\neq$ G1 = B2 $\neq$ G2 $\neq$ B1, B1 $\neq$ G1 $\neq$ B2 $\neq$ G2 = B1, B1 $\neq$ G1 $\neq$ B2 $\neq$ G2 $\neq$ B1. Several plays go further and introduce a further competitor, usually male, for one or both of the girls; so in *Aspis, Sikyonios, Truculentus, Eunuchus, Phormio*, while the astonishing convolutions of *Epidicus* require *three* girls and three male competitors for their possession (though Periphanes' interest in Telestis is not sexual). In practice, of course, some permutations are bound to be ruled out in any particular play; but this is offset by the fact that combinations recognised by the audience as forbidden may not be perceived as such by all the characters.

Table 11. Andria: *consent and bluff*

	Order 0	Order 1		Order 2
1.	P-/Chr+	PCha:P-/Chr+	SChr:P+/Chr+	
2.	P-/Chr-	PCha:P-/Chr+	SChr:P-/Chr-	
3.	P-/Chr-	PChaSChr:P-/Chr-		S:P:P-/Chr+
4.	P-/Chr-	PChaChr:P-/Chr-	S:P+/Chr-	S:P:P+/Chr+
5.	P-/Chr+	P:P-/Chr+	ChaSChr:P+/Chr+	
6.	P-/Chr-	PChaChr:P-/Chr-	S:P+/Chr-	

marry Philumena, as shown below in ending (a). But the two *senes* favour ending (b), and Chremes for his part (as Philumena's *kyrios*) has the decisive say on his daughter's marriage.

(a) Glycerium = Pamphilus | Philumena = Charinus
(b) Glycerium | Pamphilus = Philumena | Charinus.

The bulk of the play tracks a dizzying sequence of bluff, counter-bluff, backfire, and renewed intrigue, full of ironic inversions and multiple second-order confusions, around the attitudes of the two players whose consent is needed for the Pamphilus–Philumena marriage to go ahead: Pamphilus, the groom, and Chremes, the bride's *kyrios*. With the exception of Chremes, most players' zero-order attitudes remain constant up to the recognition. Pamphilus and Charinus, with their slaves, are against the proposed match (−); Simo favours it (+). But the ensemble of first- and second-order player models of what various characters want goes through some profound and complicating transformations. The essential ones are shown in Table 11.

Nor is this kind of combinatorial structure restricted to romantic pairings; it can also, as already in *Ion*, be activated in recognition plots where issues of *parentage* are at stake, as regularly in Menandrean rape plays. Since citizen identity itself is determined by who one's parents are, citizenship is itself a combinatorial quality – allowing the multiplication of embedded worlds from economically limited elements, through different characters' permutations of those elements at different orders of embedding. An exemplary case, spinning a fantastic web of deviant realities out of the smallest cast in surviving comedy, is *SAMIA*. As in *Ion*, misapprehensions multiply from permutations of a child's alleged parentage; but here the candidates are restricted to a closed set of two for each role, considerably tightening the structural economy.

[Demeas = Chrysis =] Moschion = Plangon
  | | |
  A   B   C

All players except Demeas and Niceratus know that the child's parents are Moschion and Plangon; Demeas and Niceratus are both led to believe that the parents are Demeas and Chrysis, and both assent to Moschion's marriage to Plangon on this understanding. Demeas further agrees to keep the child, apparently leaving no individual plot goals unattained. The complications begin only with the third act, where Demeas has discovered that the father is actually Moschion. Having no reason to adjust his model of who the *mother* is, he draws the conclusion that he has been the victim of a Hippolytus-style cuckoldry, of the kind understandably widely suspected in a society where sons and second wives were often of similar age. This produces the following dislocation of story models:

(before:) MCP:c | ND:A
(after:)　 MCP:c | N:A | D:B　　D:MCP:B | MCPN:D:A

In the ensuing dialogue with Parmenon, Demeas extracts what he thinks is confirmation of his belief (thanks to his ambiguous words in 320). Parmenon, however, assumes that if Demeas knows the father he also knows the mother. Thus we now have a third-order dislocation:

D:P:D:B | P:D:P:c

Parmenon now exits from the plot until Act 5, so that his version of Demeas' story model is not passed to either Moschion, Chrysis, or Niceratus. But in the meantime Demeas makes a fateful p-move: he throws Chrysis and baby out of his house and power-zone, to be rescued by Niceratus and taken into his own house. Niceratus then enlists Moschion to plead against this (to them) extraordinary move, and in the magnificent climax of cross-purposes that follows Demeas repeats his misapprehension, still in ambiguously incomplete terms, aside to Moschion. Niceratus, overhearing, grasps the gist of Demeas' accusation, but retains the ambiguity in his own outbursts to Moschion. We now have:

DN:M:DN:B | M:DN:M:c

This prompts a p-move from Niceratus identical to Demeas' earlier action: he rushes in with the intention of throwing Chrysis and baby out on the street. But in his absence Moschion, who has finally caught on, reveals the true mother's identity to Demeas at the precise moment that Niceratus, offstage, discovers the truth for himself. The play now shifts from c-moves to p-moves: all characters now know the truth, but Demeas' earlier action has placed both Chrysis and the child in the power of Niceratus, who now threatens to burn the child alive. Happily Chrysis escapes with the baby, and in a breakneck sequence is received safely back into Demeas' house, leaving Niceratus to threaten his wife (who remains within his domain). It is left for Demeas to reconcile the volatile Niceratus to his situation, and all ends happily with a characteristic fifth-act coda resolving the deeper human tensions.

For a more expansive instance yet, consider the proliferation of worlds and motives that results from the celebrated peregrination of recognition tokens in *EPITREPONTES*.[36] The ring began its story life (i) on Charisius' finger; (ii) Pamphile seized and retained the ring from her rapist; (iii) subsequently she exposed it with the child; (iv) Daos found it with the baby. The play now opens: in the arbitration scene the ring (v) is transferred to Syrus; (vi) Syrus gives it to Onesimus; (vii) Onesimus gives it to Habrotonon; (viii) Habrotonon finally returns it to Pamphilus as the false proof that she was the girl he raped. These eight physical movements of the token mark the major c-move adjustments to the game state. At (ii), Pamphile knows only that she was raped by a character x whose ring she holds, while Charisius knows only that he raped a character y who kept his ring. After their marriage, Charisius learns of the existence of x, but (with a breathtaking double standard he will later have to renounce) keeps his knowledge of y to himself. Steps (iii) and (iv) establish a new set of unknowns: B, the baby exposed by Pamphile; z, the father of the child found by Daos; z', the mother of that child. Thus the situation as the play begins is shown in Table 12.

Table 12. Epitrepontes: *pairings and parents*

[x =] Pamphile = Charisius [= y/]Habrotonon = Chaerestratus			[z = z']
|	|	|	|
A	B	C/D	E

Char: xya
CharPam: xa
DaSy: zz'e
OnHabChaerSm: (nil).

The ring proves that x is Charisius, and that therefore A is really B; but this information is only meaningful to characters aware of the existence of both Charisius and x – as yet, a combination filled only by Charisius himself. Step (v) produces the single alteration Sm:zz'e; (vi) adds On:zz'e; the first *correlation*, z=Charisius, and the correct inferences y and z'=y; and the resulting replacement of 'zz'e' by 'Charisiusyc'. Step (vii) adds Hab:Charisiusyc, and (viii), the intrigue, finally fills in the missing links by pretending that Habrotonon is y, so that

[36] Blume 1990: 31, Vogt-Spira 1992: 173–9.

CharChaer:CharHabD, with the corollary Char:(XYA)+(CharHabD).∴. A≠D. The final state thus looks like collapsing to

[x =] Pamphile | Charisius = Habrotonon | Chaerestratus
    | |
   A   D

– with Pamphile condemned to pair off with the non-existent x, and Chaerestratus (who has fallen for Habrotonon himself) left equally out in the cold. But the spatial and communicative manoeuvres finally converge when Smicrines succeeds in removing Pamphile momentarily from Charisius' house, leaving her onstage in time to be recognised by Habrotonon as she emerges from Chaerestratus' door. Habrotonon now grasps the missing connection 'Y=Z'=Pamphile', and nobly relinquishes the promise of freedom to restore wife and baby to their rightful owner. For this she is, like Stratophanes in *Misoumenos*, rewarded by events, since her new lover Chaerestratus is able to give her all that Charisius promised and more.

But the ancient world's most mind-boggling plot comes in one of its shortest plays, and arises from a unique extension of the combinatorial principle to the transactional structure itself. *EPIDICUS* features a chain of impersonations in which the objects of four separate transactions exchange identities on two different levels of misapprehension. Periphanes attempts to channel three transactions through his house (Table 13): Telestis' passage from the *danista* to Philippa, Acropolistis' passage from a *leno* to the soldier, and the *fidicina*'s hire from and return to a second *leno*. Epidicus' enchained substitutions dislocate the two stages of each transaction, moving the person and purchase of Acropolistis up into the initially vacant Telestis niche and the *fidicina* into the now-empty Acropolistis niche, allowing the real Telestis to pop off the top of the stack into Stratippocles' lap. But the fact that she *is* Telestis is unknown even to Epidicus, so that in his model transaction 1a does not exist, and what he is doing is diverting the cash for the transactional segment 1a to 2a, and from 2a to a new segment 4a.

It is apparent from the table that Epidicus' trick is highly unstable. The fault lines between the (a) and (b) sections are already under tension from the incomplete transactions (4a) and (3b), and all that is needed to trigger a slippage is for Periphanes to attempt to complete any one of the (b) stages. The weak link in Epidicus' scheme is the fragility of the central link: Apoecides apart, all the dislocations between model and reality run through the figure of Periphanes alone, and the arrivals of the soldier and Philippa offer a ready means of testing the model, for which Epidicus has not provided. The plot thus falls, like *Mostellaria*, into clear stages of

Table 13. Epidicus: *dislocations of identity*

(i) PERIPHANES' MODEL					
1a Telestis:	*danista*	→	Periphanes	→	Philippa 1b
2a Acropolistis:	*leno¹*	→	Periphanes	→	soldier 2b
3a *fidicina*:	*leno²*	→	Periphanes	→	*leno²* 3b
(ii) THE REALITY					
1a Telestis:	*danista*	→	Stratippocles		
2a Acropolistis:	*leno¹*	→	Periphanes	→	Philippa 1b
3a *fidicina*:	*leno²*	→	Periphanes	→	soldier 2b
			Periphanes	→	*leno²* 3b
(iii) EPIDICUS' MODEL					
2a Acropolistis:	*leno¹*	→	Periphanes	→	Philippa 1b
3a *fidicina*:	*leno²*	→	Periphanes	→	soldier 2b
4a *captiva*:	*danista*	→	Stratippocles		
			Periphanes	→	*leno²* 3b

complication and resolution. The *desis* phase gulls Periphanes into adopting a progressively more dislocated internal model of the story, each layer built more precariously on the last; the *lysis* begins sharply at 437, when Epidicus' handiwork starts to pull apart as the teetering stack of multiple identity-substitutions loses a brick from the bottom.

This vertiginous farce is the closest ancient plotting comes to unintelligible convolution. I frankly doubt whether any spectator or reader has ever succeeded in truly following what happens in this play, whose richness lies precisely in its wilful exploration of the limits of the genre's classical plot poetics. Such overplotting is otherwise more characteristic of Terence than of Plautus himself, who often seems impatient of classical tidiness, and in several other later plays[37] subverts or explodes the Menandrean codes altogether in favour of quite alien principles of narrative form. As early as 200, *Stichus* seems to have taken its Menandrean source apart and reassembled it into a virtually plotless montage of festive variations on a theme of home-coming;[38] yet the formal patterning is the most insistent in any ancient play, with the action patterned round an intricate structure of mirror scenes and doubled types.[39] The baffling *Poenulus* seems to proclaim *neglegentia* as a creative principle;[40] while

---

[37] *Stichus* and *Pseudolus* apart, Plautine dating is notoriously hazardous; Schutter 1952 is overbold, but the cases for putting *Poenulus* and *Truculentus* in the 180s, alongside *Bacchides* and *Casina*, are stronger than most.   [38] Fraenkel 1960: 268–81.

[39] I owe this to the 1988 production by David Wiles; see his brief remarks at Wiles 1991: 142, and cf. Arnott 1972, who calls attention to a web of unifying patterns in language and themes.   [40] See especially Henderson 1994.

Truculentus systematically violates genre rules to evoke a world bound solely by the law of avarice, with other moral, social, and narrative codes traditionally subscribed by the genre exposed in turn as wish-fulfilment myths.[41] As for Terence, his taste for complication and narrative symmetry does not seem to have been shared by his contemporaries; and there seems to have been a sense among the ancient biographers who speculated about the motive and manner of his mysterious early exit that it was prompted by some sort of crisis in translated drama – long an ideological battleground between Roman and Greek cultural systems, as his bewildering final play seems centrally to acknowledge.[42]

In the event, New Comedy's creative lives in Greek and Latin were both short. No new Greek play seems to have entered the canon after the death of Philemon (mid-260s BC), while the Latin *palliata* fades with Terence's early end (159). Neither genre died out, any more than did tragedy;[43] it was simply that the canon of classic texts was closed. As with post-Sophoclean tragedy, we should be wary of too easily assuming creative juices had run dry; but the combined output of Menander, Diphilus, and Philemon alone exceeded 300 titles, and readers who have difficulty remembering the differences between six plays of Terence will easily imagine a degree of generic exhaustion in a corpus of this size. New Comedy's straitened genre universe, so vital to its early success, may in the longer term have spelled the doom of such classically well-made plays. It may be no accident that the dramatic forms which remained vigorous into the Empire were the pointedly unclassical mime and pantomime, or that the ancient world's final, spectacular surge of experiment in classical narrativity comes from outside the existing canon of narrative genres altogether: in prose, in a genre of shadowy pedigree and readership, and in a group of uniformly mysterious writers who seem to have been largely invisible even to their own contemporaries.

---

[41] See Enk 1964, Dessen 1977, and especially Konstan 1983: 142–64.
[42] Henderson 1988, and for the wider culture-wars Gruen 1990, 1993.
[43] Horace's friend Fundanius was still writing *palliatae* in the high Augustan period (*Sat.* 1.10.40–2); a century later, Vergilius Romanus wrote Latin comedies on the models of Aristophanes as well as of Menander (Pliny, *Ep.* VI.21). Whether any of these was staged is another matter.

As Aristotle was aware, comic drama's use of *unretold stories* – the fullest manifestation of what we would term 'fiction' – was far ahead of other narrative genres, which continued to draw from the mingled springs of history and myth.[1] Aristotle has to scrape to find instances of poetic fiction elsewhere, naming only one actual title in each narrative mode: the freakish *Margites* for epic, Agathon's *Anthos/eus* for tragedy. The most striking experiments, disregarded by Aristotle, had been in prose: anecdote and dramatic invention in the historians; the pseudo-historical Socratic dialogue and fabulose Platonic myths; above all, the novelistic mutant *Cyropaedia*, a work of major influence in the ages, ancient and modern, when prose fiction was being invented. A generation after Aristotle, Menander's contemporary Euhemerus dented the mould by narrating a tale of transparent fantasy in his own first person; but even this *Sacred history* centred on familiar names from heroic myth, and none of these works aspired to a Homeric model of narrative form.

Such a *classical epic fiction* – narrated (as against performed), newminted (rather than mythical or historical) storytelling that emulates the values of economy, amplitude, and transparency in Homer and Attic drama – emerges to extant view only with Chariton of Aphrodisias in, probably, the first century AD, and with the four Greek love-novels that succeed him. Whether, or how long, the combination had existed before this is one of the many enigmas surrounding the birth of the novel; and it remains tantalisingly unclear how far other genres of imperial prose fiction plotted in the classical mode. The growing corpus of fragmentary texts has thrown much light on the diversity of Greek high and low prose fiction, but little on structure and form; while Photius' summaries of Iamblichus and, especially, Antonius Diogenes do offer occasional glimpses of astounding narrative *coups*, but it is extraordinarily hard to form much impression of their plot quality from the story synopses. The Latin *Tale of Apollonius of Tyre*, which may derive from a Greek original

---

[1] *Poetics* 9.1451b11–15; see above, p. 65.

some centuries older, has much the strongest case for consideration; but its late date, generic isolation, and pervasive narrative oddities raise too many complicating questions to be easily dealt with here.[2]

That there was, at least, a vigorous tradition of *counter*-classical prose fiction is shown by the satirical narratives of Petronius, Apuleius, and Lucian's comic novellas, which reject, even parody, Aristotelian principles of predictability and coherence. Their sprawling concatenations of episodes *allude* throughout to Homeric devices – the divine-wrath impulsion, the embedding of secondary narratives – as well as to particular episodic motifs from epic, but overwhelmingly in a spirit of burlesque. There are no constraints on setting, cast list, duration, or causal sequence, and the sense of narrative destination is erratic even in Apuleius (whose hero's metamorphoses do at least arguably demonstrate a coherent system of moral and thematic rules for narrative development, and where both the goal and the means of retransformation are kept in view even if their attainment is triumphantly *ex machina*).

The five extant love-romances, however, plainly subscribe to a different kind of narrative value. Theirs is a genre with a strong sense of destination and closure, of the rules that make the world; with economy of character and function, a low narratorial profile, and a teleological shaping of time and space; and using both the rule-bound nature of the story universe and the orderly release of narrative information to direct their reader's dynamic modelling of the total story as it unfolds in textual time. Though individual novels, particularly those of Longus and Achilles Tatius, may make a show of ironising or subverting this classical frame, none shows any inclination to break it. The love-novels' seeming isolation may not be accidental. This chapter will argue that the classicality of the love-novels, while not provably unique in the form, is a special consequence of their close generic relationship to New Comedy – a relationship that mirrors tragedy's rewriting of epic, in its attempt to transpose a distinctive set of narrative values across the boundary of medium. And that transposition forces a number of significant changes to the narrative system itself: a new ideology of the erotic, and a new role for that ideology in plotting; new configurations of politics and power; and new forms of hermeneutic play with space, time, and narration.

At first sight, the differences between New Comedy and the novel seem profound. The novelists' action is widescreen, their settings geographically expansive, and their epoch ranges from Herodotean antiquity to the reader's own day; while their storylines turn on an individualistic, symmetrical ideal of love that seems straightly opposed to New Comedy's

<hr>

[2] A comprehensive treatment in Archibald 1991.

The five novels' generic storyline, with its twin hero-goals of home-coming and beloved, originates undisguisedly with the *Odyssey* and its tragic rewritings (especially *Helen*). But whereas epic and tragedy make this love-theme subordinate to the larger defence of identity, status, and

systemic view of sex as a currency of transaction between *oikoi*. It is custo-mary to view these changes as absolute, and to explain them as reflecting historical changes in sensibility over three centuries, different cultural strata of audience, or both together. I want to suggest that the distance between Menander and Heliodorus is much less than is generally recog-nised; that the shifts in emphasis can be sufficiently understood as *narrat-ologically* driven; and that consideration of the transformations wrought by the recomposition of contemporary or historical erotic fiction in the epic mode may even illuminate, if not quite resolve, the origins of the novel itself.

Clearly, the novelists' reversion from the dramatic mode of telling to the epic puts the New Comic paradigm through an inverse of the trans-formation described on pages 164–78 above. Drama's literalistic limits to the space and time of primary action dissolve, the flow of narrative time recovers its epic elasticity, and we lose drama's practical restrictions on the number of players and types of action available to primary narrative. Multiple narrative lines become far easier to sustain than in theatre, where they require laborious shepherding of alternating player groups in and out of the static primary-narrative frame. In the novel, the relation-ship between primary and reported action becomes much more discre-tionary; direct narrative access is restored between the reader and the insides of characters' heads; restricted viewpoints are feasible in primary as well as secondary narrative, and story information is available to the reader that need not be known to a single one of the players.

And all these restored degrees of narrative freedom confront the novel-ists with challenges previously confined to epic, and never faced in unre-told narrative at all. What kind of narrative shape can be imposed on a story universe of unlimited size, contents, and duration, when that uni-verse is now created by the text *ex nihilo*? How can such plots deliver the classical desiderata of a closed and structured world, an intelligibly finite player set, a regulated set of endgame conditions, and an apprehensible system of narrative rules determining the range and outcome of permis-sible moves? From epic to tragedy to Menandrean comedy, the universe of classical narrativity had been shrinking, and New Comic plotting depends for its virtuosity precisely on an extreme acceptance of the nar-ratological confines of theatrical literalism. The novel's challenge is to knock away the walls of its world without the roof falling in.

The five novels' generic storyline, with its twin hero-goals of home-coming and beloved, originates undisguisedly with the *Odyssey* and its tragic rewritings (especially *Helen*). But whereas epic and tragedy make this love-theme subordinate to the larger defence of identity, status, and possessions (above, p. 142), in comedy and the novels *eros* is qualitatively redefined, elevated in ideological significance, and made central to plotting by a complex system of rules for erotic *competition*. It is this that sets the love-novels classically apart from neighbouring forms of fiction.

The universal narrative goal in the love-novels is secure possession of the beloved. Generically, this requires fulfilment of four conditions, all drawn from New Comedy: (i) legal citizen marriage, sanctioned (as in comedy) by the surviving heads of both families; (ii) permanent residence in the home community; (iii) freedom from erotic competition; (iv) preservation of the exclusive reproductive bond. In practice this means the lovers must find one another, marry, escape rivals, and together return home, preserving at least their genetic integrity throughout, if not always strict sexual fidelity.[3] In a sense, this goal of secure sexual possession is common to *all* the actively competing players, since it is a generic axiom that one or both of the central characters should be universally desirable; but in practice, success in this goal is determined by the fulfilment of a complex set of *ideological* requirements that remain more or less constant throughout the genre. These are the criteria of *ideal* love: in Morgan's formulation, mutual, selfless, lifelong, spontaneous, young, artless, matrimonial, chaste, sacramental, and beneficial.[4] The matrimonial criterion, particularly, enforces further limits, since married love is *a priori* heterosexual, exclusive, legitimate, public, and contracted between freeborn citizens of the same legal community.[5]

For the most part, this catalogue is a distinctively Hellenistic, and specifically Menandrean, prescription. The 'archaic' love of myth and lyric would reverse the sign on every item, and is by no means excluded from the world of the novels; indeed, as Morgan (1989a) shows for the case of Heliodorus' 'Athenian love', the sophistic novels set out early in the text a more or less detailed phenotype of this negative paradigm (Achilles' tragedy of Clinias and Longus' of Dorcon, culminating in Heliodorus' uniquely rich history of Cnemon). The one major novelty in the new ideal is Konstan's 'sexual symmetry', the presentation of desire as experienced identically by both partners. Konstan connects this persuasively with the new political map of the Empire, where the individual polis, and thus its construction of *eros* as a civic transaction, is fading in

---

[3] The *order* in which these ends are accomplished may of course vary – notably, between the founding fathers Chariton and Xenophon on the one hand (where the lovers are married before their peregrinations) and the sophistic triad on the other (where marriage is part of the endgame).

[4] This catalogue (referring to Heliodorus, but with much wider genre application) from Morgan 1989a: 107–13.

[5] The marriage of Theagenes and Charicleia is the exception: for Heliodorus' intricate manipulation of the matrimonial rules see below, pp. 255, 257–8.

importance. It is harder, however, to explain why such a model does not emerge to view three centuries earlier and across a variety of genres, and I would suggest instead that the change is determined less by political or ideological changes in the outside world than by primarily *narratological* factors: that the systemic, transactional, polis-bound world-model of New Comedy has to be modified for *any* contemporary or historical fiction in the epic mode.

The special case of Heliodorus for the moment apart, all the novels' plots – even Longus' – still begin and end their stories in the polis, and regulate their narratives by its laws, with marriages sanctioned by common citizenship and consent of the bride's *kyrios*. But whereas the conventions of the comic stage normally forbid the primary representation of action outside the polis,[6] the epic mode positively encourages it. The novels accommodate this by adopting a generic storyline of exile and return, in which standard New Comic mechanisms of displacement from the home polis – abduction, exposure, voluntary exile – are invoked to turn the lovers loose in the wider, more politically complex and threatening world of the Hellenistic Mediterranean. In this larger geography of power, where the codes of the polis no longer reign, the cosy systemic hierarchy of individual, *oikos*, and community is an ideal to which the lovers and the narrative can only struggle to return, since it alone can offer stable fulfilment of the erotic goals. Hellenistic comedy has always been interested in this complex world outside all civic order,[7] but has enormous difficulty creating it onstage; the novel, liberated from the confines of the city walls, is free to explore this global power-map for the first time.

Some important consequences follow. While drama's fixed and finite primary-narrative frame tends to a closed, systemic representation of the world, the open frame of narrated fiction favours an *individualistic* model. In drama, narrative sequence is objective and collective, guided by time and space rather than the subjective experience of characters, who simply move in and out of the narrative location; but in the epic mode, the tendency is for space and time to follow the characters. In the love-novels' rewriting of Menander, this eliminates the mechanistic Bergsonian absurdity of systemic behaviour at its extreme, making for a more earnest, less farcical tone. But the consequences go much deeper than this. One of the novel's most powerful discoveries is that several generic *values* also change once the individual is disengaged from the codes of the polis. Women, once outside the legal and familial codes that contain their identity and range of action, are empowered, while men, cut off from the

---

[6] Even in *Rudens*, the offstage law of Athens and Cyrene dictates the action, and the coastal strip is as much part of the *chora* of Cyrene as the deme settings in *Dyskolos*, *Epitrepontes*, *Sikyonios*, *Heros*, *HT* are of Athens.   [7] Hofmeister 1997.

mechanisms that give them rights at law, are comparatively disabled; as displaced persons, both are on an equal footing. Beyond the city walls, therefore, sexual traffic becomes an exchange between atomic individuals rather than familial entities, and even the narrative goal of citizen marriage can only be attained on return to the bosom of the polis and the family. In the world outside, the power to gratify desire rests with a range of local autocrats, so that the very mechanism responsible for the new ideal of eros as a bilateral, consensual contract between individuals casts that ideal adrift in a world in which rape and its cognates are part of the universal order.

And this in turn offers a solution to the old Homeric challenge of economy-with-amplitude. First, the novels build their narrative lines around *travel*: a powerful narrative device for mapping the world, and for organising and teleologising a widely open narrative space. Second, they are *episodic*, plotting epic space into distinct zones with their own autonomous rules of play, but unified by an overall closural framework of reunion and return. And third, they *thematise* this narrative framework by defining player roles around the competing power systems traversed and their relationship to larger generic goals, and building plot around the conflicts of power possible on a map divided into different political domains. As in human-rights tragedies like *Heraclidae*, *Hecuba*, and the two *Suppliants*, but also in comedies such as *Sikyonios* and *Poenulus*, the ambivalent status of refugees in an alien community leads to questions and confrontations about their position under the competing codes of local law, native law, force, and a putative 'natural' law originating with a conveniently divinised control level, where the ultimate values of genre reside as transcendent moral rules.

This relationship between transcendent–generic and secular–local rules enables player roles to be defined, with unusual clarity, in terms of the central *erotic competition*. The hero and heroine, by alone satisfying the transcendent criteria for ideal love, are flagged as dual subjects; they are also, by genre convention, universal objects, desired by all technically eligible competitors. Named, speaking, or otherwise psychologised characters who press their claims are opponents; those who recognise their deeper ineligibility (their imperfect fulfilment of the ideal erotic profile), and who consequently suppress their claims, fall into helper roles. The narrative tension then arises from carefully plotted *differentials in the competitors' knowledge and power*. To desire to compete, a player must be aware that the object of desire is available – a criterion that in practice demands a correct (or, in the case of well-meaning opponents, appropriately incorrect) internal model of the object's existence, identity, whereabouts, and state of affections. To be able to compete successfully, a player must be able to enforce his will over that of competitors – to be in the right place, with the right powers, under the right conditions.[8]

Much of the five novels' distinctive character is determined by this plotting of space and power. In principle, each has the whole of the eastern Mediterranean to play in; but in practice all five perform in an Odyssean archipelago of a few finite locations linked by a functionally defined narrative geography. All the stories, even Longus', are spatially patterned on a circle of exile and return between thematically opposed geographical zones: Greece and barbary, city and country, Europe and/or Asia and/or Africa. In all cases alienation from the home territory dissociates the hero and heroine from their citizen roots, cutting them off from family and community and finally imperilling their status as free persons rather than chattels. This traversal of categories regularly involves movement

---

[8] Achilles' fifth book alone offers a combinatorics of couples and a shifting network of dissonant secondary story-models as intricate as anything in Menander; I tabulate only the most important elements of each. A remarkable feature is the completion of the combinatorial ring of rival pairings, with the non-consensual vertical combinations threatening the two normative horizontal conjunctions. (For incomplete combinatorial rings in New Comedy, see pp. 214–19 above.)

$$\begin{array}{ccc} \text{Clitophon} & === & \text{Leucippe} \\ \| & & \| \\ \text{Melite} & === & \text{Thersander} \end{array}$$

Rules of inference:
if x:CL then x:(C,L); if x:MT then x:(M,T) – everyone accepts that the original couples are for life
if (x,y) then ~(x,z) – all pairings are exclusive
1. LT | (C,L) | (M,T) || LCM:~T || CM:~L ∴ CM:(C,~L) | L:(C,L) | T:(M,T)
2. L:(C,M)
3. M:~L | C:L ∴ C:(C,L) | LM:(C,M)
4. M:~L | L:(C,L) | CM:L:(C,M)
5. M:~L | CM:T | T:(C,M) | CL:(C,L)
6. M:L ∴ M:(C,L).

On Clitophon's arrival in Ephesus (1), he and Melite both believe that Leucippe is dead, though both know that Clitophon remains loyal to her memory until their first night on Ephesian soil. All three, meanwhile, believe that Melite's husband Thersander is dead; and after the meeting in the fields Leucippe, the only player to know the truth of her survival, believes (wrongly) that Clitophon has abandoned her and already consummated his marriage to Melite (2). Later that evening Clitophon learns, moments before he commits to Melite, that Lacaena is Leucippe (3); but Melite, who still believes Leucippe dead, imagines Clitophon is now her own. Next day 'Lacaena' discovers from conversation with Melite that Clitophon has chosen not to consummate the marriage; but Clitophon remains unaware of this exchange, and assumes Leucippe still regards him as unfaithful (4). Now Thersander turns up alive, and bursts in on Melite with Clitophon: both of them now realise that Melite must revert to Thersander, who meanwhile concludes that Melite has been adulterous with Clitophon (5). In the scuffle that follows, Melite catches sight of Leucippe's letter to Clitophon: now she knows that Leucippe is still alive, and that therefore Clitophon is lost to Melite herself (6).

between regions of contrasting political order: democracy and tyranny, polis and *chora* civic order and the anarchy of pirates or Nilotic cowboys. The five novels exploit this generic spatiality as diversely, and with just as much creative variation, as individual tragedies exploit the conventional polarities of the tragic stage. But the underlying framework is remarkably constant.

CHARITON'S narrative topography follows an especially clear political track, from democratic Greece via liminal Miletus into the despotic Persian empire and out again, placing Callirhoe progressively deeper in the power of barbarians and Chaereas in an ever more alien and disabling environment, with deadlock finally broken by Chaereas' heroic carving of a new identity and power base among the barbarians – permitting him to challenge and defeat the Great King himself on equal terms. These topographical staging-posts correspond to a series of ever more daunting abductors and rivals. Theron the pirate, who delivers Callirhoe to Miletus, is an anarchic and villainous outsider, readily (rather too readily) eliminated by *Tyche*; he has no legal or moral claim on Callirhoe, and as soon as he falls into Chaereas' hands his title to her is instantly void. From Theron she passes to Leonas the steward, by right now of purchase rather than plunder: a villa manager is at least a step up from a pirate, but neither is a conceivable competitor for Callirhoe herself. But Dionysius of Miletus, for whom Leonas has made his purchase, is a far more serious antagonist. He is Greek, rich, single, genuinely loving, and in the public eye legally married: the weakness of his claim lies solely in the fact that his love falls short of the ideal, being neither mutual nor fully legitimate. (As Chariton is careful to develop, Dionysius' marriage to Callirhoe is a sham: not an equal and contractual union of freeborn citizens, but a specious transformation of the power he holds over Callirhoe as a chattel.) Next, the rival satraps Mithridates and Pharnaces both intrigue after Callirhoe's possession: this marks an escalation from consensual Greek to despotic barbarian possession, as well as a step up the hierarchy of power and a consequent raising of the stakes.[9] But the contest barely rests there before advancing a further tier to the very apex of the pyramid, as the Babylonian *agon* between Dionysius and Chaereas under the rival patronage of Pharnaces and Mithridates attracts the involvement of the supreme player, Artaxerxes the King. From here on, Chaereas is a lone Greek alien facing the mightiest tyrant on earth, and Chariton's elegant final restacking of the odds ingeniously plots a comeback for the hero against positively Odyssean odds. This principle of escalation is mirrored in the action's striking qualitative progression – from private to public, domestic

---

[9] Note the use of an overt game metaphor in the summary of the rivals' positions at IV.4.1.

politics to international, love to war and romance to epic, so that what begins as an essay in Hellenistic sentiment takes on Homeric colours in the final books.

By comparison with the other novels', XENOPHON'S use of narrative space can easily seem random and incoherent.[10] Where Chariton restricts the scope, topology, and meaning of his zone of play, Xenophon's characters seem to pinball wildly around the Mediterranean for reasons at times known only to God and the author.[11] But an imperial reader would find the geography more familiar and followable than we do, and there are clear signs of a purposeful narrative pattern to the hugely ambitious web of storylines, characters, and episodes, whose sheer narrative density and complexity is unmatched before Heliodorus.[12] Most impressively, there is a conscious attempt to sustain double Chariton's number of simultaneous but intercut plotlines, by tracking not just the separate movements of hero and heroine but those of their wandering friends. Hägg's famous analysis (1971: 154–78) demonstrates both the complexity of this multiple narrative line and the very large number of switches. This is not simply a consequence of the sheer multiplication of episodes, which does not in itself force *transitions*; it is a deliberate narrative ploy, compelling the reader to retain an elaborate model of simultaneous lines of story in different locations. This is most easily grasped from Table 14, which may be compared with the maps mentioned in n. 11, and with Hägg's tabulations of temporal spans (1971: 156–7). I have taken over Hägg's convenient division and numeration of the alternating narrative sections between II.8.1 and V.11.2, extending it briefly at either end to cover the complete text.

All three of the principal lines of travel – Habrocomes, Anthia,

---

[10] Hägg 1971: 172–5. The status of Xenophon's strange, abbreviate text, with its erratic pace and motivational lacunae, remains unresolved: a mere incompetent farrago? An epitome of a once-longer work? A transcript of an improvisation in oral formulaic prose? The epitome hypothesis (Rohde 1876: 429, Bürger 1892, Papanikolaou 1973) has been challenged by Hägg 1966 and O'Sullivan 1995: 100–39. But O'Sullivan's rival claim of oral composition is a perilously Homeristic inference from the undoubtedly striking formulism of style demonstrated; it also, far from confounding the abridgement hypothesis, strengthens the possibility that our text may be a shorter variant of a composition that could have been known in several and longer forms.

[11] See the maps in Hägg 1983 (endpapers) and Alvarez 1996: 805 – neither of which includes the movements of Hippothous, Leucon, and Rhode. Typical is IV.4.2 on Habrocomes' journey to Italy, when Anthia ironically lies close at hand in precisely the opposite direction: one of the more difficult points for the opponents of epitomisation to explain away.

[12] Now *both* lovers are objects as well as subjects of pursuit, with Habrocomes the target of threatening attentions from Corymbus (abortively), Manto (disastrously), and Cyno (near-fatally); and the number of competitors for Anthia is tripled from Chariton's mere trio to the series Euxinus, Moeris, Lampon, Psammis, Anchialus, Amphinomus, Polyidus, the brothel punters, and ultimately even Hippothous.

Hippothous – trace a clockwise circuit from Asia to Africa to Europe and back to Asia, with the final convergence at the carefully chosen neutral territory of Rhodes (the Clapham Junction of eastern Mediterranean sea-lanes, and politically autonomous of the continental kingdoms in the period of the novel's setting). (i) The first phase of the novel, to the end of II.7, keeps the lovers together even in their wanderings – a surprising, and for some tastes bungled, variation on Chariton's sequence of marriage/separation/wandering, but with dramatic possibilities that prompted all three later novelists to keep the couple together for a still larger proportion of their adventures. (ii) When they are separated, the novel enters a phase of straightforward pursuit, but with a more purposeful and systematic sequence than in Chariton. Habrocomes remains one step behind Anthia in Tyre, Syria, and Cilicia, ironically having to return to the last to pick up the trail when he learns of Hippothous' encounter there. (iii) He comes within a step of catching her up in Alexandria (Chrysion's information allowing him to make ground by bypassing Tarsus), only for the plot to shift gear as he is shipwrecked and detained following Cyno's intrigue while *Hippothous* leapfrogs him and catches up with Anthia instead. This crucial section of the novel seems severely abbreviated, but even as the text stands we can enjoy the improbable irony that Hippothous catches, attempts to kill, and finally once more loses track of his friend's wife without once determining her identity. (iv) Habrocomes is released, and for reasons unexplained in our text goes off on a wild-goose chase to Italy. By a further stroke of what looks like, but may have once been more than, unlikely irony, Habrocomes is the unwitting quarry in this third, European phase of the chase. Like its predecessors, it teases the reader with the appearance of converging paths (as the Asian lines promised to converge in Cilicia, and the African lines in Alexandria), only to end with a *third* meeting between Anthia and Hippothous, who now threatens to emerge not as helper but as potential rival. (v) Only then do the various strands converge on the chosen meeting-ground of Rhodes, where the author has long since seeded a reason for the recognition-triggering dedication Anthia now makes on the completion of her geographical and narrative circuit.

In contrast, LONGUS notoriously rejects the motif of travel – the central narrative armature in all other ancient novels (not just the romances). The closest we get is the Methymnaeans' abortive kidnap of Chloe, which significantly prompts the most violent supernatural intervention. Otherwise, the lovers stay put until the final chapters, and their adventures, such as they are, come to them: from the sea, from Pyrrha and Methymna, from neighbouring Mytilene, but mostly from their own immediate surroundings. The geographical world of genre adventure, the

Table 14. *Xenophon, Ephesiaca: narrative strands and character movements*

Section	Reference	Events	Habrocomes	Anthia	Leucon, Rhode	Hippothous
AHLR0	I.1–II.7.5	meeting, wedding, pirates, Manto	Ephesus–Tyre	Ephesus–Tyre		
H1	II.8.1–9.1	Habrocomes in prison	Tyre			
A1	II.9.1–10.1	Anthia 'married' to Lampon		Tyre–Antioch–rural Syria	Tyre–Antioch	
H2	II.10.1–4	Habrocomes exonerated and freed	Tyre			
LR1	II.10.4	old man buys Leucon & Rhode			Antioch–Xanthus	
A2	II.11.1–11	Moeris, Lampon's ruse, shipwreck; enter Hippothous		rural Syria–Cilicia		Cilicia
H3	II.12.1–3	Manto's letter; Lampon spares Anthia; her escape and pursuit	Tyre–Syria			
A3	II.13.1–14.1	Perilaus rescues Anthia from sacrifice		Cilicia–Tarsus		Cilicia
H4	II.14.1–III.3.7	Habrocomes meets Hippothous; stories exchanged, trail resumed	Syria–Cilicia–Mazacus–Cilicia			Cilicia–Mazacus–Cilicia
A4	III.3.7–9.1	Perilaus, Eudoxus; Anthia drugged & entombed; pirates		Tarsus–Alexandria		
H5	III.9.2–10.5	Chrysion's story, Habrocomes' pursuit	Cilicia–(Alexandria)			Cilicia–Tarsus
A5	III.11.1–12.1	Psammis		Alexandria		
H6a	III.12.1–6	shipwreck, Araxus, Cyno; Habrocomes arrested	Cilicia–Pelusium–Alexandria			
H1	IV.1.1–5	search for Habrocomes abandoned, base moved to Ethiopia				Tarsus–Laodicea–Phoenicia–Pelusium–Hermopolis–Schedia–Memphis–Mendes–Tawa–Leontopolis–Coptus–Ethiopia
H6b	IV.2.1–3.1	Habrocomes condemned; Nile miracles	Alexandria			
A6	IV.3.1–4.1	Psammis' journey & death, capture by Hippothous		Alexandria–Ethiopia		Ethiopia

H7	IV.4.1–2	pardon, death of Cyno, quest renewed	Alexandria–(Italy)		Ethiopia	
A7	IV.5.1–6.7	Anchialus, the pit, and Amphinomus	(Alexandria)–Syracuse		Ethiopia	
H8	V.1.1–2.1	Aegialeus' story			Ethiopia–Coptus	
A8a	V.2.1–6	Hippothous' departure, Amphinomus & Anthia remain			Ethiopia–Coptus–Areia	
Hi2	V.2.7–3.3	departure, battle with Polyidus, Hippothous' escape & flight				Areia–Schedia–Pelusium–Alexandria–(Sicily)
A8b	V.4.1–5.8	Polyidus, Rhenaea; Anthia sold to brothel			Coptus–Memphis–Alexandria–Tarentum	
Hi3	V.6.1	Hippothous looks for work				(Alexandria)–Tauromenium
H9	V.6.1–3	quest resumed; parents' suicide in Ephesus	Syracuse–(Italy)			
LR2	V.6.3–4	old man's death & legacy; news from Ephesus		Xanthus–Rhodes		
A9	V.7.1–8.1	Anthia feigns epilepsy			Tarentum	
H10	V.8.1–5	Habrocomes in the quarries	(Syracuse)–Nuceria			
A10a	V.8.5–9	Anthia's dream			Tarentum	
Hi4	V.9.1–3	marriage, wife's death & legacy, quest for Habrocomes resumed, Clisthenes				Tauromenium–Tarentum
A10b	V.9.4–13	recognition, Anthia's story			Tarentum	
H11a	V.10.1–5	quest resumed, death of Aegialeus, convergence with Leucon & Rhode	Nuceria–Syracuse–Crete–Cyprus–Rhodes			Tarentum
LR3	V.10.6	dedication at temple of Helius		Rhodes	Rhodes	
H11b	V.10.7–11.1	Habrocomes recognises Leucon & Rhode	Rhodes	Rhodes		
A11	V.11.1–5	Helius festival, Anthia's dedication		Rhodes	Tarentum–Rhodes	Tarentum–Rhodes
LR4	V.12.1–2	Anthia's dedication found and reported to Habrocomes	Rhodes			
A12	V.12.3–13.1	Anthia & Hippothous to temple, meeting & recognising Leucon & Rhode		Rhodes	Rhodes	Rhodes
H12	V.13.2–15.4	Anthia and Habrocomes reunited, and return to Ephesus	Rhodes		Rhodes	Rhodes

wider Mediterranean beyond the coastal waters of Lesbos, never impinges at all. With the whole of the narrative devoted to the growth of love, and the consummation delayed till the final words of the text, it is as if the plot of a Chariton or Xenophon were happily stalled in book I. What is more, even within these spatial boundaries Longus seems determined to resist any formal narrative patterning. Though the novel is remarkable for its rich sense of landscape, environment, and even historical topography,[13] there is next to no sense of narrative spatiality. The recurrent landmarks of the pastoral action – the homes of Lamon and Dryas, the woods, sea, grazing, the cave, shrine, and pine tree – evoke no particular sense of relative location, and no striking structural contrasts or thematic patterns. The one elaborated spatial opposition, thematic rather than narrative, is the complex, ambivalent, and sophisticated network of interactions between the pastoral setting *as a whole* and its antitype the city.[14] Otherwise, it is the very immobility of the action that is significant, as Longus develops a fascinating *faux-naïf* dialectic between the Aristotelian classicality of the romance and its antithesis in the timeless, placeless, plotless world of the pastoral. Since it is axiomatic for Longus that the values of the latter should triumph, many elements of the classical game structure are treated with a whimsical perversity. The player set, especially, is almost parodically ill-defined: characters get introduced on a purely *ad hoc* basis, and as casually dropped once their episodic functions are discharged. In fact, Longus scrupulously avoids the classical seeding of causes ahead of effects. Plot elements appear from the blue when needed, even when it would have been perfectly possible to place them in position beforehand.[15] Again and again, the plot gives the ingenuous sense of having been improvised by a ten-year-old: in the narrative texture of Longus' world, the dreary mechanics of classical cause and effect are suspended in an all-embracing childlike innocence.

ACHILLES' treatment of narrative space, along with other elements of his narrative art, goes through some subtle modulations as the novel unfolds. In a self-conscious, ironic rewriting of the *Odyssey*, the novel falls into two contrasting halves: an archipelago of short, varied episodes whose principal plot function is to establish the essential game elements and narrative

[13] Mason 1979, Green 1982, Bowie 1985, Kloft 1989: 58–60.
[14] Chalk 1960: 48–51.
[15] Thus when Daphnis' request for Chloe's hand is rejected by her foster-parents on financial grounds, he simply prays to the Nymphs for a solution, and they inform him in a dream that the money was made available in an earlier episode (the Methymnaeans' shipwreck), though no mention was made of this at the time even by the narrator. Longus actively prefers the anti-Aristotelian *ex machina* solution, even commenting in his characteristic narratorial deadpan that 'It turned out Daphnis would have little difficulty finding the hoard' (III.28).

ground-rules, followed by a continuous mainland episode leading towards a decisive agonistic endgame. As in the *Odyssey* (and in Heliodorus, who also works from this template), the junction is not at a book-division but part-way into the first book of the second half (v.17); and it is marked by (i) a decisive landfall in an unexplored area of the board, with the introduction of a new cast of main players; (ii) a counselling-scene with a newly manifest adviser-figure; (iii) a shift from *ad hoc*, improvised individual p-moves to a sustained intrigue based on a complex chain of c-moves within a group.

This epic homage is, however, far from slavish. The first two books are comic rather than epic in their spatiality, house-bound in Tyre to Hippias' carefully ground-planned home and gardens with brief excursions to a second house (II.26–7) and the altars of Heracles and Zeus (15, 18), and Byzantium offstaged as an unvisited elsewhere.[16] Only at II.31 does the action escape its set-bound limits into an emphatically novelistic spatiality, as the comic seduction plot modulates into a more conventional intercontinental picaresque of lovers pursued, and the narratorial perspective opens up to admit flashes of epic omniscience. The two sea crossings mark off the principal remaining narrative subgames, with their contrasting narrative shapes: the itinerant, serially organised Egyptian sequence from Pelusium via bandit country to Alexandria, and the sustained, dual-stranded Ephesian segment with its giddy switches of location and viewpoint. The teasing close in Tyre, with a further voyage to Byzantium promised but never narrated, leaves the Sidonian frame notoriously unclosed.

But HELIODORUS' plotting of space is far the most elaborate and exemplary, and warrants most detailed discussion. If we roll out the story to full length, we seem to have a familiar Odyssean (and Achillean) system of archipelago and mainland, with the maritime half of the plot distributed over a string of island episodes segregated by the familiar narrative buffer of indeterminate ocean. Thessaly, Athens, Delphi, Zacynthus, Crete: the Mediterranean phases of the various storylines seem widely scattered across the map. What is more, even the mainland segment is diffused over hundreds of miles, from the Nile delta to the half-fabulous hinterland of Meroe – as opposed to the single island of the Ithacan *Odyssey*, or the city and environs of Achilles' Ephesian endgame.

Yet this is not how the *Aethiopica*'s world strikes most readers. If anything, we find it almost disappointingly circumscribed – with its handful of half-a-dozen or so principal locations, its high preponderance of indoor scenes, and its limited interest in landscape and topography outside the

---

[16] There are striking reminiscences of *Samia*, though they do not seem purposeful: for Byzantium see 98ff., and for Demeas' uniquely detailed house interior 219ff.

spectacular pictorial set pieces (the bandits' lake village, the siege of Syene). The first-time reader, anticipating a Herodotean safari through the lost worlds of Africa's dark heart, can hardly help a sense of impatience at the nine books of stalling in pseudo-Achaemenid Egypt before the borders of 'Ethiopia' (the Sudan) are even crossed.[17]

For the setting of Heliodorus' story is the most severely structured and restricted in any classical narrative outside the drama, thanks to two venerable Odyssean spatial tricks hitherto untested in the novel. The first is to draw a strict line between the spaces of primary and secondary narrative. The *primary* narrative of the *Aethiopica*, alone of the novels, is entirely landlocked: it opens the morning after the heroes' final arrival on the African continent, and none of the surviving principals returns to Greece before the end of the novel. Cnemon, whose own storyline has to return to Athens to finish, is waved goodbye from the narrative as a newly-wed in Chemmis, along with his new father-in-law Nausicles (whose return to Athens with Cnemon is also required). Even Charicles, the one character to make a sea journey within the primary narrative time of the novel, turns up artfully out of the blue in Meroe in the final pages, his pursuit suppressed even in secondary narrative until now; and nothing is said about his eventual return to Delphi, which his priesthood presumably requires of him whatever his personal inclinations at this happy time. As in *Odyssey* IX–XII, the widest part of the narrative archipelago is relegated to secondary report; but Heliodorus goes still further, effectively beginning his African *Odyssey* on the beach of Ithaca.

Second and more important yet, the vast terrain even of this primary narrative zone is shaped, like Homeric Ithaca, around a small number of very specific *locations* strung out in a unilinear narrative sequence. In the *Odyssey*, this line was the route from beach to farmstead to carefully ground-planned palace: a thematic progression from isolation and the margins of the community to its physical and political centre. In the *Aethiopica* the line is longer, but its course is similar: from the wild margin of the beach, to the semi-anarchy of the bandit swamplands, to the village of Chemmis, to the town of Bessa, to the city of Memphis, to the battle-front of Syene, to the final utopian destination of Meroe. There is thus a clear, even hyperschematic, path to be traversed from wilderness to utopia, anarchy to divine monarchy, individualism to ever greater community, poverty to fabulous wealth, the known world to the fabled. That does not mean it is an easy path to traverse: on the contrary, the scale of

[17] If *Aethiopica* was the original title, we must surely suspect a deliberate ploy of suspense; compare the remarks of Rabkin 1973: 5–6 on the title-page of Melville's *Typee*. Perhaps Heliodorus has the trick from Antonius Diogenes, whose *Fantastic adventures beyond Thule* only delivered on the pledge of their title in their twenty-fourth, and final, book.

danger increases from the crude animal thuggery of the bandits, through the more deadly urbane intrigues of Memphis, to the epic warfare at the disputed border between nations, and finally to a grade of peril known only to fabled barbarians, the Ethiopians' ritual human sacrifice. But at last the absorption of rational, civilised Greeks into their community redeems the culturally ambivalent Ethiopians from the savage excesses of their old religion.

This linear topography is no *ad hoc* narrative construct imposed from above, but a real and unique feature of the particular Mediterranean country in which Heliodorus has chosen to set his story. When we think of Egypt as a square desert country on a map, we easily forget its very different human geography, now as in antiquity. *Inhabited* Egypt, and especially the Egypt of the *Aethiopica* (where the desert is never so much as mentioned), is the demographic ribbon formed by the the banks of the river Nile, from its border with the sea where the action begins to its unexplored barbarian upper reaches. Calasiris' famous lecture on the Nile floods at II.28, like other so-called Heliodoran 'digressions', turns out to have a vital narrative function, establishing an early picture in the text of the upper boundary to the novel's Nilotic topography. At one end of the story, and its world, is the Mediterranean, the common border of all nations; at the other is only a gradual, unbounded ascent into *terra incognita*, where science and fantasy compete to colonise the blanks in our mental maps. In Heliodorus' narrative atlas, Ethiopia lies just over the border beyond Philae, a utopian kingdom suspended between history and myth. And again and again the Nile itself recurs as the one unchanging landmark of the narrative, at times entering the story directly as the instrumental means of moves inconceivable in other terrain – from the shipless pirates of the opening sentence to the exotic siegecraft of Hydaspes at Syene.

As Table 15 helps to show, all the chief players' stories draw structure and meaning from their movements along this axis of Nile. Of the six main travellers, all but Theagenes trace a loop. The main thread, and the longest, is the story's *raison d'être*: Charicleia's exile from Meroe and her return to reclaim her homeland, family, and birthright. But causally woven into this strand is the initially quite separate tale of Calasiris' own exile from Memphis, first to Meroe and then to Greece, followed by his own homecoming to city and family in the nick of time to avert a Theban tragedy. This Calasiris thread in turn connects to, and eventually converges with, that of his son Thyamis' exile and transformation from holy man to outlaw, before he too is allowed to return and be redeemed. Alongside these one Meroitic and two Memphite loops are two Greek loops: the feckless, star-crossed Cnemon's own exile from his all-too-native Athens to find his own

Table 15. Aethiopica: *principal character movements*

Step	Charicleia	Theagenes	Hydaspes	Sisimithres	Charicles	Calasiris	Thyamis	Cnemon	Thisbe	Nausicles	Mitranes	Achaemenes	Bagoas
0	Meroe	Thessaly	Meroe	Meroe	Delphi	Memphis	Memphis	Athens	Athens	Chemmis	Memphis	Memphis	Memphis
1	Catadupi			Catadupi	Catadupi	Meroe		Athens	Athens	Athens			
2	Delphi	Delphi		Meroe	Delphi	Delphi	Bucolia	Athens					
3	Heracleotis	Heracleotis			Delphi	Heracleotis	Bucolia	Bucolia	Bucolia	Chemmis			
4	Bucolia	Bucolia				Chemmis	Bucolia	Bucolia					
5	Bucolia	Bucolia				Chemmis		Chemmis		Chemmis	Bucolia		
6	Chemmis	Bessa				Chemmis	Bessa	Chemmis		Chemmis	Bessa		
7	Bessa	Memphis				Bessa	Memphis						
8	Memphis	Memphis				Memphis	Memphis					Memphis	Memphis
9	Syene	Syene	Syene									Syene	Syene
10	Meroe	Meroe	Meroe	Meroe	Meroe								Meroe

surprising salvation on the banks of the barbarous Nile; and the pious
stooge Charicles' half-comic quest from the centre of the world to its edge
in pursuit of his daughter's abductors. Thus all five circuits trace a pattern
of exile and return, precipitated by a loss of identity or position at home
that finds unexpected resolution at the farthest point of their wanderings.
Among the six principals, there is only one, telling exception to this
pattern. Only Theagenes, pure Thessalian hero from the blood of Achilles,
makes a choice and a journey such as no other Greek love-hero undergoes:
a one-way trip to an unknown new life at the other end of the earth, freely
choosing love over homeland, family, and position.

This careful zoning of characters and subplots is vital to the novel's
structural clarity. Like Achilles,[18] Heliodorus recognises the importance
in a long classical narrative of strong *episodisation* into subgames. As
Schissel long ago observed, the *Aethiopica*'s primary narrative is laid out
in five largely autonomous successive episodes, each tied to a distinct cast
and location.[19] Chariclea and Theagenes are active in the cast of only
three: the Bucolia sequence to II.19, the Memphis section from VII.9 to
VIII.17, and the endgame at Meroe in the final book. Between these fall
the Chemmis and Syene interludes, where the narrative is turned over to
supporting characters (Calasiris, Cnemon, Nausicles; Hydaspes,
Oroondates) just as the Charicleia–Theagenes action has reached a
cliffhanger at a point of transition between one subgame and another.

The boundaries to these episodes are determined by the *Aethiopica*'s
sophisticated topography of power. Chariton had attempted something
similar with the nested or competing power spheres of Callirhoe's lovers;
but Heliodorus goes further yet, in plotting the lovers' quest itself on a
map demarcated into successive individual domains of authority. The
first circle is anarchic Bucolia, where force alone rules, and supreme
power rests with the strongest – initially Thyamis, until Mitranes turns up
with his superior force. The second is Memphis, whose satrapal power
extends to the disputed borders at north and south. Here power is hierarchical: supreme authority lies with Oroondates, but in his absence
Arsace wears the trousers, with her family and subordinates partaking in
but subservient to her authority. Finally there is Hydaspes' Ethiopia,
stable and secure under his enlightened despotism. Between these three
zones lie dangerous no-man's-lands: the precarious countryside around
Nausicles' safe house in Chemmis, scoured by Persian patrols and bandit
gangs alike; and the war zone between Egypt and Ethiopia, where two
great power spheres clash at their common border.

[18] Sedelmeier 1959: 113–31.
[19] Schissel 1913: 50–2; cf. Hefti 1950: 252–4, Heiserman 1977: 189, Sandy 1982: 42.

This power-map is basic to the *Aethiopica*'s plot, whose core is a transactional chain, with Charicleia as its object, that requires the heroine to traverse a succession of power zones, passing as she does so from one transient *kyrios* to another, before she can pass into the power of her natural father – the one player with the ultimate legal and generic authority to give her in marriage to her destined lord Theagenes. The essential steps, if we omit the many detours involved in step 5, are shown in Figure 7.

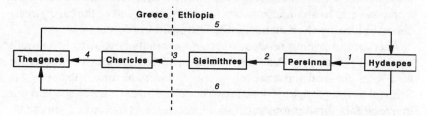

Figure 7. Charicleia's custodians

From Persinna she passes to Sisimithres and thence to Charicles; then to Theagenes (by consenting abduction), Thyamis (by capture), Mitranes (again capture), Nausicles (by contractual claim), Calasiris (by ransom), Arsace (by *force majeure*), Theagenes again (by claim of betrothal), Arsace again (*qua* enforcer of the law), Bagoas (*de facto*), Hydaspes (initially by capture), Hydaspes and Persinna (by recognition), and finally from her parents to Theagenes (in marriage). Her plight is heightened by the prevailing difficulty that her lover and helpers are technically disabled, by separation and by their own exiled status, from offering her secure protection: Theagenes himself has no status in Egypt or Meroe and spends most of the novel as a slave; Calasiris expires within hours of returning to his power base; and Charicles catches up only at the very end. Since the journey up river leads through the legal no-man's-land of Egypt, where neither lover's citizenship is defined and neither of Charicleia's fathers has authority, step 5 of the transaction is the most fragile, and constantly vulnerable to interception; it therefore makes up the spine of the primary narrative, with the fragmented 1–4 relegated to riddling backstory, and the climactic 6 the basis for the bravura endgame plotting in book x (on which more below).

In contrast to this narrative shaping of space and power, the organisation of *time* is not always an insistent feature of the novels' plotting. The fullest analysis of the novels' temporality even concludes that 'Time, as such, is not a predominant feature of the romances':[20] that variations in temporal

[20] Hägg 1971: 307; cf. Bakhtin 1981, esp. 89–91.

sequence, deadline, duration, and flow are of textural rather than structural significance, and that calendar time is neither strongly marked nor particularly functional in shaping the story. Certainly the generic pressure to temporal economy is less insistent than in either epic or drama.[21] Both *Iliad* and *Odyssey* have to compress whole decades of action into a month or so of primary-narrative time; but the novels' stories are much less temporally extended, if we exclude from the timeframe the establishing backstory in the two recognition novels. Achilles clocks in at ten months or so, Longus at around eighteen, and the less explicit Chariton and Xenophon somewhere between this figure and its double. Only Heliodorus, with his self-conscious emulation of the *Odyssey*, aspires to a truly Homeric temporality, with a primary narrative of little more than a month embedding bold flashbacks that reach ten or twenty years into the past.[22]

There is an obvious advantage here for erotic fiction over heroic myth, which has always had problems with the sheer sprawl of its inherited material. A love affair, however beset, will generally reach its narrative goal sooner than a war or vendetta. With its much tighter spatio-temporal narrative window, New Comedy was unable to take full advantage of this; thus in comedy the *beginning* of the love affair is with one exception (the Chaerea subplot in the *Eunuch*) relegated to backstory, even in those rare cases like *Dyskolos* where the entire affair from onset to settlement does fall within the Aristotelian span of a day. But the novel is not so limited. With judicious use of narratorial summaries and ellipses, the interval between love's *coup de foudre* and its secure consummation is in all cases brief enough to be fully narrated in internal story order – something Aristotle recognised was artistically impractical for either the *Iliad*'s tale of the war or the *Odyssey*'s tale of the hero.[23] It is a characteristic Heliodoran conceit that the hyper-Odyssean *Aethiopica* is the one novel to make lavish use of anachronic secondary flashbacks in narrating the love story, when it is the one novel that – by packing the whole affair from meeting to wedding into a few weeks – has least temporal need of them.

Nevertheless, consideration of the two later novels excluded from Hägg's survey suggests a more complex picture. As the genre develops, the plotting of time becomes increasingly sophisticated and significant. Not only is time *structurally* important in Longus and Heliodorus in precisely the ways that Hägg claims it is not, but all three of the later, 'sophistic' novels show an artful grasp of the centrality of narrative time to a number of storytelling values that grow in importance as the genre

---

[21] For Chariton, Xenophon, and Achilles this topic is treated very fully in Hägg 1971; I therefore limit my own remarks on these authors. For wider-ranging views of temporality in the novelists see Bakhtin 1981: 89–110, Billault 1991: 47–120, Fusillo 1991: 229–35.

[22] Hefti 1950: 125–7; Hägg 1971: 308.   [23] *Poetics* 8.1451a22–30, 23.1459a30–b2.

evolves in sophistication: the plotting of *information* within the story itself, the manipulation of the reader's dynamic modelling of that story, and ultimately the thematic implications of narrative hermeneutics for the way the text invites us to read the world.

Daphnis and Chloe, for all its resistance to classical narrativity in other respects, is the one novel to *frame* its narrative in a clearly defined temporal structure: the famous linkage between the purely temporal cycle of the six seasons spanned by the main story and the emotional phases of the adolescent lovers' coming of age. Chalk's classic analysis (1960: 39–43) demonstrated how the narrative structure follows a regular pattern within each of the seven seasonal units: a scene-setting general description of the season itself, followed by an account of the lovers' emotional response to it, leading in turn to a montage of story episodes more or less specifically generated by the seasonal conditions without and within. The part-causal, part-symbolic linkage between climatic changes in the outer and inner worlds is of course an inheritance from pastoral, but its extension to *narrative* use is Longus' own – with the seasonal movement simultaneously cyclic, evoking the timelessness and continuity of the pastoral universe, and progressive, suggesting the dynamically arrowed temporality of the novel. The second spring, summer, and autumn are not like the first: Daphnis and Chloe are irreversibly maturing, their developing sexuality and experience responding differently to the same world a year apart. Their sexual growth, in particular, summons a powerful sense of deadline. The novel's emphatic narrative destination, Chloe's defloration by Daphnis, cannot be indefinitely postponed the way Leucippe's or Charicleia's in principle could, because the blocking factors are dissoluble over time. Daphnis and Chloe are hell-bent on sexual consummation with or without the sanctions of contractual marriage. The tension lies simply in the *race* between that irresistible momentum to sex and the prior fulfilment of the various social, emotional, and practical conditions the narrative lays down for its ideal outcome. As the seasons come round again, the narrative signals – images, promises, predictions – grow more and more insistent that Chloe's virginity will not survive the coming autumn. But can a wedding be contracted and the couple's true parents recognised before the lovers spontaneously complete their education in the facts of pastoral life?

Heliodorus' handling of temporality, in contrast, is at once more conventional and more radical. The *Aethiopica*'s primary chronology is set out in Table 16.[24] An unusual feature, marked by asterisks in the table, is the appearance (in books VI–X only) of points in the narrative where a gap

---

[24] Cf. the more cautious chronology in Futre Pinheiro 1987: 19 (≈ 1998: 3152–3).

Table 16. Aethiopica: *chronology*

Day(s)	Reference	Events
1	I.1.1–18.2	Charicleia & Theagenes to Bucolia; Cnemon's story I
2	I.18.3–II.18.1	Petosiris' attack; Thisbe's death; Cnemon's story II
3	II.18.1–20.4	Cnemon eludes Thermuthis; Mitranes captures Theagenes; Nausicles obtains Charicleia
4	II.20.5–V.9.2	Cnemon meets Calasiris; Calasiris' story I; Nausicles & Charicleia to Chemmis
5	V.10.1–VI.1.1	Calasiris ransoms Charicleia; Calasiris' story II; Thyamis recaptures Theagenes, Mitranes in pursuit to Bessa
6	VI.1.1–9.1	Cnemon's story III; news of Theagenes; Cnemon's wedding
7	VI.9.1–11.1	Calasiris & Charicleia plan their quest
8–9	VI.11.1	preparations for departure
10	VI.11.1–15.5	battle of Bessa; Thyamis & Theagenes to Memphis; Charicleia & Calasiris to Bessa; interview with the zombie
*11	VII.1.1–11.1	Memphis: duel and reunions; Arsace's intrigue begins; death of Calasiris
12	VII.11.1–18.2	Charicleia & Theagenes to palace; Achaemenes' return to Memphis
13	VII.18.2–19.9	Arsace's audience with Theagenes
14–18	VII.20.1	Arsace works on Theagenes
*19	VII.20.1–22.1	Cybele reveals Arsace's passion; Charicleia & Theagenes prevaricate
20	VII.22.1–27.1	intrigues culminate: Arsace claims Theagenes
21	VII.27.1–29.2	Achaemenes, betrayed, rides to Thebes; *Thyamis confronts Arsace; Theagenes imprisoned
*22	VIII.1.5–6.2	Achaemenes informs Oroondates; Bagoas to Memphis
23–4	VIII.6.2–6	Theagenes tortured
*25	VIII.6.6–9.5	Cybele's poisoning
26	VIII.9.6–14.2	Charicleia's trial, pyre, escape, and imprisonment with Theagenes; Bagoas reaches Memphis, rescues Charicleia & Theagenes
27	VIII.14.2–15.6	Arsace's suicide; Bagoas, Charicleia & Theagenes on road
28	VIII.15.6–7	Bagoas' party divert to Syene
*29	VIII.16.1–IX.8.4	Bagoas' party captured by Ethiopians and *handed over to Hydaspes; *Syene diked & flooded round
30–31	IX.8.4–9.1	water recedes, siege continues
*32	IX.9.1–11.2	Niloa & ceasefire; Oroondates' escape to Elephantine
33	IX.11.3–23.1	Oroondates returns with reinforcements, defeated by Hydaspes; Achaemenes killed; Oroondates before Hydaspes
34	IX.23.2–X.1.1	Hydaspes meets Charicles & Theagenes; recognition postponed
*35	X.1.1–2	Hydaspes to Philae
36–37	X.1.2	Hydaspes at Philae
*38	X.1.3–6.1	Hydaspes leaves for Meroe; *Hydaspes' letter reaches Persinna
39	X.6.1–41.3	Hydaspes reaches Meroe; triumph, recognition, arrival of Charicles, and denouement.

of days is possibly implied by the action, but neither explicitly stated nor excluded. There is also an occasional tendency to expressions like 'two or three days later' or 'this went on for five or six days, and then . . .', which I have for schematic convenience interpreted as an asterisked resumption of action on the higher-numbered day. The table is thus a *minimum* chronology – some of the asterisks could in theory mask an interval of months – as well as a certainly over-definite depiction of the novel's plan.[25]

Nevertheless, it does make two important points about time in the *Aethiopica*. First, Heliodorus goes further even than Achilles in confining his novel within the Homeric limits of what Hägg (1971) calls 'day-and-night phases' – a continuous series of numerable days and nights, rather than the loose, unspecified timegaps of indeterminate length that most novels admit and Xenophon apparently prefers. We do find such intervals in Calasiris' *secondary* narrative, as indeed in *Odyssey* IX–XII; but in principle the *Aethiopica*'s primary action could be entirely contained within the thirty-nine days directly specified in the text. Heliodorus has inverted the Odyssean proportions of his two halves – as the table shows, the continuous second act is at least three times the story duration of the first – but in VIII–X, at least, the Odyssean device of progressive retardation as the endgame approaches is very deliberately, even excessively, pursued.

This figure of thirty-nine days is itself the second point. No doubt by invited accident rather than strict calculation, Heliodorus has nevertheless brought his novel in at a day below the chronological budget of the *Odyssey*. What is more, as Table 17 on pp. 252–3 shows, he embeds within that primary timespan secondary, tertiary, and quaternary action extending across seventeen years and more, as compared with Odysseus' mere decade. Calasiris' own narrative, told in two instalments to Cnemon (29–38) and to Nausicles and Cnemon (46), covers the final days from Delphi to the beginning of primary action. Calasiris' report of Charicles' story fills in the preceding decade, from Charicles' adoption of Charicleia at Catadupi to his meeting with Calasiris in Delphi. For the seven years preceding we have Calasiris' quotation of Charicles' version of what Sisimithres told him, while for the crucial backstory of Charicleia's conception, birth, and exile we have Persinna's words, reported by Calasiris from two sources: his translation of her message on Charicleia's bracelet, and his own summarised conversations with the queen in Meroe.

Such drastic narrative compression, allowing Charicleia's entire history to be told by a single speaker in the space of two conversations in a single room within twenty-four hours of one another, has no precedent in the

---

[25] There is a hiccup at 1.24.2, where we are told that Theagenes dined with Thyamis on more than one occasion, when in fact the enemy attack supervenes before any such socialising can begin.

earlier novels. Clitophon's conversation with the Achilles-narrator in Sidon, an action that takes no longer than the reading of the text, is an imperfect precedent, since the embedding frame is unclosed and its primary narrative entirely disjunct from the story; while there is no novelistic parallel at all for the extraordinary fragmentation of Charicleia's story into half-a-dozen pieces, collated for us by Calasiris from five different sources at three or four levels of remove, and told in an order that is neither their objective internal chronology nor the strict order in which he subjectively learned them.

The effects of this jigsaw narrativity go far beyond mere narrative economy. We have already noted how the novel's return to the epic mode dispenses with classical drama's fixed spatiotemporal frame to the action, so that the boundary between primary and secondary narration is now a mobile one, and the narrative is no longer bound to a real-time mapping of performance time to story time. Thus the narrating voice of primary narrative is free to vary the order and tempo of reported story events: to engage in such epic devices as narratorial flashback and anticipation, temporal ellipsis, variations between scene and summary, and the slowing or suspension of narrative time in passages of high description or ecphrasis, as well as non-narrative material such as sententious digression. At the same time, however, the novel is profoundly shaped by the narrative values of drama, and constrained in its degrees of freedom by its commitment to the classical values of narrative economy and narratorial transparency, which conspire to embed the narrating voice(s) as far as possible *within the story itself*. Drama, as we saw, does this out of narratological necessity; the novel follows willingly because it values the virtues drama has made of that necessity.

There is, however, an important difference here between the embedding practice of epic and drama. Epic is free to nest stories *within* stories at an arbitrary depth of embedding – Menelaus quoting Proteus, Odysseus quoting Polyphemus paraphrasing Posidon – without concern for the mimesis of different narrative voices. But in drama, because the narrating voice is visibly and audibly *embodied*, such Chinese-box nesting of narrators is unperformable outside certain well-defined conventional limits, such as the block quotation of secondary direct speech in extended rhesis (especially messenger reports). What the shorter performance span does encourage in its place is *serial* embedding, with secondary narrative fragmented among a succession of narrating voices from which it has to be reassembled. Tragedies of detection, such as *OT* and *Ion*, are especially interested in the hermeneutics of piecing the past together from its scattered fragments in the present, through the collation of multiple secondary voices that may overlap or contradict: thus the spoken recollections of Oedipus and Jocasta lap both with one another and with messenger reports and oracles, and collation is impeded by small but crucial discrepancies which need to be reconciled. And New Comedy takes this device further still, using the emergence of unitary truth out of fragmented multiple errors or part-truths as a paradigm of its own grand narrative, so formative for the novel: the collapse of human chaos into systemic civic and cosmic order. The challenge for the novelists is to re-create this peculiarly theatrical plotting of information in the epic mode, reinstating the narrative voice of epic to a form that still aspires to the condition of drama.[26]

Achilles Tatius' response to that challenge is a brilliant evasion. The primary narrator is confined to the opening frame in Sidon; otherwise, the entire novel forms an extended messenger-speech in a vestigial and unfinished drama, the *apologoi* from a failed epic whose primary narrator lacks even the other novelists' omniscient access to verification of the tale. Next to the very different case of Plato's *Republic*, Clitophon's story is the longest first-person narrative extant in Greek, and easily the most supple display in either Greek or Latin of the narrative acrobatics peculiar to the mode. (Antonius Diogenes may have gone much further, but Photius' summary leaves us little with which to work.) Achilles' manipulation of viewpoint is his main, though by no means his only, narrative tool in sculpting his reader's emerging sense of the story, and rightly dominates discussion both of his fictional technique and of his novel's distinctive ironic texture.[27] In particular, Achilles takes advantage of the novel's epic length to explore the ironics of framed *Ich-Erzählung* as constituted by the Odyssean *apologoi*, deconstructed by the Platonic dialogues, and satirically exploited by the comic novel (with which Achilles is surely familiar, though references to extant specimens are not easy to show).

Uniquely among the novels, Achilles' narrator and hero are the same fictional person – but at different points in time, and consequently with different models of the total story. The story model of Clitophon the *narrator* (Clitophon[n]) is synchronic and effectively omniscient: at any rate he is, *qua* narrator, by definition aware of everything that happens throughout the story he tells. But Clitophon the *viewpoint* character and lead

---

[26] In the novels, for example, *even the narrator* adopts an earthbound, speculative stance towards the epic divine machinery of wrathful and/or patron gods. Uniquely in the classical genres, there are no divine scenes – only dreams, oracles, and tentative, agnostic suggestions of a celestial purpose at work. This is plainly the perspective of drama, topped and tailed of its conventional divine epiphanies: a world in which divine agency remains immanent in the purposeful coincidences of plot, but metaphysically masked from direct apprehension.

[27] Fullest discussion in Hägg 1971; see also Reardon 1994, Anderson 1997.

player (Clitophon^v) has a very restricted diachronic view: at any given point in the story he knows nothing of the future, nothing of the thoughts of other characters, nothing of present events outside his immediate sensory experience (and sometimes even that can be misconstrued), and only fragments of the total past. Even what he does know can be edited out or revised in the narration itself, as demonstrated at length by the secondary narratives delivered by Thersander, Melite, and Clitophon himself in the trial scenes; and the narrative viewpoint is in principle free to move between the synchronic omniscience of Clitophon^n and the diachronic fallibility of Clitophon^v. Since the second of these unfolds linearly with the story, and the reader's story model develops linearly with the text, it makes clear dynamic sense to narrate the story from the restricted viewpoint of Clitophon^v in the internal chronological order that events present themselves to his consciousness.[28] This indeed, aside from one infamous lapse (XII.374–90), is the practice of *Odyssey* IX–XII, with only modest narratorial anachronies.[29]

Yet in fact, as Hägg brilliantly showed, Achilles does something far more complex. For the first fifth of the novel, the severely restricted Clitophon^v viewpoint is indeed sustained: Clitophon^n tells us only what is immediately available to the vision, hearing, and inner thought and feeling of Clitophon^v at the equivalent point in the story.[30] And then, at II.12.3, something extraordinary happens. Having just reported, in due chronological place, an omen obscure to Clitophon^v at the time, Clitophon^n suddenly jumps a day ahead in the story ('And the outcome of the omen was soon to be fulfilled'), then as abruptly leaps several months back in time, seven hundred miles in space, and into the head and viewpoint of a character whose existence has not even been mentioned till now: 'There was a young Byzantine by the name of Callisthenes . . .' Only in the final full scene of the novel (VIII.17.2) do we learn how Clitophon eventually came by this information. From this point on, by subtle increments, Achilles will selectively extend his narrator's perspective to surprising and finally to paradoxical degrees. After the Callisthenes narrative line has been pursued part (though not all) of the way through, we seem at first to revert to the restricted Clitophon^v viewpoint. But even the remaining Tyrian episodes soon incorporate action that Clitophon could

---

[28] This is not, of course, the same as the actual, objective story chronology: Clitophon does not, for example, learn of events in Ephesus following his departure until over half a year later.   [29] Collected and discussed in Richardson 1990: 231 n. 30.

[30] Plato's reported dialogues regularly leave the frame unclosed (see Halperin 1992: 96); and Most 1989 argues that the emphasis on suffering in Clitophon^n's frame is both an essential narrative strategy for a first-person love-novel and a general pattern in Greek self-disclosure to strangers. Neither explanation, however, seems to account for the move from the close in Tyre to the frame in Sidon.

248   The classical plots

not have witnessed directly: the dialogue between Satyrus and Conops, the dramatically intercut narrative lines of the abortive bedroom intrigue. And though these incidents could in principle have been reported through Satyrus or Leucippe, by the extraordinary sixth book Clitophon^n is feeding us information, such as the detailed descriptions of Thersander's inner emotion, for which no route of transmission to Clitophon^v would appear to exist – as well as switching dizzily from one parallel narrative line to another while jumping back and forth in story time.[31] A passage such as the ecphrasis on Leucippe's tears (VI.7.1–7) beggars our remaining faith either in Clitophon's sources of information or in his powers of narrative imagination.

We may believe, if we wish, that this progressive broadening of the narrative view from subject to narrator and beyond, along with the closing failure to connect the narrative fully to its narration, is a sign of incompetence, exhaustion, or unconcern. If so, the novelist's weakness is the novel's strength. Far from the 'omniscient' passages losing narrative authority, we soon discover that what Clitophon^v sees and hears directly is significantly *less* reliable than what he does not. We have, increasingly, to compare what the narrator tells us with our own internal classical projection of the story, based on what we can extrapolate from the combined repertoire of accepted genre rules and narrative signals coded into the plot. Where there seems a conflict, it is our model rather than Clitophon's that wins out.

Nowhere is this clearer than in Achilles' pervasive sport with *Scheintod*. Again and again in the narrative Clitophon^v believes, and Clitophon^n narrates, that major players are permanently removed from the game: the helper-characters Menelaus and Satyrus (presumed dead in the shipwreck) and Clinias; the chief opponent Thersander (presumed dead at sea by all before his magnificent entry at V.23); and above all Leucippe herself, three times pronounced dead and three times conjured alive. At III.15.4 we read on with astonishment as Clitophon watches one of the bandits tie Leucippe down: 'then taking a sword he plunged it into her heart and hacked her open down to the lower belly. The entrails burst out; and the bandits yanked them out with their hands, heaped them up on the altar, roasted them, cut them into pieces, and made a banquet of the bits.' No reader forgets the extraordinary double take with which one encounters this passage for the first time. The one infrangible rule in this genre is that both hero and heroine must survive to the end. This rule is so powerful that even here it overrides the explicit and seemingly unambiguous statement of the text. We continue to believe, somehow, that Leucippe has

[31] Hägg 1971: 134–5, 183–4.

survived, even though there seems no possible narrative loophole. The victim was definitely Leucippe, she was visibly hacked to pieces and disembowelled, and the pieces eaten by cannibals in full view. Yet we are right and Clitophon^v is wrong: the entire sacrifice was, amazingly, an intricate mechanical conjuring trick, the sacrificer an accomplice, and seemingly circumstantial details of the action in fact crucial moves in the stratagem of deception. We have been taught an extraordinary narrative lesson: trust the rules, not the narrator.

Throughout, in fact, Achilles' unfurling text subjects its reader to a progressive training in narrative hermeneutics, as we come to rely less and less on what Clitophon reports from autopsy and more and more on our own sense of the plot's underlying generic structure and rules. In the last generation of New Comedy, Terence had engaged in a similar experiment by eliminating the expository prologues from his adaptations of Menander and Apollodorus, leaving his audience to extrapolate the missing backstory from their own familiarity with genre patterns. But in a first-person novel, the effect is inexorably to undermine the authority of the storytelling voice itself. Notoriously, Achilles is the most ironic of the romancers: so much so, that interpretations regularly surface to argue that the tone of the work is essentially parodic, comic, satyric, or metaliterary,[32] though all such labels pin the butterfly. While Achilles may be less prone than his neighbours to pious pedestalising of erotic virtue, his deviations are mild by Lucianic or Roman standards; what he does, rather, is to plot a generically unextraordinary story in a way that privileges rules of genre over details of text and reader over narrator, evoking a world-view in which certainties are inconstant, suffering a game, and experience a web of illusions.

The contrast with Heliodorus could hardly be stronger. No less than Achilles', Heliodorus' own novelistic *Weltanschauung* is a corollary of his distinctive response to the challenge of marrying epic narration to Menandrean plotting. But where Achilles' interest centres on the ironic gap between layers of a single narrating voice (Clitophon now, Clitophon then, and the interplay of both with the reader's sense of genre), Heliodorus is concerned with the reconstruction of backstory from *multiple* embedded voices: not one Clitophon but a whole ensemble, each telling different fragments of the same story, in a way that transcends emulation of Homeric narrative economy to aspire to the condition of drama on the scale of epic, and strongly affirms the classical narrative

---

[32] The views respectively of Durham 1938, Heiserman 1977: 117–30, Anderson 1988, Fusillo 1991: 97–108.

values of teleology and closure as defining characteristics of its world. The *Aethiopica*'s actual story elements are largely generic and familiar, particularly from the novels of Xenophon and Achilles;[33] what is remarkable, rather, is their narrative presentation in plotting, and the thematic weight this presentation carries. Of earlier writers, arguably only Sophocles makes the hermeneutics of plot so central to the quest for meaning in the patterns of human events.[34]

Crucially, the *Aethiopica* is the one novel in which a substantial backstory has to be reconstructed from and in the primary-narrative present. In Chariton and Xenophon, unlike myth and comedy, the past plays no significant role in the plot, and even in the earlier sophistic novels the role of backstory is weak and limited. Longus' recognition plot spends most of the narrative suspended in pastoral dreamtime, while in Achilles *everything* is backstory to an abortive Sidonian tale that never reaches the end of its opening scene. But in Heliodorus, all but the final act of the story is already written, and the reader's work is to excavate the story from the enclosing book of the world. This is not to say that Heliodorus is uninterested in the plotting of information *within* the story itself: there are communicative restraints on the distribution of powerful knowledge, such as Charicleia's concealment of her true identity from her successive unfriendly *kyrioi*, and the repeated disguise of her true relations with Theagenes. But these latter protect Theagenes rather than Charicleia herself, and the part played by recognition in the *primary* plotline is comparatively slight until the Ethiopian endgame itself. For the most part, Heliodorus prefers to build his foreground plot around *power* relations, and to reserve his intricate shifts of *information* distribution for the secondary backstory and its communication to the reader. The first half, especially, is an unprecedented labyrinth of fragmented storylines and secondary and tertiary narratives, some true, some disguised, all one way or another incomplete, that take the reader five books to assemble into a stable model of the backstory to the opening primary-narrative scene.

Table 17 maps this narrative maze down to the reunions at Memphis early in VII – after which a mostly-new cast comes in, and the narrative reverts to a largely unembedded and unsubplotted narrative line.[35] As the

---

[33] I take it as axiomatic that Heliodorus shows first-hand knowledge and influence of Chariton, Xenophon, and Achilles, but not of Longus and not demonstrably of the fragmentary or summary novels. There is, however, still no adequate study of this.

[34] See especially Winkler 1982, Morgan 1994.

[35] The first column breaks the action down by what in a manuscript of Terence would be labelled 'scenes' (the 'French scenes' of neoclassical drama): changes in the onstage cast, which in a novel can mean regroupings within *reported* action if that action occupies the current narrative foreground. Against each, the cast of the primary narrative scene is indicated by • or name; if one of these characters is narrating a secondary action, that narrator

table shows, Heliodorus' narrative is neither as deeply nested as we may feel from the giddy impression it leaves with the reader,[36] nor as chronologically dislocated. Though there may be interruptions, the only striking departures from temporal sequence are the four top-level narratorial retrogressions (17, 23, 42, 55) and the stories of Charicleia and Thisbe. Of the former, two are summary flashbacks in the manner of footnotes, and two the familiar Achillean device of allowing an abandoned subplot to intersect surprisingly with the main action and then filling the gap retrospectively.[37] In the latter, the dislocations are surprisingly slight, though well chosen to tantalise any reader who attempts to construct a backstory model from them.

Thisbe's story is told in the order a–b–f–c–d–e (scenes 5, 6, 19, 20, 21, 23): the surprise, which is considerable, is her appearance as a corpse in Egypt (f) when she was last heard of alive in Athens (b). But the reason why the plotting of her story is so complex and satisfying is less that her presence and death (f) are simply *unexpected* at the point they enter the narrative, than because information about her story is so fragmented and distributed amongst the different players – requiring it to be *collated* from no fewer than six successive first-hand sources (Cnemon, Charias, Anticles, Thisbe's letter, Thermuthis, Thyamis). The discovery is, in fact, less of a surprise to Cnemon than it is to the reader, since Cnemon at least

is marked by an arrow or a name in bold. The casts of such secondary scenes are then tabled in the next set of columns, and where stories are told within stories the secondary narrator is similarly highlighted and the tertiary cast tabled in the next column; and so on. Temporal retrogressions by the top-level narrator are italicised, and their casts marked with ◊; false secondary narratives, whether lies or misapprehensions, are cast-listed in square brackets. In the interests of clarity and economy, I have had to make a number of simplifications and sacrifices of consistency and precision in allocating scene divisions and player status.

[36] Technically, Achilles more than once touches a depth of four levels of embedding, as against Heliodorus' maximum of three; see Hägg 1971: 128 on Achilles III.22.3–4, and compare e.g. VI.16.3–4 (where the narrator reports what Clitophon told him about what he learned from Leucippe about a soliloquy in which she quoted her own earlier words) and VIII.17.3 (where the narrator quotes Clitophon's report of Sostratus' account of Callisthenes' speech to Calligone, which Callisthenes must have relayed to him in the conversation summarised in the following chapter). But in these cases the deepest nested text is not a narrative but a statement of feeling; the nesting is much less explicit, and only apparent once the reader attempts to reconstruct a possible route of transmission; and the level-count includes the Sidonian narrative frame.

[37] Clitophon's first-person narrative has a ready-made pretext for this, since the moment such a subplot re-enters his sphere of attention is a legitimate chronological stage to report in his history of his own experience of the story, and there is generally a subplot player on hand (Clinias, Leucippe, Sostratus) to cue Clitophon dramatically in on what he has missed. Heliodorus, rather unsatisfactorily, pulls off his mask of restricted viewpoint at such moments to reveal the omniscient prestidigitator beneath. Such irritating breaches of transparency could easily have been avoided in all these cases, by merely quoting the secondary narratives in which the lead players learn the missing backstory.

Table 17. Scenes and narrative levels in Aethiopica I–VII.9

		LEVEL 1								LEVEL 2									LEVEL 3	LEVEL 4	EVENTS
		Ch	Tg	Ty	Cn	Tb	Ca	Ns	others	Ch	Tg	Ty	Cn	Tb	Ca	Ns	Mi	others			
1	I.1.1–3.3	•	•																		Petosiris' bandits arrive
2	I.1.4–7.3	•	•	•																	Thyamis' bandits capture Charicleia & Theagenes
3	I.7.3–9.1	•	•	•	•																they share a cell with Cnemon, who tells his story
4	I.9.1–11.2				↑								•									**Cnemon's story I**: Demaenete's first intrigue
5	I.11.2–14.2				↑								•									**Cnemon's story II**: Demaenete's second intrigue
6	I.14.2–18.1				↑								•					Charias	Thisbe			**Cnemon's story III**: Thisbe's intrigue
7	I.18.2–5	•	•	•	•																	Thyamis' dream
8	I.19.1–21.3	•	•	•	•																	Thyamis woos Charicleia
9	I.21.3–22.7	•	•	↑	•																	[Charicleia's fiction]
10	I.23.1–24.3	•	•	•	•																	interlude: Thyamis prepares march on Memphis
11	I.24.3–27.1	•	•	•	•																	Charicleia explains her lie
12	I.27.1–28.1	•	•	•	•											•						Petosiris' bandits attack the island
13	I.28.1–29.4	•	•	•	•											•						Cnemon hides Charicleia in the cave
14	I.29.4–6	•	•	•	•																	the bandits arm
15	I.30.1–31.1	•	•	•	•																	Thyamis kills Thisbe in error for Charicleia
16	I.31.1–4	•	•	•	•																	the attack begins
17	I.32.1–33.4	•	•	↑	•											•						Petosiris' men capture Thyamis; *flashback on Petosiris*
18	II.1.1–3.3	•	•		↑																	**Cnemon tells Theagenes** of the cave; they return
19	II.3.3–8.3	•	•		•																	Thisbe's body discovered & recognised
20	II.8.3–10.1	•	•		↑													Anticles Therm.	Thisbe Naus			**Cnemon's story IV**: Thisbe's downfall and escape
21	II.10.1–4	•	•		•																	**Thisbe's letter**: her story continued
22	II.11.1–4	•	•		•		◊															the mystery discussed
23	II.12.1–3	•	•		•		◊		Therm.													*Thisbe's story completed: the mystery explained*
24	II.12.3–14.5	•	•		•																	Thermuthis finds the corpse; Cnemon solves the crime
25	II.15.1–18.1	•	•		•				Therm.													Charicleia's dream; they plan their escape
26	II.18.1–19.2	•	•		•																	Thermuthis balks; the plan revised

No.	Reference	Narrators / characters	Event
27	II.19.3–7	*Therm.*	Cnemon gives Thermuthis the slip
28	II.20.1–2	*Therm.*	death of Thermuthis
29	II.20.3–24.4		Cnemon meets Calasiris, who drops some names
30	II.24.2–4	Oroond.	**Calasiris explains Nausicles' plan**
31	II.24.5–28.5	**Charicles**	**Calasiris' story begins: from Memphis to Delphi**
32	II.29.1–5	**Charicles** — Ccls Ch Sis	**Calasiris meets Charicles, who begins his story**
33	II.30.1–6	**Charicles** — Ccls Ch **Sis**	**Charicles, Charicleia, and Sisimithres**
34	II.31.1–5	**Charicles** — Ccls Ch **Sis** · **Sis Ch Pers**	**Simithres' story**
35	II.32.1–33.8	**Charicles** — Ccls Ch	**Charicles completes his tale**
36	II.34.1–IV.8.1	Charicles	**girl meets boy; Calasiris plays love-therapist**
37	IV.8.1–8	**Persinna** — Pers Ch	**Calasiris reads Persinna's story**
38	IV.9.1–V.1.4	Charicles	**Calasiris' plan and escape with Charicleia & Theagenes**
39	V.1.4–2.5		**Nausicles returns & reports ['Thisbe's recovery']**
40	V.2.5–3.2	[·]	**Cnemon overhears [lament of 'Thisbe']**
41	V.3.2–4.2	[·]	**Cnemon confirms [Thisbe's survival] to Calasiris**
42	V.4.3–8.6	*Mitranes*	*Mitranes' men capture the lovers; Nausicles claims 'Thisbe'*
43	V.9.1–2	*Mitranes*	**Mitranes sends Theagenes to Memphis, with letter**
44	V.10.1–2		**Nausicles reveals all**
45	V.11.1–16.4		Charicleia recognised & ransomed
46	V.16.5–33.3		**Calasiris completes his story**
47	V.33.4–VI.1.1		interlude: all retire
48	VI.1.1–3.1	(etc.)	**Cnemon tells Nausicles his story to date**
49	VI.3.1–5.1	**(lover)** · Thy Thg (Mi)	**they learn of Thyamis' recapture of Theagenes**
50	VI.5.1–4	(lover)	**Calasiris updates Charicleia**
51	VI.6.1–11.2	Oroond.	Cnemon's wedding; Charicleia & Calasiris set out disguised
52	VI.11.3–13.6	witch	**the witch tells the news from Bessa**
53	VI.14.1–VII.1.1	witch	nekyia; Charicleia & Calasiris make haste for Memphis
54	VII.1.2–4	Arsace	Thyamis reaches Memphis
55	VII.2.1–3.1	*Arsace*	*flashback: story of Thyamis's exile*
56	VII.3.1–6.4	Arsace	Thyamis fights Petosiris
57	VII.6.4–9.1	Arsace	arrival and recognition of Calasiris & Charicleia

knows (c): that Thisbe is not in fact in Athens, and may well be in Egypt. But in our model, which Charicleia and Theagenes share, Thisbe is a minor player in a secondary narrative on the other side of the ocean. For her to turn up in the primary narrative is a shock in itself, let alone for her to be mistaken for the heroine both by her assassin and, with sceptical reservations, by the reader.

Comparison with Achilles' *Scheintod* murders of Leucippe brings out Heliodorus' distinctive narrative tastes. Like Achilles, Heliodorus relies on ambiguous and selective textual detail, the narratorial suppression of give-away details, to pose the reader a formal puzzle of detection. But unlike Achilles, he abhors *ex machina* revelations after the fact – a convenient conjurer's trunk or body double, unplanted in the narrative until after the event. Heliodorus favours the classical principle of recycling existing materials: the riddle is thus not 'Who can this corpse be?' but 'Which previously mentioned player can this corpse be?' A very shrewd reader might correctly deduce that Thisbe is the only figure so far placed anywhere on the board who could possibly answer the required description. If we do not think of her, it is because we have not yet grasped the sheer classical tightness of Heliodorus' way of playing the novelistic game.

Like so much else in the tear-off Cnemon novella, the episode is an early training exercise for the reader in the narrative rules – ideological as well as technical – we will need in order to decode the real plot to come.[38] Thisbe's story is a rehearsal for the narrative strategy of Charicleia's, and only when we have mastered the Thisbe/Cnemon subplot will we be ready for the still more demanding Charicleia/Calasiris complex. The heroine's story is told in the order g–[a']–b–c–d–a–e–h–f (respectively, scenes 1–26, the secondary narrative of 9, 34, 35, 36, 37, 38, 42, 44). As the italics show, there are really only three chronological dislocations: the *in medias res* opening series (g), Calasiris' narratively legitimate postponement of the information about her birth (a) to the moment it enters his personal storyline, and the postponement of the close of Calasiris' tale (f). Once more the plot complexity lies less in the suspension of information *per se* – even the delayed revelation that Charicleia is the lost heir to the throne of Africa – than in the extraordinary hermeneutics of *collation* required from the reader. In order to assemble a complete model of Charicleia's history we have to piece together no fewer than nine different sequences, at four different levels of narration, in five different voices besides the narrator's (Charicleia, Calasiris, Charicles, Sisimithres, Persinna). To try our skill further, not only is her story nested a level deeper than Thisbe's, but the successive descents take us *back* rather than

[38] Morgan 1989a.

forward in her story; while one of the earliest of the nine narrative segments (ironically, the subject's own formal autobiography) is a dummy, a
false component that has to be discarded before the rest will fit correctly
together. Like Achilles, Heliodorus is training his readers up in the art of
plotting, of grasping the rules that make the game of the world; but his
narrative values are very different.

The consummation of all this comes in Heliodorus' astounding
Ethiopian endgame.[39] Like the *Odyssey*, the *Aethiopica* funnels its epic
action into a tight, drama-like endgame on a single set. After the epic
sweep of book IX, the final book reads almost like a theatrical transcript,
with its unity of action from 6.2 to the end, high proportion of direct
speech and scene to summary, and its small group of named characters
shuffled on and off the narrow primary stage so carefully mapped out in
6.2–4. The final narrative destination was first stated in the oracle of
II.35.55, though in a sense it is promised by the very title *Ethiopian adventures*. It was amplified at IV.13.2 by Calasiris to Charicleia ('to convey you
to your people, your country, and your parents, and to marry you to
Theagenes'); and the exact relationship between clauses was clarified by
the condition imposed by oath on Theagenes at IV.18.5–6 ('not to share in
the act of love *until* we reach my people and home'). Thus the narrative
goals are enchained: marriage is a precondition of consummation, recognition a prerequisite of marriage, and return to Ethiopia a precondition of
both. But this very conjunction will turn out to yield a seemingly ineluta-
ble paradox: under local Ethiopian rules, captive virgins are not married
off, but sacrificed.

Heliodorus' encyclopaedic narrative ambitions are already evident in
Charicleia's recognition, by far the most elaborate such scene in ancient
literature. Heliodorus seems to have gone out of his way to include every
item in Aristotle's catalogue of types: *ad hoc* birthmarks (X.15.2) and
tokens (14.3), blurting it out (12.1), collated memory (11.1–2), deductive
syllogism (14.1, 34.5–6), and natural convergence of events (35.1). Yet all
but the first have been artfully planted in the narrative, though we may
not have recognised them all at the time. The most obvious, the letter and
tokens, have been with us since II.31, but these turn out less helpful than
we have imagined. As the shrewd Hydaspes points out at 14.3, recognition tokens are transferable, and prove no more than that Persinna did
indeed bear a daughter – not that Charicleia herself is that daughter. The
decisive instrument of recognition, rather, has been lying unnoticed in the
story since that very same passage in II: the carefully unnamed Ethiopian

---

[39] The classic discussion is Morgan 1989b, taking a much wider view of the dynamics of
expectation and closure in the *Aethiopica*'s endgame; see also now Baumbach 1997.

ambassador, so hurriedly recalled to Meroe just before he could give his name and translate Persinna's message for Charicles. Now, we find he has been on hand during this whole scene under his real name, Sisimithres. But as Hydaspes also points out, even Sisimithres can only argue 'like a pleader from the heart rather than a dispassionate judge' (14.5). In the event, the only unambiguous proof is Aristotle's despised birthmark ploy – the one proof *not* previously seeded in the text, perhaps with a touch of deliberate mischief (and Odyssean allusion).

Yet the twist is that even this decisive proof turns out to decide nothing: the sacrifice must still go ahead, and Theagenes' status in any case remains unaffected. Even Charicleia's recognition as the heir to the throne is insufficient to override the sacrificial *nomos*, as Hydaspes is compelled to acknowledge.[40] It is left for Charicles, the final rabbit in the hat, to pop up in quest of his own missing daughter (who has been artfully shepherded offstage at this very moment) and, in lighting on her abductor instead, to trigger a second suspension and final annulment of the human-sacrifice rules, on the grounds that the very neatness of the plotting argues divine disapproval of the designated ending. As Sisimithres points out, the contradiction is irreconcilable: we can have either the genre ending or the rule of human sacrifice, but not both. Since the first is inviolate, we can only conclude, correctly, that the whole episode has been engineered by its divine author to do away with the second.

To understand why the *Aethiopica* ends in this tortuous way, we need to travel back up river to its own narrative springs. Heliodorus' project is nothing less than to extend Menandrean plotting to the scale of epic: to expand the systemic, transactional model of the comic polis to the level of the Hellenised world and beyond, in an inclusive Odyssean panorama encompassing the ends of the earth. And though the chains of ownership and information are disorientingly fragmented at the outset, the scattered links miraculously assemble and the pieces of the puzzle slot together before our eyes as the cast of Charicleia's story gather for their curtain-call.

In the plotting of *information*, Charicles' reappearance is merely the novel's final and most masterly programmed surprise: a character last seen (like Thisbe) in a reported plotline that dropped from sight on the other side of the ocean when the chain of information broke that linked it to the primary-narrative moment. And just as it was only at the novel's

---

[40] At x.11.3 a rule is apparently stated that only foreigners can be sacrificed. Presumably we are to understand Charicleia's argument, and Hydaspes' concession, as less than watertight; otherwise, either Hydaspes is bluffing at 16.5 when he insists that the law still demands her sacrifice, or Heliodorus has uncharacteristically nodded. Another inconsistency in the sacrifice rules is treated by Morgan 1989b: 306.

midpoint that we learned what had really been happening on the first page, it is only now, six books late, that we find what followed the end of book IV: that Charicles has spent six books tailing the lovers in dogged narrative silence just offstage. With hindsight, the clues are there: Charicles' vow of pursuit and the launch of the Delphic task force at the close of IV, Calasiris' teasing cast-off at v.i.i ('The city of Delphi did whatever it did do – for I did not stay around to find out'). The trail, too, has been laid for Charicles to follow: he can track Calasiris to his native Memphis, and there Thyamis is in residence to fill him in on the truth of Charicleia's parentage (cf. VII.11.4 with VIII.3.5, 7) and to point him on to Oroondates at Syene, who in turn is in a position (thanks to his capture and pardon by Hydaspes) to send him on to the showdown at Meroe. Now, in the novel's final and most dazzling act of narrative collation, Charicles recounts his Hellenocentric version of Charicleia's story – in Greek (keeping the watching Ethiopian masses in the dark), with the names of the principals intentionally suppressed (before we even learn how he came to know them all), and in a form that contrives to withhold all the details that would allow Hydaspes to complete the collation himself.

But it is in the simultaneous plotting of *power* that Charicles' intervention plays its comic trump, completing the Menandrean chains of information and power alike in a single coup of plotting. The narrative trap is sprung with Theagenes' nigh-untranslatable outburst to Hydaspes at 37.2: 'Not the wrongdoer but the possessor should rightly restore the wrong; *you yourself* are the possessor. Restore her – unless this man too will agree that Charicleia is your daughter.' Not Theagenes but Hydaspes is the receiver of the stolen goods, and not Charicles but Hydaspes is the victim of the theft; thus Hydaspes' own judgement requires, absurdly, that he surrender Charicleia to himself in order to reverse the already closed loop of steps 1–5 in her story (above, p. 240). Next, in the space of three astonishing sentences, Sisimithres, Charicleia, and Persinna burst into the scene to confirm the missing links in the chain of story, and to assemble its entire cast for the first and final time in full primary-narrative view. Charicles' presence, in particular, is vital to this ultimate comic transaction, because even here, at the edge of earth, Willcock's law still binds.[41] As Charicleia's legal guardian, Charicles has been robbed by Theagenes' chaste rape, and like any Menandrean father in such a situation he is required to give his assent in person to the formal legitimation of the theft in marriage – though it is, in a telling paradox, the Ethiopian Hydaspes who pronounces the Greek marriage formula that explicitly

[41] See above, p. 208 n. 28.

legitimises the fruits of the dynastic union. Thus all four of Charicleia's successive parents, Ethiopian and Greek, natural and surrogate, are present to sanction her transfer in ownership to Theagenes as husband: a transfer across boundaries of race, culture, and language, that binds the ends of earth in a rite of union.[42] The longest comic plot in history, spanning the whole of its world and the whole of its literary heritage, is reassembled on a single stage at the very moment of its completion.

The whole finale is, needless to say, fantastically overplotted. All three recognitions (Charicleia as Persinna's daughter, Charicles' missing daughter as Charicleia, Theagenes as Charicleia's lover) are massively overdetermined, the repeated interruptions and postponements eventually exhausting, and the rule-system used to generate a remorselessly inventive succession of melodramatic paradoxes. Charicleia is simultaneously qualified as sacrificed virgin and sacrificing matron; father will kill daughter, daughter will kill beloved; Charicleia has two living fathers, yet confesses to patricide before both; Theagenes can be both virgin and rapist, criminal and saint; *et cetera*. There is a mad-genius quality to it all. Yet there is also a refreshing touch of ironic sanity, in the ever more barefaced proclamations of divine purpose and narratorial allusions to stagecraft. Heliodorus knows well enough that such plotting is too perfect to be innocent. Only gods and playwrights can get away with creating a universe so unremittingly purposeful. And in a way, he was right. Despite the *Aethiopica*'s popularity in the Greek middle ages, and despite its continuing influence as a model for story, its plotting was an impossible act to follow. The *Aethiopica* is the ancient world's narratological *summa*, a selfconsciously encyclopaedic synthesis of a thousand years of accumulated pagan plot techniques, and of the game of story as a way of understanding the world. For the next millennium and more, it remained the final word.

---

[42] On the matrimonial complexities see especially Scarcella 1976.

Conclusion

Before the end, a review of the story so far. Part I argued that the idea of 'plot' is not arbitrary: that it is the best available label for a fundamental process in the way human minds decode and respond to narrative texts, by representing fictional worlds in the form of a closed and rule-bound chessboard universe. In the model proposed here, stories are understood as systemically closed possible worlds developing in time; and much of this process can be usefully formalised by appropriating terminology from the vernacular language of games, which has developed specifically to describe the elements of the structure of such worlds. Thus plots are like chess problems revealed a bit at a time: where the reader can be asked what happened before as well as after a given position, and the gradual revelation of actual moves and hints about moves allows the text to manipulate the reader's developing model of the game as a whole in the linear process of reading. The 'classical' phylum of plot privileges three special narrative values, here labelled 'economy', 'amplitude', and 'transparency': respectively the degree of functionality of narrative game elements, the clarity of the narrative system in large-scale textual forms, and the closedness of the narrative system to external elements.

Part II then used this model to tell a tale in five acts, the emergence and canonisation of the 'classical' Western sense of plotting in four seminal projects of ancient reading and refashioning: the *Odyssey*'s rendering of the narrative values of the *Iliad*, tragedy's recasting of Homer, New Comedy's rewriting of tragedy, and the Greek novel's encyclopaedic reinscription of all four. The first of these results in a pair of culturally complementary templates for large-scale narrative which nevertheless share a high degree of systemic closure and teleology: one Iliadic, tragic, or 'minor-key', evoking a world-view which denies or finally problematises human access to absolute narrative goals; the second Odyssean, romantic or 'major-key', in which goals are accessible and teleology affirmed. In both, however, there develops a set of powerful technical devices for closure, which fifth-century tragedy then transplants to the invented medium of drama. In the process, it drastically concentrates the semiotic and thematic significance of the boundary between the shown and the told – especially in types of play, privileged in later generations' sense of the tragic genre, which favour the Iliadic minor key over the Odyssean major, and make the defining feature of the tragic world the problematics of mediated experience. New Comedy then adopts this system for a major-key storytelling whose crucial innovation is the abandonment of myth for a pure form of fiction in which narrative universes are created *ex nihilo* by the particular text. In doing so, it not only proposes a uniquely condensed reading of the world in which citizen interactions are systemically organised in transactions, but also develops a close-knit system of cognitive transformations that has served as the basic toolbox for such plotting ever since. Finally, the novelists import this mature system back into the epic mode, retaining New Comedy's focus on unretold stories, but now in an unbounded narrative form with a controlling narrating voice – resulting in a novelistic paradigm for large-scale, major-key fictional storytelling still dominant in Western narrative culture.

The reasons for that dominance lie far outside the scope of this book. But we should be suspicious of the easy answer that the classical paradigm's persistence beyond the end of the ancient world is merely a result of the West's own cultural canonisation of classical antiquity – just as we should be wary of untested claims that the classical model is in certain ways more 'natural' than its rivals. Neither, I believe, is a complete untruth; but there may be intrinsic features of the classical paradigm that have helped its historical resilience. First, classical plotting is peculiarly susceptible to *appropriation*. Ideological systems that seek to assert some, any structures of power will find the simplifying, formalising tendency of classical narrative more productive than its rivals. By contrast, narrative paradigms that stress the openness, incoherence, or arbitrariness of the world have a much more limited ideological role, and tend to define themselves in contrast to, often subversively of, a dominant classical model. Second, classical models invite a collective, systemic perspective on human value, however construed, where their rivals lend themselves more easily to the sundered outlook of the individual; it is thus a paradigm that more effectively addresses the interests of larger communities. And above all, classical plotting is teleological: it asserts the deep causality and intelligibility of its world even where it denies human access to direct apprehension or control. As such, it is a uniquely powerful system for the narrative articulation of claims about the order of the world.

How far such factors steered the development of the classical model in antiquity itself is a question requiring a more nuanced historical account than the present demurely formalist narrative. Clearly there were complex – perhaps impossibly so – social, cultural, and ideological factors behind the four decisive acts of reading and remaking: the *Odyssey*'s reformulation of the heroic world of the *Iliad*; fifth-century tragedy's emulation of a Homeric paradigm; New Comedy's reconstitution of tragic narrativity in a contemporary bourgeois setting; the novels' export of polis-based comic transactionality to the total Hellenistic world. In discussing these events as primarily technical transformations, I have left untold what some may feel to be the main story. Nevertheless, a recurrent theme has been that *form itself* is a powerful engine of value; that form and ideology need to be seen as a symbiotic, mutually interacting system. If so, it is hard to have much patience with the sterile twentieth-century feud between formalism and historicism. It may indeed be that our sense of the classicality of Western classical plotting is not a purely cultural artifact; that much of its power resides in innate mechanisms of narrative processing that are part of our inheritance as occupants of human brains. But this is still a long way from explaining why such an optimally 'natural' system, if such it is, should have emerged when, where, whence, and in the form it did – let alone what baggage this bequeathed to successor traditions. It must, for example, have helped the emergence of a strongly systemic, 'gamelike' model of plotting that the two Greek monumental epics arose out of a culture of transactional reciprocity tensioned by individualistic competition. Yet this in its turn has arguably meant that the West has inherited a classical narrative culture founded on conservative ideologies of class (weighted towards the aristocracy or bourgeoisie) and gender (limiting women's subjectivity by constructing them as objects of male transactions). In asking how directly or inevitably this followed from that, we move beyond the traditional boundaries of formalist analysis; but it is a question hard to frame at all without it.

There are high stakes here for narratology's own future direction. Narrative theory is presently in schism, with cisatlantic narratologists widely in retreat from traditional formalist semiotics and a cross-platform conception of 'narrative', at the very time that North American theorists flirt increasingly with interdisciplinary cognitivism and the neo-Aristotelian dream of a grand unified narratology spanning novel, film, drama, comics, and interactive media. It will be clear where this book stands; but the challenges need confessing. If it is true, as argued here, that the most promising future for narratology is as a branch of cognitive science, we need to be sure of our claims. First-generation cognitivists do not squirm at grandly inclusive first-person plurals that erase the distance between epochs and readers – as if there were no essential difference between the narrative competence, as consumers of Homer, of twentieth-century philologists and illiterate iron-age aristocrats. They are unembarrassed by the claims of formalism to describe real things rather than *ad hoc* critical artifacts, and are happy to view literary theory as an empirical pursuit, subject in principle to the controls of scientific method. They have their work cut out if these stances are to be defended. When I began this book, I imagined that by the time of its completion the cognitivist trend would have made far greater inroads into consensus than has so far transpired. Even so, abuses are already proliferating. In the worst, the appeal to cognitivism becomes merely a pseudo-scientific rhetoric to lay meretricious claim to authority and objectivity for the same old subjective interpretations – a way of claiming that everyone else thinks what you think but is just not sophisticated enough to realise it. I feel fairly confident that the model here proposed sufficiently describes my own comprehension of 'plot' in the narratives discussed; but as a description of anyone else's comprehension it is no more than a hypothesis whose first test is the reader's own assent or dissent. Some readers may feel that this book has not even been talking about plot at all as they understand it.

For the real limits to the cognitivist project are those sites (in reading, in history, between inhabitants of different cultures and heads) where common experience of a shared text is fragmented by centrifugalising forces. One consequence, for example, of my own emphasis on deep-structural rather than surface-structural levels of narrative comprehension is that I have largely elided the 'front end' of reading, the active interface between textual signs and our own cognitive apparatus; and that in turn has steered the discussion discreetly away from many of the untidy complexities of actual reading, including much of what we value most in the experience of narrative. Yet it is perfectly possible to subscribe to precisely the view anathematised half a century ago as a revolting heresy, while readily admitting Brower's central point that there is no plot without a textual surface; and in a text marked (by genre, or reader, or internal signs) as hermeneutically 'open', that surface will be awash with ripples of nuance and signification which may entirely transform a reader's individual experience of its deep structure. We are by now at peace with the core insight of deconstruction, that the relationship between these strata of textual experience is often one of tension, and thus that language is often a weaker vehicle than other textual media for ways of experiencing narrative that assert (or ideologise) closural values. That may be one reason why the 'classical' narrative spell seems closer to the surface in cinema than in the novel.

Nevertheless, while I make no claim to privilege the notion of plot as a rival to other literary values, I do want to suggest that it may be in important ways *anterior*: logically, psychologically, and explanatorily prior to other aspects of narrative experience. Undeniably there are ways of reading, especially in re-reading, that deprivilege plot. Indeed, it is probably true that, the further we develop as readers, the less important plot becomes in relation to other kinds of textual pleasure. Yet one of the stranger puzzles about narrative is the stability of plot comprehension between different readings and readers. While we may argue, as we leave a play or film, about the significance or implications of the narrative we have just witnessed, it is unusual and disconcerting to find that companions who watched the identical performance disagree about what actually *happened*. Our experience of text seems inexhaustibly complex, individual, and diverse; and yet the deeper we probe beneath the textual surface of narrative, the more common experience we find. Why that should be is a question as old as Aristotle; but it is one that his modern inheritors have barely begun to address.

Glossary

ACTANT The Greimassian term for a function or role in the structure of a narrative situation, which may be occupied by one or more individual PLAYERS. Greimas distinguishes six such roles: SUBJECT and OBJECT, SENDER and RECEIVER, HELPER and OPPONENT, *qq.v.* In this book they are redefined in terms of the transmission of narrative POWER.

AMPLITUDE The scale of a NARRATIVE, as measured by the number of MOVES required in its narrative GAME; with ECONOMY and TRANSPARENCY, one of three qualities distinctively pursued in a CLASSICAL PLOT.

AUTHOR The actual maker of a TEXT (as opposed to the images of such a maker projected by the text, which include not only VIEWPOINT characters and NARRATORS but the higher-level images sometimes called 'implied authors').

BACKSTORY The events of a STORY preceding the point in time at which the PRIMARY NARRATIVE opens.

BOARD The spatial dimension to the structure of a NARRATIVE UNIVERSE, whose main features are (i) a set of absolute external limits on the place of the ACTION, and (ii) an internal arrangement of barriers to the flow of narrative POWER, dividing the board into smaller narrative zones and channelling the flow of power along particular routes. Generally the space of PRIMARY NARRATIVE will be more restricted than that of SECONDARY NARRATIVE.

C-MOVE A MOVE of communication, involving the adjustment between PLAYERS of a difference in their KNOWLEDGE of the GAME STATE – which may include the propagation of *false* knowledge, though the long-term tendency is for all players' beliefs to converge on the truth in the course of play.

CLASSICAL PLOT A PLOT that seeks to make a virtue of high degrees of ECONOMY, AMPLITUDE, and TRANSPARENCY.

CLOCK The temporal index of a NARRATIVE UNIVERSE, registering the relationship between the internal chronology of the STORY UNIVERSE and the conventionally analogous linear flow of the TEXT; a NARRATIVE temporality superimposed on the natural chronology of a STORY. Generally the time of PRIMARY NARRATIVE will be more restricted than that of SECONDARY NARRATIVE.

CLOSURE The narrative organisation of a STORY UNIVERSE into a complete and self-contained system; often, though not in this book, also used more narrowly of the reader's 'sense of an ending' at the end of a text.

COMPETENCE The capacity of a PLAYER to act or engage in a MOVE: determined by the three variables of MOTIVE, KNOWLEDGE, and POWER.

CONTROL LEVEL A class of inhabitants of a STORY UNIVERSE whose NARRA-
TIVE status is categorically distinct from, superior in POWER and KNOWLEDGE
to, and more or less manipulative of, the human PLAYERS; gods, fate, The
Force, unseen presences behind the scenes, etc.; generally involved under the
role of SENDER.

DIEGESIS NARRATIVE mediated through a narrating voice (as in epic, novel);
also used in film theory and Genettian narratology – but not in this book – in a
sense equivalent to S-WORLD.

ECONOMY The proportion of functional to non-functional elements in a narrative GAME; with AMPLITUDE and TRANSPARENCY, one of three qualities
pursued in a CLASSICAL PLOT.

EDITORIAL A global term occasionally used in the book to encompass the
various levels of NARRATIVE filtration and overlay associated with one or all of
VIEWPOINT, NARRATOR, and AUTHOR.

ELLIPSIS A passage of NARRATIVE where the CLOCK jumps ahead instantaneously, leaving a section of STORY time entirely unnarrated; one of five narrative
TEMPI.

EMBEDDING The inclusion within a NARRATIVE of the text of a further NARRA-
TIVE quoted from the narration of a PLAYER, normally in direct speech (see
SECONDARY NARRATIVE). Multiple embedding is possible, with quoted nar-
ratives framing further nested narratives within themselves.

ENDGAME The closing series of MOVES in a narrative GAME: the chronologically
final SUBGAME, in which remaining PLAYERS with debts to settle negotiate a
collective resolution.

ENDING The GAME STATE output from an ENDGAME; the chronologically final
configuration of a NARRATIVE UNIVERSE.

EPISODE A section of STORY marked off as a distinct NARRATIVE unit by
devices of CLOSURE in time, space, and/or PLAYER set; see LOCATION,
SUBGAME.

EVENT A change in the STORY UNIVERSE, often but not invariably associated at
the NARRATIVE level with a MOVE.

FICTION Previously untold STORIES set in post-Homeric times, as distinct from
HISTORY and MYTH.

FOCALISATION The manifestation of POINT OF VIEW in DIEGETIC forms of
narrative.

GAME A model universe in which the range of possible actions is constrained by
formal limits of time, space, number and nature of agents, and forms and distribution of power; the metaphoric system used in this book to describe the workings of a NARRATIVE UNIVERSE. See BOARD, CLOCK, ENDGAME, MOVE,
PLAYER, RULE.

GAME-STATE The state of play at a given point in a STORY; the overall distribution of GOALS and POWER between PLAYERS at a point in the GAME between
MOVES.

GOAL A GAME STATE, whether provisional or final, consciously projected by a
PLAYER as the desired outcome of a series of MOVES; the source of MOTIVE.

HELPER An actantial role occupied by one or more PLAYERS whose GOALS correspond to those of the SUBJECT, and whose POWER is added to the subject's
for the purpose of calculating MOVES.

HISTORY Retold STORIES set in post-Homeric times, as distinct from MYTH and FICTION.

KNOWLEDGE A form of narrative POWER consisting of private and transmissible information about the GAME STATE; with MOTIVE and POWER, one of three defining constituents of a PLAYER's capacity to act, corresponding to Greimas's *savoir*, *vouloir*, and *pouvoir*.

LOCATION A zone of the BOARD small enough for two or more PLAYERS to interact freely.

MIMESIS NARRATIVE by unmediated impersonation, eschewing or eliding any global narrating voice (as in drama, film).

MOTIVE The identification by a PLAYER of a GOAL to which he or she actively aspires; with KNOWLEDGE and POWER, one of three variables defining that player's COMPETENCE in the determination of MOVES.

MOVE An action by one or more PLAYERS resulting in the redistribution of narrative POWER, either directly or in the form of KNOWLEDGE.

MYTH STORIES set in or before the generation following the Trojan War, as distinct from HISTORY and FICTION.

N-WORLD The world intermediate between a STORY's own internal reality and its embodiment in a TEXT in the T-WORLD; made up of the S-WORLD and an enclosing frame of NARRATIVE rules and abstractions.

NARRATION The construction of a NARRATIVE for presentation to a READER.

NARRATIVE The '-telling' part of storytelling; the form in which a STORY is presented to its READER by a TEXT – or, more accurately, the form of the intermediate representational model from which a model of the story is sequentially constructed in the course of reading.

NARRATIVE UNIVERSE The system of NARRATIVE structures imposed on a STORY UNIVERSE.

NARRATOR The implied subject of the act of NARRATION; the owner of the voice that recounts a NARRATIVE; to be carefully distinguished from both AUTHOR and POINT OF VIEW.

OBJECT The actantial role corresponding to the GOAL of a PLAYER's MOVE; in Greimas's model paired with SUBJECT.

OPPONENT An actantial role occupied by all PLAYERS whose GOALS are antagonistic to or incompatible with those of the SUBJECT, and whose POWER is used to block the subject's MOVES; in Greimas's model paired with HELPER.

P-MOVE A MOVE involving the direct adjustment between PLAYERS of a difference in their immediately harnessable narrative POWER. A special case is the C-MOVE, where the power takes the form of information or KNOWLEDGE.

PAUSE A passage of NARRATIVE where the CLOCK is temporarily stopped, freezing on the description of a single moment of STORY time; one of five narrative TEMPI.

PLAYER A sentient inhabitant of a NARRATIVE UNIVERSE who is capable of autonomous narrative MOVES; a 'character' viewed in terms of his or her role in NARRATIVE.

PLOT The affective determination of a READER's modelling of a STORY, through its encoding in the dynamic structure of a gamelike NARRATIVE UNIVERSE and the communication of that structure through the linear datastream of a TEXT.

POINT OF VIEW The explicit or implied restriction of information about a NARRATIVE UNIVERSE reaching a NARRATOR, either to that consciously accessible to a particular PLAYER or to a hypothetical, disembodied, observing intelligence bound by more general limits of time and access; the function often discussed as FOCALISATION.

POWER The energy of a NARRATIVE UNIVERSE construed as a thermodynamic system. The distribution of narrative power determines the narrative dynamics of a STORY; though it cannot be created or destroyed in the course of the narrative, it may be dissipated, converted between different harnessable forms, or redistributed across boundaries of potential, and may attach to individual PLAYERS (where it serves, along with KNOWLEDGE and MOTIVE, to determine their COMPETENCE to act), to inanimate instruments, or to positions of advantage or disadvantage on the BOARD.

PRIMARY NARRATIVE The parts of a NARRATIVE reported directly by the NARRATOR, as opposed to those EMBEDDED in the reported words or thoughts of PLAYERS.

READER The mind that processes a TEXT – including here the audience or spectator of an oral, iconic, or audiovisual text.

RECEIVER The actantial role corresponding to the recipient of narrative POWER redistributed in a MOVE; paired with SENDER.

RULE A formal limit on the range and nature of MOVES permitted in a GAME.

S-WORLD The world of the STORY UNIVERSE, as distinct from the NARRATIVE world or N-WORLD that contains it and the T-WORLD that contains both.

SCENE (i) A passage of NARRATIVE where the CLOCK keeps analogous pace with the flow of STORY time, as in passages of direct speech; one of five narrative TEMPI. (ii) A series of EVENTS occupying the same LOCATION without NARRATIVE interruption.

SECONDARY NARRATIVE The first level of EMBEDDING: the parts of a NARRATIVE reported through the reported words or thoughts of PLAYERS, rather than in the voice of the top-level narrator. The distinction between secondary narrative and primary-narrative POINT OF VIEW is clear-cut only in the case of direct speech.

SENDER The actantial role corresponding to the source of narrative POWER harnessed in a MOVE; paired with RECEIVER.

STORY The 'story-' part of storytelling; the complete set of EVENTS recounted in a work of fiction, considered in their entirety and ordered according to the internal chronology of the STORY UNIVERSE (as opposed to that of the NARRATIVE).

STORY UNIVERSE The totality of the world within which a STORY takes place: its history, geography, people, laws of nature.

STRETCH (also SLOWDOWN) A passage of NARRATIVE where the CLOCK runs slow in relation to the timeflow of STORY, as in lingering descriptions of actions occupying relatively brief timespans in the chronology of their own STORY UNIVERSE; one of five narrative TEMPI.

SUBGAME A subdivision of a narrative GAME with its own local game structure and CLOSURE; a more or less self-contained EPISODE whose ENDING becomes an input to the larger game.

SUBJECT The actantial role corresponding to the agent of a MOVE; paired with OBJECT.

SUMMARY A passage of NARRATIVE where the CLOCK runs fast; one of five narrative TEMPI.

SYSTEM (i) A set of principles or procedures that amount to a definable category of practice; thus classical plotting is described as one such NARRATIVE 'system'. (ii) A closed environment whose contents can interact only with each other, and whose development over time depends on the system's initial contents and configuration; NARRATIVE UNIVERSES and GAMES are two examples of such systems.

T-WORLD The world in which a STORY is manifest as a TEXT: normally the real world of authors, texts, and readers, distinguished from the N-WORLD conjured by it and the S-WORLD of the STORY itself.

TEMPO The variable relationship between the flow of time in STORY and in NARRATIVE. Five narrative tempi are standardly distinguished: ELLIPSIS, SUMMARY, SCENE, STRETCH or SLOWDOWN, PAUSE.

TEXT A set of representational signs with a directional linear structure, created by an AUTHOR and consumed by a READER; any serial array of words, sounds, or images expressive of EVENTS.

TOKEN An object or person charged with narrative POWER (but incapable of exercising that power independently); thus an instrument or object of pursuit, associated as either end or means with the GOAL of one or more PLAYERS.

TRANSPARENCY The illusion of direct cognitive access by the READER to a STORY UNIVERSE; the invisibility to conscious experience of TEXT and NARRATIVE levels in the construction of STORY; with ECONOMY and AMPLITUDE, one of three qualities pursued in a CLASSICAL PLOT.

VIEWPOINT A syntactically more flexible synonym for POINT OF VIEW.

Bibliography of secondary works cited

Aarseth, E. J. (1994) 'Nonlinearity and literary theory', in Landow 1994: 51–86
  (1997) *Cybertext: perspectives on ergodic literature*, Baltimore
Adey, R. (1991) *Locked room murders and other impossible crimes: a comprehensive
  bibliography*, 2nd edn, Minneapolis and San Francisco
Allén, S. (1989), ed., *Possible worlds in humanities, arts and sciences: proceedings of
  Nobel Symposium 65*, Berlin and New York
Alvarez, J. (1996) 'Maps', in G. Schmeling, ed., *The novel in the ancient world*,
  Leiden, 801–14
Anderson, G. (1988) 'Achilles Tatius: a new interpretation', in R. Beaton, ed., *The
  Greek novel AD 1–1985*, London, New York, and Sydney, 190–3
  (1997) 'Perspectives on Achilles Tatius', *Aufstieg und Niedergang der römischen
  Welt* II.34.3 2278–99
Andrew, D. (1989) 'Cognitivism: quests and questionings', *Iris* 9: 1–10
Apthorp, M.J. (1980) 'The obstacles to Telemachus' return', *Classical Quarterly*
  30: 1–22
Archibald, E. (1991) *Apollonius of Tyre: medieval and Renaissance themes and varia-
  tions*, Cambridge
Arnott, W.G. (1972) 'Targets, techniques, and tradition in Plautus' *Stichus*',
  Bulletin of the Institute of Classical Studies 19: 54–79
  (1979) 'Time, plot and character in Menander', *Papers of the Liverpool Latin
  Seminar* 2: 343–60
Aston, E. and Savona, G. (1991) *Theatre as sign-system: a semiotics of text and performance*, London
Bagg, R. (1964) 'Love, ceremony and daydream in Sappho's lyrics', *Arion* 3:
  44–82
Bakhtin, M. M. (1937–8, 1973) 'Forms of time and chronotope in the novel';
  translated by C. Emerson and M. Holquist, in *The dialogic imagination: four
  essays* (1981), Austin, 84–258
Bal, M. (1977) *Narratologie*, Paris
  (1985) *Narratology: introduction to the theory of narrative*, translated by C. van
  Boheemen, Toronto
  (1986) 'Tell-tale theories', *Poetics Today* 7: 555–64
  (1997) *Narratology: introduction to the theory of narrative*, 2nd edn, revised and
  expanded, Toronto
Barthes, R. (1966) 'Introduction à l'analyse structurale des récits',
  Communications 8: 1–27; translated by S. Heath as 'Introduction to the structural analysis of narratives', in *Image music text* (1977), Glasgow, 79–124

(1973), *S/Z*, Paris; translated by R. Miller (1974), New York

(1975) *Le plaisir du texte*, Paris; translated by R. Miller as *The pleasure of the text*, New York

Bassett, S. E. (1938) *The poetry of Homer*, Berkeley and Los Angeles

Baumbach, M. (1997) 'Die Meroe-Episode in Heliodors *Aithiopika*', *Rheinisches Museum* 140: 333–41

Beare, W. (1964) *The Roman stage: a short history of Latin drama in the time of the Republic*, 3rd edn, London

de Beaugrande, R.-A. and Colby, B. N. (1979) 'Narrative models of action and interaction', *Cognitive Science* 3: 43–66

Belfiore, E. S. (1992a) *Tragic pleasures: Aristotle on plot and emotion*, Princeton

(1992b) 'Aristotle and Iphigenia', in Rorty 1992: 359–77

Bergren, A. (1979) 'Helen's web: time and tableau in the *Iliad*', *Helios* 7: 19–34

Bettini, M. (1982) 'Verso un'antropologia dell'intreccio: le strutture semplici della trama nelle commedie di Plauto', *Materiali e discussioni per l'analisi dei testi classici* 7: 39–101; reprinted in Bettini, *Verso un'antropologia dell'intreccio* (1991), Urbino, 11–76

Billault, A. (1991) *La Création romanesque dans la littérature grecque à l'époque impériale*, Paris

Black, J. B. and Bower, G. H. (1980) 'Story understanding as problem-solving', *Poetics* 9: 223–50

and Wilensky, R. (1979) 'An evaluation of story grammars', *Cognitive Science* 3: 213–29

Blume, H.–D. (1990) 'Der Codex Bodmer und unsere Kenntnis der griechischen Komödie', in E.W. Handley and A. Hurst, eds., *Relire Ménandre* (Recherches et Rencontres 2), Geneva, 13–36

Bobrow, D. G. and Collins, A. (1975), eds., *Representation and understanding: studies in cognitive science*, New York, San Francisco, and London

Bolter, J. D. (1991) *Writing space: the computer, hypertext, and the history of writing*, Hillsdale

Bordwell, D. (1985a) *Narration in the fiction film*, London

(1985b) 'The classical Hollywood style, 1917–60', in D. Bordwell, J. Staiger, and K. Thompson, *The classical Hollywood cinema: film style and mode of production to 1960*, London, 1–84

(1989) *Making meaning: inference and rhetoric in the interpretation of cinema*, Cambridge, MA

Bordwell, D. and Carroll, N. (1996), eds., *Post-theory: reconstructing film studies*, Madison

Bordwell, D. and Thompson, K. (1993) *Film art: an introduction*, 4th edn, New York

Bowie, E. L. (1985) 'Theocritus' seventh idyll, Philetas and Longus', *Classical Quarterly* 35: 67–91

(1993) 'Lies, fiction, and slander in early Greek poetry', in C. Gill and T. P. Wiseman, eds., *Lies and fiction in the ancient world*, Exeter, 1–37

Branigan, E. (1992) *Narrative comprehension and film*, London and New York

Bremer, J. M. (1976) 'Why messenger-speeches?', in J.M. Bremer, S.L. Radt, and C.J. Ruijgh, eds., *Miscellanea tragica in honorem J.C. Kamerbeek*, Amsterdam, 29–48

Bremond, C. (1973) *Logique du récit*, Paris

Brewer, W. P. and Lichtenstein, E.H. (1981) 'Event schemas, story schemas, and story grammars', in A. D. Baddeley, and J. D. Long, eds., *Attention and performance IX*, Hillsdale, 363–79

Britton, B. K. and Pellegrini, A. D. (1990), eds., *Narrative thought and narrative language*, Hillsdale

Brooke-Rose, C. (1990) 'Whatever happened to narratology?', *Poetics Today* 11: 283–93; reprinted in *Stories, theories, and things* (1991), Cambridge, 16–27

Brooks, P. (1984) *Reading for the plot: design and intention in narrative*, New York

Brower, R. A. (1952) 'The heresy of plot', *English Institute Essays, 1951*, New York, 44–69

Brown, C. (1994) *Screenwriter's companion: a workbook guide to developing a saleable screenplay*, Los Angeles

Bruss, E. (1977) 'The game of literature and some literary games', *New Literary History* 9: 153–72

Bürger, K. (1892) 'Zu Xenophon von Ephesus', *Hermes* 27: 36–67

Burian, P. (1997) 'Myth into *mythos*: the shaping of tragic plot', in P.E. Easterling, ed., *The Cambridge companion to Greek tragedy*, Cambridge, 178–208

Burnett, A. P. (1976) 'Tribe and city, custom and decree in *Children of Heracles*', *Classical Quarterly* 26: 4–26

(1988) 'Jocasta in the west: the Lille Stesichorus', *Classical Antiquity* 7: 107–54

Buxton, R. (1994) *Imaginary Greece*, Cambridge

Calasso, R. (1988) *Le nozze di Cadmo e Armonia*, Rome; translated by Tim Parks as *The marriage of Cadmus and Harmony* (1993), London

Cameron, A. (1995) *Callimachus and his critics*, Princeton

Carlson, M. (1984) *Theories of the theatre 1984: a historical and critical survey, from the Greeks to the present*, Ithaca

(1988) 'Semiotics of theater', in Sebeok and Umiker-Sebeok 1988: 323–53

(1990) *Theatre semiotics: signs of life*, Bloomington

Chalk, H. H. O. (1960) 'Eros and the Lesbian pastorals of Longus', *Journal of Hellenic Studies* 80: 32–51

Chatman, S. (1978) *Story and discourse: narrative structure in fiction and film*, Ithaca

(1980) 'What novels can do that films can't (and vice versa)', *Critical Inquiry* 7: 121–40

(1986) 'Characters and narrators: filter, center, slant, and interest-focus', *Poetics Today* 7: 189–204

(1990) *Coming to terms: the rhetoric of narrative in fiction and film*, Ithaca

Clay, D. (1994) 'The origins of the Socratic dialogue', in Paul A. Vander Waerdt, ed., *The Socratic movement*, Ithaca and London, 23–47

Clay, J. S. (1997) 'The Homeric Hymns', in Ian Morris and Barry Powell, eds., *A new companion to Homer*, Leiden, 489–507

Cook, W. W. (1928) *Plotto: a new method of plot suggestion for writers of creative fiction*, Battle Creek

Cooke, D. (1959) *The language of music*, Oxford

Coots, J. H. (1982), ed., *Stories*, special issue of *Journal of Pragmatics*, 6.5/6

Correira, A. (1980) 'Computing story trees', *American Journal of Computational Linguistics* 6: 135–49

Craik, E. M. and Kaferly, D. H. A. (1987) 'The computer and Sophocles *Trachiniae*', *Literary and Linguistic Computing* 2: 86–97

Crane, R.S. (1952) 'The concept of plot and the plot of *Tom Jones*', in R.S. Crane, ed., *Critics and criticism: ancient and modern*, Chicago and London, 616–47

Culler, J. (1975) *Structuralist poetics: structuralism, linguistics, and the study of literature*, London

Currie, G. (1990) *The nature of fiction*, Cambridge

Dale, A. M. (1956) 'Seen and unseen on the Greek stage', *Wiener Studien* 69: 96–106; reprinted in *Classical papers* (1969), Cambridge, 119–29

Davey, L. A. (1984) 'Communication and the game of theatre', *Poetics* 13: 5–15

Davidson, J. (1997) *Courtesans and fishcakes: the consuming passions of classical Athens*, London

Dawkins, R. (1989) *The selfish gene*, 2nd edn, Oxford

Dehn, N. (1981) 'Story generation after TALE-SPIN', *Proceedings of the Seventh International Joint Conference on Artificial Intelligence*, 2 vols., Menlo Park, 1.16–18

Dennett, D. C. (1987) *The intentional stance*, Cambridge, MA
    (1995) *Darwin's dangerous idea*, London

Dessen, C. (1977) 'Plautus' satiric comedy: the *Truculentus*', *Philological Quarterly* 56: 145–68

Dipple, E. (1971) *Plot*, London

Doherty, L. E. (1995) *Siren songs: gender, audiences and narration in the Odyssey*, Ann Arbor

Döhle, B. (1967) 'Die *Achilleis* des Aischylos in ihrer Auswirkung auf die attische Vasenmalerei des 5. Jahrhunderts', *Klio* 49: 63–149

Dolozel, L. (1976a) 'Narrative semantics', *PTL* 1: 129–51
    (1976b) 'Narrative worlds', in L. Matejka, ed., *Sign, sound, and meaning*, Ann Arbor, 542–52
    (1979) 'Extensional and intensional narrative worlds', *Poetics* 8: 198–211
    (1988) 'Mimesis and possible worlds', *Poetics Today* 9: 475–96
    (1989) 'Possible worlds and literary fictions', in Allén 1989: 221–42
    (1998) *Heterocosmica: fiction and possible worlds*, Baltimore

Dorfman, M. H. and Brewer, W. F. (1994) 'Understanding the points of fables', *Discourse Processes* 17: 105–29

Douglas, J. Y. (1992) 'Is there a reader in this labyrinth? Notes on reading *Afternoon*', in P. O'B. Holt and N. Williams, eds., *Computers and writing: state of the art*, Oxford, 29–39
    (1994) 'How do I stop this thing? Closure and indeterminacy in nonlinear narratives', in Landow 1994: 159–88

Downing, E. (1984) 'Οἷον ψυχή: an essay on Aristotle's *muthos*', *Classical Antiquity* 3: 164–78

Downs, R. M. and Stea, D. (1977) *Maps in minds: reflections on cognitive mapping*, New York

Duckworth, G. E. (1933) *Foreshadowing and suspense in the epics of Homer, Apollonius, and Vergil*, diss. Princeton

Dumont, J. C. (1974) 'Guerre, paix et servitude dans les *Captifs*', *Latomus* 33: 505–22

Dunn, F. M. (1996) *Tragedy's end: closure and innovation in Euripidean drama*, New York and Oxford
Durham, D. B. (1938) 'Parody in Achilles Tatius', *Classical Philology* 33: 1–19
Easterling, P. E. (1981) 'The end of the *Trachiniae*', *Illinois Classical Studies* 6: 56–74
  (1987) 'Women in tragic space', *Bulletin of the Institute of Classical Studies* 34: 15–26
  (1993) 'The end of an era? tragedy in the early fourth century', in Sommerstein, Zimmerman, and Henderson 1993: 559–569
Easterling, P. E. and Knox, B. M. W. (1985), eds., *The Cambridge history of classical literature* I: *Greek literature*, Cambridge
Ebert, R. (1994) *The little book of Hollywood clichés*, Chicago
Eco, U. (1979) *The role of the reader: explorations in the semiotics of texts*, Bloomington and London
  (1989) 'Report on Session 3: literature and arts', in Allén 1989: 343–55
Egan, K. (1977–8) 'What is a plot?', *New Literary History* 9: 457–73
Egri, L. (1960) *The art of dramatic writing*, revised edition, New York
  (1965) *The art of creative writing*, New York
Ehrlich, S. (1990) *Point of view: a linguistic analysis of literary style*, London
Eisner, W. (1990) *Comics and sequential art*, 2nd edn, Tamarac
Elam, K. (1980) *The semiotics of theatre and drama*, London
Else, G. F. (1957) *Aristotle's Poetics: the argument*, Cambridge, MA
Emmott, C. (1997) *Narrative comprehension: a discourse perspective*, Oxford
Enk, P. J. (1964) 'Plautus' *Truculentus*', in C. Henderson, ed., *Classical, mediaeval, and Renaissance studies in honor of Berthold Louis Ullmann*, 2 vols., Rome, I: 49–65
Falk, E. H. (1965) *Types of thematic structure*, Chicago
Felson-Rubin, N. (1993) *Regarding Penelope: from character to poetics*, Princeton
Feuillâtre, E. (1966) *Etudes sur les Ethiopiques d'Héliodore*, Paris
Field, S. (1979) *Screenplay*, New York
Finkelberg, M. (1998) *The birth of literary fiction in ancient Greece*, Oxford
Fish, S. (1989) 'Why no one's afraid of Wolfgang Iser', in *Doing what comes naturally: rhetoric, change, and the practice of theory in literary and legal studies*, Durham, NC and London, 68–86
Fludernik, M. (1996) *Towards a 'natural' narratology*, London and New York
Forster, E. M. (1927) *Aspects of the novel*, London
Fournel, P. (1977) 'Ordinateur et écrivain: l'expérience du Centre Pompidou', originally presented at 'Ecrivain-Ordinateur' conference, June 1977; in Oulipo, *Atlas de littérature potentielle* (1981), Paris, 298–302, and translated as 'Computer and writer: the Centre Pompidou experiment' in Motte 1986: 140–2
Fowler, D. P. (1989) 'First thoughts on closure: problems and prospects', *Materiali e discussioni per l'analisi dei testi classici* 22: 75–122
Fraenkel, E. (1922) *Plautinisches im Plautus*, Berlin; translated by F. Munari with addenda as *Elementini Plautini in Plauto* (1960), Florence
Frede, M. (1992), 'Plato's arguments and the dialogue form', in Klagge and Smith 1992: 201–19

Friedman, N. (1955) 'Forms of the plot', *Journal of General Education* 8: 241ff.; revised in *Form and meaning in fiction* (1975), Athens, GA, 79–101

Frye, N. (1957) *Anatomy of criticism*, Princeton

Fusillo, M. (1989) *Il romanzo greco: polifonia ed eros*, Venice; translated by Marielle Abrioux as *Naissance du roman* (1991), Paris

Futre Pinheiro, M. P. (1987) *Estruturas técnico-narrativas nas Etiópicas de Heliodoro*, diss. Lisbon

 (1998) 'Time and technique in Heliodorus' "Aethiopica"', *Aufstieg und Niedergang der römischen Welt*, II.34.4: 3148–73

Gainsford, P. (1999) 'Homer's archetypal family: a pattern of relations', diss. Cambridge

Galef, D., ed. (1998) *Second thoughts: a focus on rereading*, Detroit

Gantz, T. (1979) 'The Aischylean tetralogy: prolegomena', *Classical Journal* 74: 289–304

Gardner, M. (1989) *Penrose tiles to trapdoor ciphers*, New York

Genette, G. (1972) 'Discours du récit', in *Figures III*, Paris, translated by J. E. Lewin as *Narrative discourse* (1980), Ithaca

 (1983), *Nouveau discours du récit*, Paris, translated by J. E. Lewin as *Narrative discourse revisited* (1988), Ithaca

 (1987), *Seuils*, Paris, translated by J.E. Lewin as *Paratexts: thresholds of interpretation* (1997), Cambridge

Gerrig, R. J. (1993) *Experiencing narrative worlds*, New Haven

Gibson, A. (1996) *Towards a postmodern theory of narrative*, Edinburgh

Gilula, D. (1978) 'Where did the audience go?', *Scripta Classica Israelica* 4: 45–9

Goffman, E. (1974) *Frame analysis: an essay in the organisation of experience*, Cambridge, MA

Goldberg, S. M. (1978) 'Plautus' *Epidicus* and the case of the missing original', *Transactions of the American Philological Association* 108: 81–91

Goldhill, S. (1988) 'The Great Dionysia and civic ideology', *Journal of Hellenic Studies* 108 58–87, revised in Winkler and Zeitlin 1990: 97–129

 (1991) *The poet's voice: essays on poetics and Greek literature*, Cambridge

Gomme, A. W. and Sandbach, F. H. (1973) *Menander: a commentary*, Oxford

Gould, P. and White, R. (1986) *Mental maps*, 2nd edn, Boston

Goward, B. (1999) *Telling tragedy: narrative techniques in Aeschylus, Sophocles and Euripides*, London

Graesser, A. C., Bowers, C., Olde, B., White, K. and Person, N. K. (1999) 'Who knows what? Propagation of knowledge among agents in a literary story-world', *Poetics* 26: 143–75

Gratwick, A. S. (1993), ed., *Plautus: Menaechmi*, Cambridge

Green, P. (1982) 'Longus, Antiphon, and the topography of Lesbos', *Journal of Hellenic Studies* 102: 210–14

Greimas, A. J. (1966) *Sémantique structurale*, Paris; translated by D. McDowell, R. Schleifer, and A. Velie as *Structural semantics: an attempt at a method* (1973), Lincoln, Nebraska

 (1970) *Du sens: essais sémiotiques*, Paris

 (1983) *Du sens II: essais sémiotiques*, Paris

 (1987), *On meaning: selected writings in semiotic theory*, translated by P.J. Perron and F.H. Collins, Minneapolis

(1990) *The social sciences: a semiotic view*, translated by P. J. Perron and F. H. Collins, Minneapolis = *Narrative semiotics and cognitive discourses* (1990), London

Griffin, J. (1977) 'The Epic Cycle and the uniqueness of Homer', *Journal of Hellenic Studies* 97: 39–53
(1980a) *Homer on life and death*, Oxford
(1980b) *Homer*, Oxford

Griffith, J. G. (1988) 'Some misgivings concerning the present state of criticism of Plautus' *Pseudolus*', in *Festinat senex*, Oxford, 50–63

Gruen, E. S. (1990) *Studies in Greek culture and Roman policy*, Leiden
(1993) 'The theatre and aristocratic culture', in *Culture and national identity in Republican Rome*, London, 183–222

Habel, C. (1986) 'Stories – an artificial intelligence perspective (?)', *Poetics* 15: 111–25

Hägg, T. (1966) 'Die Ephesiaka des Xenophon Ephesius: Original oder Epitome?', *Classica et Mediaevalia* 27: 118–61
(1971) *Narrative technique in ancient Greek romances*, Stockholm
(1980), *Den antika romanen*, Uppsala; revised and translated as *The novel in antiquity* (1983), Oxford

Halliwell, S. (1986) *Aristotle's Poetics*, London

Halperin, D. M. (1992) 'Plato and the erotics of narrativity', in Klagge and Smith 1992: 93–129

Hanauer, D. (1998) 'Reading poetry: an empirical investigation of formalist, stylistic, and conventionalist claims', *Poetics Today* 19: 565–80

Haslam, M. W. (1972) 'Plato, Sophron, and the dramatic dialogue', *Bulletin of The Institute of Classical Studies* 19: 17–38

Hefti, V. (1950) *Zur Erzählungstechnik in Heliodors Aethiopica*, diss. Basle

Heiserman, A. (1977) *The novel before the novel: essays and discussions about the beginnings of prose fiction in the West*, Chicago

Hellwig, B. (1962) *Raum und Zeit im homerischen Epos*, diss. Tübingen; reprinted as Spudasmata 2 (1964), Hildesheim

Henderson, J. (1988) 'Entertaining arguments: Terence *Adelphoe*', in A. Benjamin, ed., *Post-structuralist classics*, London and New York, 192–226; revised in Henderson 1999: 38–66
(1994) 'Hanno's Punic heirs: der Poenulusneid des Plautus', *Ramus* 23: 24–54; revised in Henderson 1999: 3–37
(1997) 'The name of the tree: recounting *Odyssey* xxiv 340–2', *Journal of Hellenic Studies* 117: 87–116
(1999) *Writing down Rome: satire, comedy, and other offences in Latin poetry*, Oxford

Hendricks, W. O. (1991) 'Semiotics and narrative', in T. A. Sebeok and J. Umiker-Sebeok, eds., *Recent developments in theory and history: the semiotic web 1990*, Berlin and New York, 365–88

Herington, C. J. (1961) '*Octavia praetexta*: a survey', *Classical Quarterly* 11: 18–30

Herman, D. (1985) *Poetry into drama: early tragedy and the Greek poetic tradition*, Berkeley and Los Angeles
(1997) 'Scripts, sequences, and stories: elements of a postclassical narratology', *PMLA* 112: 1046–59

276   Bibliography

Heubeck, A. (1992) Commentary on Books XXI–XXIV, in Heubeck *et al.*
 1988–92: Vol. III, 313–418
et al. (1988–92), *A commentary on Homer's Odyssey*, revised English edition, 3
 vols., Oxford
Hirzel, R. (1963) *Der Dialog: Ein literarhistorischer Versuch*, Leipzig, 1895, reprinted
 Hildesheim, 1963
Hoekstra, A. (1989) Commentary on Books XII–XVI, in Heubeck *et al.* 1988–92:
 Vol. II, 147–287
Hofmeister, T. P. (1997) 'Αἱ πᾶσαι πόλεις: polis and *oikoumenē* in Menander', in
 G. W. Dobrov, ed., *The city as comedy: society and representation in Athenian
 drama*, Chapel Hill, 289–342
Hornblower, S. (1994) 'Narratology and narrative techniques in Thucydides', in
 Hornblower, ed., *Greek historiography*, Oxford, 131–66
Hubbard, M. E. (1972), tr., 'Aristotle: *Poetics*', in D. A. Russell and M.
 Winterbottom, eds., *Ancient literary criticism: the principal texts in new transla-
 tions*, Oxford, 90–132
Humphrey, N. K. (1980) 'Nature's psychologists', in B.D. Josephson and V.S.
 Ramachandran, eds., *Consciousness and the physical world*, Oxford, 57–80
Ide, N.M. and Véronis, J. (1990) 'Artificial intelligence and the study of literary
 narrative', *Poetics* 19: 37–63
Jahn, M. (1996) 'Windows of focalization: deconstructing and reconstructing a
 narratological concept', *Style* 30: 241–67
Janko, R. (1987), tr., *Aristotle: Poetics*, Indianapolis and Cambridge
Johnson-Laird, P. N. (1983) *Mental models: towards a cognitive science of language,
 inference, and consciousness*, Cambridge
Jones, P.V. (1991), ed., *Homer: Odyssey 1–2*, Warminster
 (1995), 'Poetic invention: the fighting around Troy in the first nine years of the
 Trojan war', in Ø. Andersen and M. W. Dickie, eds., *Homer's world: fiction,
 tradition, reality*, Bergen, 101–11
de Jong, I. J. F. (1987a) *Narrators and focalizers: the presentation of the story in the
 Iliad*, Amsterdam
 (1987b) 'Silent characters in the *Iliad*', in I. J. F. De Jong, J. M Bremer, and J.
 Kalff, eds., *Homer: beyond oral poetry*, Amsterdam, 105–21
 (1991) *Narrative in drama: the art of the Euripidean messenger-speech (Mnemosyne*
 Supplement 116), Leiden
Jonnes, D. (1990) *The matrix of narrative: family systems and the semiotics of story*
 (Approaches to Semiotics 91), Berlin and New York
Joyce, M. (1990) *Afternoon: a story*, Watertown, MA
 (1995) *Of two minds: hypertext pedagogy and poetics*, Ann Arbor
Katz, M. A. (1991) *Penelope's renown*, Princeton
Kenney, E. J. and Clausen, W. V. (1982), eds., *The Cambridge history of classical lit-
 erature* II: *Latin literature*, Cambridge
Kirk, G. S. (1962) *The songs of Homer*, Cambridge
Kirk, G. S. *et al.* (1985–93), *The Iliad: a commentary*, 6 vols., Cambridge
Klagge, J. C. and Smith, N. D. (1992), eds., *Methods of interpreting Plato and his
 dialogues*, (*Oxford Studies in Ancient Philosophy* Supplementary Volume),
 Oxford
Klein, S. *et al.* (1973) *Automatic novel writing: a status report* (Technical Report 186,

Computer Sciences Dept, University of Wisconsin), Madison, abridged in W,
Burghardt and K. Hölker, eds., *Text processing: papers in text analysis and text
description* (research in Text Theory 3, Berlin and New York, 1979), 338–412
(1974), *Modelling Propp and Lévi-Strauss in a meta-symbolic simulation system*
(Technical Report 226, Computer Sciences Department, University of
Wisconsin), Madison; version in H. Jason and D. Segal, eds., *Patterns in oral
literature* (1977), The Hague, 142–217, with discussion 218–20

Kloft, H. (1989) 'Imagination und Realität: Überlegungen zur
Wirtschaftsstructur des Romans *Daphnis und Chloe*', *Groningen Colloquia on
the Novel* 2: 45–61

Knox, B. M. W. (1964) *The heroic temper*, Berkeley and Los Angeles

Konstan, D. (1983) *Roman comedy*, Ithaca
   (1994) *Sexual symmetry: love in the ancient novel and related genres*, Princeton
   (1995) *Greek comedy and ideology*, New York and Oxford

Kosman, L. A. (1992) 'Silence and imitation in the Platonic dialogues', in Klagge
   and Smith 1992: 73–92

Koteliansky, S.S. (1927), ed. and tr., *Anton Tchekhov: literary and theatrical reminiscences*, London

Kraus, C.S. (1991) 'λόγος μὲν ἔστ' ἀρχαῖος: stories and story-telling in
Sophocles' *Trachiniae*', *Transactions of the American Philological Association*
121: 75–98

Kristeva, J. (1970) *Le Texte du roman: approche sémiologique d'une structure discursive
transformationelle*, Approaches to Semiotics 6, The Hague

Kuntz, M. (1993) *Narrative setting and dramatic poetry*, Leiden

Landow, G. P. (1994), ed., *Hyper | text | theory*, Baltimore and London
   (1997) *Hypertext 2.0*, Baltimore and London

Langford, D. R. (1997) 'Plot coupons', in J. Clute and J. Grant, eds., *The encyclope-
dia of fantasy*, London

Lanser, S. S. (1981) *The narrative act: point of view in prose fiction*, Princeton
   (1993) 'Plot', in A. Preminger and T. V. F. Brogan, eds., *The new Princeton ency-
clopedia of poetry and poetics*, Princeton, 916–18

Laurel, B. (1993) *Computers as theater*, 2nd edn, Reading, MA

Leach, E. W. (1969) 'Ergasilus and the ironies of the *Captivi*', *Classica et
Mediaevalia* 30: 263–96

Lebowitz, M. (1984) 'Creating characters in a story-telling universe', *Poetics* 13:
171–94
   (1985) 'Story-telling as planning and learning', *Poetics* 14: 483–502

Lefèvre, E. (1977) 'Plautus-Studien I: Der doppelte Geldkreislauf im *Pseudolus*',
Hermes 105: 441–54
   (1998) *Plautus' Pseudolus* (ScriptOralia 101), Tübingen

Lehnert, W. G. (1981) 'Plot units and narrative summarization', *Cognitive Science*
4: 293–332
   (1982) 'Plot units: a narrative summarization strategy', in Lehnert and Ringle
1982: 375–412

Lehnert, W. G. and Ringle, M. H. (1982), eds, *Strategies for natural language processing*, Hillsdale

Leitch, T. M. (1986) *What stories are: narrative theory and interpretation*, University
Park and London

Lemon, L. T. and Reis, M. J. (1965), eds. and trs., *Russian formalist criticism: four essays*, Lincoln, Nebraska and London

Lévi-Strauss, C. (1949) *Les Structures élémentaires de la parenté*, Paris; 2nd edn (1967) translated by J. H. Bell, J. R. von Sturmer, and R. Needham as *The elementary structures of kinship* (1969), London

Long, T. (1976) 'The calculus of confusion: cognitive and associative errors in Plautus' *Menaechmi* and Shakespeare's *Comedy of Errors*', *Classical Bulletin* 53: 20–3

Lowe, N. J. (1987) 'Tragic space and comic timing in Menander's *Dyskolos*', *Bulletin of the Institute of Classical Studies* 34: 126–38

(1988) 'Greek stagecraft and Aristophanes', in James Redmond, ed., *Themes in Drama* 10: *Farce*, Cambridge, 33–52

(1996) 'Tragic and Homeric ironies: response to Rosenmeyer', in M. S. Silk, ed., *Tragedy and the tragic: Greek theatre and beyond*, Oxford, 520–33

(forthcoming), 'Comic plots and the invention of fiction', in F.D. Harvey and J. M. Wilkins, eds., *The rivals of Aristophanes*, Cardiff

Lucas, D. W. (1968), ed., *Aristotle: Poetics*, Oxford

Lynch, A. (1996) *Thought contagion: how belief spreads through society*, New York

Lynn-George, M. (1988) *Epos: word, narrative, and the Iliad*, London

Macleod, C. W. (1982), ed., *Homer: Iliad XXIV*, Cambridge

Maitre, D. (1983) *Literature and possible worlds*, London

Mandler, J. M. (1987) 'On the psychological reality of story structure', *Discourse Processes* 10: 1–29

Mandler, J. M. and Johnson, N. S. (1977) 'Remembrance of things parsed: story structure and recall', *Cognitive psychology* 9: 11–151

(1980) 'On throwing out the baby with the bathwater: a reply to Black and Wilensky's evaluation of story grammars', *Cognitive Science* 4: 305–12

Marcus, S. (1977), ed., *The formal study of drama*, special issue of *Poetics*, 6.3/4

Martin, W. (1986) *Recent theories of narrative*, Ithaca

Mason, H. A. (1979) 'Longus and the topography of Lesbos', *Transactions of the American Philological Association* 109: 149–63

Mastronarde, D. J. (1990) 'Actors on high: the skene roof, the crane, and the gods in Attic drama', *Classical Antiquity* 9: 247–94

Mathews, H. and Brotchie, A. (1998), eds., *Oulipo compendium*, London

Mauss, M. (1925) 'Essai sur le don: forme et raison de l'échange dans les sociétés archaïques', *Année sociologique* 1: 30–186

McClary, S. (1994) 'Narratives of bourgeois subjectivity in Mozart's Prague Symphony', in J. Phelan and P.J. Rabinowitz, eds., *Understanding narrative*, Columbus, 65–98

McCloud, S. (1993) *Understanding comics*, Northampton, MA

McKee, R. (1998) *Story: substance, structure, style, and the principles of screenwriting*, New York

Meehan, J. R. (1976) *The metanovel: writing stories by computer*, diss. Yale; reprinted (1980) New York

(1981), 'TALE-SPIN', in R. C. Schank, and C. K. Riesbeck, *Inside computer understanding: five programs plus miniatures*, Hillsdale, 197–225

(1982) 'Stories and cognition: comments on Robert de Beaugrande's "The story of grammars and the grammar of stories"', *Journal of Pragmatics* 6: 455–62

Merrill, R. (1999) 'Raymond Chandler's plots and the concept of plot', *Narrative* 7: 3–21

Miner, E. (1990) *Comparative poetics: an intercultural essay on theories of literature*, Princeton

Momigliano, A. (1981) 'The rhetoric of history and the history of rhetoric: on Hayden White's tropes', in E. S. Shaffer, ed., *Comparative criticism: a yearbook* 3: 259–68

Morgan, J. R. (1981) 'History, romance and realism in the *Aithiopika* of Heliodoros', *Classical Antiquity* 1: 221–65

   (1989a) 'The story of Knemon in Heliodoros' *Aithiopika*', *Journal of Hellenic Studies* 109: 99–113

   (1989b) 'A sense of the ending: the conclusion of Heliodoros' *Aithiopika*', *Transactions of the American Philological Association* 119: 299–320

   (1991) 'Reader and audiences in the *Aithiopika* of Heliodoros', *Groningen Colloquia on the Novel* 4: 84–103

   (1994) 'The *Aithiopika* of Heliodoros: narrative as riddle', in Morgan and Stoneman 1994; 97–113

Morgan, J. R. and Stoneman, R. (1994), eds., *Greek fiction; the novel in context*, London and New York

Morrison, J. V. (1992) *Homeric misdirection: false predictions in the Iliad* (Michigan Monographs in Classical Antiquity) Ann Arbor

Most, G. W. (1989) 'The stranger's stratagem: self-disclosure and self-sufficiency in Greek culture', *Journal of Hellenic Studies* 109: 114–33

Motte, W. F., Jr (1986), ed. and tr. *Oulipo: a primer of potential literature*, Lincoln, NE and London

Murnaghan, S. (1987) *Disguise and recognition in the Odyssey*, Princeton

   (1997) 'Equal honor and future glory: the plan of Zeus in the *Iliad*', in Deborah H. Roberts, Francis M. Dunn, and Don Fowler, eds., *Classical closure: reading the end in Greek and Latin literature*, Princeton, 23–42

Nagy, G. (1990) *Pindar's Homer: the lyric possession of an epic past*, Baltimore

Nell, V. (1988) *Lost in a book: the psychology of reading for pleasure*, New Haven and London

Newiger, H. (1989) 'Ekkyklema e mechané nella messa in scena del dramma greco', *Dioniso* 59: 173–85; German version as 'Ekkyklema und Mechané in der Inszenierung des griechischen Dramas', *WJA* 16 (1990), 33–42

Nielsen, F. A. J. (1997) *The tragedy in history: Herodotus and the Deuteronomistic history* (Journal for the Study of the Old Testament Supplement Series 251/Copenhagen International Seminar 4), Sheffield

O'Grady, W. (1965) 'On plot in modern fiction: Hardy, James, and Conrad', *Modern Fiction Studies* 11: 107–15

O'Neill, P. (1994) *Fictions of discourse: reading narrative theory*, Toronto, Buffalo, and London

O'Sullivan, J. N. (1995) *Xenophon of Ephesus: his compositional technique and the birth of the novel*, Berlin and New York

Olson, S. D. (1995) *Blood and iron: stories and storytelling in Homer's Odyssey*, Leiden

Onega, S. and Garcia Landa, J. A. (1996), eds., *Narratology: an introduction*, London

Padel, R. (1990) 'Making space speak', in Winkler and Zeitlin 1990: 336–65

Page, D. (1955) *The Homeric Odyssey*, Oxford

Papanikolaou, A.D. (1973), ed., *Xenophon Ephesius: Ephesiacorum libri V*, Leipzig

Pavel, T. G. (1984) 'Origin and articulation: comments on the papers by Peter Brooks and Lucienne Frappier-Mazur', *Style* 18. 3: 355–68

(1985) *The poetics of plot: the case of English Renaissance drama*, Minneapolis

(1986) *Fictional worlds*, Cambridge, MA

(1989) 'Fictional worlds and the economy of the imaginary', in Allén 1989: 250–9

Peradotto, J. (1990) *Man in the middle voice: name and narration in the Odyssey* (Martin Classical Lectures NS 1), Princeton

Pfister, M. (1977) *Das Drama*, Munich; translated by J. Halliday as *The theory and analysis of drama* (1988), Cambridge

Phillips, M. A. and Huntley, C. (1993) *Dramatica: a new theory of story*, 3rd edn (1996), Burbank

Pinnells, J. (1983) *Style and structure in the novel: an introduction*, Heidelberg

Polti, G. (1895) *Les Trentes-six situations dramatiques*, Paris; 3rd edn (1924) translated by L. Ray as *The thirty-six dramatic situations* (1944), Boston

Popper, K. R. (1994) *Knowledge and the body–mind problem*, London and New York

Popper, K. R. and Eccles, J. C. (1977) *The self and its brain*, Berlin

Pratt, L. H. (1993) *Lying and poetry from Homer to Pindar*, Ann Arbor

Prieto-Pablos, J.A. (1998) 'The paradox of suspense', *Poetics* 26: 99–113

Prince, G. (1982) *Narratology: the form and functioning of narrative*, Berlin, New York, and Amsterdam

(1987) *A dictionary of narratology*, Lincoln, NE and London

(1988) 'Narratological illustrations', *Semiotica* 68; 355–66

Propp, V. (1928) *Morfologia skazki*, Leningrad, translated by L. Scott as *Morphology of the folktale*, 2nd edn (1968), Austin

Rabel, R. J. (1997) *Plot and point of view in the Iliad*, Ann Arbor

Rabinowitz, N. S. (1993) *Anxiety veiled: Euripides and the traffic in women*, Ithaca and London

Rabkin, E. S. (1973) *Narrative suspense*, Ann Arbor

Reardon, B. P. (1989), ed., *The complete Greek novels*, Berkeley, Los Angeles, and London

(1994) 'Achilles Tatius and ego-narrative', in Morgan and Stoneman 1994: 80–96

Rehm, R. (1988) 'The staging of suppliant plays', *Greek, Roman and Byzantine Studies* 29: 263–307

(1992) *Greek tragic theatre*, London and New York

Richardson, S. (1990) *The Homeric narrator*, Nashville

Ricoeur, P. (1983–7) *Temps et récit*, 4 vols., Paris, translated by K. McLaughlin and D. Pellauer as *Time and narrative* (1984–8), 4 vols., Chicago

Rimmon-Kenan, S. (1983) *Narrative fiction: contemporary poetics*, London

(1989) 'How the model neglects the medium: linguistics, language, and the crisis of narratology', *Journal of Narrative Technique* 19: 157–66

Roberts, D. H. (1988) 'Sophoclean endings: another story', *Arethusa* 21: 177–96

(1992) 'Outside the drama: the limits of tragedy in Aristotle's *Poetics*', in Rorty 1992: 133–53

Rohde, E. (1876) *Der griechische Roman und seine Vorläufer*, Leipzig; 3rd edn reprinted Hildesheim, 1960

Ronen, R. (1990a) 'Paradigm shift in plot models: an outline of the history of narratology', *Poetics Today* 11: 817–42; revised in Ronen 1994: 144–74

(1990b) 'Possible worlds in literary theory: a game in interdisciplinarity', *Semiotica* 80: 277–97; revised in Ronen 1994: 17–46

(1994) *Possible worlds in literary theory*, Cambridge

Rood, T. (1998) *Thucydides: narrative and interpretation*, Oxford

Rorty, A. O. (1992), ed., *Essays on Aristotle's Poetics*, Princeton

Rosivach, V.J. (1998) *When a young man falls in love: the sexual exploitation of women in New Comedy*, London

Rösler, W. (1980) 'Die Entdeckung der Fiktionalität in der Antike', *Poetica* 12: 283–319

Ruiz Montero, Consuelo (1988) *El estructura de la novela griega* (Acta Salmanticensia: Estudios Filologicos 196), Salamanca

Rumelhart, D.E. (1975) 'Notes on a schema for stories', in Bobrow and Collins 1975: 211–36

(1980) 'On evaluating story grammars', *Cognitive Science* 4: 313–16

Rutherford, R. B. (1986) 'The philosophy of the *Odyssey*', *Journal of Hellenic Studies* 106: 145–62

(1992) ed., *Homer: Odyssey XIX and XX*, Cambridge

Ruthrof, H. (1981) *The reader's construction of narrative*, London

Ryan, M.-L. (1979) 'Linguistic models in narratology: from structuralism to generative semantics', *Semiotica* 28: 127–55

(1980) 'Fiction, non-factuals, and the principle of minimal departure', *Poetics* 9: 403–22; revised in Ryan 1991: 48–60

(1985) 'The modal structure of narrative universes', *Poetics Today* 6: 717–55; revised in Ryan 1991: 109–23

(1986a) 'Embedded narratives and tellability', *Style* 20: 319–40; revised in Ryan 1991: 148–74

(1986b) 'Embedded narratives and the structure of plans', *Text* 6: 107–42

(1988) 'The heuristics of automatic story generation', in Sebeok and Umiker-Sebeok 1988: 173–88; revised in Ryan 1991: 233–57

(1991) *Possible worlds, artificial intelligence, and narrative theory*, Bloomington and Indianapolis

(1992a) 'The modes of narrativity and their visual metaphors', *Style* 26: 368–87

(1992b) 'Possible worlds in recent literary theory', *Style* 26: 528–53

(1995) ed., *From possible worlds to virtual realities: approaches to postmodernism*, special issue of *Style* 29.2

(1997) 'Postmodernism and the doctrine of panfictionality', *Narrative* 5: 165–87

Saariluoma, P. (1995) *Chess players' thinking: a cognitive psychological approach*, London and New York

Sandbach, F. H. (1973): see Gomme and Sandbach 1973

(1982) 'How Terence's *Hecyra* failed', *Classical Quarterly* 32: 134–5

Sandy, G. N. (1979) 'Ancient prose fiction and minor early English novels', *Antike und Abendland* 25: 41–55

(1982) *Heliodorus*, New York

Scafuro, A. C. (1997) *The forensic stage*, Cambridge

Scarcella, A. M. (1976) 'Aspetti del diritto e del costume matrimoniali nel romanzo di Eliodoro', *Materiali e contributi per la storia della narrativa greco-latina* 1: 57–96; reprinted in *Romanzo e romanzieri: note di narratologia* (1993), 2 vols., Naples, 357–84

Schank, R. C. (1975) 'The structure of episodes in memory', in Bobrow and Collins 1975: 237–72

Schank, R. C. and Abelson, R. (1977) *Scripts, plans, goals, and understanding*, Hillsdale

Scher, S. P. (1992), ed., *Music and text: critical inquiries*, Cambridge

Schissel von Fleschenberg, O. (1913) *Entwicklungsgeschichte des griechischen Romanes im Altertum*, Halle

Scholes, R. (1974) *Structuralism in literature: an introduction*, New Haven

Schutter, K. H. E. (1952) *Quibus annis comoediae plautinae primum actae sint quaeritur*, diss. Groningen

Scully, S. (1990) *Homer and the sacred city*, Ithaca

Seaford, R. (1994) *Reciprocity and ritual*, Oxford
  (1996) 'Something to do with Dionysus – tragedy and the Dionysiac: response to Friedrich', in Silk 1996: 284–94

Sebeok, T. A. and Umiker-Sebeok, J. (1988), eds., *The semiotic web 1987*, Berlin, New York, and Amsterdam

Sedelmeier, D. (1959) 'Studien zu Achilleus Tatios', *Wiener Studien* 72: 113–43

Segal, C. P. (1983) 'Greek myth as a semiotic and structural system and the problem of tragedy', *Arethusa* 16: 173–98; reprinted in *Interpreting Greek tragedy: myth, poetry, text*, Ithaca, 48–74
  (1994) *Singers, heroes, and gods in the Odyssey*, Ithaca

Segre, C. (1974) *Le strutture e il tempo*, Turin, translated as *Structures and time: narration, poetry, models* (1979), Chicago and London

Seifert, C. M., Dyer, M. G., and Black, J. B. (1986) 'Thematic knowledge in story understanding', *Text* 6: 393–426

Semino, E. (1997) *Language and world creation in poems and other texts*, London and New York

Sharrock, A. R. (1996) 'The art of deceit: Pseudolus and the nature of reading', *Classical Quarterly* 46: 152–74

Shaw, M. (1975) 'The female intruder: women in fifth-century drama', *Classical Philology* 70: 255–66

Shen, Y. (1989a) 'Schema theory and the processing of narrative texts: the X-bar story grammar and the notion of discourse topic', *Journal of Pragmatics* 12: 639–76
  (1989b) 'The X-bar grammar for stories: story grammar revisited', *Text* 9: 415–67

Shklovsky, V. (1919) 'Svjaz' priemov sjuzetoslozenija s obscimi priemami stilja', in *Poètika: sborniki po teorii poeticheskovo yazyka*, Petrograd, 113–50 = *O teorii prozy* (1925), Moscow, 21–55; translated by Benjamin Sher as 'The relationship between devices of plot construction and general devices of style', in *Theory of prose*, Elmwood Park, IL, 15–51

Shrimpton, G. S. (1997) *History and memory in ancient Greece*, Montreal and Kingston

Silk, M. S. (1996), ed., *Tragedy and the tragic: Greek theatre and beyond*, Oxford

Slings, S. R. (1990) 'The I in personal archaic poetry', in Slings, ed., *The poet's I in archaic Greek lyric*, Amsterdam, 1–28

Sommerstein, A. H. (1993), Zimmerman, B., and Henderson, J., eds., *Tragedy, comedy, and the polis*, Bari

Souriau, E. (1950) *Les 200,000 situations dramatiques*, Paris

Spolsky, E. (1993) *Gaps in nature: literary interpretation and the modular mind*, Albany

Stanford, W. B. (1959), ed., *The Odyssey of Homer*, 2 vols., 2nd edn, London

Stanley, K. (1993) *The shield of Homer*, Princeton

Stein, N. L. and Glenn, C. G. (1979) 'An analysis of story comprehension in elementary school children', in R. O. Freedle, ed., *New directions in discourse processing 2*, Norwood, NJ

Sternberg, M. (1978) *Expositional modes and temporal ordering in fiction*, Baltimore and London

Stewart, A. H. (1987) 'Models of narrative structure', *Semiotica* 64: 83–97

Strasburger, H. (1972) *Homer und die Geschichtsschreibung*, Sitzungsberichte der Heidelberger Akademie der Wissenschaften, Philosophisch-historische Klasse, 1972.1, Heidelberg: Winter

Sturgess, P. J. M. (1992) *Narrativity: theory and practice*, Oxford

Taplin, O. (1972) 'Aeschylean silences and silences in Aeschylus', *Harvard Studies in Classical Philology* 76 62–76

   (1977) *The stagecraft of Aeschylus*, Oxford

   (1978) *Greek tragedy in action*, London

   (1986) 'Homer', in J. Boardman, J. Griffin, and O. Murray, eds., *The Oxford history of the classical world*, Oxford, 50–77

   (1992) *Homeric soundings: the shaping of the Iliad*, Oxford

Thalmann, W. G. (1988) 'Thersites: comedy, scapegoats, and heroic ideology in the *Iliad*', *Transactions of the American Philological Association* 118: 1–28

   (1998) *The swineherd and the bow: representations of class in the Odyssey*, Ithaca and London

Thorndyke, P. W. (1977) 'Cognitive structures in comprehension and memory of narrative discourse', *Cognitive Psychology* 9: 77–110

Thornton, H. and A. (1962) *Time and style: an essay in classical literature*, London

Todorov, T. (1969) *Grammaire du Décaméron*, The Hague

Tomashevsky, B. (1925) 'Tematika', in *Teoriya literatury*, Leningrad, 137ff.; partly translated as 'Thematics', in Lemon and Reis 1965: 61–95

Toolan, M. J. (1988) *Narrative: a critical linguistic introduction*, London

de Toro, Fernando (1987) *Semiótica del teatro: del texto a la puesta en escena*, Buenos Aires; translated by J. Lewis and revised and edited by C. Hubbard as *Theatre semiotics: text and staging in modern theatre* (1995), Toronto and Buffalo

Turner, M. (1991) *Reading minds: the study of English in the age of cognitive science*, Princeton

Ubersfeld, A. (1977) *Lire le théâtre*, Paris

   (1991) *L'Ecole du spectateur: lire le théâtre 2*, Paris

van Dijk, G.-J. (1997) Αἶνοι, Λόγοι, Μῦθοι: *fables in archaic, classical, and Hellenistic Greek literature, with a study of the theory and terminology of the genre* (*Mnemosyne* Supplement 166, Leiden).

van Dijk, T. A. (1980), ed., *Story comprehension, Poetics* 9.1–3

Vickers, B. (1973) *Towards Greek tragedy*, London and New York

Visser, E. (1997) *Homers Katalog der Schiffe*, Stuttgart and Leipzig: Teubner

Vogt-Spira, G. (1992) *Dramaturgie des Zufalls: Tyche und Handeln in der Komödie Menanders* (Zetemata 88), Munich

Wales, K. (1987) 'Plot', in *A dictionary of stylistics*, London, 355–7

Webster, T. B. L. (1965) 'The order of tragedies at the Great Dionysia', *Hermathena* 100: 21–8

(1967) *The tragedies of Euripides*, London

Weil, S. (1953) 'L'Iliade ou le poème de la force' (written 1939–40) in *Le Source grecque* (1953), Paris, 9–42; translated by M. McCarthy (1945) as *The Iliad or the poem of force*, New York, and by E. and C. Geissbuhler as 'The *Iliad*, poem of might' in Weil, *Intimations of Christianity among the ancient Greeks* (1957), London, 24–55

West, S. (1988) 'The transmission of the text' and Commentary on Books I–IV, in Heubeck *et al.* 1988–92, Vol. I, 33–245

White, H. (1973) *Metahistory: the historical imagination in nineteenth-century Europe*, Baltimore

(1978) *Tropics of discourse: essays in cultural criticism*, Baltimore

(1987) *The content of the form: narrative discourse and historical representation*, Baltimore

Whitman, C. H. (1958) *Homer and the heroic tradition*, Cambridge, MA

Wilensky, R. (1978) 'Why John married Mary: understanding stories involving recurring goals', *Cognitive Science* 2: 235–66

(1982) 'Points: a theory of the structure of stories in memory', in Lehnert and Ringle 1982: 345–74

(1983) 'Story grammars versus story points', *The Behavioural and Brain Sciences* 6: 579–623

Wiles, D. (1988), tr. *Brothers*, in P. Dickinson and D. Wiles, trs., *Plautus: two plays* (Sutherland House Texts 9), Egham, 63–76

(1989) 'Marriage and prostitution in classical New Comedy', in James Redmond, ed., *Themes in Drama* 11: *Women in theatre*, Cambridge, 31–48

(1991) *The masks of Menander*, Cambridge

(1997) *Tragedy in Athens: performance space and theatrical meaning*, Cambridge

Willcock, M. M. (1983) 'Battle scenes in the *Aeneid*', *Proceedings of the Cambridge Philological Society* 29: 87–99

(1984), ed., *The Iliad of Homer: books XIII–XXIV,* London

(1987), ed., *Plautus: Pseudolus*, Bristol

Wilson, R. R. (1990) *In Palamedes' shadow: explorations in play, game and narrative theory*, Boston

Winkler, J. J. (1982) 'The mendacity of Calasiris and the narrative strategy of Heliodoros' *Aithiopika*', *Yale Classical Studies* 27: 93–158

Winkler, J. J. and Zeitlin, Froma I. (1990), eds., *Nothing to do with Dionysus? Athenian drama in its social context*, Princeton

Wohl, V. (1998) *Intimate commerce: exchange, gender, and subjectivity in Greek tragedy*, Austin

Woodman, A. J. (1988) *Rhetoric in classical historiography*, London and Sydney

Wright, A. M. (1982) *The formal principle in the novel*, Ithaca

Yazdani, M. (1989) 'Computational story writing', in N. Williams and P. Holt, eds., *Computers and writing*, Oxford, 125–47

Zeitlin, F. I. (1985) 'Playing the other: theater, theatricality, and the feminine in Greek drama', *Representations* 11: 63–94, with later versions in Winkler and Zeitlin 1990: 63–96 and in *Playing the other* (1996), Chicago, 341–74

Index